Nick Williams had a very successful conventional sales career but wasn't happy and fulfilled, so he eventually found the courage to leave and follow his heart to find out what he would love to do with his life. He is now the Director of Alternatives at St James's – a premier venue in London for major authors and workshop leaders from around the world. He also founded the Heart at Work Project. He is also an established workshop presenter in Great Britain and abroad, and works in mainline business as a consultant and trainer for the public and private sectors. He has been widely featured in the media as a leading authority on the world of work and how our work can be an expression of the best of us – our heart and soul. His work has helped such diverse groups as lawyers, teachers, managing directors, trainers, doctors, the clergy, social workers, the self-employed and the unemployed.

Praise for *The Work We Were Born To Do*:

'Nick Williams offers useful and inspiring insights to explore the infinite possibilities inherent in every human being.' Deepak Chopra, author of *The Seven Spiritual Laws of Success* and *Ageless Body, Timeless Mind*

'Nick is a great guy doing wonderful work and is an inspired teacher with much to contribute.' Dr Wayne W Dyer, author of *Manifest Your Destiny* and *Your Sacred Self*

'Whatever you do, you can use this inspiring guide to discover purpose, meaning and passion in your work … and still pay the bills.' Paul Wilson, author of *The Little Book of Calm* and *Calm at Work*

'Nick Williams is a wonderful man, and his book delivers a wonderful message.' Susan Jeffers, author of *Feel the Fear and Do It Anyway, End the Struggle and Dance with Life* and *Dare to Connect*

'Nick is a visionary at work.' James Redfield, author of *The Celestine Prophecy*, and Salle Merrill Redfield, author of *The Joy of Meditating*

'I've always believed that you should bring your heart to work. Step by step, Nick Williams shows you how.' Anita Roddick OBE, Founder, The Body Shop International plc

'A book filled with wisdom but more importantly with inspiration which will lead you to use the wisdom and save your authentic life … Read and learn how to save your life, live in your heart and have magic happen. If you get the message you'll never have to do a day's work again, because it is only work if there is some place else you'd rather be.' Bernie Siegel, author of *Love, Medicine and Miracles* and *Prescriptions for Living*

'Nick Williams has created an enormously useful way to help us discover who we are, what we want and then how to fulfil it in our work. This is a book I highly recommend.' Leslie Kenton, author of *Journey to Freedom*

'I firmly believe that we all came with a unique purpose, but finding that purpose can take a lifetime, unless of course you read this inspiring and magical book to hasten the process.' Hazel Courtney, award-winning health writer

' ... a joy to read. It sparkles with inspiration and delight, and is packed with ideas that will help you discover your life's work – and create a life you truly love. Whether you hide under the bedclothes on Monday mornings, or just feel bored or dissatisfied at work, you need this book!' Gill Edwards, author of *Living Magically* and *Stepping into the Magic*

'Nick Williams gives us a heartening and optimistic way forward.' Dorothy Rowe, leading psychologist and best-selling author

'Nick not only goes about placing our work into its true perspective in our lives but he also provides the criteria for what has meaning and value in life – happiness and fulfilment! This is an excellent and well written book on meaningful work. Nick does all the work for us in setting profound and everyday truths down in an easy and palatable form.' Dr Chuck Spezzano, author of *If It Hurts, It Isn't Love* and *Happiness is the Best Revenge*

This book overflows with the richest wisdom of the heart and positive skills for self-appreciation, open-hearted living and success. Nick Williams gets to the core of the power to make our lives what we would have them be. Read this magnificent work, enjoy, grow and soar!' Alan Cohen, author of *The Dragon Doesn't Live Here Anymore, Joy is My Compass* and *Handle with Prayer*

'This inspiring book provides the map and compass that will guide you to that sought-after destination of being able to fulfil your true potential, through your natural vocation. Use it!' Colin Turner, corporate speaker and author of *The Eureka Principle* and *Swimming with the Piranhas Makes You Hungry.*

'Nick Williams has written an inspirational book. If your work is something you want to forget as soon as you finish – then think again. Nick will help you to find meaning, hope and soul in whatever work you do. A book for our times.' Reverend Donald Reeves, former Rector of St James's Church, Piccadilly, London, Founder of the European Churches Network and author of *Down to Earth*

'Beautiful sequencing of proven principles – bursting with passion and wisdom.' Dr Stephen Covey, author of *The Seven Habits of Highly Effective People*

THE WORK WE WERE BORN TO DO

Find the Work You Love, Love the Work You Do

NICK WILLIAMS

Element
An Imprint of HarperCollins*Publishers*
77–85 Fulham Palace Road
Hammersmith, London W6 8JB

The website address is: www.thorsons.com

First published in 1999 by Element Books Limited
Reprinted 2004
Reprinted 2005

A catalogue record for this book is
available from the British Library

ISBN 1 86204 552 6

Cover photograph by Veronica Renshaw
Cover design by Slatter-Anderson
Design and typeset by Penny Mills

Printed and bound in Great Britain by
Creative Print and Design (Wales), Ebbw Vale

The author and publisher are grateful for permission to quote the following. From *Illusions: The Adventures of a Reluctant Messiah* by Richard Bach; copyright © 1977 by Richard Bach and Leslie Parrish-Bach. Used by permission of Delacorte Press, a division of Random House Inc. The lines from 'A Poet's Advice to Students' are reprinted from *A Miscellany* by e. e. cummings, edited by George J Firmage, by permission of W W Norton & Company. Copyright © 1988 by the Trustees for the e. e. cummings Trust and George James Firmage. 'O sweet spontaneous' is reprinted from *Complete Poems 1904–1962* by e. e. cummings, edited by George J Firmage, by permission of W W Norton & Company. Copyright © 1991 by the Trustees for the e. e. cummings Trust and George James Firmage. Quotes from *A Course in Miracles*, © 1975 are reproduced by permission of the Foundation of Inner Peace. Lines from 'Little Gidding' from *Four Quartets in Collected Poems* by T S Eliot, copyright 1942 by T S Eliot and renewed 1970 by Esme Calerie Eliot, reproduced by permission of Faber and Faber Ltd and Harcourt Inc. Lines from 'Healing' by D H Lawrence form *The Complete Poems of D H Lawrence* by D H Lawrence, edited by V de Sola Pinto & F W Roberts © 1964, 1971 by Angelo Ravagli and C M Weekley, executors of the Estate of Frieda Lawrence Ravagli, used by permission of Laurence Pollinger Limited and Viking Putnam. Extract from *The Mutant Message Down Under* by Marlo Morgan, copyright © 1991, 1994 by Marlo Morgan is reproduced by permission of HarperCollins*Publishers*. Every effort has been made to contact all copyright holders but if any have been inadvertently overlooked the author and publisher will be pleased to make the necessary arrangement at the first opportunity.

Contents

Acknowledgements

This is where I get to express my gratitude to everyone who has contributed to both this book and my life leading up to it. So here we go!

My partner Helen, who saw this book grow from a seed of an idea into a completed book, and loved and supported me every step along the way, sharing with me the excitement of the journey.

My wonderful parents, Pam and Harold, for their love, support and encouragment, and true desire to see me happy. To my sister Amanda for her dedication to her life's work. To Juliette Pollitzer for being an unfailing loving support over the last twelve years. Also, thanks to Linda, Peter, Jan and Catherine – fellow travellers on the journey. To *the guys*, Adam Stern, Matt Ingram and Martin Wenner, who, for eight years, have been a great source of love and encouragement. To my great friend Ben Renshaw for his unfailing love, humour and support, and his wife Veronica for her friendship and photographic skills. Thanks also to Robert and Miranda Holden for being such good friends and inspiring and showing me how to shine my light. To Maurice Simons for his enthusiasm and interest. Thanks to Sally Morris for being my friend, and her sons Matthew and Stuart. To Trish and Barry. My gratitude to Agnes Amanyi who died of cancer just as I finished writing this book. Her love of life, her encouragment and her courage will always remain an inspiration to me. To Julie Hay, a friend and mentor for many years; my bank manager, Terry Clarke, for having faith in me when my financial situation didn't reflect my dreams, and my accountant Roxy Grimshaw.

Thanks to Mandy Leonard for her friendship, Debbie Charles and Gary Hawkes. Thanks to Chris Harrowell and Susan Daniels. Anna Ziman, my workshop sister. To the guys who run the cafe over the road from our flat for the many hours I spent in there writing on my laptop and then proofreading the book. Thanks to Shirley and Sandy Matthews for their friendship, and a house with such a lovely view to write in. To Bina Gibson. My family in Malvern – Cally, Gordon, Alistair and Bethany Law and Edna Wright. Thanks to the Yamat family. Thanks to Bill Gleave and Gill Whisson. Also Elaine and Rob Shalet. From the old Wordplex days, thanks to Elizabeth O'Neill (Bets), Gary Palmer, Peter Hayward,

Kay Johnston, Chris Evans, Daksha Webb and the rest of the gang. Thanks to Roy and John and the gang at Digital. Thanks to Mike Strange, Diana Eder and Mary Patten. Thanks to Irene, Desiree and Susanna – the Swiss and German connection – and Patricia, Colin, Michael and Linda for the grand times in Dublin.

To everyone at Element, especially Julia McCutchen for seeing the potential in my writing, and having the willingness to trust that it would come to fruition. To Sue Lascelles, my editor, for her attention to detail, exquisite sensitivity, patience, encouragement and sheer hard work. To Andrew Wille, my copy-editor, for his feedback and enthusiasm for the work, and to Laura Jennings, Jenny Carradice and Tierney Fox for their sales, marketing and PR help.

It has been a great honour to meet and work with many inspired teachers in the world today; those who have especially touched and inspired me are: Deepak Chopra, Wayne Dyer, Marianne Williamson, Marie de Hennezel, Paulo Coelho, Stuart Wilde, Susan Jeffers, John Gray, James and Salle Redfield, Paul Wilson, Robert and Miranda Holden, Rupert Sheldrake, Marion Woodman, Robert Bly, Michael Meade, Malidoma Some, James Hillman, Mari Hall, Leslie Kenton, M Scott Peck, Starhawk, Gill Edwards, Brandon Bays, Alan Cohen, Ken and Elizabeth Mellor, Dorothy Rowe, Anita Roddick, Abe Wagner, Didier Danthois and Diane Berke. Thanks to Tom and Linda Carpenter whose loving presence has been a wonderful support and inspiration. Particular thanks to Chuck and Lency Spezzano for their vision and love and for founding Psychology of Vision, and whose ideas infuse my life and work. To Jeff and Suzie Allen, Julie Wookey and Peter Wise for their willingness to run Psychology of Vision in Britain, and the whole Psychology of Vision team. To Nigel Wookey for supporting Julie, being a great guy and taking me flying! To Mark Riminton and Peggy O'Hare for *The Big Events!* Great thanks to Veronique Franceus, and thanks to Dina Glouberman and all at the Skyros Centres and office.

Thanks to *The Gift of Love* by Deepak Chopra and *Benediction Moon* by Pia, the two CDs I played most constantly whilst writing.

To my family of friends at Alternatives: in the office, Jane Turney, Steve Nunn and Lea Yehud – together we make a great team. To the team themselves: Mary Priest Cobern, Tom Cook, Richard Dunkerley, Jo MacAndrews, Maria Pascual, Susannah Howe, Andrew Kennedy, Elizabeth Braun, Steve Radford, Andrea Serkin, Jelka Vukovic, John Bagwell, Christine Warmuth, Zeta Denegri, Margaret Dempsey, Jackie Butler, Gauravani and Jaganath. Thanks also to Kathy Doyle, Patrick Hine and Michael Klein for their support. Thanks also to John Hunt, Roxy Grimshaw, Janet Watts, Malcom Stern and Mary Priest-Cobern for their willingness to become trustees of the new Alternatives trust.

Immense thanks also to Malcolm Stern, Sabrina Dearborn and William Bloom for the vision to start Alternatives and for their friendship over the years. To Donald Reeves for his original vision to breathe new life into St James's, and his radical welcome of God. To the Parish Church Council at St James's for continuing to support Alternatives, especially to Petra, and to Mary Robins for her joy and open-heartedness. To Ashley and Karen, the vergers at St James's, and to Alastair for following his heart. To Winston Fraser in Aroma at St James's for providing physical sustenance and smiles for so many years.

A big thank you to all the people who have attended my talks and workshops, who have been my teachers and have shown me that the principles in this book really do work.

And last but by no means least, to *A Course in Miracles* and the Creator, the unseen, invisible, and incredible loving force behind all things, in which everything has its being.

And not forgetting Hergist.

Foreword

All worked up and no place to go?

Michael was a typical successful/unhappy executive, lost in corporate land, living and dying on the edge – the edge of exhaustion. His daily 'to do' list was his Bible, his laptop was his constant companion, and life outside of work he referred to as 'downtime'. Despite having a loving family, beautiful children and a great circle of friends, Michael hardly ever saw them, and when he did he was usually too tired to enjoy their company. Michael's plans for a great life were permanently on hold. He had no 'life-after-office' experience. There was always work to do.

'I make £100,000 a year,' he said. 'I should be dancing. Instead, I feel work is killing me.' Michael was thirty-something years old and he was already worked-up, run down and worn through. 'Mine is the tombstone that reads "Died at 30; buried at 70",' he joked. Michael and I met several times. Together we explored the possibility that it was not work that was killing him, but, rather, his belief that he had to die working.

For many of us, our experience of work is one of grind, drudgery and unrelenting slog. Work is not play; work is sweat and toil, struggle and sacrifice. It is the penance we pay for the good things in life. Like Michael, we have learned to believe that work must be serious, dull and unenjoyable. Thus, many people who go to work aren't really there. What you see is only a pale carbon copy of a real person. What these people need is a Nick Williams.

Nick Williams challenges you and I to transform our experience of work. In particular, he asks us to look at the purpose we have given to work. Work can be more than mere meaningless labour; it can be play, it can be inspired, it can be service, it can be love. Work can be whatever we want it to be. As we transform our beliefs about work so must our experience of work transform also.

Nick also challenges us to explore the gift of work. Work need not be a sacrifice; it can be a gift – a gift we give and a gift we receive. Again, the choice is ours. You and I are gift-bearers. We each of us bring gifts to this world. With great compassion and integrity, Nick encourages us not to give up on the gifts we are here to give. He supports us in using our work to express our gifts and also to express the joyful truth of who we really are. What makes Nick's vision so compelling is that he lives it. Nick has transformed his own experience of work – and continues to do so. Nick's work is his gift to the world, for through his work he reveals his best self – his real self.

Take great encouragement from this book. Read it slowly. Digest each page fully. And afterwards, go out to play!

God bless.

Robert Holden
Oxford, England
March 1999

Preface

There I was, lying on the beach in Antigua, a beer in hand, surrounded by an outer paradise of sunshine, sea and sky, supposedly enjoying the fruits of my well-earned success in computer sales. So why was I trapped in an inner hell, feeling stressed out and that the only way was down? Why was I struggling to enjoy my holiday, my mind swimming with worries about the future?

I felt I didn't deserve what I had, nor did I enjoy the price I seemed to have to pay. I was disappointed, asking myself, 'Is this it? Why do I feel so empty while I have such success?' The gulf between the outer appearances of my life and the inner experiences of myself was huge, seemingly insurmountable.

Something was missing, and I have now discovered what that something was – it was *me* and my spirit! I was failing to be authentic and true to myself; I was playing roles and putting on masks to get people to approve of me and to like me, and to show how good I was. Although in many respects I had been very successful, I still couldn't hide the fact that the *real and authentic* me – my heart, my inspiration, creativity, love and passion – were largely absent in my daily life. Because I was hiding behind masks and roles, I was *getting* and *achieving* a lot, but I was *receiving* very little. And the real me was starving.

My roles had stopped working for me; I was beginning to realize that they were covering a deep sense of my actually being a failure. I needed to slow down and attend to some of the broken parts of my heart and mind. I'd done a good job of moulding and distorting myself to fit what I thought other people would like me to be, but I had ended up losing myself in the process. I was bored and frustrated in my work, as though I was caught in a materially comfortable prison. So much of my identity was tied up in the outer *things* of my life, but I was petrified to change and let go of everything that I had accumulated through such hard work and struggle.

I sought help, went into therapy and was beginning to make progress. And eventually the pain of boredom grew worse than the fear of life-altering change, and I found the courage to listen to my inner voice. I quit my old ways to follow my heart, which told me: *If you want to find out who you are beyond all the things you are so attached to, let go and you will discover.*

As a child I always felt as if there was something inside me that wanted expression – I felt a vague calling but I was uneasy with it, like it was something of a curse, because no one around me really seemed to validate my feelings. So I ignored the call, buried it away and carried on with passing exams and gaining qualifications, including a degree in Business Studies, with no real reason other than delaying making a decision about what I would do with the rest of my life!

At the age of twenty-three I decided to be *successful*, because I thought that would make me happy. At the time success meant for me a car, salary, money, rewards, a house, girlfriend(s), toys and trappings. So I set out to get them, and by the age of twenty-eight or so got many of them: a lovely flat in Fulham in London, a high-powered job in computers in the City, a BMW and lots of perks. But I was pretty confused, as I still wasn't very happy. I often felt insecure and depressed.

I had developed such a wonderful logical mind, and yet I realized that the pain I was feeling was my soul screaming out in divine discontent, saying to me: *This isn't really you; you have another purpose and another path to follow, one that is more joyful, more authentic and heartfelt.* Gradually I learned to listen to this inner voice more often and to act on it despite my fears, my doubts and anxieties. I began to pay more attention to what I really did want to create in my life, and shifted my attention away from what I did not want.

That inner voice has been my greatest guide over the last ten years. It has led me through an ongoing metamorphosis, to the marrying of my heart and my head. This journey has made me look at what lay *behind* my old masks and roles. I have discovered places of great hurt and pain, anger and rage, senses of inadequacy and worthlessness that I have, little by little, come to acknowledge, accept and embrace. I have needed to face my shadow and slowly reintegrate many parts of myself that I threw away when I was younger. In the past I had felt bad about these shadow aspects, and from fear and guilt discarded them.

I now feel incredibly blessed to have discovered what I love to do and to have found ways of making a living doing what I love. Ten years ago such an existence was wishful thinking to me, yet today I *know beyond doubt* in my heart that it is possible – not just for me but for all of us. It is a great source of joy to me to give talks and run workshops for individuals and organizations, teaching them how to discover and bring their best selves – their heart, inspiration and spirit – into their work, and to create work based on joy, creativity, abundance and love. I coach and encourage people from all walks of life to become authentic in their own lives and work. I also help to run the Alternatives lecture series based in Piccadilly, London, where I have had the pleasure of hosting and meeting some of the greatest writers and speakers from the world of personal and spiritual development, as well as cutting-edge thinkers and innovators from science and healthcare, and healers operating in all areas of life. I also write and broadcast, and develop books and audiotapes.

My message is simple. Life is set up to support our joy, our love, our creativity and our passion, but most of us have been educated to believe the very opposite, that life demands sacrifice, struggle and suffering. I have discovered that our happiness, joy, freedom and success are often the very things we can be most frightened of. We simply need to *unlearn* much of what we have been taught so that our spirit can naturally shine through. This undoing is not always easy – it can be scary and painful at times, but we need to do it so that we can become freer. The path of undoing requires courage and trust to face doubts and fears; as one still on the path, I have had, and still do have, my ups and downs, and at times I have struggled with money, but the inner rewards are tremendous.

This process of undoing and freeing ourselves is called healing by some, personal growth by others and self-acceptance or self-realization by others still. However this process is described, at the heart of each one of us is a beautiful being, made whole and in the image of our creator, with an abundance of love, creativity, happiness and peace. Most of us have succeeded in hiding or burying the true us, but it is never lost, and the work we were born to do is concerned with remembering and re-owning this part of ourselves, and creating our lives around it.

The New Work Ethic

For several hundred years the Western concept of work has been based on a belief in some kind of original sin. In many people's lives, work has become synonymous with sacrifice, boredom and even fear – something to be endured rather than enjoyed. We've struggled on, thinking that if we grin and bear it we will be granted our eventual reward or happiness in the future (at the very least, perhaps, a decent pension).

When success is primarily measured by external criteria, positions and possessions, the split widens between the work we think we have to do to support the lifestyle we choose and wherever our heart really is – whatever we truly enjoy and feel inspired by. If our world view is one of scarcity and lack, we will feel driven to constantly prove ourselves and justify ourselves, pitching against one another, competing to survive ... Not an inspiring picture.

However, a new work ethic is emerging – one in which success is created from the inside out, based on an awareness of our original goodness. It is motivated by our inner experiences, not just our efforts to keep up appearances. Debunking our old beliefs, we are invited to accept abundance as our natural state, and realize that when we follow our hearts and spirits we will discover gifts, creativity, energy and talents within us which flow from us with ease, bringing a sense of fulfilment and pleasure.

Experiencing inner success based on love and inspiration will help us to bring about an important shift in our thinking, away from personality and ego-based views, towards a heartfelt and spiritual view of work and life.

The Heart at Work Project

Introduction

Would you like to discover what you love, where your heart lies, how to serve others and how to make a living from following it? Realizing those intentions is what this book is all about.

Today's world of work is no longer just about finding a job. More and more it means finding the best of ourselves – our heart, joy and spirit – and creating our work around who we are and how we can contribute to the well-being of others whilst establishing balance in our lives. Whether we are conscious of it or not, we all want to build our work from the inside out, to find and express what is unique and precious about ourselves. We want our work to be a vehicle for growing and expanding our sense of self, for discovering more about who we are, and even to be a vehicle for our love and our spirituality. And we will want to make money and support ourselves materially and financially in the process, doing the work we feel born to do.

To many of us raised with the Protestant work ethic, this desire to find the work we were born to do can sound either selfish or impossibly dreamy, for we have come to believe and experience that suffering in work is our *natural* state. The feeling that work should be difficult, boring and even a struggle is *normal*, but not *natural*. All of us have been born with unique gifts and talents, but most of us have not been taught or encouraged to find, develop or express those qualities; we may even have been rewarded for hiding and denying them. Consequently we will have found our way into work that isn't deeply satisfying and isn't really *us*. We can feel blind to the opportunities that currently abound for two reasons:

◆ We keep running on old programming, including attitudes, beliefs or ways of thinking about work that are no longer valid in the modern world.

◆ We have yet to develop the self-belief, self-confidence, self-awareness or skills to see ourselves changing our working lives.

Collectively we have taken a wrong turn and just kept on going, but now the tide is turning. We can only live spiritless lives for so long. More of us are declaring, 'This is enough!' Whether motivated by divine discontent with our current situation and wondering, 'Is *this* it?' or prompted by redundancy or personal crisis, or agitated by lifelong dreams that won't go away or moments of inspiration, we know we want to change, and we can.

I am proposing a radical yet ancient and perennial idea: that to build the life we want – complete with inner satisfaction, personal meaning and rewards – we need to create the work we love. By this I mean inventing ways to earn an income doing what we love and do the best, while serving others, becoming authentic and fulfilling the highest standards of our vocation. This is spiritual work, and it is our life assignment. It will need to be *self-created* from our own minds and imagination, not the product of someone else. And most of us are well equipped to do it, but were probably never shown how.

Over the last ten years, I have made the transition from doing a job to pay the bills to living my vocation, and although this is still work in progress, I want to share the journey so far. I want to inspire you to possibilities that may seem like vague ideas or impossible dreams right now, but that can actually offer the seedlings of what you have come here to be and to do, for when we cherish our dreams and visions we discover they are the children of our soul, blueprints of our ultimate achievements.

Like most of us, I used to live my life by *rules* about how I *should* be; I would invariably break these rules, then feel guilty and condemn myself. Indeed, our whole society seems to be based on rules and how we punish those who break them: we can only ever deal with rules in a right or wrong way. In creating my own life's work, I have put aside rules and discovered twelve principles that have been at the heart of my work and my thinking. Unlike rules, principles are intentions; lifegiving and inspirational, they are directions and the values by which we set our sails. We can be on or off course, but not right or wrong. Principles are how we create our work from the inside out, whereas rules come from the outside in. An essential difference between the two is that when we break with our principles, we don't use punishment, but correction.

The key principles that I have identified are:

◆ *Principle One: Defining the work we were born to do.* Each of us is a precious spirit, uniquely gifted to do something in the world; whatever gives us the experience of joy is the signpost to the discovery of the work we were born to do.

◆ *Principle Two: Undoing our conditioning.* Most of us have more negative than positive thoughts, ideas and beliefs about ourselves and our work. We are called to undo this conditioning, layer by layer.

Principle Three: Discovering the spirit of our work. What is most important is not the work we do, but the attitude and consciousness with which we do it.

Principle Four: Awakening the heart at work. True success lies in work that our heart is in, work that we love. We may need to reconnect with our own heart and passion and our true loves.

Principle Five: Knowing that money is never really the issue. We project so much of our fear on to money that we need to develop a new relationship with money and reconsider the place it occupies in our lives.

Principle Six: Working on purpose. We can move from a purpose based on avoiding our fears to a positive sense of purpose founded on creating what is most important and precious to us.

Principle Seven: Integrity, authenticity and the return to wholeness. As we grew up, we judged, buried and threw away many of our essential qualities. We need to look at our shadow selves and reclaim these parts of us.

Principle Eight: Contribution and the discovery of meaningful work. Meaningful work is created by discovering ways of making our love and joy contribute to serving the good of others and enhancing their lives.

◆ *Principle Nine: Welcoming transformation and change.* Each of us has the capacity to transform both our perception of ourselves *and* our working situation. We are not stuck.

Principle Ten: The inspiration to create. Creativity is the power we all have to be original and authentic, and to bring our hearts' desires out of our minds and into physical reality. We can create the work we were born to do even if it doesn't already exist.

Principle Eleven: Abundance and inner riches. We have mostly been trained to believe in scarcity, but this conceals the truth that within each of us is an abundance of inner riches, and that the world is naturally abundant.

Principle Twelve: Experiencing the true meaning of success. To experience the true meaning of success is to combine inner and outer achievements. Knowing and experiencing ourselves as spiritual beings is the greatest success we could ever ask for, and our true goal.

For me, the work we were born to do is a spiritual process, about knowing our own being and our creator. Although my last desire is to start another religion or create another doctrine, I would like us to discover and honour the spirit of love and ultimately the mystery that lies at the heart of most spiritual traditions and religions. The purpose of religion is to bind us back together; the root word *religio* means 'to bind together'. My purpose in this book is to bind together the essence of truth at the heart of all spiritual and religious teachings. I aim to synthesize, not reinvent. I respect and give equal thanks to all forms of spirituality that put genuine love and compassion at their heart.

We need to be willing to see ourselves with new eyes, find the power and creativity within us, so that we can then discover the opportunities to create genuinely rewarding and fulfilling work that exists for all of us right now. Einstein said that the times we live in require a new way of thinking, and this is especially true for the world of work. We can find the work we were born to do by inspiring ourselves; we can draw on resources that we didn't even know we had to bring about creative change in our own lives. The call is not to be like someone else, but to be fully ourselves. Spinoza summed it up: 'To be what we were born to be, and to become what we are capable of becoming, is the only end in life.'

One of my beliefs is that we have become too good at providing easy answers. We have lost the art and wisdom of being challenged by exciting and soul-stirring questions. Consequently, throughout the book I will be inviting you to think about and answer some profound questions that I have used to shape my life, and those of many others, over the last ten years. The point is not necessarily to have a completely formulated answer, *but to be willing to live the question*. By asking ourselves great questions we can influence ourselves and reconnect with our inner calling. Life is not a problem to be solved, but a mystery to be lived.

I'd like to suggest that before you start reading this book, you treat yourself to a wonderful journal, the best you can afford, and use it to capture your insights, ideas, inspirations and answers to the questions and exercises I shall offer you as you go. These thoughts of yours are precious, and will help you to notice the small but essential incremental changes you will need to make in the creation of the work you were born to do.

Enjoy the journey of self-discovery and self-awareness!

Nick Williams
London, 1999

PLEASE NOTE: Most of the case studies included in this book are based on actual people, but a few have had name changes for the purposes of confidentiality and a couple are an amalgam of several real people.

Principle One

DEFINING THE WORK WE WERE BORN TO DO

Each one of us is unique and precious. We all have talents and gifts. Our first task is to discover these gifts and we shall do this by finding and following that which gives us joy. As we do so, we shall find a reservoir of energy within us and begin to create our own niche in life, our part in creation, which will be found by discovering whatever comes naturally to us. The work we were born to do leads us to find previously untapped strength of will and inner power flowing from our own spirit.

WHAT IS THE WORK WE WERE BORN TO DO?

Whatever your work may be, think of your work as a channel for the expression of mind and soul. Make this thought so deep, through faith and persistence, that you can actually feel the marvels of the mind pressing for expression as you work. Then know that the greatest power within you – even genius – will, through your work, come forth. Convince the mind of this fact, and you will soon receive from within all the power and all the inspiration you could possibly desire.

EDMOND BORDEAUX SZEKELEY
Professor of Psychology and author of *Creative Work*

True work is not a job that we do to make a living, survive and pay the bills. True work is concerned with finding and expressing the best that is within us – our love, creativity, heart and spirit – and creating the money we need to pay the bills and to support our desired way of life as a by-product. This is the work we were born to do: it has greater meaning and a fullness that is deeply satisfying; it has emotional and spiritual dimensions. True work is about following our inner voice, heeding the spiritual call and living our passion and purpose by finding what is great in us and letting it out. It is work that fosters inner growth and is focused on finding our gifts.

The work we were born to do is not about pulling in a pay cheque that might allow us to retire and lie on a beach. It is about having a passion for something, then deciding and committing to putting all our love, energy and creativity into fulfilling it. It is most concerned with setting ourselves on fire again, getting ourselves inspired, excited and motivated. It is about taking risks, so sometimes, it may also mean making our plans work just so we can feed ourselves.

The work we were born to do may also take us towards new frontiers, beyond our current boundaries. We have a dance within us between the part of us that craves certainty and the part of us that wants to explore and have adventures. Both are important, so it is a matter of balance. All human and personal advances come from a new step and uncertain step. We can never be fully prepared for the unknown, but we can take care of ourselves as and when we need to. The biggest error we make is taking too many precautions.

EXERCISE

◆ Imagine what it would be like to be living, on a daily basis, the work you were born to do. What do you expect that would feel like? What experiences would it involve? How would you feel when you woke up in the morning? What would be the purpose of your life? What would your goals be? How would you measure your success? Keep this question in mind, as it will help you build up positive motivation as you become more excited about the possibility of the work you were born to do.

At the heart of our being is both the desire for our work and the inner creative power and resources to bring it into being. We may not be fully conscious of this, but we can grow in our awareness of it. It is spurred by the inner desire to experience the fulfilled life, working with as much authenticity and passion as we can. All the answers are within you right now – yes, right now. That may sound mad if you are sitting at your desk or at home thinking, 'But I haven't a clue what I want to do next. I know I am bored in my current job, but don't know what to do next.' Hold on to the precious idea that the answers are already within you, right now. The work we were born to do is a process of self-discovery, an exciting journey to discover who we truly are and what we are capable of being and doing. Like a fairground ride, it will be thrilling at times, perhaps a little scary on some of the turns, but we know we'll reach the end safely as long as we don't jump out along the way.

The work we were born to do can also be born out of a healthy disillusionment – not disappointment with people but with materialism, with pushing ourselves so hard and with allowing ourselves to be reduced to mere resources, sucking the spirit out of work.

FROM A JOB TO OUR TRUE WORK

What is the difference between a job and work? A job is mechanical, with a job description; we are measured to see how well we have performed this function, and rewarded accordingly. A job is a what, not a why. True work comes from within us, work is about us being engaged; it is where we choose to channel our life's energy. Our work can link the everyday and the mundane to our heart and soul, connecting what we do with our craving for deeper meaning and purpose. Work *can* be about consciousness – the big picture. Good work contains a *why*, not just the *what*. Work can be imbued with soul and the divine – work is an opportunity to find and express our genius and inspiration, as we participate with the divine, with spirit.

Our work is bigger than any job, though we may need to find a job in the short term while we create our work.

But what does work mean to most of us? This may seem such an obvious question that it hardly merits the answer – most of us work to make money. This is the route that most of us have taken around work – to chase material success, to please our teachers, peers or family, to fit in, accumulate things – or to rebel against the lot! But most of us have fallen under a collective spell that More of the Same (MOTS) is all that is required. Just a little more hard work, the next pay rise, the next upturn in the economy … Many of us work in jobs and careers that give us little pleasure or excitement and few outlets for creative imagination. We will have experienced just what kind of emotional environment is created when we are not doing work we enjoy.

While the majority of the world's population is suffering from hunger of the body, the minority – us in the West – seem to be suffering from hunger of the soul. The strange paradox seems to be that as our personalities get richer and richer, our hearts and souls become poorer and poorer. We are both human and divine, but somewhere along the line we abandoned awareness of our divine nature, of our hearts and souls, for our personalities alone, and we kept going without looking back. The result of this detour in human evolution has been no more keenly felt than in the world of work, resulting in a great emptiness in the human spirit. Personality, efficiency, cleverness and detachment have ruled for over 200 years but our souls are now reminding us that wisdom, connectedness, heart, love and joy are the higher ground we yearn for.

So the work we were born to do is not about being successful in the job market, but about being successful in being ourselves, and fitting our work around that. We want to shift from work as a role to work that is real. Within each of us lie the power and resources to create rewarding and fulfilling work. We can go from tediously making a living to joyfully living our making, but how?

Here are some questions to help you begin to find the work you were born to do:

◆ Where is your joy? Where is your passion and motivation? What makes you feel most energized?

◆ What experiences, throughout the whole of your working life, have you found most rewarding, inspiring, touching or meaningful?

◆ What work would you love to do if you had all the money and time you needed already, or if all the work paid the same?

(If you are unable to answer these questions easily, make discovering your answers a project.)

If you think that doing what you want in today's economic climate is a mad idea, imagine describing life on earth to an alien. 'Yes, well the way we do things here on earth is that we are born with tremendous gifts and God-given talents and incredible potential. We are born with a full and open heart, and the power to create lives as artists create their art. But what we do is ignore all that and teach people how to get jobs that they don't particularly enjoy for the rest of their lives, so they can earn little bits of coloured paper and coins.'

Doing something you hate twenty, thirty-five, forty, fifty hours a week, five days a weeks, forty-eight weeks a year for decades is mad! In searching for the work we were born to do, we are waking up from the spell and becoming sane.

HOW WE SHAPE THE QUALITY AND DIRECTION OF OUR WORKING LIVES

> Often people try to live their lives backwards: they try to have more things, or more money, in order to do more of what they want so that they will be happier. The way it actually works is the reverse. You must first be who you really are, then do what you really need to do, in order to have what you want.
>
> MARGARET YOUNG

The work we were born to do is about getting familiar with the role our consciousness plays in our life and work, as from our own consciousness we create lack or plenty, pain or joy, purpose or struggle. Creating our life's work is an adventure in consciousness, embracing new awareness and discarding old self-concepts. We can prepare and cultivate our consciousness, like preparing the soil and making it fertile for new ideas and concepts. If we don't cultivate the soil, it doesn't matter if we have a wonderful collection of seeds – they won't grow.

A great truth is that the only way to finish somewhere is to start from the same place, to travel as we mean to arrive. The work we were born to do is not about living by rules, thinking, 'Well, as long as I work hard, don't upset too many people and don't make too many mistakes, I'll be rewarded …' There is no reward for a life lived by certain rules: life itself is the reward. To experience love, live a loving and love-filled life; to experience joy and creativity, live a joyous and creative life; to experience deep fulfilment, follow your heart and give the gifts that are inside each of us. There is no place or destination; we are on a journey of growing awareness of our own being.

ATTENTION AND INTENTION

We have touched on the idea that most of us have had our attention on survival, making money and meeting the needs of our personality rather than developing creativity, love, inspiration and passion. Attention and intention are the two most powerful conscious tools we have for creating and shaping our lives. You will have noticed how difficult it is to have a totally blank mind; our mind naturally wants to latch on to something; a goal-striving mechanism, it is always headed somewhere. Through attention and intention we choose the direction our mind and our working life takes.

Attention

Whatever we focus on, think about or worship, we become. But think what our attention is mostly drawn to. The media has one of the most powerful calls on our attention, and only rarely does a day pass when we do not see television, listen to the radio or read a newspaper. And what are they mostly reporting? Bad news, disasters and things that create fear: habitually most of us end up giving attention to the very things we don't want. Yet for every item of bad news, millions of acts of kindness, love and beauty fail to make the headlines.

Likewise, we may have been taught that we find the best in us by concentrating on eliminating our faults, eradicating what we don't want and criticizing our weaknesses. But this doesn't work, because we are still focusing on what we don't want. The work we were born to do is created from finding, discovering and focusing on our gifts, our strengths, our love, our creativity and our divine nature. As Thoreau wrote: 'I know of no more encouraging fact than the unquestionable ability of man to elevate his life by conscious endeavour.'

A large part of the work we were born to do is concerned with choosing to place our attention on different things. We'll learn to look for opportunities, not problems, creativity rather than boredom, our power rather than our limitations. This discipline alone can positively transform our experience of work. Simply, what we pay attention to will grow within our mind and consciousness, so we need to ask, 'What do we want to see more of in our working lives?' and choose to keep looking for it and creating it.

◆ Add up how much time you spend thinking about what you don't like about your existing work situation, how badly you are treated, how bad things are. And how do you feel on these occasions?

◆ By contrast, how much time and energy do you spend being creative, thinking up new ideas for work, exploring new ideas for work, dreaming, envisioning and imagining new possibilities?

◆ How much time do you spend with people who love their work and are creative and inspired?

◆ And how much time do you spend with people who dislike or even hate their work and feel stuck?

◆ Finally, what do you want to find in your working life? And what do you spend most time and energy looking at and for? Are they the same, or are they different?

Therapeutic in Greek means 'to put attention on', and whatever we put our attention on can be good and helpful for us, growing and expanding in our life. Wherever we choose to put our attention, and the quality of our attention, will determine the quality of our whole existence – work, relationships and prosperity. This applies to our outer attention and our inner attention; when we notice both what we feel and what we experience.

Intention

Intention is derived from the Latin *intendere,* meaning 'to stretch, direct or apply the mind in a particular direction'. When we stretch our minds towards an idea – an intention – this has power. A research report from Stanford University into what creates success showed that only 14 per cent of success was attributable to technical skills, abilities and qualifications. The remaining 86 per cent resulted from attitude, intention and a sense of purpose. In short, the spirit in which the work was done was the greatest factor in success. It's not *what* you know, but *why* you do it that is crucial.

Intention is the choice of direction to which we set our sails in our work, as well as the way in which we travel through our working life. It differs from desire in that when we desire something we usually have a great attachment to the outcome, and unfulfilled desires can be very painful, leaving us feeling empty and disappointed. Intention is desire without attachment, a direction we are headed, and when we have our attention in the present and our intention for the future, we are at our most powerful. Conscious intention is the way we instruct the incredible power that is in our subconscious mind.

To start to get in touch with attention and intention, begin by observing and following through on some of your desires, if only in small ways to start with.

Ideas for Activating the Powers of Attention and Intention

* Formulate a list of your deepest and most inspiring desires and intentions. Look at them several times a day – put your attention on them – and remind yourself. Remind yourself early in the morning, last thing at night and before silence and meditation if you practise them.

* As far as possible, release your *demand* that they happen. Understand that you will not accomplish these intentions by hard work and struggle alone, but by understanding that an organizing intelligence runs the whole of creation, and will work with your intentions too.

* Accept the present moment and live in it as fully as possible, knowing that you are creating and directing your working life in each moment of your life.

* Notice the ways in which your intentions are being fulfilled.

As we set our intentions for the direction of our life we begin to set in place synchronistic events or meaningful coincidences. Our intention sends out ripples and stimulates possible ways of bringing it to fruition. Most things in life happen because we intend them to. We will therefore create the work we were born to do by establishing our intention. This makes no sense at all if we think we are each separate bundles of skin and bone, with our own individual and isolated mind, but from the perspective that we are each woven into the fabric of the whole of creation it makes perfect sense. From the perspective of a totally innerconnected universal force, our intentions have organizing power.

There is an intelligence running through the whole of creation, and it also runs through us. Tagore described it: 'The same stream of life that runs through my veins night and day runs through the world and dances in rhythmic measures.' It digests our food, grows our hair and nails, brings the seasons, runs the whole of the natural world, the stars and the heavens. But we seem to think we have to run our work life, and that this intelligence will not support and guide us in our work. Heraclitus wrote: 'There is only one wisdom: to recognize the intelligence that steers all things.' When we consciously, on a moment-by-moment, day-by-day basis, become wiser by aligning ourselves with this intelligence, our work and life will be transformed.

It is incredibly mind-blowing to entertain the thought that the mind of creation is on our side and working for us, not against us. It can be described as our having the intention and letting the universe handle the details. When we embrace and commit to our purpose and to helping others, life conspires to support us.

LIFE IS *FOR* US

Our fears can immobilize us, make us feel alone and unprotected, lost and confused, unable to see the many trails leading out of the woods. And there is always a way out. The way out is within. There is a sacred place within us where wisdom and clarity dwell. This is where God resides and has being. This is the simple truth we were born to discover. Awakened to this truth, we won't fear the darkness of the night.

SUSAN L TAYLOR
Author of *Lessons in Living*

We are all part of the universal mind, an inextricable part of the whole of creation; we are all part of the symphony of life. Our intentions are like seeds, and once sown they will mark the direction in which we choose to steer our lives. In the right conditions and in time, they will sprout and grow into blooms and plants in the appropriate time, but we can't keep digging up the seedlings to see how they are growing. Through the power of our intention on the object of our attention we harness the incredible creative and organizing power of universal intelligence, and when our intention is based on love and service, life gets behind us.

When we go it alone, we may experience our life and work as a series of struggles; work may even seem like a punishment and we may feel helpless to change the world of work to yield to our deepest needs and heartfelt desires. But this is only because we have set ourselves up, within our own mind and thinking, in opposition to natural principles. We don't need to know how they work, just that they do; none of us really understands how gravity, a computer or even electricity work, but we can use them and enjoy the benefits. So with universal principles.

The work we were born to do is something that is natural to us. It may require effort, but not struggle. We won't have to try to do it, we will just be it and do it. It doesn't mean being good at everything, just some things; fish swim beautifully and naturally, but don't walk so well; cats make great companions, but can't cook; babies are good at being babies, not nuclear physicists.

EXERCISE

◆ Think about when you were a child. Remember what you were told you were good at, or what you remember doing easily and effortlessly. What about when you were a teenager? And what are you told you are good at now? What do you find easy now?

Start to value more what comes naturally and easily. To let our gifts go unexpressed is one of the most terrible forms of poverty. We need to find and follow what is easy and natural to us, for love and what is natural go together.

THE POWER OF LOVE AND JOY

Someday, after we have mastered the winds, the waves, the tide and gravity, we shall harness for God the energies of love. Then for the second time in the history of the world, man will have discovered fire.

PIERRE TEILHARD DE CHARDIN

In essence, the work we were born to do is about love – discovering and doing what we love, loving our work and what we do, loving ourselves and each other, not in a superficial or hedonistic way, but truly and authentically. Somewhere deep inside we know that love is the most powerful force there is, scaring and exciting us. Somewhere in our evolution we split love and work, putting life and livelihood in different places in our mind and deciding that only certain artists or particularly gifted people should reconcile these two aspects again.

While so much modern work seems to be based on fearful thinking rather than love and creativity, we know that we are not truly motivated to be and give our best from fear or guilt, but by inspiration, the desire to be our best selves and to enhance and contribute to the lives of those around us. The greatest achievements and virtuoso performances of our lives are romanced not beaten out of us. We can develop a romance with our own heart and soul.

EXERCISE

◆ For many, the word 'work' is so negatively emotionally laden, we may even need to invent a new word for the work we love. What would you call work that you truly loved? For example, your 'creative expression', 'permission to play' or something else?

The major reason why work has become so hard is because we have learned well how to work without love – it is hard because there is no love of it or within it. We have learned to value the needs of our personality over the longings of our heart, and in doing so cut off the very source of deep satisfaction and fulfilment. The gathering back of our dispersed power begins with the realization that no work of itself is intrinsically fulfilling; we make work soulful by bringing our heart and soul to it and to the relationships we have with the people we work with.

We only struggle because we try to work without spirit and without love, which is why work can seem so graceless. Abundance, love, integrity, authenticity, ease and truth: these are the natural laws. With love, work can be art and joy.

WORK AS ART AND JOY

The work of Creation was a work of joy whose sole purpose was to bring more joy into existence. This not only gives us permission to find joy in our work but charges us with a responsibility to do so. Joy is an essential source of motivation in our work.

MATTHEW FOX

Theologian, founder of Creative Spirituality and author of *The Reinvention of Work*

Many spiritual traditions tell us joy is the goal in our work:

'There is nothing better for a man than to rejoice in his work.' Ecclesiastes 3: 22 (Bible).

'They all attain perfection when they find joy in their work.' The Bhagavad Gita (Hindu scripture).

'In work, do what you enjoy.' Tao Te Ching (Chinese philosophy).

Joy is the beacon, the compass by which we plot our course, the key to discovering the work we were born to do, because joy is of the spirit and the highest human quality. Take time to notice what does, or could, give you either a small amount of joy, or buckets full of it.

Joy is the natural result of being loving, true and authentic, of being real and whole, of being honest and living our life's purpose, and joy is within each and every one of us. Joy is an experience of now, born out of the richness of each moment, and is the fruit of our own heart and spirit. There is only one way to have real joy and that is to seek joy, not poor substitutes. Joy often arrives on the wings of discovery and surprise, and cannot be planned for or controlled, but we can cultivate our willingness to receive it.

EXERCISE

◆ Remember four occasions when, as a child, you experienced real joy. What was the outcome of these events? Was it wonderful, or was there a loss involved? What did you decide about joy as a result of these experiences?

◆ When was the last time you felt real joy? What were the circumstances?

◆ What ideas come to mind when you think how you could create more joy in your work life?

Joy comes when we excel, when we transcend what we thought we could do and be, and it comes when we surprise ourselves. The work we were born to do is full of opportunities for joy. Much as an artist creates their art for the sheer joy of it, we need to find ways of doing what we love doing for the sheer joy of doing it, and then we can also discover how we can earn a living from our own joy too. At the centre we need to match our spirit, skills, motivations and aspirations with work that can give us joy. If we love singing, we need to sing; if we love being creative, we need to create something; if we love writing, we need to write; if we love people, we must find ways of enjoying people.

The wonder of life is that all souls enjoy different things; some enjoy numbers, others nature; some offices, others open air; some are creative, others logical. The only true problem is that we don't always do what we really enjoy; we don't identify and use our gifts and talents, and so we become square pegs in round holes. Each of us is a unique expression of life, with God-given gifts and talents, each able to do things in ways that no one else can. Each of us has a song to sing, a gift to give. That calling has been placed in our heart, and it will never be lost. The greatest sadness of life would be to die with that song still in us, our gifts not found or expressed. Yet that is what happens so often.

Do what you love. Do what makes your heart sing. And never do it for the money. Don't go to work to make money, go to work to spread joy.

MARIANNE WILLIAMSON
Author of *A Return to Love*

WHAT HAVE WE SUBSTITUTED FOR JOY?

I have not seen *joy* appearing on too many job descriptions, yet it is the missing element in so much work. What do we see instead? Compliance, approval, fear, money, recognition, power.

Joy will never come as a result of a *should* or an *ought*, but only as a result of doing what we freely want to do, a creative choice. Depression is often the consequence of repressed creativity, of not giving our love and gifts. Andrew Lloyd Webber said that when he created music he was happy, but was often depressed when he was not creating.

So why don't we do what we want and experience joy in our work? Deep in our unconscious mind, handed through dozens of generations, are ancient beliefs.

REMEMBERING OUR SELF-WORTH

As you read about Principle One, you may well be experiencing some resistance. Questions and objections may already be surfacing into your mind as a result of one issue – our sense of our self-worth. Our belief in and our experience of our self-worth is at the core of the work we were born to do.

If we have had a life spent with low self-esteem or self-diminishment, the journey to the work we were born to do will be new and exciting, perhaps even scary. We'll need to examine and dissolve unhelpful self-concepts and limiting beliefs in order to liberate ourselves so that our spirit can shine. We are not here to be fearful powerless spectators, but to be creative and powerful initiators, becoming daily more aware of the incredible power of love within each of us right now. We are remembering that the power of love within each of us is in truth all that we will ever need.

◆ How many times do you remember being told recently that you were wonderful, talented, brilliant and incredibly valuable?

◆ How did you feel?

◆ What were the circumstances?

Self-worth pervades our whole working life in both obvious and subtle ways. It determines the direction we decide to take at each crossroads in our life. Our self-worth affects what opportunities we even see, how much money we will ask for and make, what changes we will make; it determines what we will attempt, what risks we will take, what help we will ask for, what we are willing to receive, how kind we will be to ourselves, how much happiness and love we will allow ourselves to experience. Our self-worth is the amount of self-love we have, the cornerstone of our self-confidence.

THE FIVE MAJOR MYTHS OF SELF-WORTH

Inside many of us there are torture chambers where we condemn ourselves for not being good enough. We push ourselves hard out of low self-esteem.

Our goal is to bring love rather than condemnation to these parts of ourselves. The work we were born to do is created out of self-love, not self-hatred, and is not a compensation against guilt or fear but is built on the foundations of self-esteem and self-worth.

We weren't created unworthy, we learned it; in coming to believe in unworthiness, we came to believe in the power of fear of not being good enough. Let's examine five major erroneous beliefs that block our experience of our own self-worth:

1 I am not good enough – I have to earn and deserve self–worth

This has felt like the story of my life! We may spend much of our energy doing good or successful things, but on one level our motivation still cries, 'Please tell me I am valuable!' We want to create appearances in order to get approval and affirmation. We may feel that life is a series of tests, a succession of hoops to jump through, perhaps hiding a fear that today we might not succeed. Those of us that have been down this route know that no amount of external recognition can satisfy. We can still feel empty, however good we are told we are.

We can't earn or deserve self-worth, but must simply accept what we already are. It is not something to prove, but to be.

2 I am wrong or there is something wrong with me – I have to improve myself to make up my self-worth.

Have you ever tried to improve yourself? Have you ever bought a personal development book or attended a workshop or course? Perhaps you have been through many books, audiotapes, talks and seminars. In 1986 I embarked on a path of self-improvement and self-development in the belief that if only I could find the right book, tape, workshop or teacher I would find that sense of myself that seemed to be missing from my life. Not only did I attend the talks and workshops, I became the organizer of London's biggest weekly platform for such ideas! I totally immersed myself in these ideas. Yet, I still wasn't happy. Then I began to understand that to be happy and at peace we have to give up all ideas of self-development and self-improvement.

Self-worth comes from accepting the Self that has been created. Through the cumulative conditioning and beliefs of hundreds, even thousands of years, we have experienced so many negative and unhelpful beliefs and self-concepts that we have almost forgotten who we really are. Our true self is the spirit, or the unconditioned self within us, untouched and unchanged by anything of this world. We can change our prayer from 'Help me be different and change myself' to 'Help me accept and experience myself as you created me'. In truth, there isn't, and never has been, anything wrong with us.

3 I am bad – I have to work off my guilt to have self-worth

We may experience events in our earlier life such as rejection, being hurt or a lack of love, and mistakenly turn that into a belief that we must be bad for that to have happened to us.

This belief can also be traced to the idea of original sin, and the Protestant work ethic: we are not good enough in God's eyes, so have to make ourselves valuable with hard and difficult work. This belief has pervaded most of the Western world, and seems as strong as ever. More people work longer hours, and seem driven to do so.

In Eastern cultures there is no belief in original sin as such, but there is the notion of karma, that if we did bad or selfish things in previous lives, we enter this world with a negative score. Our job in this life, then, is to rectify this by doing good to even the score, and receive love from our creator. In truth, there is no karma between us and our creator; we are unconditionally loved. We may believe we are bad and naughty, but our creator doesn't, seeing right through to our being, which is innocent.

4   I am nothing – I have to keep proving I have self-worth

When we believe we are nothing at heart, we are on a constant treadmill of being useful, being helpful, playing roles and sacrificing ourselves for the benefit of others to show how good we are. We will probably keep ourselves busy, showing how useful we are, how much we are needed, and allow people to be dependent on us to prove our self-worth. Being busy keeps us from having to face our worst fear – that really we are nothing.

5   I am separate – I have to make the world realize that I am special and I have self-worth

When we believe we are separate from each other, nature, God and the whole of creation – in essence, nothing special – we are constantly trying to make ourselves special in other ways, and may manipulate people to treat us in special ways, by competing, by being better or worse than someone else, by having unique problems, by being the exception. Deep down we are desperate to be anyone, to avoid what we fear would be the death of us – being boring and ordinary.

When we believe and live by any of these ideas our life to some degree is a compensation, trying to prove what we don't actually believe ourselves to be – worthwhile human beings. In essence, at the core of the work we were born to do is the idea that our self-worth already exists – it cannot be earned, deserved, proven, worked hard for or sacrificed for but has to be discovered, embraced and accepted. We can't raise or build our self-esteem and we can't be told it, we can only say 'yes' to it ourselves in our own heart. Self-worth is not based on behaviour, but on our very being.

The work we were born to do is not a compensation, but is concerned with living authentically and truly. It is concerned with finding our true self-worth and creating our work from that place of self-worth, and having our work being an expression of our self-worth. The consequence of beginning to find our self-worth is that we can't turn back, we know we are called forward to finish the job of discovering our true nature. We need inspiration, not compensation.

INSPIRED WORK

When you work only for yourself, or for your own personal gain, your mind will seldom rise above the limitations of an undeveloped personal life. But when you are inspired by some great purpose, some extraordinary project, all your thoughts break your bonds: your mind transcends limitations, your consciousness expands in every direction, and you find yourself in a new, great and wonderful world. Dormant forces, faculties and talents become alive, and you discover yourself to be a greater person by far than you ever dreamed yourself to be.

PATANJALI (*c* 2ND-CENTURY BC)
Ancient Indian philosopher and author of Yoga Sutras

We may not just want a job, we may want to be inspired. All we truly need is one inspired idea that we trust, cherish, nurture, love and have the determination to follow as far as it will take us. A small beginning can have an enormous finish! And that idea is already within us, deep in our heart or maybe just beneath the surface. We tend to undervalue ideas, yet nothing exists that wasn't just once an idea in someone's mind. James Allen summarized this beautiful truth when he wrote: 'The greatest achievement was at first and, for a time, a dream. The oak sleeps in the acorn; the bird waits in the egg; and in the highest vision of the soul a waking angel stirs. Dreams are the seedlings of reality.' The work we were born to do and the powers to create it are slumbering within us. Inspiration is not about immediately having all the answers to the practical questions of how things can be achieved, but it is about being willing to take the first step, out of the love of your heart. Then the next step will come clear, then the next and the big picture is gradually revealed.

We can't control or manipulate inspiration but we can welcome and encourage it. Sometimes it comes as a welcome guest out of the blue. We can make our heart and mind receptive by learning what can and does inspire us. Certain places in nature such as a forest or the sea can be sources of inspiration; otherwise we might find it in literature or spiritual texts, music or poetry, relaxing our body through a sauna, steam or massage, or by meditating or visualizations. Once we know what can *contribute* to our inspiration we can invite in spirit, which is the true meaning of inspiration.

Killers of Inspiration	Cultivators of Inspiration
routine	love
lies	authenticity and truth
inauthenticity	creativity
hatred	willingness
violence	positive example
judgement	giving
competition	healing
attachment to outcomes	hope
cynicism	forgiveness
desire to win	openness, listening and empathizing
hypocrisy	admitting mistakes
prejudice	imperfection
dogma	tenderness
hardness	congruence

When we see so many people failing to enjoy their work, we can easily think that work can only be based on struggle, suffering and sacrifice, rather than joy, creativity and love. Yet, since time began, there have always been those who have been determined to let their joy, their inner calling and their determination triumph over others' opinions and mass mediocrity. Awaken your attention and look for inspiration. Aldous Huxley, in *The Perennial Philosophy*, tells us that 'Perpetual inspiration is as necessary to the life of goodness, holiness and happiness as perpetual respiration is necessary to animal life.'

EXERCISE

◆ Who are the three people you know who are happiest in their work?

◆ Who are your role models for enjoying and loving their work?

◆ What would truly inspire you in your work?

The answers to these questions will be revealing. If you can identify and name these people easily, then you are feeding yourself with positive images and ideas about inspiring work. If you have trouble thinking of any, then it is not surprising that you may find it hard to get inspired. Begin to surround yourself with people who are motivated, excited, inspired and creative, and see how you feel around them, what you can learn from them, even teach them. Become a detective, seeking out inspiration, and make yourself an expert on what you find inspiring.

The essence of our work is also about the *type of* doctor, therapist, teacher, social worker, trainer or secretary we want to be, making our work a vehicle for those qualities. We can become an inspired, loving and creative dentist, lawyer, tour guide or toilet attendant. The job does not necessarily define the limits. This inspired work is not found in any situations vacant, because it is born inside us. To some extent it is easier to create this work when self-employed, but more organizations want inspired employees. The world of work is not a brick wall that we keep bashing our heads against, but a canvas that will eventually yield to our inspiration.

EXERCISE

◆ Remove all limits and allow yourself to dream about the kind of work that would really inspire you, with no thought at all for *how* you might create it.

◆ Who would you love to work with?

◆ What would you love to be doing and giving? For whom?

◆ What would you receive from that, both materially and non-materially?

Ways to Nurture Your Inspiration

* Relax your body and/or mind.
* Meditate.
* Do creative activities.
* Be with inspired/inspiring people.
* Be in nature, natural beauty.
* Listen to music.
* Read/listen to inspiring material.
* Play music/read poetry.
* Go running.
* Create beautiful atmospheres.
* Free yourself from clutter.
* Go to sacred places.
* Have dreams.
* Intend to be inspired.
* Take more time to *be* more: enjoy goal-less pleasure.
* Be by water/sea.
* Be in the elements.
* Read inspiring stories of people's lives.
* Laugh!
* Be courageous.
* Have an adventure.
* Do something totally different.
* Do something you've always dreamed of.
* Look up at the night sky.
* Perform an act of loving kindness.

DISCOVERING OUR LIFE'S WORK

Everyone has been called for some particular work, and the desire for that work has been put in his or her heart.

JALALUDDIN RUMI
12th-century Persian mystic and poet

Discovery is a beautiful, and true, word to find our life's work. It already exists! Our job is to discover and remember, to listen to our heart again, to treasure our inner longings, to experiment, and to trust that resonance, that *inner yes* experienced when we hit the truth within us. It is about what could be, not just what is and has been.

The possibilities for the work we were born to do exist right now, yet they may lie just outside our current perception. Have you ever looked up at the stars at night, and then looked at some of the pictures from the Hubble space telescope and wondered why you couldn't see that beauty? Our eyes cannot perceive that much detail right now; the light is too weak, so we need a telescope. Similarly molecular life is only brought to life for us by the *microscope* that makes it visible to us. The galaxies and the microbes existed all the time. We just weren't aware of them, we couldn't perceive them.

The same is true of the opportunities for fulfilling work. Unlimited opportunities exist right now, but we may not see them just yet.

UNCOVERING OUR STRENGTHS

Although men are accused of not knowing their own weaknesses, yet perhaps few know their own strength. It is in men as in soils, where sometimes there is a vein of gold which the owner never knows of.

JONATHAN SWIFT (1667-1745)
Anglo-Irish satirist

Do we know what we are good, competent and gifted at? There is a vein of gold in each of us, and we can resolve to find and be comfortable with it. We live in a culture that doesn't tend to celebrate being good and knowing that we are good – we tend to call it arrogance and pride. We are taught that humility is good; it can be, but I think that we have often learned a false humility, being told we are good when we put ourselves down, know our weaknesses or criticize ourselves. Yet this is unfulfilling, as we know that a light in us wants to shine, and unless we shine we are not being true to ourselves.

The opposite is not being a big-headed egomaniac but simply knowing that each of us *is* good at certain things, even excellent and brilliant sometimes, but that this is no big deal. All we are doing is owning and using our God-given talents and gifts, and it is a kind of reverse arrogance when we undermine or devalue our inner gifts. Noel Coward summed it up beautifully when he said: 'Thousands of people have talent. I might as well congratulate you for having eyes in your head. The one and only thing that counts is: Do you have staying power?'

We should resolve to find, nurture and develop the talent that is within each of us. Just as the talents of others lighten up our world, so do our talents enhance our life and the lives of others.

EXERCISE

◆ What is your response to the idea of being talented and gifted? Do you feel excitement and interest, or fear and resistance?

◆ What, in your mind, are your strengths, talents and gifts?

◆ What have been identified as your strengths by other people?

◆ How did you feel when you were told? Did you believe them?

◆ Pick four significant people in your life, such as a partner, boss, colleague or parent. In your mind, ask, 'What do I think each one would perceive to be my strengths?' Ask yourself, and hear what answers come to you. When you feel ready, ask these people for their opinions. Listen, and take note of what they say. How do their answers match your own feelings?

LISTENING TO OURSELVES AGAIN

> Your true function is not to do anything, rather, only to be willing to listen to the small Voice within. This is a voice you are not likely to be accustomed to hearing, for it is a voice that speaks not in mere words, a hearing that does not require the body's ears. It is the Voice for joy. It is the Voice for Love. It is the Voice you share with the One who created you. It is What you will someday soon become, not by change, but through remembrance and awakening.
>
> JOEL WRIGHT
> Author of *The Mirror on Still Water*

Our spirit knows the work we were born to do. It is talking to us all the time, showing us the capacity for happiness, but our personality drowns out our other quieter voices. Perhaps one of the most significant and important elements of the work we were born to do is learning to listen to ourselves and our intuitions again, discovering what we really want in our heart. There are no formulae for this, just a gradual and continual personal evolution. Mostly we have become so used to listening to the instructions and opinions of other people – the media, friends, bosses, partners and family – that we may no longer have a clear idea what we do want. Or we may know what we want, but don't know how to create it.

Creating a Sanctuary

We will not find all the answers to the work we were born to do outside us in our busy daily activities, but when we take the time to be with our being and put our attention on our inner world rather than the outer world. We can do this in any quiet place – a room in our home, somewhere in nature, a church, a park. The place doesn't even matter that much, because sanctuary is an intention and an attitude rather than a physical place. With practice we can create sanctuary in more and more situations, but we may need to start with a physical place of peace and calm.

Magic happens in this sanctuary. My best friend Ben and I get together for lunch regularly. We chat about all that is going on in our lives but as much as we can we just lie on the floor for 20–30 minutes, simply being quiet. It is wonderful. We often end up laughing at how mad we are to keep so busy as we often have incredible creative ideas and inspirations in our sanctuary times.

Real fulfilment comes only when we first tune into our inner direction and divine guidance, acting from that place and bringing our inner and outer worlds together. We need to let our own heart be the greatest influence in our lives, rather than the voices of our own doubt and fear in our own minds and the good opinions of others outside of us who seek to influence us. As Goethe wrote: 'Just trust yourself and you will know how to live.'

EXERCISE

◆ Take as much time as you need to write down what you want, think you should have and demand from work. Don't censor; just let it flow.

◆ How much of all that is truly you? How much may originate with the voices of others that you have swallowed and taken to be yours?

◆ Now ask what you in your heart truly want in and from work? What part has this voice played in your work/career decisions so far? Did you listen to it? Ignore it? Deny it? Or weren't you even aware of its existence?

See how the answers differ. In our intuitions and the ideas that we have had for years and won't go away lie the seeds of our destiny. Listening to our inner voice and intuition leads us to create our own niche in life.

FINDING OR CREATING OUR NICHE

Our uniqueness is our gift to the world. No two people have the same qualities, vision and experience, and our life's work emerges from our own melting pot.

GILL EDWARDS
Author of *Living Magically*

We all long to find our niche, a place where we belong, where our presence is valued and celebrated, where our talents and skills are known and honoured. Finding our niche is finding where we belong, a place not subject to competition, because only we can fill that place in that way, recognizing our uniqueness. We may *find* our niche if it has been created by someone else and fits us well, or we may *create* it ourselves from our own sense of inner vision, understanding how to use our own creative powers. Many people tailor their dreams and aspirations to match their circumstances, but we can adjust our circumstances to our aspirations and build from the inside out. The true joy of work is finding the best inside us, and identifying ways of sharing it and enriching the lives of others through our gifts. When we do that, money we earn comes as a beautiful by-product. A working life rich in spirit cannot be bought with any amount of money, but it can be created from our own dreams, imagination and determination. Here are some characteristics of finding our niche:

Our inner and outer worlds become more integrated and balanced.

We can be more of our natural shape, our natural self.

Work and pleasure are unified.

We feel recognized.

◆ We are in a place where we feel safe and belong.

We are home.

◆ We are in alignment with ourselves and have integrity.

◆ We are on track and on purpose.

We support the spiritual side of ourselves in work.

Our niche fits in beautifully with other people's niches.

We are the right shape in the right hole, a good fit.

◆ Our work is worthwhile and important.

Our joy in doing our work is the reward of our work, not just approval or external rewards.

In terms of the work we were born to do our niche could be:

part-time or full-time

◆ self-employed or employed or a combination

◆ a portfolio career with more than one activity or one main career

◆ a small part of our life or a major part of our life

The work we were born to do is about our choices, based on our inner and outer needs and desires. It is unique for each of us. As each of us finds or creates our natural niche, we help others to find theirs, just as we were helped by those who showed us some direction. Finding our niche means valuing again our uniqueness, our quirkiness, our moods, honesty and vulnerability, which may, in fact, be our greatest gifts. What seems different in us is the rare thing we possess, the one thing that gives each of us our worth, and that's just what we try to suppress. We claim we love life, but often suppress who we really are.

Affirmation: I know in my heart with complete certainty that there is a niche in the world that only I can fill. I am determined to find or create this niche, and not to stop exploring until I find it or be it.

No-one is born into the world whose work is not born with him.

JAMES RUSSELL LOWELL (1819–91)
American poet, essayist, critic and diplomat

We will discover the work we were born to do by putting our attention on:

◆ what we love, are inspired and excited by

◆ our strengths

◆ what we long do be, do and create

We may even have to create our niche; it may not exist yet. The work we were born to do will lead us to develop a new relationship with our own creative mind, the part of us that knows all the answers, and will lead and show us the way. It will also lead us to improve our relationship with many other aspects of ourselves that we may have neglected.

WORK AND THE CHILD WITHIN US

The return for the work you do must be the satisfaction which that work brings to you and the world's need of that work. With this, life is heaven, or as near heaven as you can get.

WILLIAM E B DU BOIS (1863–1963)
American writer and co-founder of National Association for the
Advancement of Colored People

Close your eyes quietly for a moment, and visualize yourself as a child at some age that comes to mind – trust your intuition about what age that is. Ask that child, 'How do you *feel* about your current work? How *motivated* and *engaged* do you feel?' Notice the thoughts and feelings that come to mind.

Each of us has an inner Child (with a capital C) and the work we were born to do may involve building a new and better relationship with our Child. The Child within consists of the child we were at all ages, from conception onwards, emotionally alive and affecting our life today. Our Child is home to our love, playfulness, desires and wants, our emotions, what we enjoy, our energy, power and motivation, our inspiration and sense of mystery, our dreams. Our Child is where we'll find answers to many of the questions about what we love to do. The grown-up parts of us either give or deny permission to our Child, and work out how to implement what the Child within wants.

EXERCISE

◆ When you think about work being a source of pleasure, enjoyment, fun or inspiration, what is your reaction?

◆ Who do you know that most brings their Child into their work? How do they do it? What are the benefits of them doing that?

We may have thought that the world of work is a grown-up place, and decided that our Child needed to be left out; we can only have fun, play and do what we want outside of work. Leaving our Child out of our work could be our problem.

EXERCISE

◆ Think back to before you were ten years old, and remember something that you really enjoyed, were good at and was a good experience.

◆ Think back to a time in the last ten years and do the same.

◆ Think back to within the last year and do the same.

◆ Complete the statement 'I am someone who enjoys ...' at least 20 times, with different answers.

What strands came out of this? Any common themes? What strengths and gifts must you have had and used to achieve these results?

Our Child is our powerhouse, and we can learn to cherish the Child within. An organization run by children would probably be great fun to work in, although it might be disastrous financially! But if the Child within any person in any organization is not present within their work, then energy, commitment, creativity and motivation will be low. Our Child doesn't always get the job done, but without our Child we don't have the energy to achieve what needs doing.

Our Child is also the place within us where we have been hurt, where we feel depressed, angry, frustrated and where we hold our negativity and despair, as we shall see in the next chapter.

WHAT ARE YOU WAITING FOR?

Man's main task in life is to give birth to himself.

ERICH FROMM (1900–1980)
German-born physician and psychoanalyst

What needs to happen before you'll make a change?

Success and happiness are natural. We have placed ourselves outside our naturalness through our own erroneous thinking. Our thinking creates our experience of our life, and is determined in large part by the conditioning we have received throughout our lives, the influences we have encountered and the decisions we have made.

EXERCISE

◆ Go back to your teenage years, or when you first started to make work and career decisions. Ask yourself: 'In the light of my — years' experience of work and life, what would I do differently now? What would I not do again? What would I have done that I did not do?'

◆ How, in the past, have you decided to change your working situations?

◆ What factors were present? What were the motivations? Boredom or excitement? Pain or joy? Disputes or harmony? Were you desperate to get away from something, or inspired to move to something greater?

◆ Were you decisive, or did it seem to happen to you?

◆ Did the change take a long time coming, or were you swift and decisive?

◆ What can you learn from the way you've changed in the past? What would you like to do differently this time?

◆ What are you waiting for? Are you waiting for permission or encouragement from someone outside you? What would they say? Give that permission to yourself.

When you think about making a significant life change, what thoughts come to mind? Does your mind immediately go to the joys, the material, emotional and spiritual rewards that you can experience when you follow your heart? Or does your mind go to the difficulties of change, what might go wrong and the pain involved? What is your conditioning?

Through our conditioning we set ourselves apart from the intelligence that flows through all things, but we can motivate ourselves to change. Let's now take a closer look at the conditioning that most of us receive around work, and its impact on the quality of our lives.

Simple Ways to Implement Principle One

* Choose to do what you love, or do what you enjoy in the way you love, more often.

* Notice what you most enjoy about today.

* Ask yourself what would be really inspiring for you, and do something about it.

* Remember and cherish your long-held ideas and aspirations.

* Take sanctuary time simply to be with yourself.

* Keep affirming your willingness to discover and follow where your heart lies.

Principle Two

UNDOING OUR CONDITIONING

We have stifled our natural self and our spirit through the conditioning that we have absorbed throughout our lives. Our conditioning is the beliefs, attitudes and opinions that others have invited us to take on, which we may have mistaken as facts. We are called to identify, examine and discard beliefs that are not useful and are not true for us, and to continue the emotional healing that is required.

OUR CONDITIONING – WHAT WE HAVE BEEN LED TO BELIEVE

A person is as (s)he believes.

ANTON PAVLOVICH CHEKHOV (1860–1904)
Russian dramatist and storywriter

Beliefs determine how we see the world. As Burt Hotchkiss said so beautifully: 'If I hadn't believed it, I never would have seen it.' Our true self, the human spirit, is not conditioned – it is forever fresh, free and unfettered – but as we grow up we develop our conditioned self, which incorporates our self-concepts, personalities, opinions, limitations, attitudes and beliefs about ourselves, the world and the nature of life and work. This is the substance of our personality or ego self, and it is the limitations of this self that Principle Two is concerned with overcoming.

The working life we have created is the manifestation of our beliefs; by exploring our beliefs and undoing our conditioning, we will open ourselves to the work we were born to do. Our conditioning constricts the amount of life energy that can flow through us, and the greater the erroneous beliefs, the bigger the blocks: it is as if we are trying to force the whole energy of the universe through a tiny hole in our mind. We stem the flow but can turn it back on again by undoing our conditioning and healing the wounds it has caused us. While we block, through our conditioning, the amount of life energy we receive, the amount of life energy that is available remains unaltered and is still unlimited. As we step out of our limited self-concepts we will step back into our truth.

To start the process of change we must understand our current position and what has brought us here. We do not sit down one day and decide what we are going to believe, but we make decisions based upon the thousands of influences and messages that we have received every day of our life from everyone around us. All the things our parents and family said, all we hear from teachers, church ministers and politicians, what we read, hear on the radio and see on the TV– all have had some impact. Our beliefs are largely unconscious and are like glass walls – we don't see them and only know they are there when we bump into them. To get past them, we first have to know they are there.

EXPLORING OUR CONDITIONING

Even in the best of circumstances, we are all just learning. No parents are fully enlightened. Children will unconsciously absorb their parents' fears and biases and later in life, one hopes, learn to become conscious of these conditioned attitudes and find ways to release them. This is normal; this is the work we all have to do.

RICHARD MOSS
Author and teacher

All conditioning reduces the freedom to find and live the work we were born to do because we begin to value approval and other people's opinions rather than the whisperings and intuitions of the voice of our own soul. We created many of our beliefs in our childhood and young adulthood, sometimes under stress. Psychologists say that by the time we are three years old we will already have made many of the following major decisions:

◆ We will have decided how life is – that is, safe or scary, loving or dangerous, whether we are good or bad.

◆ We will have decided how to survive in the world, and what to do to safeguard our emotional and physical survival.

◆ We will have decided what is wrong with us and what we dare never show anyone else; most of us have some kind of wounding to our self-esteem and our sense of being lovable and worthy.

We spend the rest of our lives proving that what we decided by the age of three was correct, so a significant part of our working life has been built on a three-year-old's view of the world. As adults we can go back and discover some of these beliefs that may have formed the basis of our life, and hold them up to the light of awareness and see how true they are for us as adults.

We can accept and realize that many conditioned beliefs are not even really ours, but were absorbed from those who have influenced us, sometimes helpfully, other times less so. However, blaming others, such as our parents or teachers, is not useful; they were doing the best they could with their own beliefs, and were generally just passing on what they had learned. Healing and forgiveness may be needed for us to make new choices and new decisions.

The following powerful and insightful exercise will bring into your awareness some of the major beliefs that you have developed in your life, specifically around work. Some of these beliefs will support you in creating the work you were born to do, while others will be squashing your spirit and inspiration.

EXERCISE

Isn't it amazing that we often have to make life-altering decisions about work and careers when we are young, when we have precious little experience or information on which to base those decisions? Cast your mind back to when you were younger and think about the kinds of messages you got about work – both helpful and unhelpful – from people and organizations such as:

◆ your mother or mothering influence

◆ your father or fathering influence

◆ siblings and other significant family members like grandparents, uncles and aunts

◆ school, teachers or careers advisors

◆ professional bodies

◆ the media

◆ peers

◆ religious and political leaders

Don't censor them or judge them; simply be aware and make a note of them.

You will probably identify some interesting thoughts that have forged and given birth to your belief system. Our beliefs are the software of our life, the programmes we run every hour of our life, about ourselves, work, other people and our life. As the Buddha said: 'We are what we think, all that we are arises with our thoughts. With our thoughts we make the world.' To make any significant change in our work we will need to continue to examine and change, where necessary, our beliefs.

Changing our work is an inside job, and it works! Nothing on the outside has to change before you start creating the work you were born to do! As we change, the world starts to respond and yields to us, and we start to see the world with fresh eyes.

OUR CONDITIONING GIVES RISE TO, AND IS CREATED BY, OUR BELIEFS

Our deep beliefs are like water to fish – they are the environment, the context of our lives. We are in them, quite literally, and being in them, we can't see them … We experience the world as a reflection of our deep beliefs.

PETER AND PENNY FENNER
Meditation teachers

Our experience of whatever work we do is determined largely by our beliefs about ourselves, how work should be and our beliefs about other people. Our beliefs are our reality, and what we feel to be certain about life. These certainties in turn become the limits, the fences beyond which we don't even bother trying to go. Interestingly, the derivation of the word 'hell' is an Old English word meaning fence or pen, used specifically to keep animals in. Our hell is the fearful limits with which we hem ourselves in.

Imagine an aquarium, divided into two with a clear glass wall, so you have two tanks. When you put a barracuda in one side and a mullet (a barracuda's favourite food) in the other side, the barracuda thinks that lunch has arrived, so she heads straight for the mullet, and then hits the glass wall. She tries many times over the next few days and weeks, but lunch eludes her. All she gets is a sore nose. Eventually she gives up, thinking that chasing that particular food is painful. The strange thing is that once the glass wall is removed, the barracuda doesn't go after the mullet, and stays on her side of the tank, and would even starve to death with lunch swimming a few inches away, because she knows the limits, and won't go beyond them.

This is the story of all of us; we all live in transparent boxes called our beliefs. Rediscovering our true self-worth means opening our hearts to ourselves again.

Through our beliefs, we create the source of all our experience in life. Our glass walls are the influences of teachers, families, bosses, the media … Sadly, after their voices have faded, we have internalized them and made them into our own limits. Through our conditioning we sacrifice the voice of our own spirit and follow the voice of others. We become our own gaolers, and we forget that it is we who locked the door, and that we still hold the keys to our own freedom. It is like trying to drive a car by looking in the rear view mirror; if we fail to change our conditioning, we create our future from our past. To alter the future, we need to modify our perception of our past. The most important aspect of learning is to unlearn our erroneous thinking, including the top ten spirit-squashing beliefs held by most of us.

TOP TEN SPIRIT-SQUASHING BELIEFS

1 Our purpose in work is to find approval and acceptance

From school onwards, and maybe earlier, we are immersed in a whole universe in which someone else judges, approves or disapproves of our work and even ourselves. We begin to value what others think of us more than what we think of ourselves. We are encouraged to think about how we will find a job and make employers say yes to us in a world where we believe there aren't enough jobs and we'll have to compete. So we marginalize our creativity, our spirit and joy. We sacrifice the rewards of our inner being and motivation for approval, acceptance and money, and we learn to comply. We learn to value outer rewards over inner rewards and experiences, and create roles and personas that will get us the approval we so desire. We become dutiful not beautiful, as roles are based on *ought to* and *should do*, not *want to*, as many organizations are based on the idea of encouraging the need for approval (and compliance). We may also end up doing what we are told we are good at, even though we hate doing it.

This can lead us to the experience of either feeling that we are inadequately rewarded for our compliance, or that we are well rewarded but fail to achieve joy. We may be popular, in demand and successful, but dead inside, only playing a role. Conditioning also tells us that if we are authentic and real, we will probably no longer be approved of, and may even be unemployable. If we are not motivated by approval and are not fearful of disapproval, we may be considered uncontrollable or suspect. Pay for performance becomes more like pay for compliance, and because much work is fairly mindless, we become far more concerned with the rewards than with the joy possible in doing work well and with all our heart.

2 Everything good is outside us

This is perhaps the greatest trick of the mind. We have been taught that everything good and worth having lies outside us and needs to be worked hard for, deserved, earned and competed for. Our goal then becomes to develop external power through position, authority or wealth, so we can get what we want. This has blinded us to the fact that each of us already contains all that we are looking for outside of us, as our unconditioned self is whole and complete already. Our own true nature is abundant, peaceful, loving and joyous, right now. And just as the sun never stops shining even though we may not see it for days or even weeks on end, our true nature has never altered just because we have lost sight of it and aren't aware of it.

We also look outside us all the time for wisdom, guidance, direction and a sense of purpose for we forget that we are also the source of wisdom, love, and our guidance and inspiration. Life speaks to our own heart, each of us. The work we were born to do is about remembering to ask within ourselves where our creativity and passion are, and in which direction our joy lies.

True power is power with each other, not power over each other and is not acquired but shared from our heart and unlike external power is available to all of us. Human history has been based on power over others and domination, but most of the institutions of power – church, legislation, monarchy and government – are wielding less control. We are each recognizing the power within us, and are less willing to be dominated. Our love and hearts are becoming the governing principle and we are moving from the love of power to the power of love.

3 Work is hard, a struggle, even a punishment

Or 'I believe I am here to suffer.' In the United Kingdom 6 million people work over 48 hours a week, and 1 million people work over 60 hours a week. We are working harder but not necessarily enjoying it. We are also conditioned to believe that work is a series of expectations, a series of tests, exams and hoops to jump through. This idea has one of its roots in the belief in original sin, that we are not good enough, that we are bad or even evil, in the eyes of our creator. Many of us have a deep fear of God, and believe we may need to be punished. I came across a quote from John Calvin, the French Protestant reformer, who, around the 1530s, is attributed with being a fundamental influence in the development in what we know as the Protestant work ethic:

> God, who is perfect righteousness, cannot love the iniquity which He sees in all. All of us have that within us which deserves the hatred of God ... and therefore the infants themselves, since they bring with them their own damnation from their mother's womb, are born not by another's but by their own fault. For although they have not as yet brought forth the seeds of their own iniquity, they have the seed therefore enclosed within them; yea their whole nature is a certain seed of sin.

This is obviously the product of a very darkened mind, as far as possible away from the truth of our relationship with God. Much as we would love to dismiss it as a load of rubbish, it represents something each of us may have to face at some time or another – a belief that God hates us and that we must punish ourselves through hard work in which we suffer, feel guilty, and sacrifice ourselves in the hope that God will either leave us alone or forgive us and redeem us. Or even worse we may come to believe that we are damned and that there is nothing we can do about it, so we live with a level of despair.

Many of us have come to believe that we are bad, when in truth we are good enough, born in blessing, not in sin. The work we were born to do is based on accepting that our work is not a punishment, a way of trying to pay off old guilt, but a way of expressing our true creative goodness, the spirit within us and a way of making a contribution to the good of the world.

The idea that work should be hard also automatically discounts or reduces the value of work that is soft, easy, graceful, gentle, nurturing or caring. I learned a lesson in Greece recently. I have not been a strong swimmer, and often get a bit panicky in the sea. When I was in the sea, close to the island where I was working, I thought I'd try an experiment – to relax as much as I could when I was in the sea. When I stopped being independent, struggling, and allowed myself to relax, I was supported by the sea much more than when I tried to keep myself afloat. I changed my thought and attitude. This is a wonderful metaphor for life as well as being a literal truth – most people drown because they panic.

4 Work must involve sacrifice

Sacrifice is the belief in self-denial, and the idea that self-denial will buy us something of value. We believe that sacrifice will buy us more love and approval, or that self-denial will buy us a place in heaven. So, the logic goes, if I suffer now in my work, it makes me a better person, more noble, so I will be more lovable. Images and ideas of sacrifice abound in religion – Christ on the Cross, sacrificing animals to appease gods, giving up food, sex, pleasure or joy in an attempt to find spiritual peace. The image of martyrdom being good may be very strong, but it is another trap to keep us away from our true nature. God demands no sacrifice, we have to give up nothing to be happy in our work. The work we were born to do demands no sacrifice, only the choice to relinquish our old and unhelpful beliefs and self-concepts.

A popular piece of conditioning is to say to ourselves, 'I will give up following my heart and joy, in order to have security and money' or 'I will do what I have always wanted to do, but I know I will need to go without money and security.' This belief also states that everything good has to be struggled for, deserved and earned, with sweat and tears, and perhaps even blood, so we also believe we'll be most rewarded and most secure if we don't do what we enjoy. The world is full of uninteresting work, so if you show you are willing to do boring and uncreative work it is unlikely you'll ever be short of work. We ask ourselves the question 'What would make me attractive to an employer?' rather than 'What do I love and what am I here to do and be?' We spend so much energy getting qualifications and training to become competent at things we don't necessarily enjoy but we think will provide some security. Another way our belief in sacrifice can manifest is that we feel that we can either be successful in our work and career, *or* in our family and relationships, but not both. Sacrifice can also show up as belief in needing to 'carry' people and things we care about – our work projects, colleagues, department, even our whole company, our family or friends. This becomes a heavy burden and can wear us out.

Isn't it a strange idea that we have made of God, who would create us with love, creativity, passion, inspiration, beauty and joy woven into our being and then demand that we spend the greatest part of our lives – work – totally discounting, hiding or ignoring all these gifts? We create a picture of a God who thrives and flourishes on our suffering. Somewhere we've misled ourselves, and overlooked the fact that life is set up to support us doing what we enjoy, following our heart's desires and being where our passion is. The opposite of sacrifice is not hedonism, but authenticity and truthfulness.

5   We live in a state of non-participating consciousness

We come to believe that we are a body, separate from our environment, other people and the creative force and intelligence behind all life.

Yet for most of history we have believed the world to be enchanted and alive, and ourselves as an intimate and integral part of creation, but for the last 300–400 years, since the development of Newtonian physics, we have lost this perception. Objectivity died, but was not buried, in 1927, with insights into the quantum physical nature of matter, when it became clear that there is no such thing as an independent observer standing apart from the world, and never had been, as we create the world by our own perceptions. Albert Einsten said in response to these insights: 'Everything has now changed, except our thinking.' Most of us have been taught the fossilized remains of extinct beliefs, and tried to live by them, yet the deeper truth is that the world responds to us, is part of us, and we are part of it. We are part of the web of life that runs through every living and even inanimate thing: there is only one life.

The work we were born to do is concerned with restoring the perception of spirit and soul behind the world we understand with our physical senses. Our work is shaped by invisible forces – our own intention, vision, hopes, spirit, heart and soul. As we become more aware and conscious, we can create in new and exciting ways because we are part of the whole of creation. As theologian

Matthew Fox wrote: 'Our work takes on cosmic significance when it is inner work, a work connected to the origins of the universe. Therein lies its dignity, therein lies its power; therein lies its reward.' Our true work is not just a job, but remembers our true nature.

6 Work is nine to five, five days a week, 48 weeks a year, for most of your life

This is what we have been taught a proper job is. We might also add: working for someone else; security; respectability; boring and predictable routines; something to make the family proud (or upset!); a lack of creativity. Our expectations of work are so low generally that it is almost as if we need to invent a new word for joyful, loving, creative work.

I would like to reinvent the idea of a proper job: it has many strands, a portfolio; its hours suit our lifestyle; it allows us to find and utilize the best and most creative parts of us; it incorporates and accommodates us as a whole person; it affords the opportunity to grow, expand and discover more about ourselves; it is based on win/win and co-operation; it allows us to expand into being a whole human being – mind, body, emotions and spirit. That is proper work!

The world of work and jobs is changing so fast. Most new jobs are not full-time but part-time, and more work is becoming less secure. The myth that we will be taken care of in return for our loyalty is largely over.

My friend Peter took early retirement as teacher of children with special needs, and, after around a year of not working and enjoying his freedom, decided that he wanted to resume some work. When we discussed his options, he seemed uninspired. As we talked about the possibility of him doing work that he would choose, where he would determine the hours that suited him, and who he worked with, his face lit up. The concept of being in charge of his work was new and liberating for him. He could suddenly see the freedom to work in way that he wanted, and was breaking out of his conditioned mentality.

We are all freer than we think we are.

7 We create what we want by studying and eliminating what we don't want

Much conventional psychology has a lot to answer for. Until recently the logic has been that the study of unhappiness/depression/stress/illness will lead us to an understanding of happiness, joy and wellness. If we find and get rid of everything we don't want, and eliminate the weaknesses, we will get what we do want. We've become fascinated by what we *don't* want. This is the belief of the conditioned mind, which wants us to keep our attention away from where it could really do some good. We become experts on the problem, but with little to say on creating solutions.

My good friend Robert Holden, founder of the Happiness Project, studied psychology at university but soon discovered he was studying mental illness, not wellness: 'As a psychologist, I was trained to be a problem-spotter, and initially I prided myself on how soon I could spot people's weaknesses and neuroses. As a good psychologist, I wanted to be able to spot more problems than the other psychologists!' Does that remind us of any colleagues? He explained that over a period of time he had a change of heart: 'I began to realize that the greatest therapy is about pointing people towards their own goodness, the love, creativity and health within, not fault-finding.'

The ego is the fault-finder. Much traditional management philosophy has been based on 'Let me find what people are doing wrong, badly or not so efficiently, so I can tell them so that they can jolly well put it right, and if they are doing okay, we'll leave them alone.' This does not bring out the best in us, yet it is also the thing we have trained ourselves to do, writing a long mental list of our weaknesses, faults and shortcomings and mentally telling ourselves 'Must do better!'

Yet there is a greater law and principle that we can learn. When we treasure and nurture what we *do* want, pay attention to it, become fascinated by it and celebrate it, we'll create more of it. Only rarely do we say, 'That went so well, we did it brilliantly, how can we do that again?' Yet this is the way forward. How many of us have become students of what we want, such as love, creativity, joy, peace and happiness?

The work we were born to do is about finding, nurturing, celebrating and consequently growing the best of us, our strengths and our successes. It means us realizing that it is a wonderful blessing for us and others to be talented and gifted. It involves accepting and embracing, not fighting to eliminate what we think we don't want.

8 Our work defines who we are

One of the biggest errors of thinking we make is to equate what we do, achieve and earn with who we are and how valuable we are. We all know that one of the most common ways of introducing ourselves at any gathering is 'What do you do?', as if who we are *is* what we do. We define ourselves by our *doing*, not by our *being*. This is another major piece of conditioning – we are valuable to the extent we do meaningful (in social terms), successful and financially rewarding work. Work can even become the major source of meaning in our lives if we feel impoverished elsewhere in our lives. The work we were born to do is concerned with being whole, and having meaning and purpose throughout our whole lives. Work can be just one expression of who we are.

We have learned to value other people's opinion of what we do more than we value our own experience of who we are in our work, so if we choose not to work for a while, consider changing our work or are made redundant, our whole sense of identity, value, self-esteem and self-confidence can feel threatened. Our conditioning is still very strong in that we feel we only fully participate in society and are valuable members of society when we are working hard at anything.

The way we value ourselves according to our work can be traced to another strand of the Protestant work ethic, with the idea that we arrive on earth as sinners and must make up ground through our work and then prove ourselves worthy and work off some of our guilt. Although we may not consciously subscribe to this ethic, there is still a strong belief that as children we are valuable for being ourselves, but our value as adults is determined by the hard work we do. Those who don't work hard in our society are regarded as somehow not pulling their weight. The idea is that work is dignity, and a way of paying off primal guilt and proving value.

Yet we are all bigger than the work we do. We are all the children of the creator of the universe, divine and with a wonderful inheritance. I propose a new starting point, that we are valuable because we are, because we exist and are here. Period. Nothing to prove. Who we are as a spirit, a heart and a soul is bigger than any work we will ever do; work can be an expression of who we are but is never who we are. Work when freely chosen and utilizing our best self can be a great blessing, but our value as a being is irrespective of whether we do or don't work. This is tough for many of us to believe – that we can not work *and* be valuable, be unemployed *and* loved, achieve little or nothing *and* still be precious. But it's true. Work can be a vehicle for our spirit, but our spirit is bigger than any work we will ever do.

9 There isn't enough – scarcity rules

Our whole world is based on this one major ego belief – the notion of lack, that there isn't enough of anything – love, work, money, opportunities, peace, food, hope, creativity, land, resources, likely partners … the list of lack is, paradoxically, endless. Not everybody can have what they want and need. The ego binds us up in an endless search, chasing our slice of whatever cake we are interested in, asking how we can get more happiness, fulfilment at work, financial security, sexual satisfaction, recognition, respect … again, a long list of things to strive for. And, of course, the competition must always have winners and losers because there isn't enough for everybody to have what they want. We might believe that there aren't enough jobs in the country or the world to go around, so we are in competition with each other and other countries to see who is going to win the jobs battle. Worthwhile, fulfilling and enjoyable work is at an absolute premium, and simply not available to most people. Furthermore, jobs are threatened by new technologies, cheap imports, foreign competition, and so on, so we should be grateful for any job at all. The ego works to spread fear, lower expectations, voice doubt and keep us in conflict.

One way we maintain our conditioning in lack is to continue to focus on what is missing from our lives. We don't see what we have, but become experts in seeing what we *don't have*. Like a hungry beggar on a beach of gold, we can be surrounded by all that we are looking for and feel empty. What we want is always either in the future, just around the corner or was in the past. Lack keeps us away from here and now, which in fact is dripping and effulgent with gifts, rich with possibilities, containing all we want. Abundance is our true nature.

10 Money and financial survival are the major purposes of work

Most of us have been led to believe that the goal of work lies in financial security and survival, which of course are important. Those, we believe, are what we need, so work is an expectation, not a choice. It may seem self-evident that most of us have to work to survive financially in this world, but the very feeling that we *have to* work, or have to do anything, either creates a resentment or a sense of duty, both of which preclude true enjoyment. Work becomes a necessary evil, something to hate but that we have to do, a duty, a four-letter word, necessary to survival. Our belief that we have to work can be very deep, even to the extent that we may not know what to do with our lives if we don't work. We understand from research that many men die within a year of retirement because so much of their identity had been tied up in their work. When it runs out, they believe the purpose of their life does too.

Work can only be truly enjoyable when we chose it. So although we have to work, we can choose what we do, and how we do it, finding work that uses the best of us or allows us to develop the best of us. Albert Camus wrote: 'There is dignity in work only when it is freely chosen.' We can learn to choose our work rather than feel we have to do it. Our choice to commit and give ourselves fully to the work that we are doing already, rather than feel resentful or fantasizing about different work, can be a way of transforming our attitude to work. We can discover ways of enjoying our current work and still be motivated to change.

How many of these spirit-squashing beliefs can you relate to? I expect you can identify with many of these ideas that we have been conditioned in. The work we were born to do is not about breaking the rules of these beliefs, but about replacing them with principles which, as we have seen, offer choices with consequences not punishments.

WHAT WE BELIEVE ABOUT DOING WHAT WE LOVE

When you think about *doing what you love*, what are your immediate thoughts? Are they of excitement, anxiety or disbelief? Look at the following list and note which of these thoughts you identify with the most.

Unhelpful thoughts

I might fail.
It won't last.
It's not allowed.
I don't deserve it.
Work just isn't fun, it is hard.
I won't be supported financially.
I won't be good enough.
It's too scary, I will be attacked and
    punished.
It is dangerous to be visible.
It can't be safe.
I will be judged.
I'll be vulnerable, it is inherently
    unsafe.
I won't earn money from giving gifts.
I want to be taken care of.
Money is the root of all evil.
I feel guilty about earning money.
Doing what we love is indulgent and
    selfish.

Supportive and helpful thoughts

We all have gifts and talents.
I have a niche and can find my niche.
Life supports our love, our joy and
    our passion.
I can find ways to exchange my gifts
    and talents for money.
My joy is my gift.
The world benefits from our best
    self/heart.
Work can be its own reward.
Work can be easy when we are on
    purpose.
I'll attract like-minded souls to me.
I will start manifesting helpful people,
    situations and events.
There is a lot of joy around.
I can receive.
My happiness is my contribution.
Living my vocation benefits all
    around me.

Notice the supportive and helpful thoughts you most readily agree with or believe in, as you may need to shift your attention on to the best that could happen, not the worst. Ken Bradford Brown, co-founder of the Life Training personal development seminars, puts it this way: 'Unconsidered beliefs are like fossils of experience that were once alive. The beliefs that we consciously choose are touchstones for living. And we're always choosing.' The key words here are *always choosing*. You now have the wonderful opportunity to make new choices. We can choose new beliefs for ourselves, because the original ones were never true in the first place! We've been living a lie; as Mark Twain once said: 'One of the most striking differences between a cat and a lie is that a cat only has nine lives.' Our beliefs have more than nine lives, as many of them have been passed down from generation to generation, perhaps even for hundreds of years.

In undoing our conditioning, we are clearing personal and generational history and transforming ourselves. We undertake a heroic journey to unconsciously take on, then at some stage become aware of, and then heal problems and emotional patterns that may be deep-rooted and ancient. We need grace and love to help us, as by trying to live cut off from spirit created our problems in the first place.

UNDOING OUR CONDITIONING

Michelangelo was once asked: 'How do you create such beautiful statues and models?'

His response was: 'I simply start with a block of stone and chip away all that *isn't* the beauty I want.'

This is how it is with our conditioning too; who *we are* already *is*. Our only job is to chip away at and release all that is untrue about us, all the self-concepts, judgements and beliefs we have that obscure our true nature. There are two attitudes to dealing with the emotional patterns created by our conditioning: either use them to feel a victim or attack others and blame them, or use them to heal. We don't have to create ourselves, simply unlearn all that is untrue.

It is such a simple idea, but the living of it can seem challenging. However painful our beliefs are, there is a part of us that doesn't want to let them go, and our mind is so deep that there seems to be layer after layer of them, coiled round our inner selves like a tapeworm, which is why it needs daily practice, rather than a one-off event to unravel them.

Buddha said that there were maybe 30,000 steps between us and our true nature. The following true story illustrates this idea well; I love it as a metaphor for the process of undoing.

THE RETURN OF THE GOLDEN BUDDHA

In a far away land, there was a Buddha statue as high as ten people, made from tonnes of pure gold. The Buddha sat in a lotus position in the garden of a tranquil monastery, and many people would sit at its feet and feel at peace and safe.

One day word reached the monastery that a marauding army was on its way to invade the village, which disturbed the community greatly. They knew that if the Buddha was discovered it would be plundered and destroyed. They gathered to discuss what to do, and considered many ideas. One monk suggested a brilliant idea of disguising the Buddha, so that the invaders would think it was merely made of stone.

They worked through the night, making cement and covering the Buddha. As the dawn light broke, the last bucketful was put in place and the gold was completely covered. Shortly afterwards the army arrived with its soldiers, weaponry and horses. As they passed by the Buddha, they paid it no attention. The villagers breathed a silent sigh of relief. The army occupied the village for many years, and eventually left, but by that time all those that knew the truth of the Buddha had passed on too, either through death or by leaving the village. No one who knew its true nature was left.

One day a young man was sitting meditating against the Buddha and a piece of the cement chipped away and to his surprise, a golden glint shone through. He chipped away more and more gold showed. The whole village was alerted, and everyone came to help remove the cement and reveal the beauty of the Buddha again for the first in many years. It was restored to its original beauty.

This story is true, and that golden Buddha still sits in the Temple of the Golden Buddha in Bangkok. You may have seen it; I have, and it is truly beautiful. Yet there is a deeper truth to the story. Within each of us the golden Buddha still lives, safe and radiant. We shielded it because of our fear and as a defence against pain, hurt and difficulties. We covered our divine nature in our belief about how we would be safe. But the bargain has been to keep love out, and to be less than fully alive. Layer by layer we covered our true self, replacing it with an image, invented concepts of who we are. We thought we could succeed by living out this adaptation, but the price has been the richness of our inner life and our spirit.

The good news is that while we have been wandering around in this dream and illusion of who we thought we were, our true golden Buddha nature, our spirit, has been held in safety, waiting for us to reclaim it as who we really are. As we undo our conditioning, layer by layer, we free ourselves to be the real and authentic us. The difficult and challenging work of inner transformation is not about transcendence and getting away from what is unpleasant, but is rather concerned with awakening in the midst of our difficulties, healing and seeing through the illusions of our dramas and our recurring emotional patterns and recognizing that they are but a dream, not the real us. Within us is the power to undo our conditioning and overcome our limitations, and reach the higher, but already existing, ground of spiritual awareness.

> We get down to what Buddha said was the job we have been born for, knowing that letting go of our suffering is the hardest work we will ever do.
>
> STEPHEN LEVINE
> Buddhist teacher

We can make our daily prayer 'Please help me accept the truth about myself, however wonderful and splendid that may be'; ultimately it is only our unhelpful beliefs that stop us having whatever we want.

CHOOSING OUR BELIEFS

> Your beliefs are your reality. Beliefs are assumptions about the nature of reality, and because you create what you believe in, you will have many 'proofs' that reality operates the way you think it does.
>
> SANAYA ROMAN
> Author of *Creating Money*

We don't see the world as it is, we see it as we are. By changing our beliefs we literally change the world, because the world is really only the canvas on to which we paint our beliefs. My suggestion for the foundation of a new work ethic would be based on the following idea:

Let us approach our livelihood with the belief that we can discover the creative force at the centre of our being, and then do what we enjoy most, what is natural to us, receive abundant material support and make the lives of many others richer in the process.

If we were to let this one thought alone seep deep into our consciousness and take root and grow, wouldn't our life be different? Just imagine if every day of our life, as children, we were told:

> You are an incredible creative and powerful being, and your only real purpose is to focus on your joy and do what you love doing and being. As you grow up you can find ways of using your talents and gifts to contribute and serve, and the money will follow.

How would your life be if you knew in your heart that this was true? What if you decide to believe that this is still true and begin to live it now?

WOULD WE RATHER BE HAPPY OR RIGHT?

So much of our life has been spent within our beliefs, with people who agree with them, that these beliefs become the context of our lives. We can be right about how life is, that our beliefs are how it is, and we may spend much of our life energy trying to prove how tough life is and what a noble person we are because we are suffering so much. We can be right, and subsequently righteous, but we probably won't be happy. The choice is not to be right or wrong – it does take courage to choose to give up an unhelpful belief that we've been very attached to – but to be happy and true.

Below are a list of positive beliefs that I have accumulated over the years. I offer them as a gift. Pick a few which seem helpful, and begin to choose to have them be your reality.

SPIRIT-ENHANCING BELIEFS AROUND WORK

Self-Esteem

Who I am is good enough.
I can be myself in my work.
Work is a way of knowing myself.
I can be encouraged to be creative.
Work can serve me.
Work gives me a sense of self, status and security.
I do make a difference.
I deserve to enjoy my life.
I am my own model.
Unpaid work is also valuable.

Creativity

I can create a place to fit in.

I am a creative and powerful person, able to create new work situations and circumstances.

The world needs my gifts.

I am the creator of my own experience.

We all have a unique gift to give and express.

I can create my own work and working hours.

It is safe for me to dream.

It is impossible not to get there.

I can learn and develop new skills and opportunities.

I can change my inner and outer world through work.

Success

I can excel and enjoy work.

Opportunities are more important than qualifications.

Work is satisfying.

Failure is another form of success, something to learn from.

Success is natural – life wants to give me everything.

I can always do my best.

I have known the experience of loving my work.

Abundance can come from sources other than work.

I deserve to be happy, successful and abundant.

There are always new needs and markets to be fulfilled and created.

Work is enchantment.

Spiritual

I can learn how to manifest all the people, situations and events I want.

I have faith that it will all work out.

Work can be from the heart.

Work can give the satisfaction of selfless service.

I am gifted, my life is blessed.

I trust my own path.

My work brings happiness to others.

Life is more than material existence.

I send out intentions and the Universal Mind can handle the details.

Work can help me grow spiritually and emotionally.

My true nature is spiritual.

Work can be a vehicle for making a positive difference in the world.
Work is how I express my love of life.
I am a co-creator with life.

Money

Money can be fun.
I can do easy work and earn a lot of money.
A job is not the only source of worth and money.
I can make lots of money and be happy.
I can be happy with less money.

Family

My family blesses my success.
My family wants to see me succeed.
I create family through my work.
I can create a family where I work.
Work can create a sense of community.
Work is about relationships – it's fun with the right company.

General

Take risks – don't play safe.
Work gives opportunities.
I can make the right choices.
I can give myself permission.
Let me do what I have to do with love.
I know my limits and ask for help.
I will aim high.
Work is good.
I can handle it.
I have the time and energy to see it through.
I can find out what I like.
Work can be fulfilling and enjoyable.
My present and future can be vastly different from my past.
I can discover my life's work, however far away from it I may feel now.
By seeing what others are capable of, I can discover my own abilities.
I can do anything.
I can go beyond current boundaries.

WE'LL SEE IT WHEN WE BELIEVE IT

A new idea is first condemned as ridiculous, and then dismissed as trivial, until it finally becomes what everybody knows.

WILLIAM JAMES (1842–1910)
Psychologist and philosopher

I was talking to 30 MBA students at Cranfield University. I suggested that they might consider thinking about creating their working lives by basing them on their love and passion rather than only by thinking about how they could make money and get a job. Some liked the idea, but several protested out loud, 'I'll believe that when I see it!' Their comments reminded me how so many of us have been conditioned to think that change must precede the belief that we can change, that is, we only believe what has happened not what could happen. And yet, in truth, outer change is caused by an inner change. Our thoughts are real, and if we wish to see a change in our life, we must first envisage it in our mind.

One of the most compelling examples of this is the story of Roger Bannister, the first man to run a four-minute mile. Until May 1954, hundreds of learned papers had been written 'proving' it was impossible to run a mile in less than four minutes, and that anyone who might manage it would die immediately. Despite all the 'evidence' and all the conditioning, Roger went ahead and did the *impossible*. As if that wasn't astonishing enough, within weeks, others had done the impossible too; within years, hundreds had run a mile in less than four minutes. Had mankind suddenly taken an evolutionary leap in strength? No, of course not, but one man broke off the chains of conditioning and superstition, and in doing so showed others what was possible. The leap was one of possibility and vision, and of choice, not of physical strength. Yesterday's heresies are today's truths, and that is how human consciousness, and each one of us, evolves. Most of us gather evidence to support our existing limits and beliefs, but we can also learn to gather evidence to break through these old beliefs.

HOW DO WE CHANGE OUR BELIEFS?

A mind not to be changed by place or time
The mind is its own place, and in itself
Can make a heaven of hell, and hell of heaven.

JOHN MILTON (1608–1674)
Author of *Paradise Lost*

To change anything we need to be aware of it and accept how it is.

◆ Once aware we can make a change and a new choice in the twinkling of an eye. It can be very easy. We can visualize the old belief in our mind, see it disappear and embrace the new one, or we can write the old one down on a piece of paper and burn it, then write a new one for ourselves.

◆ We can decide what we would like to be true, and what we'd like to believe instead, and decide to change what we believe. This process may take time, and we shift energy from one belief to the other.

◆ Wounding beliefs, like 'I am not good' or 'I must suffer', may seem to run so deep that we can feel as if we can never change them. We can liberate ourselves from these, in my experience, layer by layer, and perhaps through some form of daily practice. We live with them, and seek to free ourselves at the same time.

◆ Another way is to develop the witness stance to all our thoughts, including our beliefs, which is mentally to stand back and observe them. We can learn to say, 'Ah, look I am crucifying myself today,' or 'Ah, look, I am really loving myself today.' We may dissociate ourselves from these thoughts or, on other days, believe them all.

Through developing the witness position, we can realize that we are not our beliefs or our feelings, but the ones who experience them. We can get a bit of distance.

VISION – CREATING A NEW FUTURE

If we don't change our mind and our beliefs about ourselves, our gifts and talents and the possibilities for work, our life becomes just more of the same, wishfully hoping for some change. Without changing the beliefs at the heart of ourselves and our work, even if we change our work we will probably just write more chapters of the same story. Instead of living 10,000 different days, we live the same day 10,000 times. We want a new day to dawn. We can develop vision for ourselves and our working life, which will be new, exciting and inspiring, which will make us want to get out of bed in the morning and work. We can ignite ourselves and set our hearts on fire again.

You may well be caught in the trap of 'When I do it I'll believe I can do it', so let's explore some of your beliefs about doing what you love and earning money.

EXERCISE

◆ What is your immediate reaction and emotional response to the idea that you can do what you love and earn money? Take a piece of paper and write down all your thoughts, even if they run to several pages.

◆ What do you think, right now, about your ability to find what you truly love and create a living from it?

◆ What do you think and feel about people who do what they love and earn lots of money in the process?

Be truly honest with yourself, as you will do yourself no favours if you try to hide any negative responses. These thoughts will surface at some stage on your journey, so it's best to catch them as early as possible. Hopefully you will discover at least some of the reasons for your resistance to and disbelief of these ideas.

To begin to change, we must acknowledge where we are right now. The psychologist Carl Jung wrote of the great paradox that 'we can't change anything in life unless we accept it'. So accept any cynicism, disbelief, ridicule or resistance – don't fight it. You may just be discovering and becoming aware of these thoughts, but they have always been there.

FROM WISHFUL THINKING TO BELIEVING TO KNOWING

You may have heard the story about the only time Harry Houdini did not escape from the cage he was locked in. He struggled for hours to get out, tried everything that he knew how to do but eventually had to give up in exhaustion and frustration. Guess why? *The door was never locked!* Can you believe it? His mindset was so attuned to escape from being trapped that when he was free he was trapped! What a metaphor for our lives – we are both the prisoner and the gaoler through our own thinking. We can walk out of our self-made prisons and go from wishful thinking to believing to knowing.

Wishful thinking

Initially, when we hear someone else talking about changing beliefs, our response may be: 'Well, it's all right for him to talk, he's already done it; he hasn't got my responsibilities/boss/challenges.' So we have the thought that either it's all garbage or that it is not possible for us, so we fail to do anything constructive to follow through. We won't really believe it until it happens, and so make no decisions to live that way; we have weak intentions.

Believing

Now we start to get the possibility; we know that it is possible as an idea, and that it can be possible for us too. We realize that we have some power to make it happen, and become willing for the belief to be true. At this point we may well have uncertainties, anxieties, fear and conflicts, but we hold open the possibility. We can't just negate a negative belief by adopting a positive one. This creates polarities and tension. It can be like sticking a plaster on a wound that needs greater attention. This is how it is with anything new – we believe we can ride a bike before we do it, drive a car, learn to swim – belief precedes achievement and learning. We start making decisions and commit to making things happen, and living as if that belief were already true. Even though we may have doubt, we decide to commit to what we want to be true.

Knowing

When we have made it happen, we know in our heart it is possible because we have done it. We know we can ride the bike, swim or drive the car. There is no doubt, because we have achieved conscious contact. As Alan Watts said: 'We don't get wet thinking about water.' We throw ourselves in and enjoy the experience of doing what we love and knowing that it is true. I personally know that it is possible, because I have done it, and also know that when we follow our heart and do what we feel called to do, commit to it and face our fears and resistance, we can bring it into reality. Positive beliefs deepen or develop our inner strength.

EXERCISE

◆ Do you believe it is really possible for anyone to be really happy in their work? If you don't, do some research, and meet some of the thousands of people who do enjoy their work.

◆ Do you believe it is possible for you to be happy in work? If not, write down all the beliefs and reasons why not.

◆ What would you need to believe to create the next step in the work you were born to do?

The positive purpose of our conditioning is to protect our spirit or inner self, but in truth our inner self doesn't need protection but desires expression, and work can be the way that we identify and clear our conditioning and express more and more of our inner self. The great news is that no particular work is better or worse for doing this, and we can start with whatever our current situation is.

When we begin to understand that our mind is the starting point for all we see and experience, we move into genuine empowerment. Our goal is to change our thinking about the world, not just the world outside. The key is not the work itself, but the attitude and spirit with which we work. What we choose to believe about work and ourselves is our ultimate power, so let's turn our attention now to the spirit of our work.

Simple Ways to Implement Principle Two

* Spend your energy today believing 'Who I am and what I do are really important' and notice how your day goes.

* Notice people who you know, or know of, who love what they do. Meet them if possible, or learn about them and discover what their belief-systems are.

* Be clear about what you need to believe in to take the next step in your work life.

* Keep believing that you will discover what you love and that you can create it.

Principle Three

DISCOVERING THE SPIRIT OF OUR WORK

What is most important is not the work that we do but the attitude and consciousness with which we work. We can learn to transform gradually our consciousness from fear, lack and need to love, abundance and creativity. We are on an adventure of transforming our attitude and consciousness, and as we return to the awareness that we are spirit and that the basis of life is consciousness we begin to transcend our current limitations.

WHAT DO WE MEAN BY SPIRIT?

If you are called to be a street sweeper, sweep streets even as Michelangelo painted, or Beethoven composed music, or Shakespeare wrote poetry. Sweep streets so well that all the hosts of heaven and earth will pause to say, 'Here lived a great sweeper who did his job well.'

MARTIN LUTHER KING, JR (1929–1968)
American clergyman, civil rights leader and Nobel Laureate

The spirit of our work refers to two ideas: firstly, that who we are in essence *is* spirit and that there are no limits to our creative ability; and, secondly, it is the attitude and state of mind with which we work and manifest our inner spirit that are crucial – not just what we do.

WHAT IS OUR SPIRIT?

The human spirit has its source in the divine fountain which must be permitted to flow freely through man. Anyone who flows as life flows has solved the enigma of human existence and needs no other power. Anything is evil that blocks the flow of creative action, and everything is healthy (prosperous) that flows with the universe.

LAO-TSU (500 BC)
Chinese philosopher

For many the very mention of 'spirit' has them running away for fear of religious dogma, rules and guilt, yet in the simplest possible terms, spirit is our own nature; we are gods and goddesses in embryo and in essence. We may all live in a world that appears to be full of separate things – my body, your body; your job, my job; cars, buildings, computers, plants, animals and planets – all of which seem to be apart from each other. Yet true religion is a perception, a way of seeing, not an institution, which helps us realize that there is only one source of everything that appears to be separate.

A core idea that may overthrow much of what we have been led to believe is that behind all appearances of physical reality is something essential that is non-physical. The term 'substance' is actually derived from two Latin words, *sub* and *stare* which mean 'to stand under', so there is another reality that stands under all that we see, hear, feel, touch, smell and taste. Religion and spirituality have given this essence many names, the insights of modern science and quantum physics have also pointed to the reality of the non-material. Two sets of fingers point in the same direction – the source of everything we *see* is *unseen* with our senses. True prosperity is not what we make or collect, but the degree to which we are in the flow of this essence and willing to be a channel through which it can flow.

What is this substance or essence? Let's look at it from the perspective of both religion and science. Religions have given this essence many names: God or Goddess; Yahweh; Krishna; the Tao; Buddha; Rah; Brahman; the Universal Mind; the Divine or Divine Intelligence; Spirit; Life Force; Higher Mind; the Source. Studying all the scriptures from around the world and across history, they all seem to say similar things about our true nature. Consider the following:

From the Bible

◆ 'Is it not written in your Law, "I have said, you are gods?"'

◆ 'On that day, you will know that I am the Father, and you are in me, and I am in you.'

◆ 'For behold, the kingdom of heaven is within.'

From Egyptian wisdom

◆ 'And the kingdom of heaven is within you, and whosoever knoweth themselves shall find it, and having found it ye shall know yourself that you are sons and heirs of the Father, the Almighty, and shall know yourself that ye are in God and God in you.'

From *A Course In Miracles*

◆ 'I am spirit … I am as God created me.'

From Buddhism

◆ 'Look within, you are the Buddha.'

◆ 'If you think the law is outside yourself you are embracing not the absolute law but some inferior teaching.'

From Hinduism

◆ 'If you understand your own mind completely, you are not just a human being, you yourself are God.'

'Atman (individual consciousness) and Brahman (universal consciousness) are one.'

'By understanding the self, all this universe is known.'

'God dwells within you as you.'

◆ 'God bides hidden in the hearts of all.'

From Islam

'Those who know themselves know their God.'

From Confucianism

'Heaven, earth and human are of one body.'

'What the undeveloped man seeks is outside. What the advanced man seeks is within himself.'

From Shintoism

◆ 'Do not search the skies for God. In man's own heart is He found.'

Our belief about any kind of creator usually embraces several particular qualities. The creator is often seen as:

◆ distant and remote

◆ capricious and unpredictable

◆ angry, punishing and vengeful

usually male and an actual person

working through an ecclesiastical body and through institutions

◆ the dispenser of divine essence

◆ out there sending riches to fill our needs down here

In truth our creator is the field of the ever present essence in which we live, breathe, move and have our very being, and there is no distance between us and this essence, although we can feel there is. Once we know this it transforms the way we live. We may seem to live in two realms; the world of jobs and losses, fear and love, lack and abundance, joy and sadness, inspiration and meaninglessness – the world of seeming opposites that we live in moment by moment. And then there is the realm of essence, the realm of constancy and stability of the basic substance that gives rise to absolutely everything. So paradoxically it can truly be said that behind every lack is all sufficiency; behind every sorrow is joy; behind all illness and disease is wholeness. Just as music is made by the space between the notes, our lives are created by the space between our thoughts, and essence is behind everything. As Paul Valery wrote so wonderfully: 'God made everything out of nothing. But the nothingness shows through.'

SPIRIT AND SCIENCE

Everything you see has its roots in the unseen world, the forms may change yet the essence remains the same. Every wonderful sight will vanish, every sweet word will fade, but do not be disheartened, the source they come from is eternal, growing, branching out, giving new life and new joy. Why do you weep? The source is within you and this whole cosmos is springing up from it.

JALALUDDIN RUMI
12th-century Persian mystic and poet

Modern physics has studied the minutest particles that we can imagine and found that in the space between these particles is a force that keeps them in their orbits. And they have even found that particles of matter are not, in fact, solid, but appear and disappear, like stars in the heavens; on a physical level these 'solid' objects are not solid at all. There is an invisible field from which everything apparently physical comes. What is even more amazing is that scientists are calling this field the unified field and that there is no place in what we call time and space that this field does not exist. Really stretch your mind to understand this concept – the field or force from which all physical reality comes is in all places and at all times, beyond time and space, omnipresent. Isn't this what many of us have come to believe our creator to be – omnipresent?

This shows a way in which the whole of the creator can be said to be present at every place at every time, all the time, and it is probably the most important point we will ever learn: the whole of our creator, the field, is present at every place, at any time, all the time, whatever is going on. There is no place on this earth, in space or in the wider universe that this essence is not. When we grasp this point we understand what spirituality is all about. The apparently different ends of the spectrum – science and spirituality, rational logic and mystical ideas – are actually in agreement, standing together on the same ground and reaching the same conclusion from totally different perspectives.

All of the universe is made of energy, of essence; indeed, Einstein was one of the first to articulate this is in his famous equation $E=mc^2$, meaning energy is mass multiplied by the squared speed of light. This says that all matter is energy. We don't need to understand how or why, but simply that all matter is made of energy. All that appears solid – trees, planets, stars, people, desks and computers – are in fact energy in solid form. Ice, snow, water, hailstones and steam seem to be totally different and unrelated to each other, but they are all water in different forms. Similarly energy can appear in different forms, and matter is simply 'solid' or 'congealed' energy. And, as we know, every snowflake is unique and utterly beautiful.

I talked to Brian O'Leary, a scientist and former NASA astronaut, about this subject when he came to speak at Alternatives. One of his many passions is the idea of free energy, the notion that it is possible to create machines that give out more energy than they use. In theory, he suggests, this essence is available everywhere, so if we could just learn how to plug into it we could have unlimited energy that doesn't pollute. And he has been to meet inventors who have built machines that will do just that, which he has documented in his book *Miracle in the Void*. He told me that there would be enough energy in a cup of this essence to evaporate all the oceans of the world – and more!

When we can become aware of our unlimited resources and the possibility of our living in two realms at once, we start the journey into freedom. We are all trained to ask for an increased supply of what we seem to be lacking – joyful work, abundance, prosperity, peace, money, opportunity, success – but instead we can really ask to develop awareness of what is already present. There is no limitation as such, other than the belief in limitation and a consciousness of lack, which is widespread. We begin to understand that, by staying in the awareness of the wholeness of substance or essence, we too have the power to begin experiencing mastery over all that seems to happen to us and around us in this world.

THE UNENDING SOURCE OF ESSENCE

Although we can store money and riches, we cannot accumulate this essence, because there is no need to. Why would we hold on to what we can have anytime, anywhere, anyway? When we are centred in and focused on that limitless essence, it will find expression through us in terms of new ideas, creative abilities, inspiration, motivation, will, unlimited opportunities, ingenuity and even genius. When we are aware of our true relationship with this essence we realize we are like the fairground dodgem cars that move around freely after they get their electricity by hooking on to an overhead mesh. We are the same, we can hook up the universal supply at any time we want, wherever we are and fill up. Our true treasure is not what we accumulate in this world, but what we are heir to by nature of how we are created.

The most amazing thing about spiritual essence is that no one has less because someone else has more. In the realm of essence there is no competition, and we need not struggle out of fear that anyone else will get ahead of us or that we need to get ahead of anyone else. There is an unlimited supply for every living creature. When we experience any lack we can know that the essence from which that lack will be refilled is right here and right now for us. We will, in time, manifest what we feel we are lacking when we are also willing to receive it. We synchronize ourselves with the reality of this existing essence, creating a channel through which this mystical flow can work through us. But the alignment – through our consciousness – must come first.

We possess the capacity to allow this essence to flow through us. To do so we do need to let go of the conditioning that we are separate from the source, that we are guilty and unworthy and that we don't deserve. We need to claim our inheritance, the jackpot that we have already won! But we don't need to understand it, just as we don't need to be an engineer to drive a car or a computer scientist to send an e-mail; we simply need to know how to tap into this power and essence.

THE RELATIONSHIP BETWEEN ESSENCE AND FORM

Form is about facts, whereas essence is about the light and quality of our work and lives. Traditional thinking has had us believing in an almost irreconcilable split between essence and form, spirit and flesh, God and creation, creating a secular world. The Bible says we cannot serve God and Mammon. We think that spirit is holy and flesh or matter are unholy, but here is the key:

There is no split between matter and spirit, except in our minds.

When we begin to really grasp this idea, that who we really are is energy, an idea for eternity in the mind of our creator, we can really start to transform our lives. First we can understand it as a mental idea, then as a heartfelt experience, and then we begin to experience ourselves as co-creators, and know that all power is with us and within us to experience the world as we wish.

One of the greatest inspirations and demonstrations of this idea comes from

Victor Frankl, who survived detention in a concentration camp, living many further years, and wrote in *Man's Search For Meaning*:

> We who lived in the concentration camps can remember the men who walked through the huts comforting others, giving away their last piece of bread. They may have been few in number, but they offer sufficient proof that everything can be taken away from a man but one thing: the last of the human freedoms – to choose one's attitude in any given set of circumstances, to choose one's way.

Choosing wholeness is possible in every situation, and most of us are learning to expand the range of situations in we can choose a loving and peaceful response. We needn't deny the circumstances of our life, but we can choose what we focus on and how we respond.

CREATING OUR WORK FROM THE INSIDE OUT
– AND THE COSMIC JOKE

Creating our work from the inside out and from substance or essence calls us to start from a new place, from our being, which is full of all the goodies that we are looking for on the outside, right now. Our spirit always calls us to the present moment, to the creation of a compelling now.

My friend Tom Carpenter, a spiritual teacher, lives in Hawaii, and we were sitting on the deck of his house one day talking about love and spiritual things and the search for happiness. He looked me in the eye and said, 'Do you know, you are the presence of everything you are looking for.' I didn't really understand what he meant to start with, and then I understood the cosmic joke: we spend so much of our time on a wild goose chase through our work, while what we are looking for is already inside us right now, waiting to be drawn forth. We should concentrate on living in the sacred now, the only point of power we ever have. When we choose to let the past be history, and the future be now some time in the future, we have mastered life.

OUR INNER SPIRIT

It is eternity now. I am in the midst of it. It is about me in the sunshine; I am in it, as the butterfly in the light-laden air. Nothing has to come; it is now. Now is eternity; now is the immortal life.

RICHARD JEFFERIES

Who we truly are is not our physical body, not what we experience with our five senses. Who we are is invisible to our senses, but we are very real. The real us is energy and consciousness, what some people may call a spirit or a soul, a place at our centre, a place of ease where life is easier and has flow, where we are more inspired, creative, natural, loving and abundant, where things just go better. But most of us are off-centre to some degree – we are locked in sacrifice or in competition, inactivity or power struggles.

EXERCISE

◆ How much off your centre do you feel? When did this start? What events were involved?

◆ Decide to raise your arm and raise it. *Who decided to execute that thought?* It sounds so simple, and you may come up with answers such as your brain, muscles and nervous system – but who told them to do that? *The invisible you that commands your body, but isn't your body*, the you that is beyond the five senses.

◆ Think back to your earliest memory of this life. Run a quick scan of all the major events of your life and all the changes you have been through. Now run through until the end of your life, seeing yourself age and even die. Who is the witness of all those changes? The you, the spirit that you are, which is ever present and ever in charge of your life. The real you is the experiencer, not the experience.

Within us we hold our spirit, our true holy nature, an aspect of the divine whole, a wonder within our own being. Though for many of us our true self is an intimate stranger; we live with it, even if we don't know it well. As St Francis of Assisi said: 'What we are looking for is what is looking.' We are both the finder and the found.

NURTURING OUR AWARENESS OF SPIRIT

We don't have to nurture and strengthen spirit itself – it is already there, strong and indestructable. What we do need to do is strengthen our awareness of spirit. As we do so we are strengthened by it. Here are some practical ways to strengthen our awareness of spirit in our daily lives:

Take time to be in awe of the intelligence behind all the appearances of life

Allow yourself to be awestruck by the number of galaxies and stars there are in the universe. Find a book of amazing facts about the earth or your own body. Wonder at the fact that there are 24,000 species of fish alone; that a saltspoon of soil contains over 5 million microorganisms. Think of the mind that dreamed up all the myriad forms of life on this planet. Marvel at the force that maintains and co-ordinates nature. Think that every person who has ever existed has looked at the same stars and the same moon and asked the same questions. We are intimately connected to everything and everyone.

Take time in quiet and solitude

Listen to the silence in your mind, as it is the same silence that is experienced by everyone. It is pregnant with ideas and knowledge and in that silence all answers will come to you. Silence is the language that the universal mind uses to communicate.

Notice the thinker of your thoughts

Become aware of who thinks your thoughts. When you have a thought, stop and ask, 'Who is thinking it?' This is the silent witness, our own spirit, which was with us before we were born, is with us during every moment of our life and will be with us after our death.

Remember that behind all appearances is essence

Remind yourself that everything you see in the physical world had its origin in the non-physical world, in thought and essence. Essence and consciousness are the starting point of all there is.

Mindfulness

Mindfulness is concerned with simply being aware of and living in this present moment. Have you ever noticed that when you are working you are thinking about the evening or weekend, but in the evening you go home and worry about work? This is an example of failing to be mindful! Being mindful is having both our body and mind in the same place at the same time, as much as possible simply being here now. It sounds so simple, but is probably one of the most difficult things for us to do.

> Whatever the qualities you have identified as being important to you, they are already inside, now, and the best way of drawing them out is to use the affirmation,'I am', however strange or unreal that may initially feel.

There is a belief that work can repress our spirit, and it can certainly create circumstances that do not nurture our spirit, but our spirit can never be crushed, even if the circumstances are awful. The spiritual path is not about escaping our fears and pain, but using our higher power to heal and move through them.

If anyone had cause to be angry and have his spirit squashed, it was Nelson Mandela. In *Long Walk to Freedom* he writes of his time in prison: 'Men like ... reinforced my belief in the essential humanity even of those who had kept me behind bars for the previous twenty-seven years.' He didn't allow his spirit to be squashed and never even allowed himself to hate his captors. He *chose* to forgive and to channel his spirit into the creation of a new vision, which may take as much energy as being angry, but more courage. Our spirit cannot be constrained by any job, workplace or manager, unless we let it be; the inner creative power of our spirit is bigger than any power of repression over us.

INJUNCTIONS AGAINST KNOWING OUR OWN SPIRIT

We can bring our spirit into any work we do, though we may encounter injunctions against us doing so. Here are three of the most common:

It is non-material, it doesn't exist, it is based on superstition

In our scientific age anything that can't be seen, smelt, measured or touched can be dismissed as hocus-pocus, non-scientific, magic, evil or unreal.

Religious conditioning

Religious, rather than spiritual, conditioning has taught us that spirit is an idea but not an experience, and that God is remote and unobtainable, except at some vague unspecific time in the future.

We only trust outer knowledge

We think that we only trust what we learn from someone outside, and that anything that comes from *within us* is suspect and invalid because it is not verifiable in a scientific way.

Each of us is entitled to and capable of meaningful work, but this will never come from any employment as such but from the attitude and state of mind with which we approach it. So much of our struggle is based on trying to keep up appearances, getting approval, living up to other people's expectations of how we should be, or more likely how we measure up to our own idealized version of how we think we should be. This is work based on our ego or personality.

OUR EGO

Ego is the absence of true knowledge of who we really are, together with its result: a doomed clutching on at all costs to a cobbled together and makeshift image of ourselves, an inevitably chameleon charlatan self that keeps changing, and has to, to keep alive the fiction of its existence.

SOGYAL RINPOCHE
Author of *Tibetan Book of Living and Dying*

Our ego is the human self that is split off from the source or essence. It is our self-created concept of who we are based on our responses to the conditioning we have experienced. Our ego is based on one belief – we are separate from everything and everyone, leading to a feeling of incompleteness and lack. It cares for appearances and images above all else, and is always focused on the past or future, never now. Its purpose is to keep itself in business, to get what it thinks it needs, so its mantras are 'There's never enough' and 'Keep striving' (but never arriving). Below are a few acronyms I have seen for the ego and enjoyed:

Edging God Out
Enormous Guilt Often
Everybody's Got One
Ever Growing Older
Endlessly Giving Orders
Everything Good is Outside

The ego will have us for ever seeking outside of us what is already inside us. It is rarely satisfied and never at peace, and it is at the root of who most of us think we are. Much of our energy is devoted to proving our self-concepts, attacking and defending against anyone who threatens our sense of self.

We usually create our work from the urgings of our ego – which include fear, the drive for survival, guilt, struggle and suffering, attachment, drive, neediness, emptiness, the need for props, scarcity and competition – and most of us do so because that is what we have been trained to do.

For example we believe we should *work hard* in order to *have* the money to buy the things we want in order that we can *be* happy. Experience tells us that this doesn't always work; we end up working so hard, keeping so busy, that even if we have the things we want we are too busy, tired, stressed or anxious to be truly happy, at peace or fulfilled. Our ego will always have us creating a compelling *future*, but never a compelling *now*.

Our ego has many plans for our happiness, and most of these involve the pursuit of idols, things we have made into gods, such as success, money, fame or fortune. Because these aren't the real thing, they will eventually lead us to a place of disappointment, even despair and meaninglessness, and possibly a desire to die. So if one of our idols lets us down, the ego very cleverly produces another one, so we are led down another cul-de-sac. We may therefore create plan after plan for happiness, yet never ask simply to be shown the meaning that spirit would bring to our work and life. Having idols is not a sin needing punishment, just a mistake needing correction and forgiveness. Ask the heart's advice, 'What is the meaning of my work?'

EXERCISE

◆ What have you idolized in your work and life? How did it turn out?

We can either be a hostage to our ego, or a host to our spirit. We can learn to create our work from our sacred self – which is the source of such qualities as spontaneity, fun, joy, abundance, peace, wisdom, inspiration, sharing, creativity, love, vision, co-operation and compassion. The spirit of our work is determined by whichever inner us we bring to our work, and the choice is not either/or. We can take care of the needs of our ego, and be focused on our spirit.

Ego says	Spirit says
Be afraid.	There is nothing to fear.
Separation from everything.	Connection with all.
Emptiness.	Fullness.
Striving and becoming.	Already is, now.
Needs props.	No need for props.
'Look out!'	'Look in!'
There is lack and scarcity.	There is an abundance of all we need.
Withholding.	Sharing, extending and giving.
Attack and defend.	No need to defend or attack.
Fight and compete.	No need to compete – all is available for all.
Have by getting.	Have in our being, so give.
Defend.	Surrender.

EXERCISE

◆ Ask yourself, who do you mainly bring to work – your ego or your self?

Bringing our creative spirit to our work is concerned with the way we approach our work, not the nature of the work itself. It is the voice of inspiration, desire to create and is never a 'should', an 'ought' or a 'must.' We can change the spirit in which we work *now*; no one and nothing else needs to change for us to choose a new attitude. We can choose a new response to our circumstances.

THE ESSENCE OR SPIRIT WITH WHICH WE APPROACH OUR WORK

A deeper calling comes from the inside out; it is the expression of our essence, our core. Our calling is an expression of the spirit at work in the world through us. It is that mysterious voice that calls us to give our gifts.

RICHARD J LEIDER
Author of *The Power of Purpose*

I was on a cruise visit to Israel from a holiday in Cyprus, and went on a two-hour coach journey from Haifa to Jerusalem. Our guide was Micky, who had been a tour guide for 30 years. Throughout our journey and our tour of Jerusalem he told us the history of Israel, ancient and modern, told jokes, explained his understanding of the political issues and literally brought the place to life for us. At the end of the day I felt like throwing my arms around him and thanking him. I felt like he'd been our friend and teacher, historian and entertainer, healer and peacemaker and I felt deep gratitude to him. I realized he must have given that talk and tour literally thousands of times in his life, yet that day, as I expect he did on every day, he gave his heart and soul to his work, not because he had to, but because he chose to. I talked afterwards to fellow cruisers on different buses, who reported having very bored and boring guides. Micky will live in my heart for ever, as a reminder that we always have a choice about how we do our work.

I am not saying that it is wrong to focus on the physical conditions or material rewards of work: these are very important. What I am suggesting is that we have lost sight of the most crucial aspect of work and life – its spirit, its heart and soul, the attitude with which we work. The secret of fulfilment and satisfaction in our work is not to be found in any job description, but in the invisible *us* that we bring to our work.

We've forgotten a vital truth – that work will not make us happy. The circumstances of our work can contribute and help us to experience happiness, but the happiness we are looking for is inside us already, waiting to be brought out. Happiness and meaning in our work will never come from any particular form of work or any particular achievement or any amount of money, but from the spirit in which we do it.

The key to the work we were born to do is that we can change our attitude, our state of mind, our motivation, even the consciousness with which we work. We can make the transition from working with resentment, boredom or dissatisfaction to gratitude, pleasure and happiness. In doing so we can see our existing work differently and even begin to transform it, see new possibilities and begin to enjoy it in much greater ways. Changing our attitude may or may not not ultimately involve us in actually changing our job.

Mary attended one of my workshops, describing her job in PR as boring, and saying she felt unvalued and unappreciated. She was sure she wanted to leave but did not know what was next. I questioned her about her motivation and attitude, and her honest reply was, 'I go to work to get appreciation and feel important.'

'Does it work?' I asked. 'Does being that needy get you want you want?'

She responded, 'No,' so I offered her a project.

'How about you go to work for the next week with a new goal and a new attitude – to make other people feel valuable and important, to see what other people might need? In short, try giving rather than getting, and see what a contribution you could make.'

We spoke a week later, and she sounded transformed: 'All week I have looked for opportunities to help rather than feel resentful. I have got coffee for others, instead of getting angry if they didn't get one for me. I have offered suggestions instead of getting angry that no one ever asked me for my thoughts and opinions. I have offered to listen to colleagues who seemed stressed rather than get upset that no one offered me help. I have felt really appreciated, and it has been one of the best weeks of work I've had.' What had changed? Not the job, or the people or the money, but her attitude and her purpose. This may still not be the work she wants to do for ever, but she learned a huge lesson that she would benefit from in all future work.

The distinction between essence and form is at the heart of the work we were born to do, because we are all on the journey of remembering that essence is more important than appearances. When we want to change our situation, our thoughts generally go straight to new jobs or careers, and we can get caught up and scared by not knowing what to do next. But the real change may not necessarily be in what we do, but in our attitude, towards our self or towards our work. Essence is more about the *how* and the *why* of our work, rather than the *what* of our work.

EXERCISE

◆ How could you change the spirit and attitude in which you work right now, today?

Another powerful example of changing the spirit of work comes from the Tower Colliery in Wales, one of the last pits owned by the National Coal Board. It was losing money, and the NCB wanted to close it. Faced with this disaster, the community rallied together and managed to raise the money for a management buyout. Within a year the colliery had gone from a huge loss to a million-pound profit. Same coal faces, same workers, same equipment, but with a new and renewed spirit, essence and purpose that enabled them to turn it around. Once we have understood the essence we see how we can create a vehicle for it to flow through – we do need a vehicle or structure.

THE VEHICLE OF OUR WORK

There is no reality except the one contained within us.
This is why so many lead such an unreal life.
They take the images outside them for reality
And never allow the world within to assert itself.

HERMAN HESSE (1877–1962)
Novelist, poet and Nobel prize winner

Many of us been led to believe that success is largely about what can be measured and shown in physical form. In short, our work is all about tangible, measurable and touchable things. Look at most of the jobs pages in the papers and they are all about the form of the work – the results, the money, the hours, the reward package, status, the material things it can buy us, the location of work, expectations. We have come to believe that this is the Real World of work. This is what job descriptions are all about.

Yet a job description does not describe *our experience of the job*. It is us who bring the job advertisement or description to life by bringing our heart, soul, love, fear, experiences, uniqueness, gifts, humour, misery, boredom, enthusiasm or resentment to it. We create our experience of our work by the attitude of mind with which we do it and the spirit in which we approach it. A little like a suit of clothes or a role in a play, the job is inanimate until we bring it to life. When we bring who we are into our work, then we don't *do* the job, we *are* ourselves in the job. We are bigger than any work that we will ever do, and to limit our identity to what we do, rather than who we are, we diminish ourselves. To think we are of no value if we don't have a job or a good job is so sad.

MY OWN EXPERIENCE OF ESSENCE AND APPEARANCE

Mind is the creator of everything. You should therefore guide it to create only good. If you cling to a certain thought with dynamic will power, it finally assumes a tangible outward form. When you are able to employ your will always for constructive purposes, you become the controller of your destiny.

PARAMAHANSA YOGANANDA
Author of *Autobiography of a Yogi*

Quitting my corporate job was probably one of the scariest and, if I say it myself, most courageous things I have ever done. While so much of my identity was tied up in the car, the money, the flat and the status, it didn't feel like the real me. Yet underneath my fear of giving it up was a smaller, quieter voice saying, 'No, this isn't really the true you. You can discover that, but to do so you need to let go of the emotional attachment you have to all these things.' So I did. I rented my flat out, gave myself a sabbatical with a round-the-world ticket, and for three months had some wonderful adventures.

After returning, my savings had dwindled, and I signed on as unemployed for nearly a year while I conducted some personal healing and re-evaluated my life. My vision was to become self-employed, so in November 1990 I set up as a sole trader, running training courses, promoting seminars and selling books and tapes. Initially I felt very excited and free, but as time went on I realized that I had not left the anxious 'me' behind. The Buddhists have a lovely expression: 'Wherever you go, there you are.' So here I was, self-employed but still experiencing much of the neurosis, drivenness and insecurity I had felt before, when I had a corporate career.

Then I met someone at a dinner party who asked me a life-changing series of questions. 'What do you really want your work to be about, way and beyond what you actually do? What do you want to be at the heart of your work? What do you want it to be a vehicle for, other than making money? What do you want the essence and spirit of your work to be?'

I rose to the challenge of answering the questions and allowed myself to open up a new possibility of how I wanted my work to be. You don't have to know how – decide the essence without knowing how it will come to be.

Below I have outlined the possibility I allowed myself to envisage, in 1992, of what I wished my work to involve:

◆ *Communication*: I love talking about things that inspire me, and having meaningful exchanges with people.

◆ *Inspiration*: Being inspired and having vision has always been one of my major motivations.

◆ *Creativity*: I have always loved taking thoughts and ideas and making them real.

◆ *Self-expression*: I wanted my work to be a way of sharing the best of me with people.

◆ *Joy, humour and happiness*: I wanted my work to be joyful, fun and a vehicle for happiness.

◆ *Growth, challenge and stimulation*: I hate being bored, so I wanted to be able to challenge myself to grow through my work and literally be paid to grow and learn about myself and others.

◆ *Meaning, purpose and deep connection*: I wanted to know that my work had a bigger purpose than simply paying the bills.

◆ *Love*: A tough one! I wanted work to be a way of giving and receiving love and a way of loving the world.

◆ *Abundance and plenty*: I wanted generosity of spirit around my work, and not to be fearful of anything running out. I didn't want to compete, but simply do my best.

◆ *Teamwork and connection*: I had often felt lonely, so I wanted to feel connected and involved.

◆ *Miracles and wonder*: I wanted my work to unfold not just by hard work, but in a way that was miraculous and wonderful.

◆ *A connection with my creator*: I wanted my work to have a very strong spiritual message, whether or not I talked about this openly.

Notice there is no mention of what form this job would take. What I have since realized is that I didn't just want a job, but to find and share the best of me and create work that allowed me to do so. In that process I would need to, and still am, changing my beliefs and attitudes towards myself, work and life. I wanted to change myself!

When I had written these points down, I had no idea of how I might achieve them, and wondered if I was just being very naïve and idealistic. The important thing was that I felt as if I had been honest with myself. I truly wanted my work to be about these things, which represented a life well lived. I had unleashed some power here, because I had listened to my heart.

This is a different way of looking at work for most of us. It is about making our work a vehicle, something bigger and more exciting than merely earning a living. This is what I have discovered in the last ten years: we have the ability to create our own work, way beyond the capacity that most of us have been educated to believe. Little by little I have been able to draw forth those qualities from within myself and brought them into the work that I do.

FINDING A VEHICLE FOR THE ESSENCE
OF YOUR OWN WORK

Sometimes we are so caught up in old and limiting ways of seeing work that we find it a challenge even to think of work being qualitatively different to what it is now. Here is a great exercise I use to help free us up to play with new ways of imagining work:

EXERCISE

◆ Pick five positive words that you would normally *least* associate with work. Allow yourself to have fun, Here are some suggestions to get you going: tender, joyful, exciting, free, sensual, inspiring, beautiful, stimulating, wonderful, poetic, heartfelt, moving, passionate, creative, interesting, all-consuming. Be really free with the words.

◆ Now take these five words and turn them into a positive sentence, starting, 'My work is/gives me/allows me ...' Here are some examples from workshop participants:

  • 'My work gives me the *freedom* to follow my *heart*, and in doing so I *inspire* myself and others to live *unlimited* lives and experience *joy*.'

  • 'My work gives me a vehicle for my *enthusiasm*, *passion* and *love*, and in doing so I *seduce* others into a new way of thinking about their own *creative* abilities.'

  • 'My work is *fun*, with colleagues who *inspire* me, *enliven* and *support* me, and we create *miracles* together.'

The idea is to create something radically different, to unhook us from old ways of thinking and feeling. The purpose of the exercise is to light a fire beneath our frozen imaginations and to have them melt and flow with new ideas and possibilities. When you have finished, let your composed sentence bring a smile to your face, and think, 'Yes, wouldn't it be great to create that essence?' The chances are the words you picked are significant to you, so keep them in your awareness, and write them in your journal.

Another way to get to essence is to ask yourself: 'What would I like that has been missing from my current work situation, or previous situations?'

I asked this question to Andrew, who worked in local government and was struggling because he knew he didn't like his existing work but had no idea what to do next. His response was, 'I am not given enough freedom or responsibility, I am not creative enough. I either get told what to do, or tell others what to do and I don't feel valued or important.'

My reply was, 'So, you'd like work that gives you more scope to be creative, to be in partnership with your staff, managers and peers, and to know that your work is important and contributes to the whole council.' His face lit up, as within two minutes he had moved from only seeing the problem to seeing the opportunity to create what he wanted. He then began to develop a strategy from this essence.

EXERCISE

What very few of us have been taught is that we can create our own work from the inside out based on our values, what we are excited about, inspired and motivated by. So what would you like the essence of your work to be? Here are some more questions to help you define the essence of your work:

◆ What qualities do you most want to experience in your working life? For example, joy, connection, aliveness, hope, vision, abundance, love, growth, inspiration.

◆ Without using money, material possessions or what you (would like to) do for a living, describe what it means to you to live a successful life right now.

◆ What is missing from your work now, and has been in previous jobs? Write down all that is missing, and turn these points around into a sentence that starts, 'What I want to create and experience in my work is …'

◆ Is there a way that you could do what you are doing in a way that you would enjoy more, or that would support or inspire you more? Could you change the spirit of what you do?

◆ In what ways do you want to give love to the world?

Again, make sure you put the 'Yes, but how?' voices to one side while you answer these questions.

We are not looking for perfection here, simply a change of direction. Our heart knows the essence of our life's work – it is up to us to rediscover our spirit, decide what form we want that essence to take and create appropriate ways of working that suit our spirit.

LIVING FROM ESSENCE, FROM THE SPIRIT WITHIN

If you do not get it from yourself, where will you go for it?

THE BUDDHA

Below are some of the ways I have discovered to bring this essence into being:

◆ Realize and know essence is already within you, in your very being. It just needs to be drawn forth, so be these qualities. Essence is a now thing, not a future or past thing. I have always loved the following ancient Indian poem, which captures the idea of *carpe diem*, or 'seize the day':

> Look to this day!
> For it is Life, the very Life of Life.
> In its brief course lie all the
> Verities and Realities of your existence;
> The bliss of Growth
> The glory of Action
> The splendour of Beauty;
> For Yesterday is but a Dream,
> And Tomorrow is only a Vision:
> But Today well lived makes
> Every Yesterday a Dream of Happiness,
> And every Tomorrow a Vision of Hope.
> Look well therefore to this Day.

We can stop waiting to be happy, and start now.

◆ Give essence your attention. Notice where creativity or love already exist inside and outside you; look for them, seek them out, choose to create them. Don't complain or hate, create!

◆ Give essence your intention. Decide it, make it your desire, resolve it and choose it.

◆ Visualize and meditate on these qualities. Form a relationship with them, make friends with them, study them. Draw them forth.

◆ Deal with your resistance to these qualities, your erroneous beliefs and emotional patterns.

◆ Detach from the outcome.

GIVING UP THE SEARCH FOR HAPPINESS IN WORK

We may seek the world for happiness, but unless we carry it within us we will not find it.

RALPH WALDO EMERSON (1803–1882)
Essayist and poet

Getting to the essence or heart of our work is giving up the search for happiness and realizing that we are the Holy Grail; we are what we've been searching for.

David Myers is a social psychologist who has collated much of the recent research on happiness, and concluded:

> Whether we base our conclusions on self-reported happiness, rates of depression, or teen problems, our becoming better off over the last 30 years has not been accompanied by one iota on increased happiness and life satisfaction. It is shocking, because it contradicts our society's materialistic assumptions, but how can we ignore the hard truth: once beyond poverty, further economic growth does not appreciably improve human morale. Making more money, the aim of so many graduates and other dreamers of the 1980s, does not breed bliss.

The idea that nothing tangible will make us happy can lead us either into a depression of disillusionment, or into freedom, depending on how we choose to see ourselves. So what does breed happiness and fulfilment?

Robert Holden suggests that there are three ideas most of us have learned about happiness from society:

Happiness is luck

It happens to some people and not to others; the gods are capricious and unpredictable and our happiness is dependent on the roll of our or someone else's dice. Some people are clever, some are not, some are gifted, others are not. In this scenario we are powerless victims, unable to affect our situation.

Happiness is circumstantial

When we have the right work or job, win the promotion, become a manager, get the right amount of money, start our own business, get a new boss, start a family, move house, the economy picks up … all are circumstances that we dream will make us happy.

And so we spend much of our time and energy trying to manipulate our environment instead of enjoying the moment. In truth we know that these things will not make us happy, but they can encourage and contribute to our happiness. We hope that a change of circumstances will make us feel differently, but know there is no guarantee. Most of us have probably experienced happiness being single and in a relationship; happiness working and not working or resting; sadness with no money and with a load of money.

When we make our happiness circumstantial, even if we have the right circumstances now, we may live in fear of them changing – losing our income, our work, our partner leaving, losing our looks and youth. Circumstantial happiness is still not the real thing. We may know people who, in the most unfortunate of circumstances, seem to find happiness or peace nevertheless.

Happiness as a decision

This doesn't mean 'I am going to clench my teeth, harden my heart and not let anything get me down' but that whatever our circumstances and whatever our apparent 'luck', we can choose a loving or a fearful response, happiness or misery. The key word here is choose, as happiness is ultimately a choice. This is a radical idea, which may seem to contradict the common belief, that we are victims of our circumstances. Attitude, rather than the situation, is of primary importance. It doesn't mean that happiness is guaranteed, because we may have had many years of practice of making decisions that lead to unhappiness and it may take a while for us to choose again.

Robert Holden then adds a fourth category, inspired by all the great teachers who have ever lived on earth:

Happiness as a state of being

You probably will have experienced times when for no apparent reason you feel at peace and happy, if only for a short while. The very radical idea is that our true nature, our spirit, is happiness. We just have to see beyond the conditioning. Like the sun that can be obscured by clouds, it never stops shining. Our true nature never stops being happy, but we may be more or less attuned with it. When we are in tune with ourselves and natural, we tend to be happy, when we are out of tune we will experience unhappiness. That is why naturalness is so important to the work we were born to do.

PEACE OF MIND IN OUR WORK

We have been taught to believe that peace of mind is some far off-goal that is the reward for years of struggle, hard work and achievements. To start we may want to change our understanding of what peace is. The world tends to equate peace with the absence of war or conflict. But true peace is beyond *absence* – it is the *presence* of calm, love and power, and a mind at peace can be in tune with the whole of creation. A peaceful mind is open to receive – ideas, inspiration and guidance – while a conflicted mind is less open. Peace can be a deeply rewarding and healing spiritual experience, and it is available right now, within us, and attained through choice, willingness and discipline.

Spiritual traditions and mystics tell us that joy, peace and love is who we are behind all our conditioning, not something to get but something to be, so the starting point is the finishing point.

TRANSFORMING ESSENCE *WITHIN* OUR WORK

We were born to love people and use things, instead we love things and use people.

LEO BUSCAGLIA
Author of *Born to Love*

A question I am often asked is, 'But if I did what I really wanted, or did it the way I wanted, would I have to leave my current job?'

It can sometimes seem that the only way to be authentic is *outside* the traditional organizational structures and work situations, so deep is our conditioning that we can't be ourselves and be successful in work. I meet doctors whose achievements are measured by how many patients they see in an hour and how much money they save. In their hearts they know that they aren't able to give their patients the *quality of attention and care they need* and feel frustrated. Lawyers are judged by the amount of money they bill, not the quality of service, and teachers are measured largely by exam results and league tables and not by the love they give. Commercial companies are completely measured on the form – the results. Look at the financial papers and that is all we see. We need to find ways of moving beyond the status quo, but this doesn't necessarily mean abandoning it altogether.

Therese loved teaching six- and seven-year-olds, but was finding the other administration work around teaching too much. She knew that raising self-esteem, nurturing the children's spirits and helping them feel capable were essential ingredients of the learning process, more so than any technique, and she knew that this was where her heart really lay. In her own time she trained to become an educational consultant, and now continues to work part-time in the same school as a teacher and part-time as a consultant helping raise the self-esteem of teachers and children in schools. Her school sees the value of her consultancy work, and incorporates it into their culture.

When we focus on the essence of our work rather than the appearances of success, we find that the success we may otherwise have striven for and chased begins to find us naturally. It can seem quite a magical process, by which we make ourselves a magnet to attract the people, situations and events we need in our life.

James is a doctor who nurtured an interest in healing and spirituality, which didn't readily fit in with conventional medical practice. He decided he wanted to run a surgery that integrated holistic and mainline medical treatment, and he felt in conflict because he felt he might have to choose between being a holistic practitioner or a doctor. I asked him, 'What kind of work would you like to do as a doctor?' His answer included integrating traditional and alternative medicine, empowering and educating patients to be well and running open days to help patients live more holistically. I asked him if he could become this kind of doctor and, after thought, he realized he could do it without leaving. Along with his other partners, he developed a new vision for their practice and is now creating it.

Both Therese and James show that our spirit can outgrow the existing form of our work, but we can create a new form within our existing work.

EXERCISE

◆ If you are in a job, what kind of person do you want to be in that job?

I love being invited to go into organizations and help them change the spirit in which they work. Sometimes the changes can initially be small, but their cumulative impact over time can be huge. One family-owned company in Wiltshire asked me to run a course called 'Enjoyment and Employment' in which I asked employees to look at ways in which their work could be more fun and nurturing of their spirits. Their top team of directors and senior managers spent several days with me over a period of months. I was struck by how formal they all were, all wearing business suits and meeting in hotel rooms, and I pointed out to them that they had no external shareholders and were free to work in whatever clothes they decided. They did in fact have a great sense of fun. I suggested they think about how they might like to have their meetings, and when one of the women suggested they have their next top team meeting over a picnic in the park, in casual clothes I was delighted. They had begun to change the way they worked, and to step into their own freedom.

Stepping out from behind formality and inner rules can also be very challenging for some people. A local council asked me to design and run some stress management courses for their middle managers, and part of this day involved lying on the floor in the conference room learning some relaxation techniques. At some point in the day, usually halfway through, I would invite them to lie down and then dim the lights, and ask them to *do* nothing for twenty minutes, and be paid for it. The horrified expressions on some faces sometimes made me think I'd made a mistake and asked them to run around the civic centre naked! As we discussed the matter, I realized that they felt a huge pressure on themselves so that they felt guilty at the idea of doing nothing and were afraid that if their bosses saw them they would be in trouble for slacking, yet each of them knew and agreed that relaxation actually made them more centred and consequently more productive and better managers. We talked at length about this guilt and how to unhook themselves and transform it into positive energy. By the end of the day, they were committed to bringing those ideas into their teams.

THE COURAGE TO BE WHO YOU ARE, WHERE YOU ARE

About ten years ago, Lisa, my girlfriend at the time, was a lawyer with a top West End law firm. To help her deal with the stress and develop her own personal sense of well-being, she was beginning to learn to meditate. She was sharing a flat with a another professional, and practised meditation some evenings in her bedroom, pulling her chest of drawers across the door to feel safer. One evening her flatmate tried the door to come in for a chat while she was deep in meditation, and questioned why she had barred her room. Flustered, Lisa replied, 'I'm … I'm masturbating!' That, to her at that time, was preferable to admitting to meditating!

When we are on the early steps of reclaiming our true selves, we can feel very vulnerable, like a sapling just rising from the earth. We may need to fence it off for protection, but as our sense of self gets stronger, we flourish and can remove the fences and quit hiding. Then in time we become a strong tree, able to offer protection and sustenance to others. I lost touch with Lisa … maybe she's a meditation teacher now.

Richard Barrett is a good down-to-earth Yorkshireman who worked at the World Bank in Washington. As a result of several experiences, he began to wake up to his own spirituality, realizing that he was not just a body but a soul. He began writing his first book, *A Guide to Liberating Your Soul*, while working at one of the most conservative organizations in the world. As you can imagine, he experienced a dilemma: 'I felt torn apart and could not see how to integrate practical spirituality into my career.' In 1992 he asked six like-minded colleagues to give him feedback on the ideas in his book, and they had a series of lunchtime meetings to discuss bringing spirituality into work. As Carl Jung wrote: 'Conflict exists strictly as an opportunity to raise our consciousness.' Richard decided to raise his consciousness.

Soon afterwards he was promoted into a challenging new role at a high level, and two of the lunch time group asked him to set up a spiritual study group, though he thought he'd be too busy. He was well practised in asking for inner guidance, and within a few days had been contacted by two employees whom he didn't know, saying they had read the report of a lecture he had given on the subject of his book. They asked him to set up a spiritual study group at the World Bank, and even offered to organize it for him. That was his sign.

Within a month or so they had their first meeting, attended by over 40 people, and although some of those attending had fear about being judged by colleagues it soon became perfectly respectable to be associated with the Spiritual Unfoldment Society. Within another few months a very complimentary article appeared in the *Washington Post*, and soon membership grew to 400, with many enquiries from other organizations in the area. They created special interest groups, monthly meditation sessions, retreats and two newsletters. 'Members said their souls had been fed, and that the work of the group had a profound impact on both their personal and professional lives,' reported Richard.

There followed an international conference to explore the link between spiritual values and sustainable development, which the World Bank agreed to sponsor. It was packed out with 350 delegate from 20 countries. The real significance was that the Bank staff now had the permission to talk about spiritual values in development, and bringing hearts and souls into work. All this came about because one man had the courage the speak his truth with love rather than shrink through fear.

Richard encourages anyone to do the same. He explained to me, 'For anyone experiencing a similar dilemma, let me encourage you to integrate your spiritual journey into your working life. There is a great need to bring spiritual values into the corporate setting, either by providing a forum for people to meet and discuss spiritual matters, or persuading your organization to shift from a paradigm of competition, exploitation, and self interest, to co-operation, empowerment, and the common good ... When you accept the challenge to implement your soul's purpose, you will soon move from career to mission.'

Richard's story shows the influence a single person can have. No one gave him the power; he simply took the power of his own heart and integrity and influenced others with his vision, courage and inspiration by showing what he stood for.

Michael is a very conservative-looking chartered surveyor, but beneath the pin-striped suit a radical heart is beating. His goal is to live a peaceful and loving life in a stressful world, so he meditates every day in his London office of chartered surveyors. He is quite up front about it; he tells his colleagues, 'I am unavailable for 30 minutes now as I am meditating,' shuts his office door, and meditates. 'At first they thought I was bit strange and would tease me,' he told me. 'Then I noticed that people would come and ask to have a quiet word with me. They would tell me that I always seemed so calm, ask how I managed – was it the meditation, and how could they find out about it? And others would ask me for a hand with their specific life challenges.' He discovered that by deciding to be himself and authentic he became a very positive influence in the office.

These are all examples of people who have decided to bring their spirit, willingness and determination to be themselves into their work. They changed their minds about how they wanted to do their everyday work. Each of us is the power to love, to be kind, to help, to inspire, to touch the lives of all the people we meet, in large and small ways. These qualities are already within us, waiting to be drawn out and nurtured.

Remember: what we are here to give and to be are actually the same thing.

CLAIMING OUR INHERITANCE – OUR OWN SPIRIT

Here are some ways to bring our spirit into our everyday awareness:

◆ Bring it back to now. Affirm this moment that, whatever the appearances and experiences, you are fully connected to the whole of the essence of creation. Do this now and every day.

◆ Know that life is on the side of overcoming blocks and limits, of healing, of prosperity, abundance, creativity and of success.

◆ Each of us has the whole of the universe on our side; we are each precious and gifted, no one any more so than another.

◆ Focus on what is present in your work and life. Count all the blessings that you already have and be willing to receive more.

◆ Turn your attention away from lack and turn in to find the essence within.

◆ Practise the presence of essence – that we are always in the presence of the infinite, eternal essence from which all things proceed.

REALLY ONLY TWO ATTITUDES

Every decision is a choice between love and fear.

A Course in Miracles

While it may seem as if there are thousands of different attitudes and states of mind, there are only two sponsoring thoughts with which we can work: the thought of fear and the thought of love, and what is not love is always a form of fear. The forms in which these two thoughts can seem to show up are unlimited.

The spirit of fear can show up as: survival, guilt, doubt, blame, clinging, problems, demanding our needs be met, defensiveness, competition, scarcity, lack of opportunity, roles, sacrifice, win/lose, fighting, battles, tantrums, separation, judgement, using, manipulation, criticism, withholding, domination, control, power struggles, attachment, projection of feelings, conflict, struggle, striving, resistance to change, living in the past or future, traps, lies, deception, not trusting dreams, cynicism. Fear requires manipulation and struggle to maintain it, and is focused on externals.

And the spirit of love can show up as: truth, integrity, giftedness, true creativity, openness, spirit, joy, inspiration, forgiveness, defencelessness, trusting and following dreams, sharing, trust, happiness, innocence, peace, vision, abundance, support and sharing, naturalness, co-operation, joining with, forgiveness, valuing, appreciation, acknowledgement, treasuring, making precious, open communication, intimacy, releasing the past, old thoughts, beliefs and habits, healing, owning feelings, willingness to change, living in the present moment, moving forward. Love is centred in the present moment; it is ease, is inside and much less stressful.

We may not fully realize it but the choice is always ours. We may have been so used to choosing fear we may not see that there is an option, and we may need some help to choose again. At the core of the work we were born to do is the belief that we are in a transition, individually and collectively, from a fear-based view of work to a return to a love-based view of work. To create from our spirit invites us to focus on what we want to create, not on getting rid of what we don't want. We can apply this principle to the realms of the heart, with appreciation, feedback and recognition.

APPRECIATION, FEEDBACK AND RECOGNITION

I now perceive one immense omission in my psychology – the deepest principle in human nature is the craving to be appreciated.

WILLIAM JAMES (1842–1910)
Psychologist, philosopher and teacher

There are two things people want more than sex and money – praise and recognition. We all crave appreciation and feedback for the energy we expend in our work. Like an incomplete loop, work done without feedback is not complete, as if we are left hanging in mid-air. A research report stated that 46 per cent of people who quit their jobs reported that they did so because they felt unappreciated. In my 25 years' working life I have never been to an organization where people reported, 'We feel so appreciated working here!' Appreciation and recognition seem to be the great secrets waiting to be discovered by so many employers.

I suspect women are a little better than men at giving and receiving appreciation and value, though not always. In many work environments the belief seems to be that a need for feedback is a sign of weakness and insecurity – you should know how you are doing, or shouldn't need to know. We seem to have come to accept that we are more likely to receive criticism than positive feedback, and that therefore no news is good news. We think that by humiliating, ignoring and demeaning people they will be more motivated to care about product and service quality – we believe that fear motivates more than positive encouragement and appreciation.

I was once invited to give a 30-minute presentation to an audience at the Industrial Society, the largest corporate training provider in the UK, to help launch a report on stress in the workplace. I suggested that I would like to speak on the importance of love, appreciation and valuing people in the workplace, as I believe that the absence of these is a great cause of stress in most workplaces. They looked surprised, but agreed.

As I rose to deliver the talk on the day, I felt great anxiety about speaking to such an audience on such a subject, but went ahead and did what I intended to. At the end it seemed like there was a split in the room; half the people wondered which planet I was from and how I had been invited and the other half truly resonated with the ideas and said it was like an oasis in a otherwise uninspiring day. One man came up the me and said, 'I have been working for my boss for 20 years, and he has never once said thank you or appreciated me.' I was staggered and saddened that it could be that bad, but this reminded me of the belief that is commonly held that if I haven't told you that you are doing a bad job then assume you are doing okay.

We forget that we are humans with hearts, not machines, and that feedback is vital for learning, appreciation is essential for motivation and feeling valued is imperative for growth and creativity. Self-esteem and creativity are such delicate flowers that praise tends to make them bloom, while criticism and discouragement often nip them in the bud. Any of us will produce more and better ideas if our efforts are appreciated. Often appreciation can be spontaneous and about finding beauty in the moment.

I was invited to facilitate a day for a team of social workers. I asked the question, 'Do you ever tell each other what you enjoy and appreciate about working with each other?' My question met blank expressions. I invited them to spend some time appreciating each other, and asked each person to take it in turn to receive feedback from the others; the person receiving was only able to sit, smile and listen, not respond; my experience tells me that we tend to block receiving when we talk, saying, 'Yes, but ...' As the process unfolded it was like rain in a desert, and the whole mood of the team changed as they all began to feel appreciated. The manager wrote to me afterwards to tell me how there was a difference in the team from then on.

I always ask teams I work with to do that exercise, and suggest they also make it an agenda item at each team meeting from then on, giving each other feedback as regularly as possible. Another great exercise is to tell people in the team to write each other a card, as if they were leaving. Often we give truly heartfelt feedback only when somebody leaves a job, and I've often heard people say that they would not have resigned if they had heard that appreciation earlier.

Heartfelt appreciation is a wonderful way of dissolving competition and nourishing the soul. I love the following passage from *Mutant Message Down Under* by Marlo Morgan, a tale of her time on walkabout with Aborigines in Australia:

> During our journey there were two occasions that we celebrated by honouring someone's talent. Everyone is recognised by a special party, but it has nothing to do with age or birth date – it is in recognition of uniqueness and contribution to life. They believe that the purpose for the passage of time is to allow a person to become better, wiser, to express more and more of one's beingness. So if you are a better person this year than last, and only you know that for certain, then you call for the party. When you say you are ready, everyone honours that.
>
> One of the celebrations we had was for a woman whose medicine or talent in life was being a listener. Her name was Secret Keeper. No matter what anyone wanted to get off their chest, or vent, or confess she was always available … The woman knew her strong points and so did everyone else. The party consisted of her, sitting slightly elevated, and the rest of us … various people took turns telling her what a comfort it was to have her in the community and how valuable her work was for everyone. She glowed humbly and took the praise in a dignified and royal manner.

There is a common belief that we have a need for appreciation that cannot be fulfilled, as if we are bottomless pits. Often as children people do not give us the attention we want for fear of spoiling us. I had a great insight when I read a wonderful book by Jean Liedlof called *The Continuum Concept*, which is the story of her life with indigenous people in South America, whom she discovered were the most confident and self-assured people she had ever met. When she looked at why, she found that their attitude with children was that they gave the children whatever they needed by way of attention. They assumed children only asked for what they needed, and babies were given human contact all the time for as long as they needed it. They had no concept of spoiling children, and their belief was that the child simply asked for what it needed, and when it filled up it went away contented. They had no notion of scarcity, knowing that there is enough for everyone, and knew that children only had a certain number of needs for love and attention. From this Jean Liedlof considered that most of the problems of anti-social behaviour with adults in our culture resulted from failing to meet children's basic needs, not from spoiling them. This contrasts with many of our childrearing philosophies that say if you run to comfort a baby every time it cried, you'll become a slave to it.

In most working environments we seem to have hundreds of manuals, rules and regulations outlining punishments, grievances, things you must not do and what to do when things go wrong. How many manuals show how to encourage, appreciate, honour, encourage, value and recognize people? What is the procedure for things going right? This is a key for fulfilment in any work situation: letting people know they are valuable and important.

We can express our appreciation in the simplest of ways – a word, a note, a gift, a prayer, a thought, e-mails or faxes. The key is to catch frequently and praise the small stuff, then the big stuff will take care of itself.

Expressions of the heart and work can seem to be at loggerheads, but need not be. Let's now concern ourselves with how we can follow our heart and bring our heart into our work.

Simple Ways to Implement Principle Three

* Do what you love, enjoy and like more often.

* Throw yourself into doing your work without concerning yourself with the outcome.

* Do a little less, be a little more.

* Put fresh flowers on your desk at home or the office.

* Write a card to a colleague as if they were leaving. Write down what you would say to them then, and tell them now.

* Take a piece of paper and write down the names of six significant people in your work. Drop them a note to tell them of your gratitude for them.

Principle Four

AWAKENING THE HEART AT WORK

Our feeling heart is our guide and compass, showing our true path through joy and our false paths through pain and suffering. It is our guide to love, and we can learn to bring our love and compassion into any work we do or create new work from the inspiration of our heart. Our heart knows while our head supposes and throws up doubt after doubt; we can rely on our heart.

THE HEART AT WORK

The heart has its reasons, which reason knows nothing of.

BLAISE PASCAL (1623–1662)
French philosopher, mathematician and physicist

One of our major struggles occurs when our heart is not in our work; in short, when we don't do what we love or love what we do. What moves and touches the heart is what makes us human, and when we fail to engage our heart we are more likely to be going through the motions. Our heart is vital to us in many senses, and literally seems to have a mind of its own. We are often experts at knowing what we don't want in our lives; our heart is where we turn to discover what we do want.

Our heart is our authentic compass. When we make friends with our heart again, it happily guides, advises, is a fountain of inspiration and wisdom, shows the direction we are called to and leads the way for our visions from conception to completion. When we consult it, our heart can tell us whether we're headed in the right direction, or if we've made a wrong turn or when it's time for a U-turn. For many of us, this is information we are reluctant to acknowledge, as knowing it might mean choice, and choice often means change. It never forces us to change, but it does offer options that will lead us to freedom and authenticity. Our heart never deceives us, nor will it lead us into trouble; it may lead us into what feels like scary places but only in order to heal, to cleanse us and clear away old emotional scars.

The work we were born to do is not a cerebral process of rational analysis, but a process of noticing what touches our heart, inspires and moves our heart. We can then use our head in service of our heart. Our head can only *suppose*, while our heart *knows*.

Our heart works in two realms – the physical realm and the realm of feelings.

OUR PHYSICAL HEART

Even as a simple mechanical pump, our heart is a miracle machine. The biggest muscle in the body, but weighing only 12–14 ounces, it pumps between 40 and 80 million gallons of blood in an average 70-year life span. In one day alone, 8 tons of blood passes through the heart, and the heart produces enough energy to lift a ton weight 3 feet off the ground, a truly phenomenal little machine. We usually only think about when it goes wrong, although it never usually stops or needs a service.

Its reduction in our minds to a mere mechanical function started in 1648 when the English physician William Harvey discovered that the heart was the pump that sent blood around the body. Until then history had regarded our heart as our emotional and spiritual core; there does in fact appear to be a scientific basis for this belief.

Psychoneuroimmunology is the study of the mind-body connection in medicine. It shows us over and over again that patients who are seriously ill make dramatic recoveries, sometimes against all odds, when they know they are loved – when the feeling heart influences the physical heart. Love literally heals.

Dean Ornish is a doctor who has been fascinated by the scientific evidence of the healing power of love and intimacy. In a study of 159 people undergoing coronary angiography it was found that those who felt most loved and supported had substantially fewer blockages in the arteries of the heart. In another study, 17,000 people between the ages of 17 and 24 were studied for six years, and those who were most isolated and least connected had almost four times the risk of dying prematurely. The capacity to nurture and be nurtured – to have an open heart – is vitally important to having a long and healthy life. Loving truly is miraculous. We can become well by wishing others well, and we can become ill by competing and wishing them ill.

Acts of love, nurture and affection and connections to other people stimulate the immune system. Love arouses the body's inner pharmacy, producing healing chemicals and wonder drugs to fight illness; things that cannot be bought in from the outside. Scientists know that love heals, regenerates, renews; it makes us younger biologically and can make us feel safe and secure.

OUR FEELING HEART

Our feeling heart is our physical heart's invisible twin. In Indian Ayurvedic medicine the heart is the seat of the soul, and in Chinese medicine it stores *shen*, which is a sense of appropriateness and right behaviour. Ancient warriors would eat the hearts of their victims to gain their strength. Aristotle believed the heart to be the centre of thought and sensation, and the Hebrew Bible has more than a thousand references to *lev*, the heart, which was regarded as the centre of knowledge and morality. In the Middle Ages prominent people would have their bodies buried in one place, and their hearts in another. Love poetry has romanticized the heart, and it is regarded by many as the link between the physical and spiritual worlds. In the chakra system, the heart is at the centre.

We all talk of feeling 'heartbroken', that someone 'touched our heart', or something was 'heartwarming'. Indeed the Oxford English Dictionary has well over 100 entries for the heart – more than for any other organ of the body. And yet the heart seems unwelcome in most modern workplaces. But, no one can stop us bringing our heart into our work. We can choose to listen to it and act on it.

THE LANGUAGE OF OUR HEART

Our heart will never tell us what we should, ought or must do; it will never tell us how to win or to beat someone else: those are the commands of our personality. Our heart will simply show us how to be true to ourselves, our own nature. Our heart will never chastise us or get angry with us, however long we may have ignored it, but will always tell us how to correct our wrong thinking or wrong path; its only desire is correction, not punishment. It only ever speaks to us in loving terms.

When we listen to our heart we listen to the voice for love, our conscience; we can consult it to discover what it is telling us, guiding us, prompting us to be and do. Here are some ways that our heart communicates to us:

◆ Through words. Simply sit quietly and ask your heart a question and see what answer comes.

◆ Through feelings and sensations. We know that something doesn't feel right any more, or that we feel excited and interested in an idea or project. We sense what is true and false for us.

◆ Through dreams or symbols. Make a note of dreams or symbols that you are aware of, and explore them.

INTUITION

It is by logic we prove. It is by intuition we discover.

JULES HENRI POINCARÉ (1854–1912)
French physicist and mathematician

We struggle when we listen only to others instead of to ourselves and our heart. While outer support and encouragement can be wonderful, the work we were born to do unfolds from the inside out. Intuition is a form of intelligence, of inner knowing and inner understanding that transcends the laws of cause and effect. Intuition is the language of the soul speaking through the heart.

We may need to learn to value our intuition again, as we have mostly been trained to trust and value logical analysis and rational deduction over inner knowledge. Our intuition may not make logical sense, but it makes heartfelt sense to our need to be whole and have integrity. I often wonder how frequently we actually make intuitive decisions and *then* justify them. I have worked with so many business people who are proud of their rationality, but speak of hunches, gut feelings and sixth senses. I think a mystic hides behind many a business suit.

Intuition, rather than logic, is often the way we break out of old struggles, mindsets and limitations. Insights concerning the work we were born to do are more likely to come through intuition rather than logical deduction. Intuitions are not normally about the past but are about some way of freeing ourselves from our history for a new now and a new future, a new level of awareness. They are the means by which innovative ways forward come to us. Intuition is about seeing things anew and discovering new territory. It is not even about the one best or only way, but about guiding us through options.

When we follow our intuitions, we rarely see the complete picture, but are shown how to take each step one at a time. Our working life becomes an adventure, perhaps taking us to new places in the world and within ourselves. When we our faithful to our intuitions, our work will become our guide and teacher, as described in an Estonian proverb: 'The work will show you how to do it.' We don't have to figure it all out ourselves and can discover providence working in beautiful, unpredictable and even unimaginable ways. When we are inspired by our heart, we get answers and ideas for the situation of that moment.

EXERCISE

◆ When have you felt most intuitive, guided and inspired in your life? What events, situations and circumstances were present?

◆ What would you do in your life if you knew that you would be guided to say and do the most appropriate things in each moment? How do you feel about that level of trust?

I have always been fascinated by intuition and ideas and where they come from. They obviously originate from a hidden part of our hearts and minds that we are not aware of all the time, but are they plonked into us by some outside force? And if so what is this force? It is ultimately a beautiful mystery, one that we don't have to understand to appreciate, use, enjoy and benefit from.

The most beautiful thing we can experience is the mysterious.

ALBERT EINSTEIN (1879–1955)
Mathematical physicist

E X E R C I S E

Many of Einstein's greatest ideas came to him while he sat by his fire with a large brandy, half drunk and half awake. He was receptive to ideas in that state. We can become aware of when we are most receptive.

◆ Take time to be quiet every day, and several times a day when possible. If you think you are too busy to do this, you need to do it even more!

◆ Simply listen out for your intuition. What is the quiet voice behind all the loud voices telling you to be or do?

◆ Thank that voice and offer to build a stronger and stronger relationship with it.

WHO ARE WE IN OUR HEARTS?

In our quieter and more private moments, each of us is aware of a greatness inside of us – a power and a beauty and a magnificence. We tend to reserve the idea of greatness for special and usually very public people, or we may have been told to be humble, not great, and that if we blow our own trumpet we are arrogant and big-headed. Yet because we are spirit in essence, we are literally the stuff that God is made of. It doesn't make us special, because it is in all of us. We are all precious, and it is our arrogance to diminish ourselves and pretend we are less than wonderful.

So, in your grandest vision, who do you see yourself being? What have you come to contribute? What light have you come to shine? What glory have you come to make manifest?

WHAT IS YOUR HEART IN?

If you follow what you love, you will be amazed how often it leads to a job.

Barbara Sher
Author of *I Could Do Anything If Only I Knew What It Was*

Where does our heart fit into our work? Most of us have been encouraged to make the market king or queen in our work choices. Our decisions may have been based on questions such as, 'Where can I make money?' and 'How can I make myself attractive in the marketplace?' Largely we've come to believe that our heart and our deeper emotions should not be involved in our work. As doctors, lawyers, therapists, accountants, social workers and other professionals, we are taught that professional distance is good and that we should avoid getting too involved with feelings. Boundaries are always important, but it is our very caring and connection through our heart that makes all the difference.

We need to separate two questions that often get put together, which are:

◆ What do I love and where is my joy and inspiration?

◆ How can I discover and create ways of supporting myself financially doing what I most love and enjoy?

We may not know the answer to either question, but by trying to answer the second question too soon the creative promise of so many ideas can be stillborn. We need first to focus on and build up our enthusiasm, excitement, love and inspiration. The mistake we make is to try to figure out how to travel every inch of the journey before we have even set our direction. Our job at this stage is not to know all the hows but to get excited and motivated and strengthen the whys.

EXERCISE

◆ Keep noticing what you enjoy and love; make it an object of your attention; record what you observe in a journal. Remember that what we pay attention to grows and expands. Do we love other people enough to love ourselves?

◆ If you aren't clear what you love and enjoy, or don't have an unfulfilled dream, notice what you could love and enjoy, or think about other people's ideas that touch you.

◆ If 'But how could you ever make a living out of that?' arises, say, 'Thank you for sharing, we'll come back to that question.' If we don't get excited enough about ideas everything can seem insurmountable, but when we set our heart on an idea we will discover the ways how as we go and deal with the obstacles.

LOVING WHAT WE DO

Nothing is impossible to a willing heart.

JOHN HEYWOOD

A great starting point is learning to love what we do now, as we have already discovered the key ingredient in loving our work is not what we do, but the spirit and attitude with which we do it. K Bradford Brown, founder of the Life Training programmes, expressed it this way: 'Drudgery is a state of mind, not the task we refuse to enjoy.' We may think that it is easier to change our job and think that different circumstances might bring happiness but these may just be excuses.

Unless we are self-employed, most of us think we work for someone else, but what if we realized that we work for ourselves, whoever pays the salary or wages? When we don't give our best because of what we regard as a lousy boss, we are the ones who really suffer. We go home angry, frustrated and resentful and are the ones who get ill, but we blame *them*. Do what you love and give of your best, and have the fulfilment of a life well lived. Be like the bird who sings in the morning, whether anyone listens or not. It is wonderful to feel appreciated by others, but more wonderful still to appreciate ourselves for living the life we want.

EXERCISE

◆ Try to notice what you are satisfied with in yourself, in others and in situations in your work and life. Conditioning may keep you striving for more, and will have you focus on what is missing rather than what is present. This is a good exercise in shifting awareness from ego to unconditioned self. And even beyond the feeling of loving your work is working with the attitude and spirit of love. Love is not, at core, an emotion or a feeling, but a choice and a decision, and a willingness to extend ourselves.

GRATITUDE – THE ART OF ENJOYING WHAT WE ALREADY HAVE

If the only prayer you say in your whole life is 'thank you' that would suffice.

MEISTER ECKHART (1260–1328)
German mystic and theologian

One of the most powerful mechanisms for loving our work right now is the process of gratitude. It focuses on what is present in our work and life right now rather than our ego's desire to notice what is missing. How well are you doing with what you already have? Whatever we appreciate, we get more of, and when we are grateful, we are added to. Gratitude breaks through the need for more and the constant yearning we feel.

I remember listening to Mother Teresa talking about seeing so much material wealth and yet vast spiritual poverty in the West. She told a story of a man starving in the street in India sharing half a banana with another starving person. There was scarcity within those circumstances, but love and abundance within them too. That, she said, is true wealth, the ability to feel blessed with whatever you have and a willingness to share whatever you have. Mother Teresa said that in the West we have many bananas, but we don't share them.

Often we use stories like this to feel guilty, which is a trap. The key of the story is to feel blessed and grateful for whatever we do have, and to desire to share whatever we can. We can move from the trap of guilt to the joy of gratitude.

We can take so much for granted, as I continually notice as I work with people from all walks of life. Truly grateful people are not the norm. Most of us spend our lives focusing on what is missing from our work, where our lives are lacking, how lousy our boss is, how badly paid we are, how unappreciated we are, how busy we are, how the economy isn't really getting any better, how little time we have, how overwhelmed we feel, how lousy the weather is, how we've put on weight, how we're getting older, feeling guilty, worrying about our future … This is not to deny any of these circumstances, but to choose what we look for and notice in our current situation. All these things keep us away from our joy.

I have always loved the sentiment of a song by Mike and the Mechanics: 'I'm a beggar, but I'm sitting on a beach of gold.' We are all sitting on a beach of gold, the richness of our own heart and soul, and yet we often experience ourselves as beggars. As we remember who we are and commit to regain our true spiritual identity as our most cherished possession, we find the true wealth of spiritual love that is our essence.

◆ What do you most notice as being scarce in, or missing from, your life?

◆ How do you feel when you observe that?

◆ Why do you think you feel that way?

A DIET FOR GRATITUDE

Show me one happy, ungrateful person.

ZIG ZIGLAR
Author of *See You at the Top*

Doing this exercise daily *will* change your life. Gratitude is the way of giving thanks from our heart to everything in the universe. Every day, simply take at least ten minutes to notice how in your life you are being blessed and what you have to be grateful for. Not much, you may answer, as we can often be so good at noticing what we don't have. Maybe a useful way of stimulating your attention would be to imagine you were a peasant in India or some other developing country, and notice what they don't have that you do, appreciating what you have by contrasting it with what others do or don't have. Here are some ideas to focus on:

How are you blessed by nature? How much beauty is there around you, how much life is going on all the time?

What about the cosmos? Just think that the stars and the moon are shining for you, and the sun always sends light and heat, usually without a word of thanks from us.

Closer to home, who likes, cares for or loves you?

Which experiences have been most important to you?

Which people have been the most strong loving influences in your life?

Do you have a home? Consider every single possession you have, that you have a bed.

What is your favourite colour?

What is your favourite vegetable, or fruit, or sweet?

What flowers do you most love?

What countries have you visited?

What emotions do you most enjoy?

What are your favourite tastes? And smells?

What about physical sensations?

If you have some kind of job, what are the benefits of it? You may hate it, but what does it allow you to do, to have, to be? Does your job allow you to have holidays? Pay your bills?

Do you have friends at work?

What do you enjoy at work, or could you enjoy at work?

What skills and qualities have you developed through work?

What meaning and purpose does work give you?

If you could not work, what would you miss?

Even if you hate your work, what does it allow you to do outside the workplace?

What have you learned about what you need because you are not getting it?

What material things has your work allowed you to accumulate?

If you are unemployed, what are the benefits of being unemployed?

Did you get any birthday or Christmas cards?

If you died shortly, would any people be at your funeral?

How many things are available to you freely in this country? Depending where you live, a telephone call may lead you to all of the following for free: health and dental care, libraries, TV stations, roads, parks, the right to vote, legal advice, police, ambulances, social services, emergency counselling ...

Your body is constantly working for you, digesting food, renewing cells and bones, with no conscious effort on your part.

Can you walk, see, talk, smell, taste?

What skills and talents do you have?

What freedoms do you have to talk, speak, write what you want? Billions lack the freedom of self-expression ...

Take a mental wander through your life and see who and what is precious to you and would be missed if you lost them.

We can go on for ever, literally. There is so much to be grateful for, yet much of the time we only notice a little of our abundance. Often our attention is on yearning for more, or noticing what we don't have, or who has more than us. We fail to see our own treasure, but we can choose to begin to cultivate a sense of awe, wonder and gratitude. When we can live in the awareness that all life is happening right now, we realize that there are no ordinary moments. We are the miraculous expression of life, and are surrounded by the miracles of love.

WORK AND LOVE

Books don't mean a lot unless you open them, hearts are the same …

RICHARD WILKINS
Author of *10/10*

The love that flows through our hearts is our greatest resource, even in the world of work. However, much of what we understand to be love is actually more like neediness and attachment, so we associate love with hurt. Chuck Spezzano, a teacher of mine, puts it this way: 'If it hurts, it isn't love'. This turns around much of our thinking. The pain of love, love dying, the loss of love, unrequited love – these are not forms of real love, but the substitutes we have created. Actually love never hurts, contrary to popular love songs and poetry. Most of what we call *love* is actually need and attachment, which is why it can feel painful.

Ideas about love

◆ *Love as need*: When we say 'I love you', we often mean 'Don't you dare leave me or do anything to upset me – I will try to control and manipulate you so that I can feel safe'. It is based on behaviour, and it is conditional and something to get. We can spend much of our energy trying to earn and deserve love by being special. At the heart of specialness is not love but need and manipulation.

◆ *Love is an emotion*: It is the joy, happiness and pleasure that we experience when we are involved in activities or experience that are pleasant and enjoyable for us. Love is something to experience.

◆ *Love as a choice, as our being*: Wise people and mystics have said that we reside in a world of illusion, and beyond this illusion is a world so wonderful that we can't even imagine it, where we realize that love is the very fabric from which all we know is created. M Scott Peck described love as the willingness to extend ourselves for the spiritual growth of ourselves or others. Sometimes we don't feel as if we want to be loving, but we can choose to even though we don't feel like doing it. Then we realize that love is what we are, and our purpose is to extend and share it. When we express unconditional love, we are expressing our own divine nature, and an open and generous heart draws the very best to it, because it wants to withhold nothing. A generous heart is self-initiating – it waits for nothing, and just extends itself.

The work we were born to do is the adventure through these different awarenesses of love.

Misguiding Myths about Love

* Love can be earned through hard work.

* Love is only achieved through deserving it.

* Love can be and needs to be continually proved.

* We have to be special to earn or deserve love.

LOVING OURSELVES

Where you find no love, put it, and you will find love.

ST JOHN OF THE CROSS (1542–1591)
Spanish mystic and poet

In Confucianism, a principle called *Jen* refers to the belief that there is goodness, pure goodness, at the heart of each of our beings, where our true self or spirit resides. We would do well to share this belief as we progress towards the work we were born to do. The more we are able to love and be happy with ourselves, the more we will be able to love what we do and we will be at peace with our work. If we find it hard to love ourselves, we will find it hard to be satisfied with whatever we create or achieve.

EXERCISE

◆ What does 'self-love' mean to you? Does it have a positive or negative connotation, or both?

◆ How lovable do you consider yourself to be?

◆ What does the concept of unconditional love mean to you?

Love underpins all joy, happiness, creativity and peace and is the major purpose of life; as Leo Buscaglia said, 'When it comes to giving love, the opportunities are unlimited; and we are all gifted.' Remember this: we were all born to love and be loved, and in essence loving *is* the work we were born to do.

Miracles can and do occur in the presence of love. In my experience each of us has parts of ourselves that we think are unacceptable, so we create masks and dances to hide them and hope people will love our masks or performances instead. Yet there is a deeper part of us that wants someone to come see through the mask and love us anyway. We all do this to some extent, and the one that we are hiding is the one that is most needed – the real us, with our strengths and vulnerabilities, our joys and fears. The real us is far better than any mask we can patch together.

The process of learning to love ourselves more is the process of acknowledging, accepting and loving all the hidden, denied and buried parts of ourselves, which we shall explore in more detail in Principle Seven on wholeness and integrity. To really know love in our lives we must be willing to reveal ourselves to those we hold at arm's length or try to protect ourselves from. We can learn that there is nothing we need to hide.

HARD WORK OR HEART WORK

If you come from your heart, you will have the strength to do whatever you need to do. You will walk without fear, for what Spirit guides you to do must easily be accomplished.

ALAN COHEN
Author and workshop leader

Let's remember that work is only hard when it is performed without love, either love of the work or love within the work. We may well have experienced the misery of doing work every day that our heart just isn't in. At best it is boring, and at worst it is excruciatingly painful. Hard work is a role we play, and even if we are successful we feel a distance between us and other people because we only show them the role, not the real us. It is as if our heart steps back from connecting with other people; as if we are working and caring by remote control, from a distance. In a role we are cut off from our heart and have no criteria to measure and establish what is true, so there is always doubt.

Heart work is easier because it brings us into alignment with ourselves and gives us a strong sense of purpose. When we listen to our heart, we may face fear or doubt, but we know that we can and will deal with those challenges. Our heart receives the strength it needs to rise to challenges, and narrows the distance between us and others. We get the courage we need to venture by venturing and by giving ourselves, and by being willing to give what we are scared to give without a need for anything back. We get to work together to connect and engage, in teams and in partnership with others, which makes success much easier. Heart means seeing that other people are not just resources and stepping stones or blocks for us, but are whole beings – just like us.

EXERCISE

◆ What keeps you from giving your heart and getting closer to other people? Think of six answers to the following question: If I get closer to other people through my work, what will happen to me or them?

THE POWER OF KINDNESS

No act of kindness, no matter how small, is ever wasted.

AESOP (620–560 BC)
Greek author of fables

I was walking back to my car after working out at the gym, and had bought a bunch of flowers. I saw a lady probably in her 80s, whom I didn't know, standing at her gate and a voice in my head said, 'Give her the flowers.' I immediately thought that was a mad idea, so I just carried on walking to the car, but the voice repeated, 'Give her the flowers!'

So I put my sports bag in the car, walked back, and rather sheepishly said to her, 'Would you like these flowers?'

Her face lit up. She took them and told me, 'Nobody has given me flowers for years.' We chatted for a few minutes, and then I left her at her gate and went to my car. I probably made her day, but the joy she gave me was huge – she made my day too. That £2.50 bunch of flowers created great joy.

I have often thought to myself, 'If I had to condense the essence of my work, my beliefs and what I think it means to be loving or spiritual, it would have to be *kindness*.' I found these words echoed by Aldous Huxley who, at the end of his life, wrote in *The Perennial Philosophy*: 'It's a bit embarrassing to have been concerned with the human problem all one's life and find at the end one has no more to offer by way of advice than "try to be a little kinder".' Daily human kindness is the greatest power each of us has to transform our own life, and the lives of those around us.

An indication of the real measure of how much we have chosen a life rich in spirit is the extent to which we have chosen to view and treat all people and things with basic decency, kindness, true respect, love and compassion. All spiritual traditions have at their heart the teachings of kindness:

Islam: The Koran teaches that 'the deep human response for which Allah calls is the commitment to justice that transforms daily life into continual acts of generosity and kindness'.

Judaism: In the Talmud it states: 'Kindness is the beginning and the end of the law.'

Christianity: Jesus said that his disciples will be known by their acts of loving and caring.

Buddhism: Emphasizes a loving heart and kindness to all living beings; the Dalai Lama states: 'My religion is simple. My religion is kindness.'

Hinduism: Paramahansa Yogananda wrote: 'Be … a cosmic friend, imbued with kindness and affection for all God's creation, scattering love everywhere.'

So the essential idea of all religion is loving kindness. But what happens when ideas get organized? That is another story. Imagine what the world would be like if all religions treated each other with loving kindness. Wouldn't that be an interesting world?

Being immersed in the New Age and spiritual world, I meet hundreds of people who are involved in the latest therapies, chakras, healing and meditation techniques, mantras or crystals. For the first few years, I felt in awe of all these people and how clever and esoteric some of them were. More recently I have come to use a new yardstick to gauge any teacher or guru: How kind are they?

◆ Think of some of the acts of kindness throughout your life that have been most important to you, at home, school, work and socially.

◆ When can you remember being told that *your* kindness had touched somebody?

We all need to know that people care. We can nourish ourselves and each other by the numerous small and large acts of love and kindness every day. When we are caring in our work we will inspire others to care in their work. We will help ourselves and our colleagues to work from the heart.

CHARACTERISTICS OF WORKING FROM THE HEART

The best and beautiful things in the world cannot be seen or even touched. They can only be felt with the heart.

HELEN ADAMS KELLER (1880–1968)
Author and lecturer

Kindness is one simple way to bring our heart into our work. The actual characteristics of working from the heart are no more complex and no less powerful.

The heart sees only itself reflected in thousands of guises

We meet ourselves time and again in a thousand disguises, but there is a place within us that embraces all the apparent opposites we experience. The heart unites, integrates and embraces everything, all aspects of human nature which the intellect has divided and pulled apart. It embraces all opposites: the sinner and the saint, generosity and greed, love and hate, joy and depression. Many of the spiritual traditions of the world say that it is through the heart that we see truly, and with the eyes we see only illusion and appearances. Antoine de St Exupery wrote beautifully: 'It is only with the heart that one can see rightly; what is essential is invisible to the eye.'

The heart doesn't judge and embraces all our imperfections

The heart doesn't judge feelings as good or bad, so the path of the heart requires the willingness to feel all our feelings, including the ones we have judged as bad, such as envy, hatred, jealousy, hurt, revenge and pain. This doesn't mean we have to act on them or encourage them, but that we should honour and own them. In doing so we integrate them, and have their energy available to us. Splitting them off has taken up so much of our energy, and by fighting them we have even strengthened them. This also stretches to embracing and forgiving every unkind act or thought of our own or another person.

The heart doesn't judge behaviour, but looks to see that all behaviour is either loving, or if it is not loving, that it is a call and a cry for loving. The heart sees beyond appearances to the essence of the person. For much of my life I have experienced depression, and I have judged it to be awful and I don't like it. Nothing I ever tried really seemed to shift it. What really has begun to help is stopping judging it and just accepting it. This hasn't meant being a victim to depression and letting it overwhelm me, but stopping fighting, because I could never win the fight.

A truly enlightened attitude is to be kind, loving and accepting of – while not condoning – *all* of our feelings, even the most painful and least socially acceptable ones. The work we were born to do is about moving beyond neediness and mere survival, and about truly living and giving, embracing life fully in all its hues and colours. Every day above ground is a good day.

The heart doesn't see anyone else as inferior or superior – behind appearances we all come from the same source

The heart sees only the spirit behind the appearances and knows that behind our masks and personas we all come from the same source, we are all one and are all on the same team. Mother Teresa once described her work as tending for and loving Christ in all his distressing disguises. That is the heart at work, knowing that behind all appearances of behaviour and all distressing physical appearances is another heart and soul, just like us.

The heart sees only love or calls for love

Because we are all from the same source, we are all connected, and love is what connects us all. Love is what is true, and if we perceive unloving behaviour, it is because we and/or the other person have forgotten who they are in essence and need help in remembering, not through punishment, but through love, support, compassion, forgiveness and good boundaries. Everything unloving calls for correction and is a call for love. The heart creates no rules for loving, it just wants to love. Love melts the distances and the blocks between how we see ourselves and others and the truth of who we are. Love takes us home. We can let go of attachments to outer things and hold on to our heart.

The heart does not dominate or manipulate

Our ego demands power over others or to be a victim in order to be special. The heart has no desire or interest in specialness, but sees itself on an equal level with everyone. You may remember reading stories about Princess Michael of Kent, a member of the Royal Family, regularly volunteering at a homeless shelter, anonymously serving soup. She said it gave her the greatest satisfaction, because it cut through all her apparent specialness and privilege and simply allowed her to be natural. The heart knows that there is an abundance of what we need; it doesn't manipulate to get it, but just asks and expresses.

The heart is the seat of intuition

We have already seen how listening to our heart means listening to the source of wisdom that lies within each and all of us. It will lead the way, guide and inform us, and it is always offering to do so when we listen and trust it. Our heart will never lead us to what will hurt us; it is in the realm of the heart that the most precious discoveries are made.

The heart's only desire is to give

Our heart, as the home of our spirit, is full, and seeks for nothing for itself, and wishes only to extend itself. Love, being whole, needs nothing and desires only to extend itself.

Following our heart is not about *not* having problems

Following our heart is not about some romantic idea of sailing off into the sunset, living happily ever after, but is about being true to what is most important to us. We may in fact have further problems, but what is more important is that our life will have more meaning so we have the motivation to deal with them. When we follow our heart we can choose to see the obstacles that we encounter along the way as having a gift for us, somehow for our highest good. But it is a choice to see problems this way.

When things don't go the way we wanted them to or how we thought they should go, we can ask ourselves questions: 'What am I being called to understand? What self-concepts am I being asked to release? What would be the most loving and compassionate response in this situation?' Ultimately we can see that all problems have only one purpose – to teach us forgiveness and love. Sometimes we may be overwhelmed with such opportunities.

I used to have a joke that when someone asked me how I was doing I would say, 'Oh, another EGO,' and they would ask me what I meant and I would respond, 'Another Enormous Growth Opportunity!' The trick is not to get caught up in the drama and indulgence of the problem, but to spot and get the gift more quickly.

The heart holds no grievances, it forgives

Grievances, hatred and resentments obscure the love in us, and forgiveness is the process by which we release these blocks. We've come to understand forgiveness as *overlooking* but true forgiveness is *seeing differently*. Through forgiveness we release ourselves from our own prisons of judgement and condemnation, and bring the miracle of love forth again.

On an episode of her TV show, Oprah Winfrey enabled victims of crime to confront the criminals. She described how a teenager who had been beaten almost to death, and needed seventeen operations to restore her face, forgave the perpetrator so that *she* could get on with her life. Oprah shared; 'To this day, it is the most powerful thing I've ever seen. In that moment, she expressed why we are here – to learn to love in spite of the human condition, to transcend the human condition of being fearful. We get so bogged down in worldly things we don't understand that we're here for a spiritual quest. Understanding that this is a journey is the most exciting part of being human. It has revolutionized my life.' Love is for-giving.

THE HEART AROUSED

A true heart is like a desert rain, inspiring and bringing hope to tired, parched and disillusioned souls. One aroused and awakened heart can touch and feed millions of people with love and nourishment.

The power of our heart aroused is enough to break down any limitation or barrier and to overcome all obstacles, because love is the most powerful force that exists. Many of the icons of the second half of the twentieth century – such as Gandhi, Mother Teresa, Nelson Mandela, Martin Luther King, Princess Diana

Changing Your Real Boss Without Changing Your Job

We have mostly chosen to be employed by our fearful thoughts and anxieties, but we can also choose to be employed by our hearts and spirits in our work. Our heart makes a much better employer; the reward package is huge and the terms and conditions are great. We can choose to have a new executive decision-maker.

Chris is an English political co-ordinator working in Brussels who took a holistic holiday in Greece. When he arrived he was his usual tough and armoured self, close to picking fights with many of the people he met. He became friendly with some of the people learning Reiki, a way of sending loving energy to people. As the week progressed he began to melt, and began hugging people around him. His heart began to open, and he liked it so much he didn't want to close it again, so when he got back to Brussels he decided to stay that open. A couple of months later he decided to learn Reiki himself, which was when I met him. He seemed very open, and I found it hard to believe that this guy worked in the tough world of politics.

'How do you do it?' I asked him.

'I've just decided what is most important to me, and decided to live that way.'

– touch and capture our hearts because they have been teachers of love and forgiveness. Deep down we all know that love is what it is all about, and when we see others having the courage to choose love, contribution and forgiveness over revenge, judgement and condemnation, we are inspired because we know it to be true.

Our natural heartfelt response is to want to help others. You may remember the story not so many years ago of some South Pacific islanders who just started to receive television and radio for the first time. Their culture had stayed pure and intact for many centuries. On TV they heard a story of a family in America who had been made homeless by a hurricane, and their immediate response was to gather together a food package and send it to them. It was such a natural response for them to extend themselves, and had not yet learned that it is impossible to help and sensible to close their hearts.

One of Bruce Springsteen's greatest songs has the line 'Everybody got a hungry heart, you lay down your money and you play your part'. We all have an aching in our heart for something greater, deeper meaning or purpose, and the quality of our life is the attention we give that hunger and longing. Yet along the way we've all experienced heartbreak and disappointments, usually enough to justify us closing down on any other great risks.

We all have good reason to have closed our heart, but do we have enough good reasons to risk *opening* our heart again? Without our heart there is no joy, no purpose and no true feeling of aliveness; our heart brings life to life. Will we commit to venturing our heart again, for the sake of love and in the name of regaining our vitality and gifts, and will we do that not just for ourselves but for the sake of all those we come into contact with? Will we venture it all again? Are we willing to bring ourselves to life again? The way to win our heart back is to venture again, to risk giving, receiving and trusting again, and of course to risk getting hurt again, but deciding to forgive and to no longer use the hurt or fear to keep ourselves in prison.

EXERCISE

◆ When in your life have you most followed the desires and callings of your heart? What were the results?

◆ At what times in your life have you felt your heart was most open?

◆ This is a question to be answered by intuition, not logic. What would make you venture your heart again in your work now?

◆ If you were to be an inspiration to yourself, what would you have been, become or achieved?

◆ Take time to nourish and invest in your emotional heart – be with those who love you, immerse yourself in beauty, treat yourself, bring intimacy and laughter into your life.

WHAT IS YOUR EXCUSE FOR *NOT* FOLLOWING YOUR HEART'S DESIRE?

Any unfulfilled dream or desire speaks of valuing an excuse more than our passion. We say things are impossible rather than inconvenient or scary. We say we are stuck, but in fact, unlike a tree stuck in the ground, we are free to move and choose and change, yet we pretend we can't.

John, for example, claims that he wants to leave his job in accountancy, perhaps retrain and do something new, but he's been saying this for the last five years. What he really means is that he isn't prepared to (a) take a risk, or (b) adjust his lifestyle in the short term, or (c) take the time to discover what else he loves and is good at, or (d) make the effort to go back to studying, or (e) maybe do some part-time work while he is studying. Yet if John fell ill and went to the doctors and was told he had six months to live, do you think he would find the motivation to leave and do what he wanted? Of course he would.

The question is never one of 'Can I?' but of 'Am I motivated enough to?'

EXERCISE

◆ Pick an unfulfilled ambition, dream or heart's desire.

◆ Write down all the reasons and excuses why you haven't followed it through.

◆ Ask yourself 'What *would* create enough motivation for me to get going on this dream?' See what comes into your mind.

◆ Start anyway!

THE WAY BACK TO OUR HEART

Anything that helps you get in touch with your heart will move you closer to your life's work.

LAURENCE G BOLDT
Author of *Zen and the Art of Making a Living*

The journey back to our heart is our life's journey and our soul's journey. Each of us has our own way of doing this, and the most important ingredient is our intention to want to. It is the path of opening up to greater levels of capacity for loving. We believe that love is an emotion, but it is actually a choice, so how do we choose a path for our working life that has a heart to it? Here are some ideas:

◆ The heart is the seat of feeling, so we get back to our heart by feeling. We have all blocked off and repressed painful and difficult feelings. The trouble is that we can't be selective, and by hiding *some* feelings, we dampen *all* feelings. So the way back into our heart is to be willing to feel all feelings, the joy and the pain, the love and the hate, the laughter and the tears. It can be a bumpy ride, but it is the way to regain our wholeness, to regain our integrity. As Kahlil Gibran wrote in *The Prophet*: 'The deeper sorrow carves into your being, the more joy you can contain ... they are inseparable.' Feelings have only one purpose – to be felt, so we should be willing to feel our feelings, not to indulge or manipulate others with them, but just feel them. Our resistance to certain feelings can keep us struggling for a lifetime or more.

◆ Listen to your intuition.

◆ Notice what you love doing, who you love being with, which circumstances inspire you and touch you. Be aware of your strong feelings of love, fun, passion and motivation. As you notice them, give them more attention. Make sure you spend at least a little more time doing what nourishes you.

◆ Practise living from your heart, speaking your truth, being strong and being vulnerable. Richard Green, who worked with Diana, Princess of Wales on her public speeches, once explained that she had been very anxious about giving them. He said that his advice to her was very simple: 'Speak from your heart.' When anyone speaks from their heart, it strikes a chord with us, inspires us and moves us to greater action. Heartfelt communication is more powerful than any 'techniques' and is beyond mere skill. Heartfelt intentions are a gift we offer of our very being. As Jeremiah Burroughs said: 'That which cometh from the heart, goes to the heart.'

◆ The heart is the seat of caring, so notice what you really care for and care about. Make caring for people, animals or the environment your work.

◆ Notice what you complain about most at work or generally. Whatever you complain about reveals where you are called to make a difference.

DEDICATING OUR WORK

Through dedication we set intentions, and when we commit to our intentions amazing things can happen.

In August 1995 I was coming to the end of my first trip to India with Ben Renshaw, Robert and Miranda Holden and Therese, my girlfriend at the time. Robert, Miranda and I were in Rishikesh, in the foothills of the Himalayas, and having been in India for nearly a month, I had gone native, wearing lots of beads and a white cotton suit (quite embarrassing when I look back)! If you have been to India you know that for a few rupees you can buy flowers, incense and a candle that will float in the water. The three of us sat by the Ganges, and decided to write a note and throw it, with the package, into the river, said to be the holiest in the world.

I wrote a note, not even knowing who I was really sending it to – perhaps to my own soul – saying that I felt my life was about bringing love and spirit into the workplace, and if that was my calling then I surrendered to that and was willing to serve and contribute in whatever ways I could, and I dedicated my life to that. And then I threw my little bundle in the extremely fast-flowing river. It was a symbolic gesture, but I did feel good about it, and since then my work, my career and sense of purpose have strengthened. Who knows?

Also in India, as in many other countries, people often dedicate their daily work to gods, goddesses or other deities, in order that their work be of service and bring them good fortune.

EXERCISE

- ◆ If it feels appropriate to you, pray silently to yourself or whoever you feel close to, and offer your work to be for the highest good of you and everyone you work with.

- ◆ In your own work, and even better if you can influence others too, take a moment of quiet and dedicate your work or the meeting to be for the highest good of all concerned.

- ◆ Pause before you start work and ask yourself silently, 'What would love have me do here, now, today?' Listen to and act on the response.

- ◆ Play with the novel idea of falling in love with your work. What might that be about?

Prayer is an Attitude of the Heart

I remember seeing a newspaper headline just after the devastating bombing of the government building in Oklahoma. It read: 'When all they could do was pray.' It struck me that this is a commonly held attitude, that prayer is a last resort, not a first resort. Images of prayer tend to have us speaking with a distant, old, white-haired male, pleading for God to dispense some favour for us or someone we love, or to punish someone who is not our friend.

I like to think of prayer as setting our intention by communicating with the divine and the absolute. Prayer is not something we do but something we are. It can be silent, in words or thoughts, and it is not a substitute for action but a prelude and a partner to action. I like the Quaker idea of 'praying with your feet moving' and the Arab proverb of 'trusting in God and tying up your camel'. Here is a favourite prayer I use at the Heart at Work project:

Please help me discover the gifts and love that are inside me.
Instead of wanting brilliant work, help me to be brilliant and to bring that to all the work I do.
Help me to find the love that is in me, so that I can find what I love and love what I do.
Help me face and set aside my fears and be willing to be inspired and to inspire.
Help me to contribute to the lives of everyone I work with – colleagues, customers and suppliers.
Help me to know that it is not the quantity of work I do that matters, but the love behind any action I take.
Thank you.

THE MARRIAGE OF THE HEAD AND THE HEART

Buddha always emphasized a balance of wisdom and compassion: a good brain and a good heart should work together ... These two must be developed in balance, and when they are, the result is material progress accompanied by good spiritual development. Heart and mind working in harmony will yield a truly peaceful and friendly human family.

THE DALAI LAMA

Given the importance of our heart physically, emotionally and spiritually, and that most people don't have their heart in their work, is it any wonder that heart disease is one of the biggest killers in the Western world? We have seen how the modern workplace seems not to be the most welcoming place for our heart. We may even believe that work and emotion are – and should be – separate, and that the workplace is where rational efficiency resides.

We're mostly good at rational thinking but may find heart-centred work more challenging, whereas too much thinking tends to get bad press in the spiritual world. Both rational thinking and heartfelt response have value, and the way to ease into it is to let our head be in service of our heart. Let our heart show the way, and let's use our head and mind to figure out how to travel, what to do and how to get there. The ego is a great servant but a lousy master, yet most organizations have the ego in executive control.

One of my greatest joys is helping people who have come from the commercial world to find their heart and then recycle all their old skills in its service. At the Samye Ling Buddhist Centre in Scotland, the Lama asked me what I did for a living. 'I bring spirit into business,' I told him.

'That's interesting,' he replied. 'We're trying to bring business into spirit!'

We need both – business sense and spirit. The Lama was telling me that Buddhists can be great meditators but lousy managers!

We will always doubt if we let only the rational mind decide, as it is its nature to be uncertain. Certainty and knowing are of the heart. The only way to begin to rid ourselves of doubt is to commit to our heart's calling and then deal with the doubts of our mind as we go. If we waited until we had no doubts, we would still be waiting on our deathbed. This courage and commitment, more than any skills or knowledge, will contribute to our success.

The difference between our heart and our mind is that our mind tends to separate, exclude, withhold, judge and discriminate, while our heart wants to keep sharing, joining, extending itself, including and embracing and expressing compassion. This is why our heart can frighten us if we've neglected it. In a work and business situation we may fear feeling or being regarded as soft when we are not hard and judgemental, but the trend is for us to want to bring more of the whole us into our work, including our heart and our whole range of emotions. Let our head chart the course inspired by the heart, and let the cleverness of our mind compliment and support the wisdom of our heart. Just make sure the head knows the heart is boss!

Towards a New Working Environment

I've often thought that babies and pets should be compulsory in workplaces, helping us feel warm during the day. I spent a day at The Body Shop headquarters in Littlehampton where they have a creche. It was beautiful to see the children paraded past the office windows by the carers so their parents could see them. They all smiled, felt connected and their hearts were wide open.

EXERCISE

◆ What would it mean to you to work heartedly?

◆ Why don't you? When will you?

◆ Who do you know who works most wholeheartedly? What could you learn from them?

DOING WHAT WE LOVE WITHOUT SACRIFICE

When love and skill work together, expect a masterpiece.

JOHN RUSKIN (1819–1900)
English writer, critic and reformer

Finding and doing what we love is a trajectory, a direction and intention, not a fixed place to arrive at for ever but a fluid and evolving journey. It opens the doors to joy, abundance and a purposeful life. One of the greatest confusions is the difference between love and sacrifice. Sacrifice is the ego's version of love, the belief that to achieve or gain anything, there is a price to pay. The crucial understanding we need is that love demands no sacrifice. We may also mistakenly believe that the only choice is between doing what we love and starving or doing what we don't enjoy to earn a living. We can in fact do both – integrate love and money.

It is important to find our love and our joy somewhere in our life; it's not necessarily the case that we have to leave what we don't enjoy in order to find what we do enjoy. We can do work to pay the bills during the day in order to fund our passion in the evenings and weekends, and to discover how we could eventually give up the day job; the form of work that we love is unique for each of us. Here are just a few examples:

> Renee is passionate about healthy living and organic food and opened the organic supermarket, Planet Organic, in London.

> Simon loves Japanese cuisine and after two years of research opened the Yo! Sushi Japanese restaurants.

> Erica is passionate about the environment, and started the Oxford Rickshaw Company to benefit students, visitors and the environment.

> John loves modern military history, and turned his hobby into a business collecting military equipment, renting to film, TV and magazines and becoming a consultant to the film industry about creating authentic battle scenes.

> Kristos loved water sports as a child and trained to become a professional waterskier; after having to retire through injury, he started a beachfront water sports business.

> Roxy loves being an accountant, helping people keep their finances together and negotiating the intricacies of dealing with the Inland Revenue.

> Richard hates being an accountant but discovered that he loves playing, acting and clowning, so trained as a clown and runs workshops on play while working still as an accountant.

We may be experts at what we dislike or even hate, but how well do we know what we love?

EXERCISE

◆ When you think of doing what you love, what are the first thoughts that come afterwards? For example, '... and I'll starve' or '... and I'll be really happy' or '...and the money will follow' or '... and people will be jealous' – write down six of your immediate responses. Interestingly, many people go blank when they think about this because we actually have precious little conception of what would happen. Take time to flush out some of your fantasies, both helpful and unhelpful.

◆ What in your work, and outside it, gives you most joy and pleasure?

◆ Think back to all the work and jobs you have ever done, and remember the parts, even if they were small, that you most enjoyed and found most rewarding. What people, circumstances or attitudes were present there and then?

◆ What did you most enjoy when you were eight years old, or twelve, or sixteen? And what did you dream you might most like to do when you were an adult?

◆ If you worked for love, not money, what would you love to do?

◆ Think about the work you would do if you only did work that delighted you.

◆ Who do you know, or could you know, who could be a mentor, helping, guiding and encouraging you to find and follow what you love?

Many people are now being forced to review the belief that work is a duty with little place for joy as they discover that they are no longer secure employed in doing something that they don't enjoy. The old contract with employers is rapidly disappearing, so we're thinking that if an employer is not going to take care of us, we'll have to start taking care of ourselves. We can create what we love, but first we have to discover what it is we love. Finding our heart in our work requires us to make a shift in thinking from what we could do and what others want us to do to what we *want* to do. To view money as an incidental benefit to doing what we love in our life is the most blessed of all experiences.

Here are three principles for doing what you love in your work:

◆ Work for the joy of it, *as if* you don't need the money.

◆ Love *as though* you never have been or will be hurt.

◆ Create and express yourself *as if* no one is watching.

To find what you truly love, you may need to try many things first, eventually finding what you love and then figuring out how to make a living out of it.

So far I have deliberately kept us away from thinking about money too much, in order to start getting us to think about the crucial questions of identifying our love, inspiration and joy because this will generate the momentum we need to start making changes. Once we have positive motivation, we can start thinking about responsibilities and paying the bills. Let's now turn our attention to mastering money and marrying our highest visions with the down-to-earth practicality of earning a living.

Simple Ways to Implement Principle Four

* Really appreciate someone you work with, and communicate your appreciation to them.

* Do something for your boss to make them feel valued and appreciated.

* Find something special and precious to celebrate.

* Get your team together and pose the question to everyone, 'How can we work together in ways that are more fun, supportive, inspiring and loving?' Brainstorm the answers, and carry out a few.

* Take some quiet time to picture your favourite colleagues and customers, and in your mind say to them all, 'I wish you happiness, peace, love and abundance.'

* Take some quiet time to picture your *least* favourite colleagues and customers, and in your mind say to them all, 'I wish you happiness, peace, love and abundance.'

Principle Five

KNOWING THAT MONEY IS NEVER REALLY THE ISSUE

Money is essential to life but not to the purpose of life, and lack of money is not really the reason why we don't do we want to with our working lives. Money is not, in itself, a scarce resource; what may seem scarce are creativity, will power, determination and self-awareness. As we develop our inner strength and are willing to follow our heart, we will create and manifest opportunities to bring money into our lives. When we are willing to receive it and remove our blocks to it – our sense of guilt or unworthiness – we will bring it to us.

THE VALUE THAT WE GIVE MONEY

There is little likelihood that your life can become fully functioning with prosperity unless you have a positive and creative attitude toward money … You may go into the day with the highest intention to walk in the light of Truth. But if you have not resolved the 'money enigma', you quickly lose your lofty awareness the moment you dip into your wallet.

ERIC BUTTERWORTH
Author of *Spiritual Economics*

To be truly successful in the work we were born to do, we need to carefully and honestly examine our beliefs about and relationship to money. If we don't, even our most beautiful, loving and creative ideas could flounder. Money is like oxygen, it is essential for living but not the purpose of living. For many of us money is still one of the most emotionally laden subjects. According to Relate, the UK marriage guidance service, it is the subject *least* talked about by couples.

The fear of not having enough money or of money running out or of financial insecurity is probably the biggest block to creating the work we were born to do. We carry this fear with us at practically all times, so that physically and emotionally we are too close to actually see it clearly. We have so much conditioning that we need to unravel, but before we can do so we need to become clearer about what we currently think and feel about money.

EXERCISE

◆ Cast your mind back and remember your earliest memories about money. What did you decide about money as a result of that? For example, Steve's first childhood memory was of finding half a crown (12^1/$_2$ pence or 20 cents) in the street and his father taking it from him as he wanted to spend it himself on going to a football match. Then and there Steve decided that having money is pointless, as someone will just take it away. His adult life certainly reflected this decision. Does your adult life still reflect the decisions you made as a child? Would you like to make new decisions?

◆ When you think of money, what are the first ten words that come to mind in association with money?

◆ When you think of money, what are the three qualities that you would least associate with money?

MONEY AND BASIC SURVIVAL – OUR PARENTS' INFLUENCE

Depending on our age, our parents could have grown up during or just after the Second World War, and perhaps lived through the Great Depression, rationing, bombing or other hardships. On some levels their lives were a struggle for material and financial survival, and they did well, both for themselves and for us. Now that most of us live in a society that provides for most people, where survival is not the key motivating force in life, but those memories may still live on in our minds.

Our parents would probably have loved to pursued more creative and artistic activities or more spiritual paths, but were too busy surviving and providing. Their unintentional influence can lead to two dynamics in our own minds:

◆ We feel guilty that we have more opportunities than our parents and are able to pursue our creativity and higher expressions of life. The way out of this is to move from guilt to gratitude, to thank those who have gone before, either in reality or in our minds, for building so that we could stand on their shoulders and create even greater things.

◆ Deep down we may still have a fear based around our survival and be driven to fight for our survival way beyond the time when our immediate material needs have been met. Rationing and hoarding may be alive and well in our minds.

MONEY AND SPIRITUAL BELIEF – THE INFLUENCE OF ORGANIZED RELIGION

Many religious teachings have created guilt and fear around money. 'It is easier for a camel to pass through the eye of a needle than for a rich person to get to heaven' and 'blessed are the poor' and similar doctrines don't exactly support an attitude of innocence about money; they invite guilt. But did you know that the 'eye of a needle' in fact described the entrance to a city in olden times? All the camel had to do was lighten its load and crouch down a little to pass through, so this saying has been greatly misinterpreted: it simply means that it is overattachment to money that is the problem, not the money itself.

Yet many of us fear that we can't be both materially and spiritually successful. We believe that material riches prove we aren't spiritual. This is a form of spiritual snobbery. We may even believe that when we embark on doing more loving, pure, spiritual and service-orientated work that the bad money will taint our work. None of this is true. Being involved with the spiritual world I see many people who claim to be above money and beyond those earthly concerns. Some of these have been very enlightened people but others are probably on ego trips. At a conference exploring different approaches to money that I attended, there were various speakers, including successful business people, therapists and a Buddhist monk. The monk had taken a vow not even to touch money, and needed a novitiate to travel with him to carry money and pay for food and travel. The monk was a lovely man, but I felt uncomfortable with the idea that he needed to be above the earthly concerns of money to be spiritual.

Albert Camus, the existentialist writer, said: 'It is a kind of spiritual snobbery that makes people think that they can be happy without money.' I believe that we can reach the higher ground of spiritual awareness in the midst of our daily earthly concerns. The goal is transformation, not transcendence. Money can help or hinder our growth – it depends on our attitude, not the amount of money itself.

Indeed, the established churches have become some of the most wealthy institutions in the world by teaching the 'give us all your money and you will get to heaven' policy, although many churches do put money to wonderful uses. No wonder we have become so confused about its spiritual status!

WHAT MEANING HAVE YOU GIVEN MONEY?

Let's examine some of the misunderstandings we may personally have acquired about money so that we can start liberating ourselves and be freer to pursue the work we love and feel called to do.

Below are a series of questions to help you identify some of your accepted beliefs, and understand what meaning you have given money.

What meaning did your parents or parental influences give to money?

How much was money openly talked about in your family?

What are your deepest fears about money?

What are your positive fantasies about money, and what you think it can do for you?

Who is your most positive role model around money? Who inspires you most?

What do you think of incredibly wealthy people?

What do you think about very poor people?

How much money would be enough for you to lead a fulfilling life?

What do you most fear happening in your financial life?

What do 'affluence' and 'abundance' mean to you?

What religious ideas do you have about money? For example, how do you think God views poor and wealthy people?

If you don't have enough money, what does this prove in your mind?

To what extent have you tied up your sense of identity with financial success?

Be as honest as you can be in answering these questions, and you shall reveal to yourself some of your major conditioning around money.

HOW IMPORTANT IS MONEY TO YOU NOW?

This may sound like a silly question, as your immediate response may be that it is very important, but perhaps it is not as significant as you might think. As our culture values economic success and money so much, it is easy for us to think that making, saving, keeping and spending money should be important to us. We are told from school onwards that we should be concerned about money.

Once we develop a clearer understanding of the value we give money, we can choose how much of it is enough, and therefore what is sufficient for us. It may be that we can survive and thrive on less money and choose what is being called voluntary simplicity – less money, which gives more freedom in other areas.

EXERCISE

◆ Who in your life has particularly negatively influenced you around the importance of money? See which names pop into your mind. For a moment give them their opinions and attitudes back, and do this for several people if necessary. Recognize that these were never your thoughts.

◆ Ask yourself honestly: 'How important is money as a goal in itself to me?' Is it truly one of your greatest values? Discover your own true values and attitudes.

WE THINK MONEY WILL GIVE US A FEELING ...

If you are going to let the fear of poverty govern your life ... your reward will be
that you will eat, but you will not live.

GEORGE BERNARD SHAW (1856–1950)
Irish-born playwright and author

EXERCISE

We probably think that money will make us a feel a particular way and will give
us some experience we yearn for. Close your eyes for a moment and just
imagine that you won the lottery last week and that money is no longer the
motivating force in your life. With your eyes closed, survey your life and see
how you actually feel. Are you at peace? Are you happy and contented? Will
your life be easy and trouble-free?

If just imagining it makes you feel that good, try an experiment, which is to live
your life as if you had millions of pounds in the bank. This doesn't necessarily
mean that you have to spend the money! Try to fool your unconscious mind by
telling it that you are rich, and it may respond by helping you create the
confidence that you would have if this were the case. Our unconscious mind
doesn't know the difference between what you vividly imagine and what you
actually experience, so fool yourself into feeling that sense of assurance and peace.

If this exercise helps you discover that vast sums of money bring new concerns,
anxieties and fears, it is a great insight into the idea that money is not the issue, but
our state of mind is. Practise feeling at peace and confident now, as these states of
mind are available to us right now, regardless of how much money we have.

RESOLVING OUR TOP 15 MONEY
MISUNDERSTANDINGS AND MONEY WOUNDS

1 Money is a game – money has no value

On one level, money isn't serious stuff at all – it is a big game that we all play.
Money has no intrinsic value! It is worth nothing! For centuries the Gold
Standard allowed you to swap a bank note at a bank for its face value in gold,
but that was stopped in the Great Depression. Now we pretend that notes, coins

and bits of plastic are worth something and work hard doing what we don't enjoy so that we can accumulate more of them. It is we who give money value by endowing it with power.

2 We have too many negative associations around money

On a piece of paper write down all your negative associations or thoughts about money. Here are some examples, but add your own:

◆ Money is the root of all evil.

◆ Blessed are the poor.

◆ It is easier for a camel to pass through the eye of a needle than for a rich person to get to heaven.

◆ We must manipulate, cheat or be unpleasant to create money.

◆ Financial success always has a high price tag.

◆ We will be envied for having lots of money.

◆ We'll feel guilty for having more money than others.

◆ Money is not spiritual.

◆ Money destroys and corrupts relationships.

◆ Money creates meanness.

◆ Money is just a compensation, and won't make me happy.

◆ I can't earn good money, I have nothing to offer.

◆ We have to betray our heart, soul and authenticity to earn money.

Do you recognize any of these judgements and thoughts? Most of us have some, perhaps many, of these beliefs somewhere in our awareness, often quite buried. It is very important to be honest and not to deny them, because these thoughts affect our willingness and ability to engage successfully with money.

A popular belief is that ''Sooner or later it all comes down to money' but actually the problem lies in the fact that we *believe* that money will give us all the answers. This is true of many of us, although more and more people are realizing that money doesn't solve everything; indeed, the Henley Centre for Forecasting reckoned that 12 per cent of people in 1998 in the UK were actively planning to downshift or voluntarily simplify their lives and live with less money.

3 Money, or lack of money, doesn't create fear

Money and fear don't go together because money of itself is neutral, like everything else in this world. Give a child money and it will simply play with it. Every thought, belief and emotion about money we have learned from people around us or decided for ourselves and it is possible to learn some new ideas, attitudes and strategies around money. By giving money its meaning, we generate emotion. Fear and desperation are not in money, but in our mind, and we project on to money our fear of running out of it, of poverty or of never being able get enough of it. I have had times when I have lain on the floor and cried with fear and desperation about money, but looking back my lack was not money but self-belief. Even when I had money it didn't fix the underlying problem – my poverty consciousness and lack of self-belief. But, whilst money doesn't fix all the problems, it is still nice to have! We may say it is our fear of not having enough money that is the block for us, but in truth it is the fear of not having enough of what we *think* will create the money for us that is the problem.

Money Talks?

At the beginning of the money workshops I run, I often have people take money or credit cards and place them in front of them on the floor. I then have them point their index finger at the money and say out loud, 'You are the problem in my life; it is your fault I am not doing what I love, that I do what I hate and that I can't be happy!' They often report that they feel pretty stupid, and that is the point – it is stupid and it is what we do. But we can stop and realize that as we grow in self-confidence and creative power we become more detached about money and it flows more easily.

4 Money can't and won't make us happy

We think that money has a magic power to make us happy or unhappy. If this were true, every millionaire business person, entertainer, musician or film star would be happy, but we know that is not the case. Did you know that the wealthiest 325 individuals on the planet own around as much as the poorest 2.4 billion people? Do you think that you could easily identify those 325 people by the extent of their joy, freedom, peace of mind and happiness? I doubt it very much – some would be content, others would not.

Money can contribute to and support our happiness, and the absence of money can contribute to, encourage and support our unhappiness. Try this question – were you unhappy as a four-year-old because you didn't have a regular income? Of course not! Will you be unhappy on your deathbed because of money? Of course not! Let's put money in perspective; we *can* be happy with and without money, so let's keep it in its place as a very useful object but not the sole objective in our life.

EXERCISE

◆ How much money exactly would make you happy? (The honest answer is that you probably don't have a clue – you can only guess.)

A way to dissolve any fear is to get specific. Think about and calculate what is enough to pay your basic bills and give you some comfort. Know with complete certainty that there are hundreds and thousands of ways of earning that amount of money.

We confuse cause and effect, seeing money as the cause of affluence and prosperity, rather than the effect of a prosperous mind. Everything has its source in mind, in consciousness, so everything that we see in this world, including money, is an effect, not the cause.

5 The amount of money available is not a problem

If you took all the money and wealth that exists in the world right now, and put it an obviously huge pot and then shared it out equally, there would be enough for all 5 billion people on the planet to have over £1 million pounds each! Our thoughts of money being scarce are simply not accurate. We may experience a personal lack, but this is very different from there simply not being enough money overall. So what is the problem with money, other than unequal distribution? Our attachment to it is the problem.

A few years ago the World Watch Institute calculated the cost of a six-year programme to clean up the global environment and repair all the damage. It came to £456,000,000,000, which seems like a lot until you compare it with the £625,000,000,000 spent in *one year* on arms worldwide. We have the money, we lack the will. I shall be bold and say that the amount of money available in the world is enough to solve every social and environmental problem on the planet. The problem is the lack of will, greed, fear and scarcity of vision to use this money for loving purposes.

6 We have too few positive associations with money

We need to see how easy it is to become enthusiastic about money and see it as wonderful thing. Here are some more positive associations and thoughts:

◆ Money is wonderful.

◆ Money is just an energy.

◆ Money can provide security.

◆ Money is a blessing, a gift from life.

◆ Money is fun and can be used to express and share love.

◆ There is an unlimited supply of money; all we need do is tap in to give and receive our part of that flow.

◆ Receiving money is a demonstration of rendering some useful service.

◆ Money is a symbol of divine and unlimited energy.

◆ Deciding what is enough money frees me to pursue higher goals.

How did you rate with positive versus negative associations with money? In my experience, most of us make it through childhood with more negative associations than positive ones about money and then wonder why we have such problems with money. Make it a project for yourself to start seeking out people who use money in very positive ways, and to create positive thoughts, beliefs and affirmations about money for yourself.

7 Our emotional attachment to money is our biggest problem

Have you ever noticed that when you've really wanted something, been desperate for it and chased it, that you didn't get it? That's attachment. Desperation tips us into a downward spiral: the more desperate we become, the less attractive … and so on. Desperation throws us off balance. On one level most of us are slaves to money. You may think you are not attached when you have an adequate amount of it, but just close your eyes and imagine not having it for a few minutes ...

How do you feel, then? If you are confident, great; if you feel afraid, that is a demonstration of attachment, this can serve as a huge block to creating the work we were born to do. It can stifle our creative ideas because if we can't see an immediate way of commercializing our skills, gifts, dreams and desires we may immediately drop them as pie-in-the-sky, not realizing that the first year of business may be a bit tough, but that in the second and third years things will start to take off, and in the fourth year you may end up making more than in your previous job. Attachment kills dreams, creativity and willingness to follow our heart, and is one the major ploys our ego uses to keep us stuck. The more emotional we are about money, the more control it has over us.

But how can we not be desperate about money? It all comes back to choosing our attitude. If we need money, we can't pretend that we don't, but we can choose to relax a little about it.

8   Money and doing what you love do not go together

We may well believe that it is an either/or choice, a dilemma, which is another way of staying stuck, as in truth it can be an and/and or a win/win choice. We can do what we love *and* make money from it. We'll have more ideas, fun, energy, creativity and willingness to put the energy into something we really believe in and enjoy.

If you are ill and need an operation, would you rather the knife be in the hand of a surgeon whose major motivation was business and making money, or one whose motivation was loving, caring and helping people to recover? Obviously the latter. Would we rather have our home decorated by someone who saw it as an easy way to earn a buck, or by someone who loved the creativity of colour, texture and creating ambience? Obviously the latter again. We can apply that logic to our own work; aren't we going to more successful when we do what we love? Aren't we going to be more hireable, popular and successful?

Another popular belief is that we have to do lousy work to get filthy lucre. When we are more focused on negative thoughts around money, we tend to believe that we have to do unpleasant things to acquire money, and that may have been our experience. If we have money as a compensation rather than a joy in itself, we go for work we don't really enjoy in order to have money as the reward, creating rather an unpleasant spiral. Money can take on such an exaggerated sense of importance. Because there can be so few other rewards, it is what we think we deserve for the amount of unhappiness we feel in our work.

Real poverty consciousness is believing that we must do what we don't enjoy to earn money. We are, in effect, saying to ourselves, 'I don't believe I have the talent, imagination or courage to make a living doing something I enjoy.' If you believe that is true, you may have fallen into the cycle of earning money in order to enjoy the rest of your life – apart from your working life, that is. But do we truly know how to enjoy the rest of our lives? If we put unreasonable pressure on ourselves, our pleasurable pursuits, our family and friends to make us happy to compensate for work we don't enjoy, we may be in for trouble. There is no way to buy back enough pleasure to make up for what we miss through not enjoying our work. So stop sacrificing and start living, even through your work! Stop punishing yourself and those around you.

If we've only ever met people who didn't enjoy their work and haven't known many who have loved it, it would be easy for us to believe that doing things we love doesn't pay the bills. We may also have known somebody who experienced some kind of failure in doing what they enjoy, and that adds to our belief. It is vital that we actively seek out everybody who has found and followed through on what they enjoy and are working at what they enjoy. Unfortunately we don't necessarily find these people in the newspapers, so make it into a project to find a number of people who are successfully doing what they love.

Try this lovely affirmation: 'Financial abundance comes to me through easily, lovingly, generously and joyfully giving and sharing of my unique gifts.'

9 Being spiritual and having money aren't compatible

In a workshop a participant said, 'You can tell what God thinks of money by seeing who He gives it to.' She meant that only horrible and selfish people can have money. Needless to say, she wasn't doing so well financially.

When we ask what it means to be spiritual, images of poverty, worldly renunciation, begging bowls and leaving the distractions of the world behind are often conjured up. *It could seem that money and holiness don't go together.* But even the greatest spiritual leaders had their ministries supported by money – Jesus and his disciples were given money, Mother Teresa received huge donations – every charity, church and good cause does. Even a follower of Gandhi, famous for owning only a loincloth and few possessions and teaching 'Live simply so that others may simply live', once said, 'It takes an awful lot of money to keep Gandhi living in poverty!' It took much money to feed, water, transport and accommodate his entourage, and Gandhi was supported by wealthy business people. We really need to understand that money, love, God, spirituality and a higher calling can go together.

Much of our religious conditioning has led us to believe that God favours the poor and suffering, not those who are rich and successful. None of this is true. God loves us all equally, regardless, and there is nothing we can do to earn more favour with God.

Affirmation: No amount of money I have or don't have can make me any more or less lovable, even in the eyes of the creator.

EXERCISE

◆ What are the most joyous, creative, loving, abundant and glorious things that you do or would love to do with money?

If you find this exercise hard, I encourage you to develop more positive and life-affirming associations to money.

10 We have become confused, and equated money with wealth and prosperity

True wealth and prosperity are attitudes and states of mind through which we determine how we will see and experience the world. They are also choices and decisions. True wealth and prosperity are about how much love flows in our life, to us and from us, how generous of spirit we are and how free we feel. In the past, my neighbours included a Filipino family; both parents worked as porters, and were relatively poor, but they were two of the most welcoming, generous, loving people I have ever known. They were poor but prosperous. I bet you know people like that, and others who seem to have much more materially and financially but are poorer in mind and attitude. We can have inner riches of the spirit regardless of how much money we have.

We may also play the 'if only' game with ourselves, so that money becomes an object of huge fantasy, and we believe that most of our problems in life would be solved if only we had more money.

A friend of mine was always talking about how bored she was with her work, how she craved more adventure and excitement but couldn't afford to take risks.

Then out of the blue she inherited a considerable amount of money. It freaked her out! Instead of celebrating, being grateful and planning the creative and exciting life she had talked of, she went into major denial, saying she didn't deserve this money. For many months she did not even spend a penny of it. Gradually it dawned on her that the problem was not money but her attitude to money, her lack of self-confidence and most importantly her lack of passion, purpose and excitement in life. Her problem was *poverty of aspiration and purpose*, which she had fooled herself into thinking would be solved by money. Slowly, with help, she began to get a sense that although she didn't need that much money to achieve what she wanted, she could start to celebrate, enjoy and have fun with her money.

A research company asked 276 people who were not millionaires, 'Do you think you would be happier if you were a millionaire?' Hardly surprisingly, 76 per cent responded, 'Yes!' Then they asked millionaires, 'Did your first million make you happier?' and the answer was a resounding 'No!'

Underneath our unreasonable fantasies about money lies yet another big fear – the fear of disappointment. We know deep down that we could be disappointed, that money won't change our lives that much, so we actually push it away, preferring to cling to the hope of our dream rather than to the reality of a possible disappointment and a shattered dream.

EXERCISE

◆ When you say to yourself, 'If only I had money I would ...', what difference do you believe it would make? What do you think or tell yourself you would do if you had more money?

◆ Be honest with yourself. Is it lack of money that is *really* stopping you having what you want? What is it really a cover for?

◆ Start doing and being what you want right now, with the money you have right now.

11 We judge people with money or wealth

Be as honest as you can with the answer to this question: 'When I think of people I know or know of who have more money than me or are very wealthy, how do I feel?' If you are honest to enough to admit to jealousy, envy, judgement or superiority, then you must be human! Many of us have great judgements around money and people with money, thinking they did bad, exploitative or greedy things to earn their money, and some may have done, but this obviously sets up inner barriers to us earning more money in case we end up like them! We need to release our judgements about money and those who have more than we do. Money and integrity can go very well together, and money does not automatically corrupt. As Oscar Wilde said, 'The only people who think about money more than the rich, are the poor.'

12 Money only ever comes from hard work

A major by-product of the Protestant work ethic is the view that, by its nature, work should be difficult and a struggle, and that by association earning and creating money should be difficult and a struggle too. This need not be true. Hard as it may seem to believe right now, making money can be very easy when we have a strategy and when we are willing to receive.

EXERCISE

◆ Close your eyes for a few moments and imagine yourself relaxed, happy and at ease. Imagine somebody coming to you in your imagination and saying, 'You're great. Here, have some money for nothing.' Visualize them giving you a considerable amount of money, for no reason, for free, without conditions. How do you feel? Do you have mixed emotions – joy, gratitude, happiness – or any guilt, fear, thoughts that this must be a mistake, that you must get rid of it straight away? Notice any mixture of feelings.

This exercise will help uncover any thoughts you have about receiving money easily. If you felt resistance, this speaks your belief that getting money must be a struggle and difficult.

I have come from a background of believing that money must be difficult to come by and I made sure I worked damned hard for every penny I earned. As I started creating my new career, I wanted to believe that money *could* come to me more easily and through joy rather than struggle, and it began to. One day I was running a course at a hotel opposite a lovely park and, as it was a beautiful day, the group decided that it would be fun to work in the park in the afternoon, so we did. I noticed I wasn't feeling good as we sat in the park, and I wondered what was going on. Then it dawned on me – I was feeling guilty! A voice in my head was saying, 'How dare you just have a good time and make money?!' Luckily I could just smile at this voice, but it is one that probably exists in many of our minds. We can have money with ease when we are willing. The work we were born to do is about learning how to make money more easily.

EXERCISE

◆ What is the easiest money you have ever earned?

◆ What is the most enjoyable money you have ever earned?

◆ Who do you know who seems to earn or create money most easily, joyfully or effortlessly? What could you learn from them?

Steve is a member of the team at Alternatives. After working in the City and local government for many years, he was used to earning his living the hard way. He loved books and tapes, so I asked him to serve on the bookstall. The first night he worked there he earned perhaps £20, but he came up to me afterwards and said, 'That was the most joyful and easy money I have ever earned.' Although it was a small beginning, it actually represented a turning point for him through the simple realization that it was possible to earn money with love and have fun. He has since left local government and is working as a healer, counsellor, speaker, workshop leader and administrator.

13 We limit our sources of money

Most of us see a job or a career as the only way we can earn money to support ourselves and our family. Yet money can come to us in many different ways.

EXERCISE

Take five to ten minutes to remember all the ways that money, in any amount whatsoever, has ever come to you, from birth onwards. Here are some ideas:

◆ Did anyone put money away or in a bank or other investment scheme when you were born or when you were young?

◆ Did you ever get pocket money?

◆ Did you have a paper round or any other work as a child?

◆ Did you have money given as a gift at birthdays, Christmas or other occasions?

◆ Did you ever win any money?

◆ Did you ever find any money?

◆ Did you ever make money through gambling or playing the lottery?

◆ Did you ever inherit any money?

◆ Were you ever just given money?

◆ Were you ever tithed money (given as a gift)?

◆ Have you ever made money on investments?

◆ How many jobs have you ever had that paid you money? Were you ever paid a commission on anything? List all the ways that you have ever earned money, from newspaper rounds and Saturday jobs onwards, even if it was only a few pence.

◆ How many different ways has money ever come to you? And how many had you forgotten about?

◆ Which ones did you enjoy most?

Let it seep deep into your consciousness that you have already bought money to yourself in many, varied and interesting ways.

◆ Roughly calculate how much money has flowed through you – your pocket, wallet, purse or bank account in your life so far.

◆ Write down ten ways that you could earn money right now, given the ways that you have previously made money.

This should help show you that there are many ways that money can come to you, not just one way or from one job. You could create a portfolio of income.

Given the mixture of positive and negative thoughts that most of us carry about money, we end up feeling quite confused about money – we love it yet feel guilty, we want it yet push it away, we want to be generous around money yet have our fears around it. These confusions and the dance we do with money will determine our financial comfort and success, and the work we were born to do is concerned with developing a really healthy and mature relationship with money, making it into a great tool and servant but not our master.

14 We have no real understanding of how money works

It is easy to look around and see who has money and who hasn't, people who have worked hard all their lives and never made much money and then people who don't seem to work hard and yet create vast sums of money. You may end up thinking that the laws of money are capricious and unfair. There are so many different views on economics too that we may wonder if there are even any predictable laws. In fact economists can never predict the emotions and motivations of human beings. We operate on love and care, as well as fear and anxiety. Billions of pounds can and does disappear from stock markets around the world in seconds, solely through fear and lack of confidence. The reason we don't understand how money works is because it is tied up with human emotion, which can change moment by moment, day by day.

15 We have no clear strategies for earning money

For some people, it appears that those making money are simply lucky, but you only need look a little more closely to see that anyone who attracts lots of money to themselves has a strategy. Most likely they have an inner strategy – giving, prosperity and willingness to receive – and an outer strategy – a product or service they offer in return for money. We must find our gifts and be willing to offer them. We must be positively motivated, with enough reasons why we want money that are positive and life-enhancing, rather than fearful. We must also have a strategy for ways to exchange our talents, gifts, skills, energy and enthusiasm for money, and be ready and willing to receive money in return. This means commercializing our skills.

There are unlimited ways of earning money. It is possible to receive money in return for doing practically anything! People get paid for house-sitting, helping people choose clothes, cheering people up, dancing, walking dogs, easing stress, enabling relaxation, loving, supporting and encouraging. There is probably nothing that you can do that somebody somewhere wouldn't pay you for doing.

MONEY IS NOT THE ISSUE

There is no scarcity of opportunity to make a living doing what you love, there is only scarcity of will to make it happen.

WAYNE DYER
Spiritual teacher and author of *You'll See It When You Believe It*

I hope you are beginning to grasp that money is not really the issue. There is enough money for everybody; there is no lack of money. There is lack, but the lack is of will, or purpose, of courage, of vision or inspiration. And these qualities are all within us, waiting to be drawn out. Most of us dream of having a fortune, but forget that we are a fortune in ourselves. But there is little point in having a fortune of any kind if you've forgotten how to play, laugh, love and feel, and follow your heart's desire.

FOLLOWING OUR HEART'S DESIRE – BUT WHERE WILL THE MONEY COME FROM?

The universe will pay you to be yourself and do what you really love.

SHAKTI GAWAIN
Teacher and author

Strange as it may sound, questions about where the money will come from are not our greatest problem, but being overconcerned with this issue could be one of the biggest traps we will ever fall in to. The most pressing object of our attention should be how to develop our creativity and motivation, and what to offer in return for money? Our ego will preoccupy us with worrying and even obsessing about money in order to keep us from a single truth: that when we find and commit to our heart's desire we will be supported financially, even if it may only be in the fullness of time rather than immediately. Logically, does it make sense to believe that we won't earn money doing what we were born and put on this earth to do with joy? Do we really believe in our heart that life is set up to financially support our misery, but not our joy?

When Maharaji Mahesh Yogi, founder of the Transcendental Meditation movement, was asked where the money would come from for a major project he was planning, his response was, 'From wherever it is at the moment.' He was secure in the knowledge that life would support his purpose. The money we want to receive for the work we were born to do exists right now and is happily circulating around the economy right at this moment. Our job is to offer ourselves, our skills, gifts and talents, step through any doubts and fears, and to look at where we might be blocking ourselves from receiving abundance in the form of money. And, yes, we may need to do a job to support us financially while we build up our creative career – but that is fine.

EARNING MONEY AND ASKING FOR WHAT WE WANT

The strongest single factor in prosperity consciousness is self-esteem: believing you can do it, believing you deserve it, believing you will get it.

JERRY GILLIES
Author of *Money Love*

One of the worst forms of thinking that we have is magical thinking, the idea that we don't have to ask for what we want but that it will come to us magically. This is not the same as believing that life will support us once we set our intention, for to have most things in this world we need to ask both ourselves and the world outside.

While on holiday in Greece, Ian became clear about what he wanted, and decided to ask for it. He had been dissatisfied with his work as dean of postgraduate medicine, and had the courage to answer honestly the question, 'What do I really want?' The answer that came to him was that he wished to cut down from five to two days per week in his job, and to spend the other three studying and developing a practice in alternative and complementary therapies. Realizing that this was his truth, he knew that to be truly happy he needed to create that situation, either achieving it within his existing work or by leaving it.

Still motivated by his clarity, on his return he approached to his boss, with some trepidation, but certain of his direction, and as far as possible unattached to the outcome. He sat and explained what he wanted, and the answer was yes! It required planning and negotiating, but within three months Ian was working two days per week, with a pro rata pay increase and a renewed enthusiasm for his work, because he had been given a new freedom that he didn't previously believe was available.

An even greater bonus that his boss was even grateful to him! It forced her to look at more flexible ways of working for other staff too, leading to the realization that more flexible working arrangements could often lead to greater productivity and motivation. We can have what we want when we clarify what we want and simply ask for it. As Ian told me his story, I was struck by the power of his own self-belief, and the level to which he was able to be detached in asking for what he wanted. He had a strategy.

EXERCISE

◆ What do you want that you are not asking for right now?

◆ How could you ask for what you want? Who do you need to ask? Ask for it.

THE TWO KEYS TO MAKING A LIVING DOING THE WORK YOU WERE BORN TO DO

Key Number One: Whatever you do, do it with more energy and the willingness to discover, develop and give your gifts. Be willing to give more and simply be good at what you do. Build your self-confidence. Choose to invest a lot of your time, energy and money in yourself, in your work and your ability to do your work.

Can you easily name six people, suppliers or organizations you spend money with that truly impress you with their wonderful service? I doubt it, which illustrates that it is not difficult to be successful, because there is such mediocrity in work and business.

Authentically and genuinely, do your work with generous amounts of: love, beauty, energy, care, enthusiasm, expertise, inspiration, openness, knowledge, intelligence, passion, sincerity, courage, humour, fun, integrity, kindness, aliveness, self-belief, vitality, gentleness (or whatever else you have identified in Principle Three as being the essence of your work).

How can you fail to rise above that mediocrity? It is impossible not to be successful when we shine, as long as we are willing to value ourselves, our gifts and skills. As Emerson wrote: 'If you love and serve man, you cannot, by any hiding or stratagem, escape remuneration'. The key is the desire to shine your light, give your best, to serve and make a difference, because that puts us in the flow and we are giving and receiving at the same time. We can develop both competence and confidence.

Who are some of the most highly paid people in our culture? Often entertainers, singers, comedians, artists. Why? Because they have created and developed such an energy that people are willing to pay money to experience it on stage, video, TV, radio, in the press, on CD or cassettes. We enjoy the way they make us feel. I remember seeing Victoria Wood, one of Britain's most popular and loved comediennes, perform live, and as soon as she came on stage all 5,000 people stood up and applauded her for five minutes before she had even said a word! Her presence touched people.

We all have our own natural and unique energy. Know it and trust it, as it is your key. Shine and you will be irresistible! We don't have to set the world on fire, just those in our immediate circle who may be potential or actual customers. Discover that the more you give of yourself freely in service, the more you are given to give. Give for the joy of giving.

You have a unique way of being yourself and expressing life, and that is crucial to the work we were born to do; treasure your own uniqueness and preciousness. Maggie was a great massage therapist, but often found working on someone for an hour unsatisfying. So she offered a whole service – people would arrive at her flat and first she would chat to them and run them a bath with suitable oils in it. She'd be playing beautiful music on her hi-fi, and would create a wonderful atmosphere in her massage room, so people could relax and leave their cares behind. She would massage them for 90 minutes, let them relax and then offer them tea, fruit and a chat afterwards. They left feeling truly nurtured, renewed, and relaxed. She really put her love and care into her work, and was very successful as a result.

EXERCISE

◆ Think about your own uniqueness. There is no one else like you. Write down any unhelpful beliefs and resistance you have to this idea.

◆ Identify your unique talents and the way that you do things well and beautifully; become aware of your niche.

◆ How can you raise your energy, and bring more of your unique being and presence into your work?

Some people find this first key fairly easy, others will need to develop self-belief first, but as we shine, serve and help others we cannot help but start attracting people to us. The next step is to ask for money – to receive.

Key Number Two: Be willing to charge or ask for money, value yourself and your work and be willing to receive. Be willing to market and promote yourself, at least in the early days.

The second half of the equation is to create an exchange – to get money in return for what we give, to be comfortable with money, to value ourselves and what we do. This process can be a journey of growing in confidence, yet too often we are reluctant, unwilling or scared to charge for our work, our goods and services. We fear rejection, guilt, humiliation, put-downs and even acceptance and success. Often, in ways that we aren't very aware of, we can resist the very things we consciously want. So how do we stop ourselves?

Guilt. More guilt! Even more guilt!

I joke, but our sense of guilt is often an enormous block. It may show up as unworthiness, self-denial, judgement and criticism of others who have lots of money, self-sabotage, turning money down, putting ourselves last, and losing money.

EXERCISE

....

◆ Are you aware of feeling guilty, or even feeling that you can't receive money for being good at what you do? Write down any thoughts you have about this.

....

We were not put on this earth to feel guilt. We are here to free ourselves from the belief that we need to feel guilt. Many of us think that the creative power behind all life wants us to suffer and to do without. This is just not true, yet we mostly believe that suffering has a value that will bring us a reward. We can begin to learn to feel really innocent around money, to know that we are innocent to want money, that we are also innocent if we have as much as we want, and that our having money does not necessarily deprive others.

Other blocks to asking for what we want:

◆ Fear of rejection.

◆ Not being clear about what we want.

◆ Not asking the right people.

Ideas on asking for what you want:

◆ Check that you are not demanding out of anger.

◆ Be specific – how much do you want? When? Why?

◆ What are you offering in return?

◆ Check out how you would feel if you got a 'no'.

◆ Check out how you would feel if you got a 'yes'.

◆ Make sure you are asking the person who has the power to make a decision.

By giving our gifts and receiving money, an exchange of energy is taking place and that lies at the core of the relationship between money and the work we were born to do.

MONEY AND WORKING FOR OURSELVES – THE DIFFERENCE BETWEEN CONFIDENCE AND COMPETENCE

When starting out, don't worry about not having enough money. Limited funds are a blessing, not a curse. Nothing encourages creative thinking in quite the same way.

H Jackson Brown

It requires great courage to know and believe in your own creativity, love, skills, knowledge and experience – all the intangible things that can't be touched or counted – and to ask for money in exchange. It is also the greatest of all fulfilments to support ourselves financially from our own gifts.

Money comes in exchange for some service rendered. A great way to realize how simple it is to bring money into your life is to be aware of the simple formula of all financial transactions. It is:

I render you some service, using my gifts, energy, love and talents, with the intention of making your life more rewarding and fulfilled,

and in exchange

you give me some money or other service that feels like a fair exchange.

It is remarkably simple, yet we can get in such a pickle because of all the emotion we attach to the transaction: we don't feel we have anything to offer, we don't feel good enough, we don't feel we can charge or deserve money in return, or we feel guilty about wanting, needing or receiving money. Money can come from easy exchanges and without involving forcing, manipulation, fighting or power-tripping.

This is where we can get confused about money and its many purposes. One simple purpose of money is that it serves as a common medium of exchange, to allow people to trade different goods or services in a common currency. Our gifts are valuable, even if we don't get money in return for them – money alone does not give value.

The exchange may not even be financial, as we can barter, swap or exchange. There are hundreds of LETS (Local Exchange Trading Schemes) throughout the UK and elsewhere and their purpose is to allow people with products, services, gifts and skills to exchange what they have with no need for any money to change hands. Participation in them continues to grow hugely.

Money doesn't have to be involved for a good exchange but one of the most erroneous thoughts is that the less we charge, the more business we will get. The key is not to charge less, but to give more. I often choose to give talks for nothing or very little and I can still feel like a good exchange has occurred. I get to do what I love and enjoy, and in return I have the joy of giving, attention and appreciation. I love the maxim that if we give more than we are paid for, one day we will get paid for more than we give.

Either by misunderstanding, lack of self-esteem or fear we can underprice what we do. We are sometimes unable to objectively understand what others are willing to pay. I have worked with many people starting their own businesses, and loved a story I heard on one seminar I ran. A woman had started to produce and sell beautiful handmade candlesticks and, like many, was dithering about whether to spend money on advertising. She managed to negotiate a good deal at the last minute with a women's magazine, but because of the lateness of her decision didn't get to see a copy of the advertisement before it went to print. She excitedly waited for the magazine with her advert, and was horrified when she read the advertisement. It had mistakenly priced the candles at £300 instead of £30 per pair! Her dismay turned to joy over the next few weeks as she received orders for six pairs. She made more money selling six pairs at that price than from dozens of pairs at the 'correct' price.

Louis is an accountant who was well qualified and in private practice, charging £200 per day, but he wasn't creating much business. He had expressed an interest in becoming an accountant specializing in the entertainment and music business. When I met Louis again, he was incredibly busy and financially successful, and he explained to me that he began getting busy when he put his fees up to £1,200 a day.

In 1998 Alternatives hosted a talk for Paul Wilson, author of the best-selling *Little Book of Calm*, and we sold 50 tickets at £6 each for an evening talk and workshop. A little while later he came back to the United Kingdom from Australia and was hosted by a major business conference organizer, which sold hundreds of tickets at £370 for a day, even though he gave the same talk. The perception of the audience was that charging more money must provide more value.

These examples wonderfully illustrate the untruth that the cheaper we are, the more successful we will be. None of us are likely to buy the cheapest of anything. Rather the more we value ourselves the more successful we can be. It is up to us to determine a financial value for our work that we feel comfortable with and others seem to agree with. Price is just one of a basket of tools that go to make up our offering to the world.

We can be clever at marketing and finding the people who want to and are willing to pay more money. It is simple enough to understand that if you want people to pay you a lot of money, you should aim what you do at those who have the money and the need.

HOW DO WE EARN MONEY DOING WHAT WE LOVE?

Find what we love and what we are good at, what gives us joy

If you are in an uninspired place in your life, it is vital to find some things you enjoy, feel passionate about and that excite you, even while you may be doing what you don't enjoy. Begin to do what you love and love what you do, else the prospect of earning money through joy may seem too remote. Take it on as a project entitled 'Six months to re-find my passion' and set a goal of trying at least one or two new things a week. Be determined to find a number of things you enjoy.

Practise and develop skills, confidence and abilities in your chosen area and just go for it

After most talks I give someone will say, 'I want to do what you are doing. How do I go about it?' My response is usually, 'Just start.' Woody Allen said that 80 per cent of success is just turning up, and that is very true. For example, if you want to become some kind of public speaker, start by gathering six friends (or strangers) around for the evening, telling them, 'I want to get passionate for an hour with you. Will you listen to me present what I am most excited about, and at the end of it give me some feedback and ideas?' Cook them a meal if you want to, and by the end of it you will have made your debut as a public speaker.

Tony Robbins, an incredibly successful personal development trainer, tells how when he decided to be a trainer and public speaker people told him it would take years to get good enough. He worked out it would take years if he did one presentation a week, so he simply offered to talk to any group that would have him speak, and did so up to two or three times a day. So after just a few months he had the experience, confidence and skills that should have taken him years to develop. The issue need not be finding the time itself, but having the courage and willingness to make things work.

Be willing to start asking for and charging money

If we feel okay with money we may have no problem with this, but many of us do. We think we have to be perfect before we can start charging. Some people I have met become perpetual students, always learning more, but are secretly scared to say that they know enough to charge for their services. And of course money can change the dynamic in what you offer, but needn't do; for example, Eleanor has incredible knowledge of astrology, but precious little confidence, and she is unwilling to charge for her readings because she reckons she isn't an expert. Yet I know her to be highly gifted, more so than many people I know who charge £50 per hour; until she changes her self-perception I think she'll always struggle. Skills are only half the answer.

Be willing to learn and ask for feedback

Especially when we are new and nervous and think we are getting by by the seat of our pants, we can be very reluctant to ask for feedback, fearing it will only be negative. When we do have the courage to ask for and believe positive feedback and constructive criticism, we can learn much that can help us to use our gifts in an even more useful way for those we are wanting to help and serve.

Also be willing to ask for information about pricing. I once conducted presentations for a number of law firms and was never sure what fee to ask for. After one presentation, the director of training and education said to me, 'Yes, interesting – so how much do you charge?' I quickly turned it back into the question: 'I have recently been told I don't charge enough for my services. What would you expect to pay?' She told me how much to charge!

Separate out your own expectations of yourself from clients' expectations of you

In the last example, asking what I was worth, I was well outside my comfort zone, despite how calm I may have actually looked. My big fear was that the more money I charged, the more would be expected of me. Along with that I feared I would not be able to deliver. As I have ventured into these areas, I have discovered that expectations work in strange ways. I realized, through my work with lawyers, that they often paid the most for the services of others, because they were professionals themselves and expected to work with other professionals, but that didn't necessarily mean that they expected to get all that much in return. I soon discovered that I didn't find working with lawyers rewarding on non-financial levels, so stopped.

At the other extreme, I have worked with organizations such as charities that would have precious little money and huge expectations. One I worked with was only able to pay a small amount for a half-day, but this represented practically their entire training budget for the year, and their expectation that I help them fix all their challenges in three hours was huge, and unreasonable. I needed to set a good boundary and agree what I could do in three hours despite their great needs. Expectations are relative and do not necessarily increase with the amount of money I charge. I have reached a point where I simply do what I love and enjoy; sometimes I get paid large sums, sometimes small sums and sometimes nothing, but I aim to give of my best every time.

Start marketing, presenting and communicating who and what you are – create an identity

It is important that whatever we are communicating about ourselves and our identity be congruent. Marketing is simply about letting people know who you are and conveying the spirit of whatever you do. Everything we do on an outer level can convey this; brochures, letterheads, the actual product or service itself can all convey the essence of what we are about. If we have service and contribution as our core love, this will shine through. Sonia Choquette summed it up beautifully:

> When you work with love you draw others to you. Embrace this truth.
> The reason for this is that love is the highest vibration on earth. When

you work with love people feel it, are helped by it and return to it. It's a positive vibration that draws people naturally into its sphere. Those who love what they do reveal that love through their work, and others are drawn towards their energy. That's why love is the best marketing tool around. Because it is so attractive, it pulls to you what you need.

We don't need hype, manipulation or lies – just let your honesty and integrity shine and be a blessing.

Be willing to give your best right from the start

A singer I met said she resented having to give her all to such small audiences, and I suggested that when she put on her best show for everyone who turned up more people would turn up. She was caught in the trap of attachment, forgetting that success lies in doing what we love, in her case singing, rather than enjoying singing when enough people turned up for her to earn lots of money. I told her to recall her initial joy for singing, focusing on that as well as how to get bigger audiences and not resenting the ones who turned up now. Be grateful *now*.

Be willing to receive

If you resonated to any of the negative conditioning we looked at earlier in the chapter, you may find this one a challenge. If we judge or dislike those with money, we'll limit how much we'll be open to receiving. Be willing to receive money for easy and natural work, not just toil and struggle. Two years ago I received a cheque out of the blue from a woman who had been on a workshop of mine a few months before. It was a tithe (or donation) for me, with a note saying, 'Thank you for being an inspiration to me!' It blew my socks off – I felt I hadn't earned it or deserved it. I sat down and examined why I felt guilty, and found remnants of all my beliefs about needing to work hard for money. Eventually I was able to receive it with grace. I do still find it amazing that when we get what we say we want we can find it a challenge.

Learn to deal with all the resistance you encounter

As we choose to return to our natural state, all our learned responses will be stimulated, so we need to be willing to encounter our fear, guilt or anger and know that they are not true. But we can't deny them; we accept our experience of them but not their reality.

Charge what you truly feel you are worth

As we grow in confidence, we get to really know that we are good and may raise our sights. After attending a money workshop Frances, a journalist, decided to write a list of all the magazines and journals she'd like to write for rather than just accepting the commissions she was offered. She was nervous about approaching them, but as she made an inner shift about her own skills and worth, this was soon mirrored back when she was given a series of wonderful commissions and received more money and less hassle than before.

Be in the flow of money

We come into the world with no money and as far as we know we don't take it with us. There are no prizes for how much we manage to accumulate during our life, but our real joy will come from how much we have enjoyed money and let it flow through us during our lives. Our ego will tell us that the goal is to have and own as much as possible, while our spirit will tell us that the key is to let money represent a flow of giving and receiving, being a channel. Practise being in the flow and deriving equal pleasure from earning and receiving money, as you do from spending and giving money. Practise giving money away too.

Capture all your money-making ideas

Keep a notebook in which you capture all your ideas, and do your best to remember ones you have had in the past. Make it a grand and luxurious notebook, as it could be one of your best ever investments. Also notice how other people's ways of making money may fascinate you. Keep answering the question, 'What would I love to be receiving money in return for being or doing?'

MONEY, FLOW AND EXCHANGE

True affluence is not about accumulation but about the flow of money. Nature is never static: with each breath in and out we exchange billions of molecules with every other living being, so even our bodies are in a constant state of flow. Everything in creation is involved with change, flow and growth. We are channels of flow, and we should not impede that flow through fear and clinging. Both giving and receiving are joys, and to block either blocks the whole flow. Affluence comes from the Latin *affluare*, meaning 'to flow', 'to abound', and from *affluencia*, meaning abundance.

To trigger the flow, simply identify the block and unblock it, which will mean

either giving more or receiving more, or both. Giving is the best starting point –
whatever you want, give it: if you want more love, be more loving; if you want
more respect, be more respectful; if you want more money, be more generous,
both financially and with your time, energy, ideas and presence. The only way
this won't work is if you give, but are unwilling to receive. This is called sacrifice,
and is familiar to many of us, often leading to stress, burnout and frustration.
We'll learn more about this when we look at contribution and service with
Principle Eight.

We can only reap what we sow. Nature shows us that we don't get fields of
wheat without sowing kernels or an oak tree without sowing an acorn, and we
won't get money unless we sow the seeds of generosity. All that we think, say
and do is a seed, so let's consider the harvest we want. Nature is always giving of
itself, and doesn't worry about running out, and so with our own true nature.
Many point at nature to justify a scarcity belief in the survival of the fittest and
that not everyone can succeed, but in nature much is provided for daily, without
having to store and accumulate. All of nature interconnects so that generally
everything gets what it needs.

The best way for us to get what we want in life is to help others get what they
want, by being of greater loving service (not sacrifice). One of my greatest
teachers, Dr Chuck Spezzano, lives an incredibly abundant and prosperous life;
he inspires me so much because I know of few people with such willingness to
give all they have and hold nothing back. This I see clearly is the cause of his
prosperity. Each of us can always look for new ways of loving and contributing
and making a positive difference.

The flow of money is really the flow of energy, and we've learned already that
there is no lack of energy. And we have seen how money has no intrinsic value,
its value comes from the exchange that it has facilitated. So what are we willing
to give in order to receive money in exchange? The world owes us nothing. The
more we choose to become a giver, the more we become a magnet. The law of
success is service and exchange.

In the work we were born to do, money is a by-product of doing what we
love, which is living the purpose we are here to fulfil. In Principle Six we will
look at how we can find and strengthen a positive sense of purpose in our life
and work.

Simple Ways to Implement Principle Five

* Work today as if money didn't matter.

* Let satisfaction, not money or recognition, be the measure of your success today.

* Give some money away today to someone really needier than you, and notice their response.

* Pretend that today someone has promised you a million pounds if you give your all to your work today. Give 100 per cent anyway.

* Write down all the reasons you think you are worth promotion or a pay increase. If you can't think of enough, work out what would make you worth it.

* Ask for something you'd love to have or you need, but that you have been afraid to ask for.

* Identify which pleasurable activities you would like to receive money from doing.

Principle Six

WORKING ON PURPOSE

We will find our purpose when we follow our inner knowing, discover and work at what we love, and in so doing channel our life energy into creating what matters most to us rather than avoiding what we fear. Being on purpose will offer us many opportunities to move through doubt, obstacles and fear to a greater awareness of our true spirit. There is something that each of us believes in; that each of us has a vision for and which will make our heart content as we fulfil it.

WHAT DO WE MEAN BY 'PURPOSE'?

It is better to follow your own life's mission however imperfectly, than to assume
the life mission of another person, however successfully.

BHAGAVAD GITA

So what is your purpose? Is it to pay the bills, be good and to try not to get into
too much trouble? Or is it to listen to your heart, to choose love over fear, to
find and live the divine creative spirit inside of you in the most beautiful way
possible?

EXERCISE

◆ Write down the first ten answers that come to mind to the question, 'What is
my purpose, right now?' Then answer it five more times. Be sure to answer
honestly rather than thinking of what you'd like it to be or what it ought to
be?' How do you feel about your answers?

We are here to live the truth of who we are, which is more magnificent than
anything we can imagine, but try telling that to your boss or mentioning it at
your next interview! In finding our purpose we feel fully alive, rather than living
a half-life, because we get to heal old hurts and in doing so we become free. We
start to feel whole and experience the greatest joy of all – to live the life we were
born to live.

When we know that our purpose is 'to create the good, the beautiful and the
holy', as the mystic poet William Blake wrote, then only doing that will satisfy
us. Our true purpose and vocation lies where we find the intersection of our
gifts and talents and the needs of the world and our fellow beings. This is why
our true purpose is a gift to others too, and being on purpose is a win/win
situation.

EXERCISE

◆ What would be a mighty purpose, other than survival, for your life?

HOW DO WE DISCOVER OR REMEMBER OUR PURPOSE?

Purpose is unique for each of one of us, and subject to our emotional or financial position in our lives. If we are agoraphobic, going outside on our own may be a great purpose; if we are blind, being able to find our way around a city is a heroic purpose; if we have been stuck in a job for 20 years, finding the self-esteem and courage to make a change may be our purpose. Each of us has something that our spirit is calling us to do that will take us beyond our current perceived limitations.

Start by knowing that your purpose is already within you, in the software of your consciousness, in your heart and soul. Most of us only discover our purpose late in life, after some wrong turns, although some people know theirs clearly from the beginning. My school friend Matthew, for instance, always knew he wanted to be a stockbroker; sure enough, he has become a very successful one.

For most of us it is not that simple. We may have started with a clear idea but through lack of support or encouragement, or active discouragement, we may have dimmed our sense of purpose and compromised ourselves. It is a huge crime that young people today are often pushed towards careers based on money alone rather than their true purpose and their desire to contribute to society. The sad state of many of our professions can probably be traced to young people entering them because of the promise of lucrative careers rather than because they love the work. Don't we know it and appreciate it when we are served by someone who loves their profession? But the concepts of calling and its denial have been with us a long time; Plato described it over 2,000 years ago in The *Republic*, saying that early in life we usually know what our calling is, but we get sidetracked into jobs, careers, duties, roles and pleasing others.

So the bad news is that no one else can tell us our purpose even if many have tried – parents, teachers, religious leaders, politicians or employers. We may still be waiting for them to tell us, as we have been trained to give our power to external experts. Often I have people ask me, 'What should I be doing with my life?' The answer I give is 'Nothing'. What I mean is there is nothing any of us *should* be doing.

Purpose is not a duty, but a calling and a choice based on a feeling of inner rightness, of integrity and truth to ourselves. My friend Adam once put it this way: 'The cells in my body really seem to align themselves and there is a *big* change in me when I am on purpose. I am like two different people, on and off purpose.'

EXERCISE

◆ Are you on purpose? Ask yourself, 'Does this feel true for me?' Answer honestly.

◆ In simple terms, write a short statement that feels true and real about your life purpose. It doesn't have to be about your precise direction in life, but the one in which you feel you are headed. Purpose can be the compass by which we guide our lives.

At some point in our lives we've probably all had the experience of being on purpose, although our experience can go by many names – on track, a peak experience, in the flow, in harmony, unity, epiphany or a spiritual experience. You might just call it having a good day! Although the sense of being aligned with our true purpose can be experienced by people in different ways and at different times – while playing football, running, nursing a child, making love, giving a presentation or watching a sunset – there seems to be a shared transcendent quality to these moments.

I remember hearing Nigel Kennedy, the violinist and Aston Villa supporter, speak of his experience of being on track and on purpose while playing the violin. He would sometimes feel himself being infused with the spirit of the music he was playing, and even the spirit of the composer, bringing the music to life from the page. He also spoke of how at times his awareness seemed to leave his body; he became detached and was able to observe himself playing from another part of the room.

When we are on purpose all flows well, easily, gracefully, although not necessarily without problems; however we can handle these problems without being derailed and we can use our creativity to find solutions to them. Indeed we can even find that what first appears to be a problem is actually a gift and a lesson in disguise. We can feel unstoppable, not because we are tough and relentless but because we are in alignment and our energy flows. We are in tune with our soul's purpose and often manifest the people, situations and events we need.

OUR SOUL'S PURPOSE

The desire to create does not go away, it seeks expression. When you create, you align yourself with your most natural state of being. As a consequence, many of the difficulties of your life will either disappear, or no longer be important issues for you. This alignment will not come from attempting to solve your problems but from creating what most matters to you.

ROBERT FRITZ
Management consultant, composer and author of *The Path of Least Resistance*

Purpose is about having things to really live for in your work, giving your days and months a direction of your choice. The idea that we all have a life purpose and a calling can seem either a little archaic, like a hangover from another era, or an overinflated ego trip that tries to make us out to be more important than we are. The truth is that each of us has particular gifts, qualities and talents to give in this life. We each have a vocation, a gift we have come to give.

The Price of Being Inauthentic

We know it can be hard to walk our talk, but what is the cost of being inauthentic?

* We are cut off from our natural energies, our spontaneity of anger, sadness, love and happiness. We then put so much energy into repressing these emotions, and rob ourselves of energy twice over.

* We spend a lot of our energy defending ourselves, and fear deeply being exposed or people seeing behind our masks.

* We get bored doing more of the same, and we don't grow and discover more about ourselves, what we are capable of and what resources lie hidden and dormant within us.

* We are out of control, failing to steer our own destiny from the inside. We tend to react to circumstances and defend ourselves rather than creatively responding and seeking new meaning.

* We don't get to experience the beauty of who we truly are.

No two people have the same qualities, vision and experience, and our life's work emerges from our own melting pot. Purpose is about giving what we came here to give and what only we can give; it means ensuring that we don't die with our song still in us. The Bible says: 'Each of us has our own special gift from God, one of one kind, one of another.'

In Indian culture, the Sanskrit word *dharma,* means 'life purpose'. Dharma involves blending our unique gifts and talents with a spirit of service, which will then lead to our feeling truly fulfilled. Each of us is uniquely equipped to meet some particular needs of others, and this is the key to our abundance and success. The three components are:

◆ To discover our true self, to know that our nature is spirit, not our ego.

◆ To express our unique talents, or talents that we use beautifully, lovingly, inspiringly, leading us to the experience of joy, of losing our self or ego, when we go into a timeless awareness. For me this can be talking, for others parenting, playing an instrument, solving problems, making love or being in nature.

◆ To serve humanity. How can I help all those I come into contact with? This final aspect gives rise to plenty and abundance. A dialogue with spirit, helped with meditation, inspires us in each moment to contribute in an appropriate way.

As we suggested with Principle Three, the form or manifestation that our purpose takes is less important than its essence, but our work can be the vehicle that we use for discovering and fulfilling our purpose. Some of us do have particular talents and skills in particular areas. My purpose is to be inspiring and creative, a purpose which many other people share too. Try to get me to sing or draw creatively and I am lost. Stick me in front of a radio-station microphone, an audience or a word-processor keyboard and I am in my element.

Purpose is about finding both the essence that we resonate with and a suitable vehicle to express it, living our truth.

Here are some more questions to help you rekindle your own unique sense of purpose:

What is my life really about and what do I want it to be about?
If I found I only had six months to live, how would I choose to spend it?
When have I previously felt most purposeful in my life?
Who do I know that seems to live a life of integrity and purpose?
When do I feel most in my element?

SETTING OUR INTENTION

Our intention decides our purpose. As we discovered in the previous principles, the intention of our purpose creates the experience of our work. Intention is a force of motivation.

For several years, I have known and admired Richard Olivier, who in order to find his purpose has had to undo his share of family conditioning, being the son of the world's greatest actor. Nevertheless he felt his purpose was also to go into the theatre in some way. He was often confused about his own motivation, and even at one stage directed his mother (Joan Plowright) and sister in a play. Through trying many avenues he discovered that his purpose was to combine mythology with theatre, using ritual, poetry, drumming and storytelling to creative interactive theatre. He is now artistic director of the Globe Theatre in London, and generally loves his work.

One aspect of his work is a workshop he runs on fame, linking it to Shakespearian ideas of Inner Kingship and Inner Queenship. 'Like everything in life, it is not what you have, but the purpose to which you put it,' Richard explained to me. 'I have been around fame all my life, and see that you can use it either to try to get your needs met out of your own insecurity and get the love you don't feel for yourself, or you can use that power to influence people positively, to inspire, to help, educate and bless other people.'

It can take some courage to be on purpose and to decide to create work based on being authentic. The poet e e cummings wrote, 'To be nobody but yourself in – a world which is doing its best, night and day, to make you everybody else – means to fight the hardest battle which any human being can fight; and never stop fighting.' Rather than fight I would suggest you face some of the most challenging choices you may have to make.

FINDING THE COURAGE TO BE ON PURPOSE

> When you accept the challenge to implement your soul's purpose, you will soon move from career to mission. You will need to become fearless and disciplined. Soul work cannot be undertaken halfheartedly; it demands total commitment. This commitment does not require you to become a workaholic. On the contrary, soul work is joyful and light. Advanced soul workers do not labour hard to achieve results. They manifest what they want through the power of their minds and by understanding the principles of manifestation.
>
> RICHARD BARRETT
> Author of *A Guide to Liberating Your Soul*

Our conscious purpose in life can be either avoidance of what we fear or the creation of what we most love and value, but it is usually a combination of both motivations. Rather than creating what we want and what is precious to us, we may decide to play safe, defending ourselves against the harshness of life, simply trying to avoid too much pain.

EXERCISE

◆ What are the situations and experiences you spend most time and energy simply trying to avoid? Think for a moment about what you least want to experience in life; is it pain, failure, poverty, rejection, loneliness, life being meaningless, conflict, feeling lost, getting things wrong, looking stupid, disappointment – a combination of these or something else? Write them down.

◆ Ask yourself: 'How much of my energy do I put into trying to avoid these experiences?' See what answer comes into your mind. Is it 10 per cent, 40 per cent, 60 per cent or 70 per cent?

◆ What is the consequence of this in terms of the quality of your life?

Whatever results you have, you will have discovered a crucial point: you are human! We all spend much of our energy avoiding or protecting ourselves against what we fear. The result may be a life half lived, safe but uninspired, predictable but boring, with few mistakes but probably many regrets about what we didn't do. We may have survived and avoided pain, but we have not flourished and bloomed. It's like playing not to lose; winning isn't necessarily even on the agenda. We can't score goals by only defending our own goal mouth. The best we can expect is to minimize the number of fears that become real.

Choosing to commit to answering our call to purpose may take us to all sorts of emotional places within ourselves – joys and fears, vision and desperation, exuberation and poverty – as we may need to do a certain amount of emotional, mental and spiritual spring-cleaning. Experiences and feelings that we buried away will resurface to be examined, felt and healed. It is an adventure in self-discovery. We may also want a guarantee of the outcome – that we won't get hurt, that we'll be able to pay the bills, that it will have a happy ending, all will turn out well and that people won't be upset with us. But as a good friend told me, 'You want a guarantee? Buy a toaster.'

In the late 1980s when I was sitting at my desk in Holborn, London, well paid but bored, someone asked me, 'On your death bed are you really likely to say, "I wish I'd put in more time at the office, I wish I hadn't taken so many risks and seen so much of the world?" ' As Helen Keller said, 'Life is either a daring adventure or it is nothing at all.' The biggest risk of all is taking too many precautions.

What I later discovered, and deep down knew all the time, was that much of my life purpose was trying to prove that I wasn't nothing. My deepest fear seemed to be that I thought I was nothing, so I set out to be somebody successful! I had fun and good times along the way, but my achievements were mainly a way of trying to prove that I wasn't the inner failure I really believed I was instead of demonstrating what I truly believed – that I was a great person. I always felt like a fraud, as if I didn't deserve my material success. It sounds mad, but I have come to discover that I am not the only person to feel that way, to feel like a fraud; perhaps even the majority of us do. Nearly all of us have beliefs about ourselves and self-concepts that we dread anyone else discovering. This comes through living out a role, a life purpose based on fear, rather than one based on truth ... So what is the choice?

I began to ask myself 'What my life would be about if I wasn't motivated by guilt or fear, what would my life's purpose be?' I needed another perception of myself that would lead to a new purpose. Sometimes we can do that for ourselves, but mostly I think we need mirrors, people who see the good we cannot see in ourselves. A friend can do this, or a counsellor or therapist, or a spiritual teacher who helps us see whatever is good in us and therefore where our gifts are.

Once I start to change my perception of myself, doors in my mind began to open and I began to see new possibilities and new directions. As I lifted the emotional debris off myself, I found my heart and spirit still waiting underneath, dusty but willing to go again. I was able to start changing the purpose of my life, moving from avoiding to creating. Slowly, little by little, I have been doing that ever since, changing the purpose of my life to being about love and creativity. My life has become like an ever opening flower, opening to newer and greater levels. This usually also involves healing, facing further dark beliefs, fears and guilt, but each demon confronted leaves me a little freer to be authentic and real. If someone can show me a way of doing this without having to deal with the lows, please do so, but in my experience there are always new demon thoughts to be brought to the light to be healed.

The only purpose of going into the darkness within ourselves is to shine a light to illuminate and chase away that darkness. One of the most beautiful and powerful teachers for me has been the book *A Course in Miracles,* which, in its 1,300 pages, speaks only of our innocence in the eyes of God and tells us that we are still whole, without any guilt, fear or sin, and loved without conditions or limits. A major teaching of the Course is that every decision is a choice between love and fear; I often joke that at 1,300 pages, it strikes the fear of God into most people! Here are some of its major ideas:

◆ There is no separation between us, or between ourselves and God. God is love, eternal and infinite, and all there is.

◆ We are God's one creation.

◆ God only creates like himself, so we remain as God created us, innocent and whole.

◆ Only what God created is real.

◆ God did not create pain, death, guilt or fear, so although they exist in our experience, they are not real.

Rather than trying to change external circumstances, the Course teaches us to change our perceptions of the world. Likewise finding our true purpose involves us in choosing to evolve from a reactive life based on dealing solely with urgent matters and everyday survival to also being honest with ourselves about what is important and precious to us, and building our life around those things. Urgent is not always important; living purposefully is often not urgent, but it is always important.

PURPOSE CALLS US TO COMMITMENT

Until one is committed, there is hesitancy, the chance to draw back, always ineffectiveness. Concerning all acts of initiative (and creation) there is one elementary truth, the ignorance of which kills countless ideas and splendid plans: that the moment one definitely commits oneself, then providence moves too. All sorts of things occur to help one that would never otherwise have occurred. A whole stream of events issue from the decision, raising in one's favour all manner of unforeseen incidents and meetings and material assistance, which no man could have dreamed would come his way.

Whatever you can do, or dream you can, begin it now.

Boldness has genius, power and magic in it.

JOHANN WOLFGANG VON GOETHE (1749–1832)
German poet and scientist

To change the direction and purpose of our life involves a decision and a commitment and regular recommitments as we face new challenges, perhaps even every day. Our life is like a huge ocean tanker with a mass and a momentum; it takes time to change direction and it is a gradual and even lifelong process. My experience is also that a commitment can be a surefire way to flush to the surface any doubts and fears that were lurking just beyond our awareness. Through commitment, though, we focus the whole power of our mind on a positive outcome, and are able to dissolve our doubts and fears as we continue to commit, awareness of our vocation and calling continually evolving.

Our job is not to figure out all the details but to get excited and passionate and make a commitment to the essence of our heart giving ourselves completely to life. As the saying goes, 'When the student is ready, the teacher will appear'; to this we can add, 'and the people, circumstances, situations and events that will help us will also appear'. I cannot stress enough the fact that our intention – our will and commitment – is an organizing force that literally orchestrates people, situations and events to happen to support us.

How precisely this works, we are still coming to understand, but two schools of thought lead our understanding in the same direction – one of which we looked at in Principle Three. Firstly there is the romantic idea that we have the power within us to make our dreams come true when we think positively and persevere. The second school of thought is scientific rather than romantic, based on the idea that all the world is energy, all matter is energy, we as beings are energy, and that everything in the universe is energy and information, constantly changing and in a state of flux. Because energy resonates at particular frequencies, we are in tune with everything else that vibrates at that level. When we are on purpose we are more in harmony with ourselves and with the supporting universe, the essence of creation.

Commitment is nevertheless a choice, but not a single decision, more of a process. It is easier to commit when things are going well, but we also need to commit when when things are tough and when we don't want to. To commit means to keep giving continuously, not out of sacrifice but out of choice. By choosing to commit, we will face and burn through layer after layer of resistance.

Living a Vision

My friend Alexandra is an inspiration to me because of the size and challenge of her life purpose. Born into an aristocratic family, she has never needed to work as such, and has a huge gift for treating all people with the same respect, and is as at home with a Queen or a homeless person, a woman of true grace. Married to a Lebanese businessman, she has homes in London, Beirut and Paris, and with four grown-up children her life might appear to be perfect and needing for nothing. Yet her home in Beirut was torn apart by the war in Lebanon, and she decided to stay in the heart of the conflict to try to help bring about peace.

Years later, the war is over but there is still hatred between different religions, factions and personalities. Yet Alexandra has a vision – a garden of forgiveness and reconciliation in the heart of Beirut, bringing people together and acting as a beacon to help healing occur where the emotional scars still remain. Based in London, she is now working extensively, travelling the world meeting the various religious, business, civic and community leaders involved in the regeneration of Beirut.

But why bother with such a seemingly impossible task? Why not just settle for an easy life? What is her motivation, that she would even put herself in physical danger? Alexandra's response to this question was, 'The inner calling came from a vision I had, and the confirmation of that

WE CAN'T BLOCK OUR PURPOSE

Once you learn what your life is about there is no way to erase the knowledge. No matter how afraid you become you have no choice. If you try to do something different with your life, you will always sense there is something missing.

JAMES REDFIELD
Author of *The Celestine Prophecy*

Purpose only becomes painful when we resist it or try to go it alone without asking for help. Answering the call to live our life's purpose is inevitable and, once we respond, there is no turning back. This compulsion takes us back home to our heart and soul. Although the journey may feel bumpy, the destination is assured.

At the Atsitsa Centre in Greece, I met Gabrielle, a successful lawyer in her mid-thirties. She had all the trappings of success, but something was missing

vision came in a spiritual experience, so strong and compelling that I have never really had the choice since to turn aside. Sometimes my logic has tried to persuade me that it is crazy to attempt to do this project, and often my ego has come in with disbelief. However, on the whole faith has so far prevailed and the guidance is such that I feel tremendously trustful. I hardly dare say how easy it has been, though at times I do feel as though I am carrying it all energetically at a place outside of myself, like keeping a huge balloon in the air through the belief that it should be there and that I am somehow the guardian of it.'

She explained that her vision wouldn't let her go, and led her to all the right people and places, 'The inner calling is as a result of my years of work with myself and my clients and the consideration of the agonies of the war in Lebanon ... that war will repeat itself if something does not change in the way people think. Revenge is not an option any more, only healing is. The main vision was to do with releasing the ancestral patterns which bring us to act the way we do.' Alexandra's vision and purpose requires commitment to the belief that love will always prevail over fear and her example shows that the work we were born to do may not be work in its conventional sense. Her calling costs her money, not makes it, but she feels called to contribute her energy and love in a way that can feel deeply fulfilling for her.

from her life. As we talked over dinner, watching a beautiful sunset, she explained, 'When I was younger, I wanted to do something creative. There was always a voice inside that kept pointing me to creative things, but I kept telling myself that being a successful businesswoman would make me happier.'

I asked her, 'Is there any way that you think you could still be happy and fulfilled in the law?'

She hesitated, and said, 'Maybe'. After a pause, she then said, 'Now here I am in my thirties, and that voice has never gone away. I guess it is not a matter of whether I change direction, but when. No, the law doesn't do it for me anymore.'

We can delay ourselves but not turn back. Living our life's purpose is also a journey of healing, and it may involve us going back to look at some of the unhelpful decisions we made earlier in our lives in order to survive. A conscious purpose that can trap us is the need to prove ourselves right. Once we've created an identity for ourselves and adopted a set of beliefs and opinions, we can almost feel that *is* our identity, so we feel we have to prove ourselves right in its light, else we feel the alternative to being right is being wrong. As we discovered in Principle Two on conditioning, our beliefs make up a huge part of our sense of who we are. To follow our purpose successfully we need to be willing to find that we have been incorrect in some of our thinking about ourselves and the world of work. In doing so we don't get to be wrong, but happy.

Here is a list of some of the major blocks we create to living a purposeful life that I have discovered in my own mind and the minds of the people I have worked with over the years.

1 Guilt

As we've already seen in Principle Five, guilt is the glue that keeps us stuck where we are in our work, using existing ways of doing and thinking. It hides and obscures our innocence, and can either stop us doing what we'd enjoy or stop us enjoying it. Guilt can be vague and non-specific, so that we feel guilty just because we exist, or may take on specific forms such as feeling we don't deserve something or that our parents and family struggled and sacrificed for us, so we mustn't let them down by going against their wishes.

We've all made mistakes, and the way out of mistakes is correction, not further guilt and inner condemnation. Our spirit is innocent and knows nothing of guilt, and its grace heals the illusion of guilt and affirms the core spirituality of us and others, refreshing and cleansing our vision and flinging the doors wide open to giving and receiving. Innocence dissolves judgement.

2 Fear

Whatever our gifts we may also experience fear or even terror to stop us owning our best skills and talents. Our purpose is likely to be found underneath our fear or even terrifying thoughts and feelings, so listen to your fear and ask what it is trying to hide and block:

◆ *Fear of failure*: These fears are often on the surface; we think if we do what our heart calls us to do, we will fail, look stupid, be humiliated, embarrass ourselves, go broke, be rejected. We may also fear that we would sabotage, undo or destroy what we had created that we loved.

◆ *Fear of success*: This is often a deeper level of fear. Obviously we all consciously want to be happy, fulfilled, rewarded, successful and loving, but sometimes just under the surface we are scared because we think we will lose something by having these qualities. It's said that in our work, finances, love and relationships we have what we feel we deserve, which is not what we actually deserve, but is defined by our own self-created limits.

◆ *Fear of the size of our purpose*: We often know on a deep level that we have come to do something beautiful, magnificent and wonderful with our lives, and that we didn't come here just to pay the bills and to do a nine to five job. But we look around and see most of the world living a half-life and think that perhaps we are being overambitious, and begin to sell out on our purpose. Purpose is only difficult or overwhelming when we feel we have to do it all on our own, and forget that our purpose is done through us, not just by us. Our true purpose will be achieved in partnership with other people and with spirit.

As we face and step through our fears, vision and possibilities automatically open up within our mind. We shouldn't forget that we can call on help from other people and will best fulfil our purpose in partnership with others, and that we can also partner with God, life, spirit or whatever word we feel comfortable with. Then our purpose moves from being a chore to being done through us. It becomes easier and more graceful. We are never given a job without also being given the resources, guidance, support and help we need to complete it when we are willing to receive that help. One of the ways through fear is to choose to make reaching out and giving to someone else more important than your fear.

3 Hiding

We hide from our own power, our own love, even our own gifts and greatness. We get scared of them, so we hide them. We deny what we are capable of so that we don't have to risk not succeeding. In my workshops I often ask participants to sit opposite a stranger and do something which may initially feel quite challenging – to look at this person you don't know and guess, intuit or hunch what their strengths, gifts and best qualities are. This makes no logical sense, but at the end of this exercise most people report, 'They were right!' We can hide from ourselves but a total stranger can see us anyway, so why don't we just quit hiding and let ourselves be the best that we are – to shine our light, not keep it hidden under the bushel (or bullshit!) When younger we may have even decided that our safety and security depended on not drawing attention to ourselves. Our deep fear is actually how powerful and wonderful we are, and how much we'd like to be seen, not how powerless, terrible, invisible and insignificant we are.

4 Victimhood

We feel a victim to circumstances, unable to change the world, our relationship to it or even our own thoughts and feelings. The truth is more likely that we don't want to change circumstances; we are scared to or simply don't know how to. Also there is enormous power in being a victim. We get sympathy, recognition, support and we can manipulate other people's feelings. But it doesn't actually get us what we want – our freedom. Complaining is a manifestation of feeling a victim, as when we complain we feel we don't have the power to contribute to change, or make any changes ourselves.

5 Fantasies

We may dream and fantasize for years about changing our lives to do what we love, having wishful thought after wishful thought, but never actually deciding to follow through, and failing to take positive action. Conversely we may also create negative fantasies, leading to self-absorption and worrying ourselves silly, but we still take no action to create change. Worry is a substitute for taking any positive and creative risks, so we can break through fantasy by taking positive action in our purpose.

6 Holding On and Revenge

We may still be holding on to something from the past, an old hurt or disappointment, using it to stop ourselves moving forward. We use excuses such as: 'Yes, but if you'd had my childhood you'd understand why I can't do that' or 'Yes, but I tried taking a risk 23 years ago and it didn't work out, so I can't now'. Even if we aren't aware of it, we may also be getting revenge on somebody, like parents or teachers, saying to them, 'By not being happy in my work, I am proving you didn't do a good enough job!' The trouble is that we can be right that they were wrong but *we* are the ones who suffer! Revenge is like having a gun with one barrel pointed at them and another barrel at us. We shoot ourselves and hurt ourselves with revenge. Happiness is the best revenge.

7 Sacrifice, Compensation and Roles

Sacrifice is about giving without really receiving, doing work out of a role and duty rather than out of choice and freedom. We do it as a compensation for feeling not good enough or unworthy, and because we aren't receiving we can easily get stressed and burn out. Any more successful or greater purpose just feels like more of the same – more sacrifice and burden, so we resist it. This stems from the belief that we can't have what we want without paying a price, that to get something we want means to have to lose something.

8 Neediness

When we are very needy, we expect others to save us, and everyone and everything becomes a way of filling the gap inside. Neediness can also be a desperation to get away from the work situation we are in at present, which also blinds us to what is good in our current situation. We look to the world to take care of us, and are very dependent on others, which blinds us to our own sense of purpose or desire to help others in turn.

I wonder if many of us have trouble with just how needy we are. When we are uncomfortable with our own neediness, we may block help, because people feel they are only there to meet our needs. We can end up pushing away the very things we think we want, so neediness can show up as lack in our life; it may be a lack of money, but it could also be a lack of fun, time, love, ease or success.

Neediness and desperation keep us focused on what is missing and what we feel is missing from our work and lives. The solution is to learn to acknowledge and embrace our own neediness, and honestly and maturely ask for help, love and support. The way through neediness is paradoxically profound self-acceptance of how we are, a willingness to focus on what is present in our lives, not absent from it.

9 Self-attack

Our true purpose will be achieved through self-love, not self-attack, but self-attack is another way of staying stuck. We put ourselves down, tell ourselves we are not good enough, rubbish or at least underestimate our own gifts and talents. We may also condemn and punish ourselves for past mistakes. There is luxury in self-reproach; when we blame ourselves, we feel no one has the right to blame us. We may be in hell, but at least we reign over our own hell and know the rules! We get to stay in charge. As with all traps, we think self-attack will buy us something. But it doesn't, it just delays us.

10 Independence

We can mistake independence for freedom, as it is the major example of relationships in Western culture, symbolized by the attitude: 'No one messes me around. You do it my way or you take the highway.' Rebellion is also a form of independence. Independence covers the fear of dependence, as somewhere back in our life we got so hurt or felt so much pain in a relationship that we decided we would never let anyone be that important to us and that we would never be that needy or vulnerable again. Independence forms a defence, covering unmet needs and pain from that past, and imposing our plan for happiness on the world. The biggest problem with independence is that it blocks true partnership and doesn't allow us to be interdependent with other human beings. When we are independent all relationships have an element of competition rather than equality. Purpose creates true freedom which comes from partnership.

11 Feeling Unwanted

We may have perceived ourselves as not being wanted when we were young, so if our parents or family didn't want us, who on earth would? And if we aren't wanted, neither are our gifts and talents, so we don't bother. Feeling unwanted is a feeling of throwing ourselves away, a form of revenge and withholding that hides a deeper fear of standing in our own power and being wanted.

12 Competition

Our life purpose is between our heart, us and our creator, yet we block ourselves when we are intent on competing and winning. We equate success with winning, rather than being our best self and celebrating others being their best selves. We are caught in jealousy traps and the curse of comparison. We may win, but for us to win someone else has to lose, and if they lose they will probably crave revenge. We have to compete again, and the cycle continues.

13 Meaninglessness

'What is the point? Is there any meaning to this world?' Without love in our work and life, life is meaningless, but our ego will trap us into believing that other things are more important than love. This trap is common among successful people who have achieved much materially but feel the pain of it not filling up the hole inside them where something is still missing. They have holeness, not wholeness. Meaninglessness can be incredibly painful, and we often cover it up with hard work or addictions so we don't have to face it, inventing other major purposes to hide this feeling and act as a compensation. Our ego really seems to fight our spirit (although our spirit doesn't fight), and even says we should die because life is so painful. Our ego tells us that death is the release from our pain, but it is not; spiritual truth is the way out. We experience the pain when we put all our value in the impermanent things – money, fame, success, recognition or relationships – rather than in the permanent source.

The way out is to ask our spirit, not our ego, to give us meaning. The answer will be quite simple, like love, peace, happiness or inspiration, which then reconnects us to true meaning.

14 Judgement

If we judge or condemn others for having a wonderful, loving, successful, abundant or creative life, we are actually judging ourselves too, and thereby blocking ourselves from receiving and enjoying what we want. Whatever we judge in others we secretly judge in ourselves.

15 Appearances

When we place more value on how things look, their appearance rather than the substance behind them, we can block our purpose. This ties up all our energy in externals rather than in spirit. The way through is to be willing to release attachment to appearances and focus on the essence of our purpose.

Our Dark Stories

As we begin to follow our purpose, we may find that our worst beliefs about ourselves come up into our consciousness. We may feel like a hypocrite, or that we are out of integrity, or that if people knew that secret about us they would recoil in horror. So rather than make ourselves more visible we continue to hide or play roles so that our secrets won't be seen. All these dark stories are ultimately untrue, simply a ploy by the ego to keep us feeling small and stuck.

Quite a list! Now it becomes clearer why we can feel resistant to following and living a purposeful working life. These dynamics can delay, but not stop us, for the goal is ultimately assured.

THE CALL TO PURPOSE

Each of us possesses an exquisite, extraordinary gift: the opportunity to give expression to Divinity on earth through our everyday lives. When we choose to honour this priceless gift, we participate in the recreation of the world.

SARAH BAN BREATHNACH
Author of *Simple Abundance*

We are often reluctant to answer and follow the call to our purpose, because we know that doing so may lead to major inner and outer changes in our work, but once we begin to clarify our purpose we can arrange our life around it. Like iron filings around a magnet, our life will form around our purpose. There may be disruption for a while as our life is rearranged to be more true and more supportive of our purpose. Our purpose has always been there, like an invisible path that we may see out of the corner of our eye but never really focus on. Joseph Campbell described it: 'If you follow your bliss, you put yourself on a kind of track, which has been there all the while, waiting for you, and the life you ought to be living is the one you are living.'

Listening to the Call

The work we were born to do *is* calling to us, but are we listening? I sometimes wonder just how good we are at listening to ourselves. I often imagine that we ask to be shown what to do in our life, but sit there with our fingers in our ears, scared to hear. We may not heed our own unhappiness, illnesses and frustration as a call to change either our situation or our perception. We carry on as if those signals were a nuisance rather than our body's and heart's way of telling us that we are off track. Take the case of Vicky, who had been off work ill for months; every time she recovered a bit and returned she fell ill again very quickly. She was literally sick of her work and direction in life, but hadn't yet decided to see this as a call to a change of direction. Our body does speak our mind, often very loudly, but sometimes we have to be truly desperate before we listen to ourselves.

We may have a blinding flash of inspiration, but that too may come after a process of change and upheaval. Tom Cook experienced this when he was bedridden for nearly a year with hepatitis after being totally stressed out and exhausted as a TV executive. As he recuperated he knew he didn't want to, and couldn't, go back to TV production. He went to art galleries during the days to lift his spirits. As he looked at the art, it suddenly hit him. He was already at heart, and wanted to be, an artist. He has learned to paint and even teaches people how to get in touch with their own creativity. His 'call' came during a process of personal change, illness and contemplation, and he chose to follow his call. He told me, 'My illness saved my life!'

It is for us to discover our purpose individually by listening to our own inner selves, our own hearts and bodies, through intuition. Sometimes, to find that love again, we have to reach deep inside ourselves to discover our true sense of purpose at its source. Simply take time to be in silence. The language of the universal mind is silence. The one who created us wants us to hear the messages about our life purpose, and we can learn to take more time to listen.

EXERCISE

◆ Take time to sit every day and be quiet and peaceful. After a while in the quiet, simply ask the silence, 'What purpose would you have me fulfil?' Listen to the answers that come.

Yours could be a great and public purpose, or one to minister in a low-profile way in your life. No purpose is greater than any other, because they are all forms of love. Our ego does frighten us into thinking that we can't fulfil our purpose, which is partly true, but our purpose can be fulfilled through us, when we are willing to say 'Yes' and turn up and be inspired by grace in the moment. Purpose is not figuring it all out in advance, but being willing on a day-by-day, moment-by-moment basis. And there will be challenges, but when we do embrace our purpose, many of the problems just fall away.

EXERCISE

◆ Simply, what would you like the purpose of your life to be? Here are some examples: to help, to be your best self, to spread happiness, to serve, to inspire. You can apply this question to work, to relationships, and to your life in general.

Articulating Our Purpose

Below are some of the purposes that have been articulated by people I have worked with:

'My purpose is to produce the purest foods I can to help people be healthy and free from disease so they can follow their path.'

'My purpose is to inspire people through my art, and to encourage them to try art too.'

'My purpose is to bring more laughter into the world, and to lighten the way for people.'

'My purpose is to live an inspiring life, and by example encourage and give permission to others to do the same.'

'My purpose is to create joyful work, follow my heart, and to show others how to do the same.'

'My purpose is to show people maps home to God.'

'My purpose is to help people die with as much peace, love and dignity as possible.'

'My purpose is to love and appreciate nature and inspire others to love and preserve it too.'

FINDING OUR PURPOSE HELPS OTHERS

Another way of viewing our way home is to describe our universe as big jigsaw puzzle, with a unique shape cut out for every living being, a little space in the cosmos that only one special person can fill. The miracle comes when, as you find your place in the jigsaw puzzle, you form the pattern for me to find mine. We serve each other most powerfully by finding our own place.

ALAN COHEN
Author and workshop leader

Far from being selfish, finding our purpose is also a gift to others. Your giftedness blesses the world, because the more we receive, the more we help and show the way for others. It is our joy to share your giftedness, because it is a way of joining with others and creating a better world for everyone we come into contact with.

We can find our purpose in the most unexpected situations, and often after much personal distress. Nick's story is a good example of this. After some success Nick's life hit rock bottom. He lost his business and home and struggled with addictions. Yet, deep down, almost at a soul level, he knew he was being prepared for a new life, being stripped back down to the basics, to what was essential. As he began to recover, he trained to become an addiction counsellor himself. His assignment was to work in prisons, helping inmates recover from their own addictions. 'When I walked into prison,' he explained to me, 'for some reason I can't explain, I felt like I was home. I had an empathy and an understanding for the men, not judgement, condemnation or a need to punish. I felt a genuine desire to help.'

For five years Nick has worked with Category 'A' prisoners – murderers, bank robbers and the like, and most recently with Section 43 prisoners – who include child abusers and rapists. Yet he laughed as he told me that *every day* he has looked forward to his work. 'It's funny – the wardens hate being in prison, the prisoners hate being there – but I love it! What I've discovered is that 90 per cent of the inmates have had a drink or drug problem, and nearly 100 per cent have experienced abuse in their early life. They have been on the receiving end of criminal behaviour themselves, and I am often surprised that they have kept their lives together as well as they have. When I hear their stories, I actually admire and respect them.'

Nick saw his purpose as being able to break the cycle of abuse, condemnation and abuse that these men have lived all their lives. Instead of condemning them, which is the widely held prescription, or even feeling sorry for them, he holds a space open for them in which they can feel loved and accepted, perhaps for the first time in their lives. In that space amazing things, even miracles, happen. He separated their behaviour from their being, and helped them realize that 'criminal' was not their true identity.

Nick's love can be very tough. He earns their respect, but sees beyond the appearance of their guilty behaviour, to an innocent being, a spirit inside, and that is how healing occurs. 'I teach them spiritual principles, based a lot on the twelve-step programmes of AA and NA.' He gives and receives real respect, not out of fear, but out of a genuine bond and connection he establishes with the men.

He knows he helps them to change their lives when he manages to get beyond their tough, streetwise defences, to the tender heart that lies a little further within. He fights, laughs and cries with them, often establishing a soul-to-soul relationship with them. 'My motivation is that I know they can change with the help of a higher power, and by the quality of our relationship I try to have belief in them and help them develop it in themselves. Most of them have never had anyone believe in them. The letters I receive from prisoners who have been released – telling me that our relationship has helped them build a new life on the outside – give me the greatest satisfaction and touch my heart. I really know I am living my purpose, and doing the work I was born for.' Nick also has a vision to change the way that prisons operate, breaking the cycle of guilt and condemnation to introduce boundaries, love, even intimacy and genuine spiritual healing.

His example of purpose is concerned with going beyond appearances. In the world's eyes the men in prison deserve condemnation and punishment, yet his purpose is to help them remember their true identity.

Our own purpose in the work we were born to do is ultimately about remembering our spiritual identity and going beyond the appearances of the world, and all the stories we tell about ourselves. We must come to realize that we are the gift under the Christmas tree, and we are just remembering to unwrap ourselves.

REALIZING OUR WHOLE NATURE

It is our fear of giftedness that complicates life. All problems have at their root the fear of taking the next step in life and the fear of acknowledging our gifts and talents. These so-called problems are resolved with ease and simplicity by simply acknowledging our life-enhancing gifts and unwrapping our Presence.

DR CHUCK SPEZZANO
Author and visionary psychologist

The blocks to a purposeful life seem to be outside us: money (as we saw in Principle Five), the economy, lack of resources or support. But mostly they are actually within us, in our own mind. On a deep level we are scared stiff of our purpose. Indeed, my friend and mentor Chuck Spezzano suggests that 85 per cent of our problems in life are on some level a way of conspiring against ourselves and not having to live our purpose, because we are actually terrified of how great we are. Marianne Williamson expresses this idea beautifully in her book, *A Return to Love*, in which she writes about our deepest fear:

Our deepest fear is not that we are inadequate. Our deepest fear is that we are powerful beyond measure. It is our light, not our dark that frightens us. We ask ourselves, Who am I to be brilliant, gorgeous, talented, fabulous? Actually, who are you not to be? You are a child of God. Your playing small doesn't serve the world. There is nothing enlightened about shrinking so that people won't feel insecure around you. We are meant to shine, as children do. We are born to make manifest the glory of God that is within us. It's not just in some of us, it is in everyone. And as we let our own light shine, we unconsciously give other people permission to do the same. As we're liberated from our own fear, our presence automatically liberates others.

Living our purpose is about being willing to receive more and more gifts and share them, and to re-own those gifts we may have thrown away out of fear when younger. It invites us to become whole and powerful again. Many of us spend our lives waiting to be discovered! Purpose calls us to rediscover ourselves, not to wait for someone else to do it for us. It calls us to choose to bring out the best of ourselves for our own benefit and the benefit of others, to win our heart back and share what is precious. The irony is that it seems we would often rather live in pain and sorrow than swap that state for liberation.

That is not to say that the path to the work we were born to do is without its own troubles. Travelling on it can sometimes be confusing as we may suddenly hit some resistance that had been buried just out of our awareness. We may need to attend to some of these buried and hidden parts of ourselves, known as our shadow. Yet our shadow contains many valuable treasures as well as many potential traps, so let's look in the next Principle at how we created our shadow and how we can start to integrate it successfully into our lives.

Simple Ways to Implement Principle Six

* If today were the last day of your life, how would you treat people? Do it anyway.

* Be as authentic as you can be today.

* Drop a note to a colleague/boss from a previous job, telling them how important they've been for you.

* Make 'successes and things to be proud of' into agenda items at your meetings.

* Set a good and supportive boundary for yourself today.

* Tell a client or customer how much you value them.

* Write a 'life-purpose' statement for yourself.

Principle Seven

INTEGRITY, AUTHENTICITY AND THE RETURN TO WHOLENESS

We have buried much of our energy, qualities, gifts and talents deep in our mind because we felt scared that they weren't approved of, and now we see them only in other people. We judge and fight our shadows by judging and fighting other people. We are on a journey of regaining our inner power by integrating these buried and split-off parts of ourselves.

Our spirit requires no approval or validation as it knows no fear, it is only our roles, self-concepts and personalities that are based on fear and require approval.

THE RETURN TO WHOLENESS

When opposites no longer damage each other,
Both are benefited through the attainment of Tao. ...
Therefore, the wise identifies opposites as one,
And sets an example for the world.

Tao Te Ching

Each of us is a diamond with many facets and seeming flaws, some well seen and others more hidden. Wholeness and authenticity are about uniting and integrating the many fragmented parts of us, and returning to our original wholeness, which is a direction rather than a destination. By discovering our wholeness through this seventh principle, we will be aligned with our real nature which is at the heart of the work we were born to do.

As we move towards the light of our true selves, we may be beset by shadows; as we move towards wholeness, we may feel torn apart; we reach for a dream but are rudely awakened. Each movement has an opposite, an opposing force or a duality, and as we move forward, towards our hearts' desires, there can be a force with us that wants to go back, stay put or sabotage our efforts. These forces are our shadows. We crave to become whole and authentic again, to have more of our integrity available to us, and identifying and integrating our shadows are the ways to do this. We do this not by denying but by becoming comfortable with these seeming opposites within us.

We were all born in original blessing; we arrive on earth bearing the light of heaven, and a heart full of love and gifts. We also come bearing all the opposing energies, and contain all opposites. Poets, mystics and spiritual traditions across the world remind us of this, as the denseness of life on earth makes it easy for our light to be obscured. 'Intimations of Immortality' by William Wordsworth suggests the true source of our soul:

Our birth is but a sleep and a forgetting:
The Soul that rises with us, our life's Star,
Hath had elsewhere its setting,
And cometh from afar;
Not in entire forgetfulness,
And not in utter nakedness,
But trailing clouds of glory do we come
From God, who is our home

In Bali, each newborn child is constantly held for the first 150 days of life because the culture regards each child as a gift from heaven and knows their memory of heaven can fade quickly. When the child's feet are allowed to touch the ground after five months, it is done as a ritual with prayers and blessings to help lessen the shock. In the Hawaiian spiritual tradition, each newborn child is regarded as a bowl of light, containing the beauty of heaven.

However many of us were not welcomed into this world as a gift from another realm, with an attendant sense of awe, reverence and mystery. We were more likely received with bright lights, a slap on the bum, and a mother who was semi-conscious or perhaps even cut open. Our light can be dimmed from the beginning. I have heard from several people the story of a four-year-old girl who, after her brother was born, asked to be left alone with him for a while. Fearful of her possible jealousy, the parents allowed the child to be alone with the baby, but stood outside with the door slightly ajar for safety's sake. What they heard touched their hearts as the girl, leaning over the cot, whispered, 'Tell me about God, I'm beginning to forget.'

We begin to split off from our own inner being very early on in our lives, putting our energy into matching ourselves to what we think the world will want of us, even if it goes against our true inner nature. But our purpose is not necessarily to return to our divine nature – it is simply to cease resisting it. Let's explore how we refuse or give away our innate power, and how we can claim it back again.

WHAT HAPPENED TO THE CLOUDS OF GLORY?

Our problem is not that we are weak, but that we do not believe we are strong.

ALAN COHEN
Author and workshop leader

The poet Robert Bly creates an image of our being born as a radiant 360-degree sphere of shining energy. All qualities are there: light, joy, inspiration, divinity, purpose, vitality, love, magic, imagination, joy and compassion, as well as greed, hurt, deadness, darkness, competitiveness, anger, depression. It's all us – our minds are whole. As we grow we discover which parts of us are acceptable to family, teachers, friends or religious teachers. Whatever is unacceptable is split off and hidden away in a bag that we carry behind us. By the time we are 20, we may have gone from 360 degrees to perhaps some 30 degrees of radiance, and the rest of our energy is dragging along behind us in a big bag, like a dead weight, and we hardly feel alive. And that is what we have come to regard as a mature and civilized society – cardboard cut-out people!

Let's consider a couple of examples of how this works:

◆ We are told to be sensible, to be good and not to be so childish, so we bury away much of our exuberance and excitement and present a mature and grown-up face to the world.

◆ We are told off for being angry, so we bury away our anger and present a happy and calm face to the world.

◆ We are told that big boys or girls don't cry, so we bury away any feelings of hurt or even sensitivity and present a stoic face to the world.

◆ We get teased, criticized or ridiculed for some creative endeavour so we bury our creativity, believing it causes us only pain, and spend the rest of our lives telling ourselves we are not creative.

Every time we bury any one of our natural energies – our very gifts – we replace them with self-concepts, ideas about ourselves, which we build into our personality. Our personality becomes our self-created identity rather than our natural energy, and may have thousands of different, often conflicting, elements to it.

SOMEBODY TRAINING

Through influences at home, school, church and work, we come to believe that there is something wrong with our real self, our spirit, and we all go into what spiritual teacher Ram Dass calls 'somebody training', replacing who we truly are with trying to be somebody else. We create self-concepts known as our personas, egos or personalities to replace and compensate for selling out on our real self, but all self-concepts are based on doubt and need to be constantly proved. Indeed the Greek meaning of the word *persona* is 'mask'. We develop the deep fear that who we are is not good enough, so we hide our naturalness under layers of masks through roles and images. The irony of all this is that we end up spending our energy trying to prove what we already are. But life is always calling us to greater real integrity, so the work we were born to do is concerned with being real, rather than playing a role, and makes work a greater opportunity to grow and reclaim neglected aspects of ourselves.

◆ What are some of your worse self-concepts that you hide away?

Most of us believe we are less than good enough, so we create less than good enough work, endure boring chores, play roles, go through the motions and wonder why we aren't happy. Many of us feel inferior for one reason or another, either because of our gender, our skin colour, religion, sexual orientation, place of birth, income or accent. We may cover this up by acting and finding roles. Feeling inadequate is almost a prerequisite to creative achievement – it is our starting point but not our finishing point.

HOW DO WE GET FROM US TO A ROLE?

We are born with God-given naturalness but then we hear criticism and put-downs along the way to adulthood. By the time we are 18 years old we will have been praised, supported and encouraged about 25,000 times – 50% of these occasions will have been by the time we are three! By the time we are 18 we will also have been criticized, told off, told we're stupid or ridiculed around 225,000 times – a ratio of 9:1. No wonder we often grow up with low self-esteem. We respond to not feeling good enough by trying to be perfect, or by living with a feeling of inadequacy, or we end up neurotic.

We all have our own stories. So we believe that our naturalness is wrong, dangerous or painful – that there is something wrong with us. We take on a role to cover that hurt and disappointment, finishing up with layers upon layers of ourselves:

Our roles of being good employees, bosses, partners, nice people, our
social faces, what we show the world, what we are trying to prove we are

form the covers for the next layer which is:

the fear that we are not good enough, boring, inferior, defective, or
even that we're bad, angry, even evil people, nasty, greedy.
These are all illusions about ourselves

which themselves are a cover for:

our true goodness, our innocence, our natural love and beauty,
our true spirit. This is the truth about us.

THE US WE ARE TRYING TO HIDE

All the significant battles are waged within the self.

SHELDON KOPP

Author of *If You Meet the Buddha on the Road, Kill Him*

Beneath our social roles lies the shadow. It is what we really believe and fantasize about in our own nightmares. These are the parts of us that we don't like, or don't think we should be, and they stop us being really happy, truly intimate or successful. Our fear is that if people really saw this in us they would recoil in horror. My friend Malcolm Stern, who has been running workshops on loving relationships for 15 years, said to me once, 'I think most people would rather stand in front of a charging rhinoceros than be intimate with another human being.' We really fear people seeing behind our social mask. Yet the Latin derivation of the word intimacy is *in terme*, which means, 'without fear'.

The path back to the real us is easy in that it simply requires us to go 'Oops!' every time we hit an illusion about ourselves and be willing to accept the truth instead. The reality is that we are rather attached to these self-images, however awful they may be, and we have trouble letting them go. But true intimacy is the place in which we begin to drop our social masks and show our beauty and our vulnerability.

SUCCESS AS A ROLE

Even success can be a role: we can have all the right things, meet the right people, have all the badges, get all the acknowledgements and recognition, but the problem is that the role gets all the rewards, not the true us. We still feel that there is something missing. It is like we are behind a suit of armour, and everyone tells us how wonderful the suit is, while the true us is inside the suit crying, 'What about me? Don't you see me?' We can feel quite lonely.

The gift is to see beyond our own appearances to the real us beyond the success. The personal experience of so many people I meet is, 'Yes, I am doing okay, but I feel like a fraud, like it is somebody else who deserves all this. It is not the real me. The way out of the role is to choose to be authentic, to venture our heart again, to risk feeling all our feelings. This is a daily choice and practice; we can choose dozens of times a day whether we show the persona or the real us. Otherwise our life is nothing but compensation. We are trying to prove we are wonderful and great, when in fact we feel awful and valueless.

From a Role to Playful Authenticity

Peter and I used to work together as salesmen. He was one of the most confident people I knew and was very public about his desire to be a millionaire by the age of 30. Before I lost touch with him in about 1987, he was well in sight of his goal. As life works so wonderfully to conspire, I met him at St James's in 1996, the day after I found an old photo of him. We met up again at the gym where we both happened to be members, and talked about our paths. He had been well on the way to be becoming a millionaire using the money made in sales to get into property, but the market had fallen apart. He was now in debt, but happier than ever and working as an actor. He had come to realize over the years that his desire for success was a cover-up for his deep insecurity. He was trying to prove he wasn't a nobody. Now he loved acting and was passionate about it, and using his old determination to pursue something he truly loved. I couldn't miss the irony, though, that he did not find happiness playing a success role but in bringing himself to roles as an actor. I also saw he was never as confident as I thought – he was just driven, and had created a convincing persona.

We all take on roles – helpless, helpful, useful, saviour or persecutor roles, even success roles. This is how we go from the work we were born to do to the work we are conditioned to do. We need to remember that what is true simply needs demonstrating – we don't need to prove anything to anybody – and to see our roles for what they really are. In doing so we will need to face our shadows.

TURNING TO FACE OUR SHADOWS

Everyone is a moon and has a dark side which he never shows to anybody.

MARK TWAIN

The work we were born to do is concerned with reclaiming some of our lost treasures, which means that we may need to visit uncomfortable or scary places that we hoped we would never need to return to. Yet in order for us to be whole and authentic we may need to shine the light of awareness on them and heal them so that their shadows bother us less. We may need to feel some of the unpleasant feelings that we buried away in order to be free. As Joseph Campbell wrote: 'It's only by going down into the abyss that we recover the treasures of life. Where you stumble, there lies your treasure. The very cave you were afraid to enter turns out to be the source of what you were looking for.' We need to look again at the areas where we learned to reject ourselves, that we outlawed to our shadowlands. Our very best gifts and qualities may well be underneath our worst pain, fear or addiction.

The ground-breaking psychologist Dr Carl Gustav Jung described the shadow as the sum of all those aspects of ourselves that we have denied, devalued and disowned: in short, all that we insist we are not. We take what we don't like and see it outside of us, finding in others what we hide in ourselves, using the mechanism of projection. Basically, through projection we give to other people what we don't want to feel in ourselves. We look for others to blame for how we feel.

FACING OUR SHADOWS

Our shadow contains disowned and abandoned parts of our identity, which, like lost children, need to be reclaimed and embraced. The ego is so clever – what better place to put our gifts than in a place that we are scared to go – our own shadow. Paradoxically, the more we make friends with our own shadow, the safer we become for those around us, because we are less likely to unconsciously dump our projections on them, the more attractive we become because we have more energy available to us, and the more we are able to live and experience life more richly, fully, and deeply. Our job is not to get rid of the shadow parts of ourselves but to acknowledge, accept and embrace them, learning to come to be comfortable with the opposites within each of us.

The benefits of choosing to do shadow work are:

◆ genuine self-acceptance

◆ inner power and resourcefulness

◆ greater freedom and choice

◆ healthier relationships

◆ defusing negative emotions that erupt in our lives

◆ the reclaiming of disowned parts – gifts and talents

◆ the release of guilt and shame

◆ the unleashing of creativity

◆ less blame and greater responsibility

BUT ISN'T IT RIGHT TO REPRESS OUR SHADOWS?

That I feed the hungry, forgive an insult, and love my enemy – these are great virtues. But what if I should discover that the poorest of the beggars and most impudent of offenders are all within me, and that I stand in need of the alms of my own kindness; that I myself am the enemy who must be loved – what then?

C G JUNG (1875–1961)

Swiss psychiatrist and founder of analytic medicine

Our egos can get us two ways here – they tell us we were awful in the first place for feeling so angry, jealous or nasty and make us bury those feelings, blaming them on someone else, and then they tell us that if we ever let those feelings out of our bag again they will run amok and kill or destroy us or others around us. So we lose great energy by hiding that part of us, and tie up another amount of energy suppressing it and denying it. No wonder 80 per cent of people in a research programme reported feeling exhausted in the morning! So much of all our energy goes into hiding and standing still. Yet what we repress festers, and as Sigmund Freud said: 'Secrets make you sick.'

Our culture tells us that the two options for dealing with strong emotions are to repress them or express them, and we are not particularly encouraged to do the latter. We can choose another option as we grow in emotional maturity, and that is to simply experience and be with those feelings without acting them out. When we can have the courage to feel them with as little judgement as possible, they can be healed little by little. We can say 'Yes, I am feeling like this, but I won't act on it.'

Judgement is a form of resistance, and whatever we resist persists. The Buddha taught that the way to inner peace is: 'Desire and need nothing. Resist nothing.' The Bible teaches: 'Resist not evil. Be not overcome of evil, but overcome evil with good.' Our job is to accept and embrace all our judgements. All of our feelings are okay, it is our judgement of them and resistance to them that causes our problems.

'Depression and low self-esteem have been a big part of my life, and I used to let them rule me,' Michael explained to me, 'There were so many things I wouldn't attempt because of low esteem, and so many things I would cancel or make excuses for because I was feeling so low.' Michael is now successfully self-employed as a personal development trainer, and I asked him how he made the change to doing what he truly enjoyed. 'What I have chosen to do little by little is get a distance on these feelings and say that they are my feelings but they are not *me*. Who I am is bigger than any feeling I ever have. I used to feel very hypocritical thinking how could I teach other people to be happier in their lives when I often felt like I struggled in my own.' He explained that what worked for him and his work relationships was not to deny his shadowy and darker thoughts and feelings, but to be honest with himself and others about them and to choose to continue with his life despite them. Michael learned not to let his shadow rule his life. He is a wonderful living example of the maxim 'we teach best what we most need to learn'.

Colin Caffel had a life experience most of us would dread. His ex-wife, two children and ex-parents-in-law were murdered in the case known as the Bamber murders. It was eventually found out that the his ex-wife's brother was the murderer. His life was torn apart, and he experienced emotional places of anger, despair, rage and revenge that most of us cannot imagine. He faced many shadows. Yet in time, as he dealt with his feelings, he came to some peace and realized he was not the only one to need support to go to such dark places. He now helps run a variety of workshops, including some helping men to face and handle anger, rage and violence and to be able to reach places of peace and forgiveness. Out of his own experience of such tragedy he has chosen to help others. He said: 'If I could turn the clocks back, I would obviously rather this hadn't happened, but I have learned and grown a huge amount from it, and am glad that I can now help others.'

Before we can become fully divine, we must become fully human.

St Ignatius

The purpose of doing all this shadow work is not to wallow in how awful we think we all are but to see that all these beliefs are simply self-concepts. They are not the truth of who we are but beliefs we use to block our awareness of our own divine nature. The mystics tell us that only love and loving thoughts are true and that anything else is an illusion. By fighting the illusion of evil and darkness we give it energy. Once we have looked our unloving thoughts in the eye, we can see through them to the light behind.

THE DARK SHADOW – ENEMIES

If we could read the secret history of our enemies, we should find in each man's life
sorrow and suffering enough to disarm all hostility.

HENRY WADSWORTH LONGFELLOW (1807–1882)
American poet

All that we don't like and have judged in ourselves we project out and give to
our enemies. The names change with each age, but the themes and patterns are
timeless: we're nice, so they must be nasty; we're not selfish, because they are so
greedy; holistic medicine is wonderful, because conventional medicine is awful;
the New Age has integrity, because conventional religion is corrupt; the sales
department only care about sales, so the accounts department have to keep
charge of financial management; they are criminals, because we are law-abiding.
These are the false polarities that we've created. We may even have coped with
the rejected, painful parts of ourselves by labelling them as bad, evil, nasty or
unacceptable, then accorded them to other people, countries, races, colours,
sexes, sexual orientations, departments or organizations through prejudice,
ignorance, stereotyping and rationalization. The scenarios show up in
thousands of ways, but the underlying dynamic is the same – if we make you
bad then we feel good, and we need you to be bad so that we don't have to deal
with *our* bad feelings.

This seems to be human history – the history of enemies, wars and battles. In
time our enemies may become our friends, and we need new enemies. So what
if we gave up the need for enemies, and just recognized that the only battles
were really within ourselves, between aspects of our own minds?

Alexander Solzhenitsyn once wrote: 'The line dividing good and evil cuts
across every human heart, and who would cut a piece of their own heart?' It is
true that some groups demonstrate or act out certain qualities, but the reality is
that we all embody all aspects of the human condition. This does not mean that
everyone is bad, but it does mean we all believe on some level that we are bad.
The Austrian-born psychologist Elisabeth Kübler-Ross has helped thousands of
people deal with facing death and the feelings that brings up in people. She said:
'I have come to realize that within each of us is an Adolf Hitler, and we must
learn to recognize and acknowledge and deal with that part of us, rather than
keep projecting it onto others.'

We are encouraged to do things such as hate, judge and fight our enemies even
though we may know in our hearts that they are our brothers and sisters in

disguise. I remember as a child watching the May Day parades through Red Square in Moscow, seeing all the weapons and armaments as my Dad got angry at the Russians. I couldn't get angry. I knew in my heart they were just people, like us. I vowed one day I would go and see for myself and in 1974, very much before Glasnost, I spent a week in Leningrad and Moscow. Standing in Red Square, I didn't see an enemy but a people on the breadline, queuing all day for food and basic amenities. They were ordinary people living through difficult times.

We make our enemies – those that cannot be trusted, who are out to get us, who are threats to us. We feel we need to defend ourselves against these people. Yet every enemy – every judgement – is like shutting a door to a gift in our creative mind. John 14:2 says: 'In my Father's house there are many mansions,' which refers to the many aspects of our own mind; most of us have a mansion full of closed and locked doors. Wherever we have judged, we have stepped back from life and our authentic selves into a role instead. Because the conflicts are within us they can be healed within us, and our outer world will change accordingly.

The easiest way to identify what we have turned into our own dark shadow is by looking out for what we can't stand in other people.

EXERCISE

◆ Who most irritates you? What qualities about them most irritate you?

◆ Who do you most judge, and for what behaviour and qualities?

◆ What most hurts and upsets you when somebody accuses you of being like it? For example, being accused of being selfish, insensitive, angry or uncaring?

◆ What are you most ashamed of being or doing?

◆ Who do you most hate at or through work?

◆ What quality would you deny is in you, which you can see clearly in other people?

The answers are by definition hidden, and therefore require honesty with yourself, but they give greater insights into your personal shadow. These qualities are not bad or evil, although they may feel so because we have judged them so harshly. Our shadow does not make us a bad person, but can perpetuate the belief that we are bad, which is obviously unhelpful for our sense of self-worth and true success.

EXERCISE

◆ On a weekly basis pick someone who really pushes your buttons or winds you up, and place your judgements aside as much as you can and join with them. Talk to them, get to know and understand them, recognizing that they are simply a part of you that you don't like. Get to see if you can accept or even like them.

◆ When you feel out of integrity, ask yourself 'If I were being authentic in this situation, what would I do or say?' Be with that and see how it is appropriate to act on it.

SHADOWS OF LIGHT

When one projects, one is really giving away an energy or power that rightfully belongs in one's own treasury.

ROBERT BLY
American poet and mythologist

Psychological literature has tended to focus on our projected image or 'shadow' as containing the dark and nastier aspects of our personalities, but it is also true that we deny much of our goodness, light and spirit in the same way: we have a dark shadow and a light shadow. We may give away our power to gurus and teachers, to our idols, as well as enemies. Just as much as we give our darkness to our enemies, so we also give away much of our goodness to our messiahs, saviours, cults and spiritual teachers. Once, at a talk at Alternatives we had a lovely Buddhist monk speaking, and when he finished and people were eating and chatting, I noticed many of the audience were sitting at his feet, even prostrating themselves. He was a lovely gentle and wise man, but it seemed that because he had a shaved head and was wearing robes, he was somehow holier. Yet he was as holy as everyone in the audience and you reading this book. We are all holy!

Celebrate those, like the monk, who have a greater awareness of who they truly are, but don't confuse the message with the messenger. Zen philosophy has a saying about not confusing the finger pointing at the moon for the moon itself. Teachers can *show* the way, but they *aren't* the way. Remember that the great teachers are the ones who produce most other teachers, not the most followers. I like the idea that when you spend time with a good teacher, you leave knowing how wonderful and holy they are, but when you spend time with a truly great teacher you leave knowing how holy and wonderful you and everyone else are. Great teachers simply remind us of what we have forgotten! They are our wise elder brothers and sisters – not people to be in awe of, but to be grateful for.

Being involved in the spiritual world, I have seen many leaders and followers be spiritual as an escape. They can all love and appear enlightened, but they may enter spiritual work to deny their anger, hurt or pain; many spiritual traditions support this. For me true spirituality is not a denial of anything human, but the willingness and ability to embrace everything human, including the seemingly darker and yukkier stuff.

EXERCISE

◆ Identify your shadows of light. Who do you most admire or even worship and respect in or through work, but feel you could never be like?

Much conventional religion has conditioned us to believe we should defer our divinity and thereby give away our own connection to God. We cannot actually do this but we think we can; what we can do is lose awareness of our own divine nature, although that does not stop us being divine in our core.

The true meaning of religion comes from the Latin *religio* meaning 'to link back'. Religion's true purpose is to link us back to God, to our own divine nature, to release us from fear and to let us know that we have never left God or lost our connection with Him/Her. I have spent years reading and listening to many spiritual teachers who all seem to have a single message – that God is within and is our true nature. They claim(ed) nothing for themselves that they didn't claim for the whole of humanity. Buddha said that the Buddha nature is the state of awareness that we all share. John 10:34 says: 'Is it not written in your Law, "I have said, you are gods?"' So we are all God and Goddess in embryo whether we know it or not, and whether we like it or not.

◆ Close your eyes. Let the thought 'I am the stuff that God is made of' roll through your mind. What response and reaction do you have to that? Note your immediate reactions. Be aware that these may be the erroneous thoughts that the ego uses to keep us from the awareness of our true nature.

Imagine for a moment that every good quality you see in someone else also lies within you. That doesn't necessarily mean you can sing like Celine Dion, cook like Delia Smith or tell stories like Peter Ustinov, but when we spot creativity, humour, beauty and an open heart in another person it is because that possibility exists within us too. We can say to ourselves, 'I intend to find what's good in me too, my best self.' Rest with that thought for a while – great things are inside you right now, and you can resolve to find them.

WHAT DO YOU *REALLY* THINK ABOUT DOING WHAT YOU LOVE?

Consciously we all want to be fulfilled, happy and abundant in our work, but we may well have judgements about others who are doing what they love. Think about your responses to the following questions:

◆ What is your opinion of happy and successful people?

◆ What do you think about people who have downshifted or done what they wanted in their life, dropping out or breaking the rules of convention?

◆ What is your opinion of people who are very creative and seem to have an easy life?

◆ What do you think of people who don't struggle or work long hours and are self-determining, not motivated by fear?

If you have any strong negative feelings in response to any of these questions, be aware that these people may represent yet another part of your shadow. If you judge them, it is going to be harder for you to develop these qualities for yourself. If you don't like qualities in them, you won't want to become like them or share their contentment. You will need to make peace with these qualities before you can integrate them in to your work.

From High Flier to High Wire

As we discovered in Principle Three about Spirit, some people find they can become more authentic within their existing work, while others feel a need to make more radical changes. Rachel Caine is one of the latter. She spent years being successful in business suits with padded shoulders as a manager in a recruitment firm. She had nearly as many shoes as Imelda Marcos, a flash car and tons of opportunities, but it all began to fade as she realized it wasn't really her. 'I knew that what I was doing wasn't really me, I was just pretending. I wasn't fulfilled, and on a soul level I knew I wanted to do something else,' explained Rachel. She knew she was playing a role, and it was killing her not be real. Her shadow was that she'd hidden away much of her playfulness and her childlike qualities to be all grown up and sensible. She needed to reclaim them.

She found the courage to quit and do some of her own healing, and decided to enrol in training to be a sacred clown, and other training as a massage therapist. She has struggled with money, but overall has no regrets, and has decided to strengthen her commitment by selling her flat to join Zippo's circus, learn more circus skills and become a full-time clown. She told me, 'Doing something which gives me so much peace and joy more than compensates for the lower financial reward.' The rewards of being real are the biggest pay cheque she could ever receive. Often she clowns for people in hospital, and told me, 'The joy I see in the eyes of the people is the best reward I could ever ask for. It makes my life truly worthwhile and worth living.'

WHO DO YOU REALLY THINK IS SUPPRESSING YOU?

We forget that we were the ones who originally hid away certain qualities in our shadow. As a result we blame other people for doing it to us. Do you ever experience some really horrible feeling and then find someone else to blame for making you feel this bad? This leaves us powerless, so to be able to reclaim the ability to change our situation we should start identifying how we do this. We may have suppressed our knowledge and awareness of what we love, and when we finally we admit what we've denied, we must meet ourselves honestly.

EXERCISE

◆ Who do you think is stopping you doing what you love or stopping you being yourself? Your partner, boss, employees or children?

◆ When you think, 'If it wasn't for ... I'd be doing something else', who or what comes to mind?

◆ Who do you feel has had most control over you, your career or your life?

◆ Whose permission do you feel you need to change, to be yourself or to do what you love?

There may well be some reality to these feelings of being influenced as these people do have some power in our lives, but only as much as we give them. They do not actually have the power to stop us doing anything; we don't need their permission to be ourselves. When we give our power away to other people, we often end up fighting with them, either outright or passively, but remember that for you to be right, they don't have to be wrong. Power struggles can use up a huge amount of our creative energy, and they often hide a deeper fear of actually being free! Freedom means being responsible and giving up blame, trusting and acting on our own inner wisdom rather than believing what others tell us to be true.

EXERCISE

◆ Who are you fighting with, either silently or outright?

◆ What *don't* you have to do because of this fight? What is your deeper fear?

WHY ARE SO MANY WORKPLACES REPRESSIVE?

For many of us work has become 'the great escape'. We can put on our suit or overalls, play a role and avoid facing many of our feelings. Work can be a place where we don't have to open up and be real, where our denial of our spirit and authenticity, our hypocrisy and even our downright lying may be both encouraged and rewarded. We are rewarded for doing and not reflecting, and paid to do as we are told and not to question authority or suggest better ways of doing things. In essence, much work and many workplaces are based on control and command, roles and repression, not partnership and openness.

Most work is about results and profit, not process and human growth. If our personal conditioning matches that of the organization, then we are fine and fit in, but at least as many of us are growing, changing and reclaiming our heart and our spirit, finding that we don't want to continue denying so much of ourselves. More of us are beginning to develop emotional intelligence, the ability to think with our hearts. We are recognizing the value of emotion in and within work. And as we change, we want work that matches and fits our inner changes, but in leaving behind the very qualities and neuroses that made us 'good employees' we may suddenly begin to be seen as suspect.

Vicky's story is a good illustration of our growing need for a more profound sense of achievement at work. Vicky had a mother who told her she was never good enough, even though she was capable of achieving anything; and because Vicky's father died when she was very young, she was taught to be independent and self-reliant. Consequently she became incredibly competent, speaking six languages, getting more and more qualifications and easily becoming a very successful and high-flying City lawyer. In other words she set out to be perfect – but she never felt good enough. She told me, 'I always told myself that perhaps if I had more qualifications I would feel better about myself. I got all the qualifications easily, but never did feel good enough.'

Her turning point came after she had worked seven days a week, six weeks in a row for her firm and asked for a Sunday off. They told her, 'You obviously aren't committed enough and aren't cut out for a City law firm.' This of course devastated her and confirmed her feelings of not being good enough. At that point she began to see that her need to prove herself had driven her to that level of self-sacrifice and outer success. But none of it gave her the one thing she craved – peace of mind and a sense of feeling good enough. She got help and support, and realized that she didn't want to sacrifice her life that much to prove herself and that ultimately she couldn't prove herself. She decided that she wasn't cut out for that kind of corporate lifestyle and eventually moved sideways into a government legal position, while reconsidering her whole career and where next she wanted to go with her life.

While we talked Vicky began to see that for her the question was not about the work she could or should be doing. She was eminently qualified and capable of doing thousands of jobs. The issue for her was how to let go of her need to be perfect all the time, and be happy with who she was. As she learned to become happy with herself, she started to become happy with her work. When she was unhappy with herself, no work, no success and no amount of qualifications would compensate for her feeling of inadequacy. She was blind to her own self.

Vicky's account holds true for many of us. If certain emotions aren't openly expressed in any work setting, that doesn't mean that they aren't there; they are usually simmering away just beneath the surface. In boardrooms, offices, conference rooms, classrooms and factories we have created vast emotional undercurrents, worlds of repressed and unexpressed emotions and feelings that represent vast amounts of untapped energy and vitality. But we are generally afraid of emotion and work becomes the place to cut ourselves off from it. We can easily become more and more rational and analytical to deny and repress these feelings. Ironically, we fear the expression of our emotions in case we are labelled irrational, a trouble-maker, soft or that we have lost our edge.

One reason we might put the lid on emotions in the first place is that they can seem like a can of worms. I was once invited to do a day's team-building with a small group in a local authority. I soon discovered that team-building was a euphemism for 'They are not talking to each other, please go in and sort them out'. There were only five members in the team and they all sat within a few yards of each other, but they were barely communicating.

We ended up spending three days together over the next few weeks, but the first few hours were simply spent trying to create a feeling and agreement of safety so that they could express some of this reservoir of feelings, and start re-establishing relationships. Their work had suffered terribly. I was reminded of the message of a book written by my friend Abe Wagner called *Say it Straight or You'll Show it Crooked*. He argues that when we have any strong emotion, whether it is *positive or negative*, it will show up in some other way, usually unconsciously, if we don't express it.

EXERCISE

◆ Which 'negative' qualities or hostile emotions are least openly discussed or expressed in your current or previous workplaces? For example, competition, jealousy, anger, resentment, hurt, pain, scapegoating, frustration, difficulty?

◆ Which 'positive' qualities are least openly expressed or discussed in your current or previous workplaces? For example, love, care, inspiration, fun, laughter, creativity, vision, hope, co-operation, beauty, joy, tenderness, compassion?

WHY ARE MANY WORKPLACES LIKE BATTLEFIELDS?

Many workplaces seem to be the modern-day equivalent of the battlefields of old, rife with politics and alliances, coups and overthrows, plotting and betrayal. But why? Perhaps the most pervasive cultural belief and conditioning that we play out at work is the belief that everything good is outside of us. Work becomes the battleground for competing for the apparent scarce resources of power, money, privilege, approval, good jobs, security and victory – the things our ego tells us are the source of our happiness.

At their core workplaces are where we play out our belief in scarcity, and the need to win. And because through work we earn our money, work seems like a survival issue, so we repress ourselves to survive. As work is a major source of identity for us, perhaps especially for men, we are even more scared to lose out at work. Work becomes a big facade, a game we all play. What this totally misses is that the greatest rewards of all – joy, creativity, integrity, authenticity, love, peace – cannot be won. They can be chosen, and they are within each of us. This is the greatest joke and sadness of all – we compete outside for what we already have inside. We try to prove self-worth when we are already worthy; we try to get happiness when we already have unlimited resources of it; we try to compete to win when we can have it all from inside for free.

LIVING WITH THE CONTRADICTIONS
AND PARADOXES OF LIFE

The human journey is truly heroic when we consider just what it takes to be fully human. Consider the following, adapted from, and inspired by, an original idea by Stuart Wilde. We are called to:

◆ seek to express our true essential nature when we have been told to conform and play a role

◆ seek to feel safe in a world that seems to thrive on fear and insecurity

◆ value ourselves when we are constantly told we are not good enough, criticized and belittled

◆ believe that love is the greatest power when we are told that hate and anger are

◆ seek our personal power in a world that wants us to feel a victim

◆ believe in and surrender to a loving God that we can't see and have been told to fear

◆ believe in abundance in a world that focuses on shortages, what is missing and lacking

◆ seek our freedom in a society that seems intent on controlling us

◆ live fully and be detached knowing that we have great emotional attachments

◆ be loving, kind and gentle in a world that seems uncertain and full of hate

◆ see beauty in a world that is full of ugly appearances

◆ embrace our infinite nature in a limited mortal body

◆ live fully knowing that our body will die

◆ believe we are all from the same source, even though the world focuses on differences

◆ co-operate and share in a world that encourages greed and competition

◆ trust in what we can't see in a world that encourages us to only trust in our senses

To live fully requires us to acknowledge and embrace these paradoxes, to accept that life is full of apparent opposites, yet this is not normal to our education. We are taught to resist, to only have one pole, to take stands against things. Mastering life requires the mastery of these paradoxes, and we certainly encounter plenty of lessons in this every single day. The more we become comfortable with these opposites, the more inner power we reclaim and the more attractive we become.

Ultimately we should recognize that we are all harmless. We came here to venture in to the darkness, but we did bring a torch – our own heart and our divine nature – to chase away all the shadows and laugh at how we could have been frightened by them, because the spiritual truth is that there is no darkness.

JUDGEMENT, CONDEMNATION AND EXAMPLE

I loved a story told about Gandhi. A mother was imploring him to tell her child to stop eating so much sugar as his teeth were rotting, to which Gandhi replied, 'Bring him back in two weeks.' So the woman duly took her son away and returned two weeks later, and Gandhi told the boy, 'You really should stop eating so much sugar, and you will preserve your teeth.'

The mother thanked him, and then asked, 'But why couldn't you do that when we came two weeks ago?'

Gandhi responded by saying, 'Because I was still eating sugar two weeks ago!' This is probably why one of Gandhi's most famous sayings is, 'We must be the change we want to see in the world.' But how often do we criticize others for doing precisely what we do?

Judgement and condemnation of a problem simply do not work, as they can maintain and even strengthen the problem, keeping the 'split-off' parts of us alive and well in other people. We give them energy and feed them, because what we resist persists. What we perceive in others, positively or negatively, we strengthen in ourselves.

Fighting shadows doesn't work because we are fighting a part of ourselves, so are really only fighting our reflection in the mirror. Judgement seems to keep us safe because it keeps that behaviour or attitude over there while we stay safely over here, but it also keeps us in gaol with the ones we have condemned. We can either judge or love but not both, as judgement blocks the awareness of love. Love is the absence of judgement, and that is why we can heal our judgements by joining and connecting with those we have judged, by loving them even from a distance, by having contact of some kind with them, finding common ground and similarities with them. Joining – creating a connection with people – melts the invisible wall of guilt, fear and separation that judgements create. Often when we feel hurt or angry we want to blame and distance ourselves, when we can only really resolve matters by understanding and moving towards. And we all crave to belong.

Deep down we feel guilty because we judged, so we might even feel shame that we have judged so harshly, which keeps us further distant from people around us. When we judge we usually adopt either an inferior or superior role, but we don't feel equal to the person we judged. Some of us live in fear of what we call *Judgement Day*, when all our sins and misdemeanours will be presented to us by God and we will probably get sent to hell.

In truth, Judgement Day will be when we realize that God has never judged us, because God doesn't judge. The ultimate cosmic laugh will be when we realize that *we* created the idea of a vengeful and punishing God, and that God only loves! We will walk away free and innocent, understanding that we always were. This is our release from hell. There never was any punishment from God – it was all self-inflicted.

Emmanuel, speaking through Pat Rodegast, sums this up beautifully:

> Not only is there no punishment in God
> but there is no punishment in the universe

You dear human beings seem to feel
that punishment had better be self inflicted
before God gets to you.

HOW CAN WE INTEGRATE THESE DENIED PARTS OF US AND RECLAIM OUR POWER?

We reclaim our power by joining with those we are projecting on to or judging, seeing through to the divine core in our self and the others, knowing that we all come from the same source. Some people call this hugging a monster, or feeling the fear and doing it anyway. When we hug a monster, we integrate the power of what we were splitting off into ourselves and we become more strong and truly whole. Here is a process to achieve this:

1 Be willing to acknowledge and simply be aware of your discomfort, judgements or thoughts of criticism or attack on other people.

2 Two ways of dealing with them are presented with the next step:

   ◆ You may be willing to say, 'oops, yes, I do that too,' and without guilt or judgement simply accept it, forgive yourself and the other person, and release it. You will automatically feel a release, a lightness and an integration.

   ◆ The other response is, 'Not me, never, I'd rather die than own up to that, I couldn't possibly be like that.' Which doesn't mean that it isn't you; rather you are unwilling or unable to accept that you too are doing that on a level of which you are not conscious. We are so terrified of being seen in such a way that we feel that our whole identity could be in jeopardy. Alternatively we would rather kill the person who is making us feel this uncomfortable, and we keep trying to pass this bad feeling, as we have seen happen in the West's relationship with certain dictators. We call them evil, they call us evil and we keep the game going.

3 Communicate with that person if you can. Transformational communication is achieved through simply naming how you are feeling, without blame, then being willing to listen to the other person without defence or prejudice, which is a real challenge. Don't even respond to start with, simply listen and breathe.

4 Draw images or intend to have dreams about this shadow side and ask for integration through these processes.

5 Close your eyes and imagine that in each hand you have what seem to be the opposites and conflicting poles, for example good and bad, love and hate, judgement and acceptance, greed and selflessness, sensitivity and insensitivity. Visualize those energies, one in each hand, and then see, sense or feel them merging together. Bring your hands together and see a merging, a joining and an integration into a new strong whole. When we integrate opposites there is real power, because when parts of our mind are united and start to move in the same direction, we discover true power.

6 Be willing to see your innocence and the innocence of the other person in their actions. You cannot do that with your physical vision. You may need to call on the help of some greater power to do that – whether you call it God, Buddha, the Holy Spirit, love, truth – whatever you call it doesn't really matter. The key is simply to be willing to see with the vision of a force that can see beyond appearances. Be willing to see it differently, and when your willingness to release that prison is strong enough, you will succeed. This is what many would describe as a miracle. When we feel fear, it is because we are calling on our own power, and when we call on love with its many names, we are never alone.

7 Humour – be willing to laugh and see the silliness of some of your self-beliefs. Humour is a great healer.

A Course in Miracles describes a miracle as a change in perception from fear to love, and teaches us not to deny our darkness because that leads us to maintaining a feeling of separation. We should bring all our darkness to the light for healing and release, it teaches us, and there is nothing we can think, feel or do that God would ever hold against us. We don't actually need to be forgiven; we simply need to forgive ourselves. We need to take our armour off, so we can get back in touch with ourselves and others.

This is almost the opposite of many religious teachings that tell us to bring bad thoughts or actions to God in confession with the hope for forgiveness or to hide them from God in guilt and fear of punishment, although we are told then that God can see all our secrets anyway, so we've had it. It is hard yet the truth to realize that we need to let ourselves off the hook. God has never judged us. It is the accumulated guilt, anger, rage, fear, hatred and violence that we won't acknowledge that keeps the game going. We can simply recognize these as mistakes and ask for correction. We simply need to be willing to forgive. It is our only true function, and the way to happiness.

EXERCISE

◆ Begin to join with those who you have judged, separated and split off from. This may mean sitting down and talking with them if they are alive and accessible, but it may also involve people or groups who live in other parts of the world, whom you may have never met or who are no longer in their bodies. If you are unable to do it in person, simply sit down and close your eyes and do it in your mind. The unconscious mind cannot actually tell the difference between what you vividly imagine and what you actually experience anyway, so it is the joining and healing in your own mind that is vital.

Let me share with you some of my own experiences of healing through owning projections and joining.

I was invited to make a short presentation at St James's Church to a group of visiting Swedish clergy. I had been told that they were being very threatened by the New Age in Sweden, and that they were undergoing major reform. I felt quite honoured, and as the day drew near I wondered what I might say that would be useful, and trusted that I would be guided to say the right things. When the afternoon arrived, we sat down at the altar at St James's, and I realized that there was only one other person than me not in clerical garb. I suddenly felt quite scared, wondering what authority I had to speak to them; they had all undergone years of training to become priests, and I used to sell computers. I thought that they would be defensive, seeing me and what I stood for as a threat, and for a moment I entertained the thought that 300 years ago these very people may have burned me at the stake! Within a few moments I had projected so much on to them.

As it was my turn to talk, I decided to speak from my heart, saying what I believed in and stood for. I didn't criticize the Church at all but said I stood for love and healing, and I didn't care whether that came from Buddhism, Christianity, *A Course in Miracles*, Hinduism or atheism. I said I believed in one God who loves us all unconditionally, and that differences are ones *we've* made so it is up to us to dissolve the individual distinctions that we've created. I said I believed in joining, even with those I didn't like, and wanted dialogue between all faiths and traditions. I also said I thought there was a huge amount of naïveté and some ignorance in the New Age movement, and that we were often intent on looking at the light and ignoring the darkness.

After I finished I felt I had been in integrity. Although I had no idea of how I had been received, I had tried to be as unattached as possible. To my astonishment I received some very warm and grateful feedback, and had several very intimate conversations with individual clergymen and women, in which they shared their anxiety and their questioning of the Church and its purpose. For me it was a major lesson. As I took back my projections about them and simply shared from my heart, *I was healed* and made more whole. There was me thinking I was there to try and change them, and what I learned was that I could change my perception of them and suddenly they were different. I had burned off one layer of projection, and came away feeling more powerful, because I was less fearful of them and their judgements, which in truth were only my judgements of myself.

Our real attractiveness in work comes from being comfortable with our own inner opposites – within each of us is the sinner and the saint, the love and the greed, the cynic and the believer. True personal integrity also means honouring and valuing the true masculine and true feminine in each of us, having them in partnership inside. In doing so we become less judgemental and much safer because we don't act out unconsciously.

HEALING

I am not a mechanism, an assembly of various sections.
And it is not because the mechanism is working wrongly, that I am ill.
I am ill because of wounds to the soul, to the deep emotional self
and the wounds to the soul take a long, long time, only time can help
and patience, and a certain difficult repentance,
long, difficult repentance, realisation of life's mistake, and the freeing oneself
from the endless repetition of the mistake
which mankind at large has chosen to sanctify.

D H LAWRENCE (1885–1930)
English poet and novelist

Why not let sleeping dogs lie? Why bother to do all this shadow work if it can be scary and painful? Because we know in our heart that judgement is not the way, and that somehow we diminish ourselves when we split off. There are many, many good reasons:

We have greater compassion

It is better to light one candle than curse the darkness for eternity. As we realize that everything we judge in others we are actually judging in ourselves, we become less hard on our ourselves and consequently on others. As the Native American saying goes, 'Do not judge someone until you have walked a mile in their moccasins.' We all have our reasons, not excuses, for being as we are and behaving as we do, and understanding and correction, not condemnation, are the way to change. We may not understand the reasons why, but we are more willing to assume that we are all doing the best we can at the present moment. Knowing that love is at the centre of each of our beings, we can ask, 'What is going on for them that they are so far off their centre?'

Shadow work is not about catching and condemning ourselves, as we would a criminal, but having compassion. Judgement drives the feelings or behaviour deeper underground, so the way to remove darkness is to shine the light of compassion into our dark places. It takes great integrity to experience all our feelings when our whole culture tells us not to, by keeping busy, shopping, drinking, drugs, TV, radio or exercise. It takes huge courage simply to sit with how we feel, letting feelings flow, welcoming them and letting them wash through us.

We expect perfection from our leaders, and condemn them when they are less than perfect, because we believe we aren't without guilt either. Albert Einstein told us that the amount of energy in the universe is fixed, so we don't get rid of the dark energy but transform and transmute it into a different kind of energy. Denial and repression maintain shadows, while only love, acceptance and compassion truly transform.

As we understand ourselves better, if we choose to, we are also able to help others more, accepting them as and where they are, rather than where we expect them to be. We can see where they may be stuck and where they are on their journey, and be willing to help if they want it.

We become more whole, authentic and real

We may have spent much of our life and energy hiding our shadow side and presenting personas in order to be liked. Paradoxically we find that as we embrace our shadow we are more authentic and more lovable, because we are more whole and real. We develop a greater repertoire of moods, feelings and tendencies and become more multi-dimensional. People feel safer around us because they feel less likely to be judged and more likely to be accepted. We become more truly self-contained and less needy in relationships, and we have more energy, as the energy that we put into repressing feelings is freed up as we become more comfortable with them.

We learn to dance and flow, releasing rigid extremes

Every shadow place in us is like an Achilles heel that we must defend at all costs, else we fear it could be our downfall. Every defence is a rigid place, so as we embrace each one new energy and aliveness flows. The iceberg becomes the flowing water and fossilized beliefs start to melt. Shadow work is bringing about a spring thaw after a frozen winter. We become more able to dance, move and bend with the extremes of emotional poles, more like a willow than an oak.

We become lighter

The point is not to stay in the dark shadow place, but to be more comfortable with it and more accepting of it. Every shadow hides a gift, so we have more gifts of love and compassion to share. When others are stuck in their pit of darkness, we can throw a rope to pull them out, but we don't have to throw ourselves into the pit too.

We become freer and more in charge of our working lives

When it is not integrated and accepted, our shadow controls us because we are either unaware of it or aware and scared of it. We all know stories about politicians who preach morals but have affairs; TV evangelists who accumulate fortunes and sleep with prostitutes; health freaks who binge out on ice cream, chocolates and crisps in private; spiritual gurus who denounce worldly possessions but have stashes of cash.

None of these are bad or evil: they simply haven't integrated these shadow aspects. We need not deny our greedy side, simply choose generosity; don't deny our anger, but choose not to act on it; acknowledge violent feelings but find another channel for that energy.

Through integration, when broken or fractured parts of us are bought together there is a healing. Healing comes from a Middle English word *helen* meaning 'to make whole'. The work we were born to do will likely stimulate our doubts, fears, old broken parts and blocks, but we can begin to see them not as problems but opportunities to heal and create greater wholeness. Everything we heal becomes wisdom. Integration leads to integrity.

ALL SHADOW IS ULTIMATELY ILLUSION

> By passion for the 'pairs of opposites'
> By those twin snares of Like and Dislike, Prince,
> All creatures live bewildered, save some few
> Who, quit of sins, holy in act, informed,
> Freed from the 'opposites' and fixed in faith
> Cleave unto me.
>
> Bhagavad Gita (Hindu Scripture)

If we can relate to the metaphor of reincarnation and believe that we live many, many times then we'll begin to realize that we have been the sinner and the saint before, the murderer and the victim. They are all in us and within us. When we really understand this we can give up shadow boxing and start embracing it all. Recognition and integration, not going to extremes, are the purposes of this shadow work.

FINDING INTEGRITY IN OUR WORK

Our heart craves and yearns for integrity and authenticity. Integrity is derived from the Latin *integer*, meaning 'untouched' or 'unharmed'. If we have no integrity, we may temporarily gain some symbols of success, but we will be empty inside. Integrity is characterized by honesty, truth-telling, consistency, congruence and being real, not playing a role. A wonderful example is Howard, an advertising sales director for several magazines. He refuses to sell space to a company he doesn't think will benefit from advertising in his magazines. He actually turns away business if he doesn't think that it will be a win/win outcome. His purpose as a businessman is obviously greater than just making as much money as possible.

A woman who inspired me with her sense of integrity is Jan. Gaining a degree in psychology in the 1970s she moved into social services, and was one of a few people at the cutting edge of the values-based revolution occurring in the areas of mental health and learning disabilities. Until then, those with any form of mental illness were given psychiatric labels like Mongol or mental, but Jan was helping to make these people be seen as important and valuable, with identities, gifts and talents the same as any other person. Jan said, 'I was inspired to be one of the people championing to help them become integrated within, rather than isolated from, the community, and was able to be an influencer of many people who made decisions and shaped policy.'

Jan, along with a great friend and colleague, Chris, was able to put training packages and courses together, showing people how to live their values and change their attitudes, involving everyone from a cook or gardener in a residential home to a director of social services. The essence of her work has always been to live, demonstrate and inspire caring, respect, mutuality, meaning and satisfaction, as well as giving people a voice where they hadn't one before.

In 1987 she was made redundant and was struggling with two children at home. She threw around lots of ideas for the next 12 months with Chris, who was still working. Jan told me that in 1988, 'With a £2,000 investment from Chris and I, we started Pavilion Publishing from the back bedroom of my house in Brighton, developing and publishing training pack material for special needs. Luckily, it was the era of new technology for publishing, and we were able to do a lot with a little money.' They did it all themselves with no previous experience of running a business – Jan's husband did the accounts on an Amstrad computer, Jan did the editing although she'd never done it before, and Chris worked on sales and marketing. It was a real 'learn as you go' experience, and they could have easily gone bust, as even with their strong professional background they knew little about running a business. But by the end of the first year, they had developed eight training packs and were still going.

In 1990, Jan's second daughter was born amid folders and photocopying, and it was time to hire the first employee and find a small office in Hove. 'Our lack of resources made us more creative, we had to be. We've never borrowed money and always have grown incrementally.' Today Pavilion turns over £2 million a year and employs 30 people, and it also has a thriving conference business. 'We have grown through consciously intending to serve and support in a way that covers our costs and makes a profit, but profit has never been our first goal. We have only ever done what is personally meaningful to us. It is quite unusual for an organization to keep the spirit of service and be commercially aware. Some people do actually think we are a public service, not a private company, because we've never taken a brash aggressive stance.' I find this deeply reassuring and inspiring, as it shows that integrity and financial success can and do go together – the split is in our mind. Bringing them together may not always be easy, but is possible.

Jan explained to me that as well as empowering people with disabilities, she loves forging partnerships with other organizations whose message needs to reach a wider audience. 'We have now worked with dozens of other organizations including NHS trusts, academic researchers and charities of all sizes. For example, I was particularly proud of working with a small charity called Respond that provides psychotherapeutic support for people with learning disabilities who have been sexually abused, which is a real taboo subject. They had no resources to organize their own conference, so we did it with them, had 60 people attend, made a small profit and created a real win/win situation. We aim to be, and see ourselves as, real enablers.'

I wondered how this philosophy operated within Pavilion. 'We do grow our people, and know that Pavilion is bigger than Chris or I, and create a fun place to work. We aim to delegate, empower and encourage the creative potential of our staff as much as possible. Even as founders, we do try to let go of control and become dispensable, developing people so that they can take on more responsibility. We also take people on for work experience, have taken on people with learning disabilities and take on some school leavers.' She concluded by saying, 'Our intention is to run the business successfully, not make it successful and sell it on.'

On a more personal level, I asked Jan about her own goals of developing personally through her work. She replied, 'I have come from a background where I gauged my success by the good work we did as a company and the number of ticks against the to do list by the end of the day. In the last couple of years I have consciously tried to bring more of me into work, and move from a role to being real, and bringing my own heart and soul into what I do. I now aim to *be* more in work, take the time to talk to people, connect, listen and not just come up with quick and clever answers but deeper and wiser solutions to challenges. I am being with the question, "How can I bring more of myself and my spirituality into my work?" and observing the ideas and answers that come. I am aiming to be less head-driven and more heart-inspired.'

Obviously this is not the usual language of most companies, so I was curious to know how this works. Jan explained, 'I am letting work unfold rather than being so goal-orientated, and playing with possibilities of how work could be. I am also learning to laugh more, and am getting to a place where I don't feel a split between my work and my family. I used to spend my whole life with a layer of guilt; I used to feel guilty at home because I thought I should be working, and at work felt guilty that I wasn't with my children. Now I feel much more like a whole person, and don't feel this split at all. I think this is because of regular meditation, and am committing to doing this every day, as I think it strengthens my feeling of wholeness, even the less pleasant parts of me. Obviously I do have support from my employees, but have a feeling of greater personal wholeness.'

Jan is keen to point out that she isn't perfect, and still often shouts at her kids or becomes task-orientated under pressure. When I asked her what she was most proud of, her response was, 'My family, and having them be a part of my whole life, and the love and support we give each other.' Her second response was intriguing: 'Who I have become in this whole process. I no longer feel a victim to my work but want to continue growing through my work, and see it as a wonderful vehicle, with so many possibilities to help and do good. I am also becoming much more inner-directed, gauging my success through being true to myself and my own inner integrity, rather than through profit or even public recognition. I am recognizing that the journey and the destination are the same thing.'

EXERCISE

If you worked with your greatest integrity, how would you work and what might you do?

As we become more integrated and whole in our self, and as we become more comfortable with the opposing forces within us, we develop a greater level of inner power, of authenticity and the ability to contribute on a greater level. Once we have that power back, we can put it into creating the work we were born to do rather than denying and defending our shadow. So let's now turn our attention to what can make any work truly meaningful – our ability to contribute to the lives of other people and have our lives enhanced by the contribution of others.

Simple Ways to Implement Principle Seven

✳ Notice someone who you really compete with. Find a way of co-operating with them, working in partnership and creating a win/win situation with them.

✳ Apologize to someone you've been harsh with, without justifying or putting yourself down.

✳ Think of somebody you are angry with or resentful of in your work sphere. Close your eyes and send them, and yourself, forgiveness. Wish them well..

✳ Sit down with and really listen to someone you work with without judging them.

✳ Allow someone you work with or around you to get angry with you but do not take it personally and react.

✳ Notice who you are most angry at or irritated by in your working sphere. Ask yourself, "What are the qualities I most dislike about this person?" List them on a piece (or pieces!) of paper. Recognize that those qualities are ones you most dislike, or have most hidden, in yourself. Accept and become more comfortable with the qualities in yourself. See how *they* change!

Principle Eight

CONTRIBUTION AND THE DISCOVERY OF MEANINGFUL WORK

When we find our gifts and contribute them to enhance the lives of others, there lies our greatest joy. Knowing that each of our lives weave together and that we are intrinsically connected makes our work meaningful. We can choose the kind of contribution we want to make and consciously discover the joy of giving and making a difference.

WORK AS CONTRIBUTION

Could it be that the lost art of loving what we do and making it a gift to those we serve, is the lost art of our civilisation? And might it also be that those who seek for their work to reflect the divine have discovered the secret to satisfaction in human vocation?

ALAN COHEN
Author and workshop leader

Making a Difference

He stood up in front of the group of 300 people who were the employees of the company that manufactured pacemakers, and put his hand on his heart and said, 'You literally keep me alive with the new pacemaker I have fitted every year. Because I am alive I can continue to run my company and to employ dozens of people and feed and support their families. The impact you people have is huge.' At the end of his presentation they all left the room feeling great, knowing with every fibre of their being that their work was important and made a difference. Whatever part they played in that company took on greater meaning.

What makes much work truly meaningful is the contribution it makes to our own life and the lives of those we work with and whose lives we touch. We live in a culture that seems to devote so much time and attention to communications of all sorts – telephone, fax, e-mail, letters, television, radio, advertising and marketing – but there is still such loneliness in the world and a pervading sense of isolation. We can be surrounded by people at work or socially and still feel disconnected. What many of us seek is a quality of connection and contribution within our work and within our lives as a whole.

I was standing on a platform at the station, pondering the Principle of contribution and the ideas associated with it, when the train pulled in. I wondered, 'Does the driver of that train ever get to speak to the passengers? Is he aware of the incredibly important way that he contributes to the lives of thousands of people every day?' I doubted it. There is an old Greek proverb that says, 'How do you get a man to appreciate his donkey? By taking it away!' It is a sad reality that we often take so much for granted, and only realize the importance of what we do have when we lose it, and then we are often angry at the inconvenience.

In truth, because our lives are so interwoven it is impossible for our lives not to have made an impact and contribution to thousands of other lives. If we had the opportunity, like George Bailey in the classic fim *It's a Wonderful Life*, to see the world as if we hadn't been born, we would feel very differently, seeing how our life had touched others in ways that we never even knew about.

EXERCISE

◆ Think about your current, or recent, work and raise up your awareness, looking at an overview of how many people you have met and helped through your work. See the ripple effect. How many do you think it might be?

◆ How aware are you of the contribution you've already made to society? Do you feel a sense of connection, and a feeling of 'Yes, I have made a difference'?

We never can and never will know just what contribution we do make, but what we do have power over is our intention, the contribution we intend and want to make.

WORK, CONTRIBUTION AND COMPASSION

As wisdom and faith emerge from within us, we recognize that we are always in God's presence …Until we allow peace and joy to unfold from within us, we will forever be distracted from doing our larger critical work. Only when we expand the promise of our lives will we have the courage, the vision and the will to provide a lifeline to those who are suffering still.

Susan L Taylor
Author of *In the Spirit* and *Lessons in Living*

We say we want meaningful and purposeful work or that we want to make a difference, but what we actually mean – whether we are conscious of it or not – is that we want to serve and contribute. As John Gardner summarized, 'When people are serving, life is no longer meaningless.' The search for meaningful work begins with the realization that we are each part of the human community, and that everything we do sends a ripple out through the entire human family. The major shift in awareness that is happening on this planet now is the realization that we all belong to the human family – we are all interconnected. We live on a round planet that has no sides; you can't see borders from space. Boundaries and separations, such as the Berlin Wall, exist primarily in our minds, and the world reflects that: when we take down the wall inside, the one outside follows rapidly.

We know in our hearts that the 1980s maxim that 'there is no such thing as society, we are all individuals now' is untrue. We cannot separate ourselves from the rest of humanity. Atoms in our body came from explosions billions of years ago, and we literally contain the essence of the sun, stars and moonlight. We are in constant state of flux – the atoms in my kidney today could be in your nose tomorrow! As Walt Whitman wrote: 'Every atom belonging to me as good as belongs to you'; each of us contains atoms that were once in the body of Buddha, Allah, Christ, Hitler, Mother Teresa and Saddam Hussein. Our bodies, far from being solid and stable, are part of a constantly changing dynamic field of energy.

A good starting point for discovering your meaningful work is to ask your heart to allow its natural compassion to suggest and guide you to creative and even joyful ways of serving this interconnected family of ours. We won't find meaning in any particular form of work, because we ourselves discover or create its meaning. We can, for example, be an enlightened fishmonger, or carpenter or teacher. The key is knowing how our work influences and impacts other people and to do that work consciously, for the benefit of all; then we will create true win/win situations.

Compassion arises when we realize that as human beings we all have similar experiences – we all have hopes and disappointments, pain and joy, loneliness and friendship. Compassion is the choice not to judge ourselves or others for the pain and mistakes we all make, but to soften rather than harden our heart. Compassion is the antidote to judgement.

Compassion cannot be forced or demanded, but comes naturally from the gradual dawning of who we are and understanding that what we do for others we are actually doing to and for ourselves. Some people use this idea fearfully, doing good deeds because they want to ward off punishment for not doing them. This is a form of untrue service to others; true service is motivated by love and compassion, a desire truly to make a difference.

We each need to follow our own mission and heart's desire rather than be driven by the dictates of guilt, fear or obligation. True contribution is chosen by us. I doubt Mother Teresa woke up every day and said, 'Let's make myself look good today and help those wretched poor lepers.' She often said it was her joy to serve, because she saw the face of Christ in every person, and as she gave love she felt it and experienced it herself. Love simply flows through us as we continue to commit to contributing. It requires no sacrifice, and follows from our own strengths, aptitudes, joy, interests, inspiration and passion. True contribution energizes us and makes us feel that we have arrived home in our heart. The desire to be truly helpful is the wish to serve.

The Doctor who Cared

My friend Adam is a medical doctor in general practice and is involved as a volunteer in personal development training in his spare time. He was explaining to me the conflict he can feel between looking after the true needs of his patients and the drive to be seen to be an efficient and business-like doctor, seeing as many patients as possible and treating them as economically as possible. 'I so enjoyed being able to spend 20 minutes with this one patient, to really understand why she had been having heart problems. We had real intimacy and true communication for our time together. When she thanked me at the end of the session, I felt touched, because I so much enjoyed helping her.' What I really heard was his joy at being able to truly help beyond the prescription pad; to be of real service. As Dr Karl Meninnger wrote, 'Love cures people, the ones who receive love and the ones who give it, too.'

THE TRUE NATURE OF SERVICE

Consciously or unconsciously, every one of us does render some service or other. If we cultivate the habit of doing this service deliberately, our desire to serve will steadily grow stronger, and will make not only for our own happiness, but that of the world at large.

INDIRA PRIYADARSHINI GANDHI (1917–1984)
Indian Prime Minister

When I initially thought of serving, ideas such as domestic service, social services and national service came to my mind. These have connotations of duty (even a mild form of slavery in the case of domestic service). But the word service has its roots in a Latin word *servare* meaning 'to protect', so when we serve we protect and look after, and this can be a very uplifting experience.

Serving involves the dissolving of *me* doing a good turn or favour for *you*, because – as we saw in Principle Six – we are aware in a fundamental way that we are the other. Some of us are called to serve many, some of us to serve a parent, a partner or our family. Quantity is unimportant, but a quality of willingness to love is. If we only ever truly learned fully to love one person, our ability to love all of humanity would increase enormously. In big and small ways everything we do touches the lives of all we come into contact with.

EXERCISE

Think about your answers to the following questions:

◆ Who, either individuals or a group of people, do I feel particular compassion for?

◆ Which human suffering am I most called to relieve?

◆ Which unmet human aspirations would I most like to help people fulfil?

◆ Where does my motivation to serve come from – is it from guilt, love or a combination of the two?

◆ Why doesn't the idea of serving and contributing appeal to me?

In a world obsessed with external power, control and domination, serving with our hearts full of love cuts across boundaries and sees through appearances, and reminds us of the power that resides in the centre of each of our beings – the power to do good and to be good.

We have probably grown up with many untruths about making a contribution and what that means, so let's examine some popular but misleading myths.

SOME MYTHS ABOUT SERVICE

You have to be a kind of saint to serve

We may think we must have achieved perfection before we can be of help to anyone else, and be close to heaven, when in truth all we really need is the willingness to help. We can all serve and we can do it now, it doesn't require qualifications, cleverness or huge intelligence, just a willingness to open and share our heart. Martin Luther King Jr put it beautifully: 'Everybody can be great. Because anybody can serve. You don't have to have a college degree to serve. You don't have to make your subject and verb agree to serve. You don't have to know about Plato and Aristotle … Einstein's theory of relativity … (or) the second theory of thermodynamics in physics to serve. You only need a heart full of grace. A soul generated by love.' And that is within all of us.

Service must involve sacrifice

Our ego will always tell us that to gain something we must lose something else, and says that depriving ourselves is a virtue. We may love music and fear that to serve we may have to be an accountant, doing something we hate because it would be good for our soul. But to truly serve means giving the best of ourselves, that which gives us joy, not the worst of ourselves, which is a drudge. No sacrifice is required. We serve most when we are spreading love, respect, humour, creativity and laughter – as this is what spirit is made of – and when we align ourselves with the natural laws.

Another element in the belief in sacrifice is the idea encapsulated in the concept that it is somehow holier to give than receive, that to serve means to be in self-sacrifice. This is a common misunderstanding, and I often wondered how it is supposed to work – we all go around giving but no one really receives what we give, so our gifts are wasted. It is equally holy to receive. I enjoyed the way Bernard Gunther expressed it, saying: 'It is better to give *and* receive.' True service is about being given more gifts of the spirit – being willing to receive more – so you can give and share more. Giving and receiving in truth are one, and we all know the experience that when we have given our best, we feel refreshed and fulfilled.

When we are giving out of sacrifice, we may seem to be giving a huge amount, but we are actually withholding, we withhold our heart, we give our duty not our Self. Service and sacrifice can actually look the same from the outside, but are based on different attitudes and experiences. Sacrifice is also a form of manipulation, because we sacrifice ourselves in order to get something from other people. Sacrifice is giving in order to get. In true service we can open ourselves for all the gifts of creation to flow through us. Sacrifice is a form of control, whereas true service is about being a channel.

Service is the way of making ourselves useful

This implies that we are not intrinsically useful, and have to make ourselves so, another hangover from the Protestant work ethic, that says we are bad and need redemption. We are intrinsically lovable and worthwhile, and need not prove it. Serving doesn't make us valuable, but demonstrates and affirms that we already are valuable. Otherwise we create an unhelpful dependence, in essence communicating, 'I need you to need me so that I can feel good about myself. Please need me.'

A life of service doesn't pay

This is another strand of the sacrifice belief. We either sell our soul to earn a living or do what we love and starve. Our ego will have us believe that only selfishness pays. As markets become even more competitive, the one element that will differentiate us is the spirit in which we do our work, make our products and provide our services. Real and genuine caring is a powerful business tool, sadly because of its relative scarcity. The language and mentality of the market-place is that the market is king, a battleground of limitation, all about chasing profit, while service is concerned with intending to help and enrich the lives of others, and the profit comes as a by-product. And we may choose to serve somewhere in our life for no financial reward. The work we were born to do may be about creating a working life that allows us to volunteer a day a week cleaning up the environment, working on a cancer ward or in a nursery.

Serving begins a shift of thinking and intention from 'What is in this for me?' to 'How can I help?' The financial rewards gradually become a by-product of service rather than the primary goal. Do what you love and the money will follow, even if after a period of transition.

Service is heavy and no fun

One of the most striking examples of people's genuine desire to serve was taught to me by Patch Adams, a clown and doctor, and the subject of the film *Patch Adams* starring Robin Williams. He visited Alternatives and spoke of his dream to build a hospital called the Gesundheit Institute, where people would be treated with love, humour and fun. The hospital would be a community and no one would be turned away and payment would be by request. He has been speaking of his dream around the world for nearly 20 years, bringing some light into places such as Russia and Bosnia, where lives have been torn apart. He told us, 'When we treat an illness we either win or lose, but if we treat the person, listen to them and love them, we can't fail. The unencumbered life of service is worth paying to do.' He receives dozens of letters every week from doctors and nurses wanting to come work at his hospital for free! Such is their heartfelt desire to practice medicine with love and fun that they want to come work with him and help serve others. People are crying out to serve and contribute. And Patch is one of the most alive, vibrant and outrageous people I have ever met. Following the release of his film, he told me: 'Finally, the work I was born to do has borne fruit.'

You must leave the commercial world to serve

We have lived in era where commercial success and caring have seemed to be incompatible. I am excited that we are waking up to the realization that they are in fact compatible (perhaps necessarily so). The commercial world is made up of human beings, and we all have caring at our core, and we have moved so far away from the caring core that the pendulum is swinging back in the direction of service very rapidly. That is why so many have become disillusioned with work – they want something with a heart.

In our minds we seem to see our life as a choice – to live for ourselves *or* live for others. We either work and spend money for our own gratification, or we deny our own needs and look after others. This apparent split manifests in the difference between the charity/voluntary/religious sector and the commercial sector. The charity sector cares for others, the commercial sector only cares for itself. This split is false and exists first in our minds. There are some very uncharitable charities and some very caring businesses. The key lies in the intention and purpose of the people running them, as you discovered when you met Jan in the previous principle.

The work we were born to do is responding to our inner call to serve. The truth is that we will live a very rich and full life when we also seek to contribute to the lives of others through our work. The two actually can go beautifully together, and indeed must do. Each of us has a generous spirit and a desire to give, and our work can the become a major vehicle for our giving.

Service is a luxury, and we can only do it after we are successful

We may say to ourselves that once we've been successful, solved all our problems or made our million we can then afford to be of service and help others. But service to others is the best way to guarantee long-term and sustainable success.

Service is the journey, not the destination. Instead of waiting for all our problems to go before giving ourselves fully, we should try giving ourselves now and see what happens to our problems. Once we have tasted the joy of service, we want to do more, as Leonardo da Vinci expressed: 'I am never weary of being useful ... In serving others I cannot do enough. No labour is sufficient to tire me.' If you've still to taste the joy of service, try volunteering just an hour or two a week of your time to help people you don't know, and you will most likely experience the truth of what William Blake described: 'The most sublime act is to set another before you.'

The key to serving is to give for the sheer desire of it, with as little as possible anticipation of being appreciated or thanked – it is a need of our ego. True service goes from heart to heart. It may feel like it breaks our heart at times, but it will break our heart open with love and compassion for our fellow humans.

Service is an ego trip to make us feel superior

Some people try to use serving others as a way of being superior. For many years I volunteered at Alternatives as an act of service, and when I was offered the opportunity to start earning a small salary, only about £40 per week, I noticed I resisted it. I needed the money, but was aware that a part of me felt superior; here I was, doing all this wonderful work for nothing! Didn't that make me a truly wonderful being? Although it was unpleasant, I needed to examine that feeling. It took me a while to realize that the work I did was just as important, whether I was paid or not. Money does not establish the importance of the work; much of the most important work on the planet is unpaid, such as parenting, caring for family, work in the home and charitable work.

Service can be an ego trip, but it is also a wonderful way of going beyond our ego into a greater sense of ourselves. Joseph Campbell wrote: 'When we quit thinking primarily about ourselves and our own self-preservation, we undergo a truly heroic transformation of consciousness.'

Service is hard work

Service is not necessarily hard toil. The best service we can perform is sometimes simply to be with people and share our presence with them, as seen in the work of Marie de Hennezel, a Jungian psychologist and one of the founders of the French hospice movement. She felt called to serve by helping people, including President Mitterrand, die with as much peace, love and dignity as possible, usually from causes such as cancer or HIV. She explained to me that opening rather than defending our hearts gives us more energy: 'One is actually less exhausted by a total involvement of self – provided one knows how to replenish one's reserves – than by the attempt to barricade oneself behind one's defences. I have often seen for myself how the medical personnel who protect themselves the most are also those who complain the most about being exhausted. Those who give themselves, however, also recharge themselves at the same time.'

Having dedicated her work to being of service, her success followed. She wrote her book *Intimate Death; How the dying teach us to live* about her experiences and desire to tackle two major taboos – death and intimacy. It became a worldwide bestseller, selling over 500,000 copies in France alone. She didn't set out to be successful, but to love and care. The success is not that important to her, and I found her one of the most loving and compassionate people I ever met.

While much modern medicine is about drugs and cures, the work of her team focuses simply on being with people. She explains: 'There can be moments of humanity, gentleness, love, intimacy and connection even in the darkest moments before death. We have to let go of the idea that there is anything we can *do* to help, and simply *be* with people, be honest and authentic, and be real. We can create an atmosphere, which has as much do with *our own* thoughts, feelings and intentions as anything we actually do. Our simple physical, emotional and spiritual presence and acceptance can be wonderfully powerful.'

Marie has spoken twice at Alternatives, and she does have a remarkable presence. Qualities of love, compassion, peace and acceptance exude from her. She explains that the dying need a presence with them, maybe simply to hold their hand. 'I cannot deny the suffering and sometimes the horror that surround death, but alongside this suffering I feel I have been enriched, that I have known moments of incomparable humanity and depth, moments of joy and sweetness that I would not exchange for anything in the world. And I know that these experiences are not unique to me.' But we all have and need that presence throughout our lives. All of us have those qualities in our very being, which we can deny and hide but not destroy. I have noticed that when a speaker at Alternatives gives their all, signs books and chats to whoever wants to talk afterwards, they are often more refreshed than those who ask to be shielded or leave straight after the talk without wanting to speak to anybody.

GENUINE SERVICE

In spite of all the myths, the answer to the question of whether people are still interested in serving is undoubtedly 'Yes'. Millions of people volunteer time and energy to causes they love and support. Any job can be carried out as an act of service, but we have tended to think that we either serve or go into business and commerce. We can serve and be commercial; indeed I am suggesting that the most likely way you will be commercially successful will be by serving. We have a belief that service doesn't pay – it does and can. Service is not a luxury when we are already successful, it is the path to true success.

EXERCISE

◆ Do you volunteer your time, energy and skills anywhere in your life? Why? Why not?

◆ If you could, who would you like to volunteer to help?

◆ What do you want to contribute to them?

◆ Contact the National Council for Voluntary Organizations or your equivalent local body and explore the thousands of ways you can contribute your time, energy and skills.

It can sound like a cliché, but there are always people worse off than us. While I was unemployed I served for a while making protein drinks on a cancer ward in a local hospital. I found it tough at times, seeing men younger than me with cancer, but knowing that I wanted to help in any way that I could, I was touched by their honesty and bravery. It filled my heart with gratitude.

Genuine service is the ability to focus equally on the needs of others without sacrificing your needs, and the willingness to get into other people's skins to understand and give them what they need. Ask the magic questions:

◆ What do they want?

◆ How can I help?

◆ How can I create a living helping others get what they want? How can I succeed by helping others succeed?

Cultivating Hearts

Catherine Sneed presents an immensely moving example of the desire to serve. Catherine founded the Prison Garden Project in California, pushing to get a derelict piece of land made available for the prisoners to restore, tend and grow their own vegetables and plants on. The prisoners found that working with the earth gave them a great sense of purpose, encouraging them to build relationships with each other and giving them a sense of connection they never had before. She explained that some of the younger inmates were raised on fast food and fizzy drinks and had never even eaten a vegetable let alone grown one! It was a life-affirming and purposeful experience for many of them. What touched my heart so deeply was when she explained that some prisoners, when their sentence was over, didn't want to leave prison! They had found more meaning and purpose in prison by the contribution they made through the garden project than they ever did in their life outside before prison.

Catherine has now taken the project to many other prisons throughout the United States and has converted many other derelict and polluted plots of land, and helped to reform many other lives in the process.

WORK, SPIRITUALITY AND COMPASSION

Many of the spiritual traditions of the world have taught that service is the way back to God. Cicero wrote, 'In nothing do men more nearly approach the Gods than in doing good for their fellow men.' The work we were born to do is about serving the world in a way that we enjoy and that we are uniquely talented, gifted and equipped to do. Baha Allah, founder of Baha'i faith said: 'Work done in the spirit of service ... is considered as worship.' In the Hindu scriptures, the Bhagavad Gita teaches: 'Strive constantly to serve the welfare of the world; by devotion to selfless work one attains the supreme goal of life. Do your work with the welfare of others always in mind ... The ignorant work for their own profit; the wise work for the welfare of the world.' God, by any name, is the spirit of giving, not taking away. When we truly give we can experience our own divine nature, and that which is in God, essence, is available through us to give and share. We become the hands and feet, mouth and ears through which love can flow.

Service can also restore the truth of our own wholeness and even our holiness. In *A Course in Miracles* we are taught: 'When you meet someone it is a holy encounter. As you see them, you will see yourself. As you treat them, you will treat yourself. Never forget this, for in them you will find or lose yourself.' Bhakti yoga, in the Hindu tradition, is devotional service, which teaches that if you serve Krishna – the divine – in everyone, it is the way you find the divine in yourself. Contribution can be a way to find the divine in ourselves and others.

We are not here to contact our higher self, but to become it, or more precisely, to become aware of what already is – that we are already a divine being, and service is one of the greatest ways to restore that awareness.

GIVING AND RECEIVING

I don't know what your destiny will be, but one thing I know; the only ones of you who will be truly happy will be those of you who have sought and found how to serve.

ALBERT SCHWEITZER (1875–1965)
German theologian, medical missionary and Nobel Laureate

Giving and receiving are two sides of the same coin, and are but different manifestations of the same universal energy – spirit or love. No one can take away from us what we have given. True giving – from one heart to another – dissolves the emotional distance between us and lessens the feeling of loneliness and separation. What we give is ultimately what we get back, and what we give is what we value and what we strengthen. Spirit doesn't differentiate between giving and receiving – it is just one flow. But mostly we have come to believe that there is a limited supply of everything, so what we give we have less of. Let's say I have £20 and give it to you; unless I received something good for my money I appear to have lost out on the deal. That is the way the world seems to work – when I give more I have less.

But there is also a deeper principle at work at the level of essence or consciousness. In order to give you a gift like love, inspiration, forgiveness or happiness I must have received it myself in order to be able to pass it on to you. *A Course in Miracles* teaches that 'to give and receive are one in truth' and that, paradoxically, the way to have our gifts truly is to give them away. The world tells us that if we have a gift we should copyright it, protect it, fight anyone who tries to use it without our permission and exploit it as much as we can. But our natural desire is to share it and let everyone else have it, and be adequately rewarded for it. When we contribute what is precious, we send an unconscious message that says, 'You are significant', which others recognize and appreciate.

When we truly give, we are transformed. Every time I give a talk or run a workshop I am changed a little bit, as some new idea will come to me, or a question is brought to my attention, or I receive some feedback, or I am challenged. When our intention is to give we become channels and are altered. As you contact the joy of sharing your abundant spirit, more spiritual wealth will pour down from the heavens, filling you with ideas and inspiration that wouldn't have been given unless you had made the initial commitment. We often confuse cause and effect – commitment triggers receiving.

Our inner growth can be gauged by how much we are willing and able to give, and the way we can choose to grow consciously is to choose consciously to give more of ourselves and the greatest gift we can give is a part of the true and authentic us. Most of the giving we have experienced in our lives is conditional, by which I mean that it is done for the purpose of controlling or getting something in return. The trick is to learn to give more without wanting anything back, because when we expect something back we are attached to results, blocking the flow so that less happens. The paradox is that when we do not expect anything back we will receive in vast quantities, because we didn't need a return and weren't attached.

We can burn through some of our own pain through choosing to give instead of staying stuck. We can be in pain and give, and make loving, joining, helping and connecting more important than staying separate and isolated. It can take incredible courage to be that vulnerable and reach out when we are hurting.

BLOCKS TO GIVING – WHY DO WE WITHHOLD?

To get something without working for it – that seems to be the acme of delight. But why is the desire to get something for nothing so strong in so many minds? For no other reasons than this: we do not understand the true nature of work, and therefore dislike it. When we learn to understand work, however, and learn how to work, we shall go to our work with just as much delight as our pleasure. And when we consider the real purpose of work and discover that work builds ourselves, we will consider it a far greater privilege to work for everything we need or desire, than go to a free mine and take all the gold we can carry away.

PATANJALI (2ND TO 3RD CENTURY BC)
Indian sage

Why do we withhold? What do we think we gain from holding back on truly giving the best of us. My own 'favourite' reasons for not giving include:

Scarcity

I have believed that I have always needed to hold something in reserve, not giving it all because if I do then the cupboard will left bare. I have held back, but then have gradually learned that the more I give, the more I am given in return to give again, so the cupboard can never be bare.

Fear of rejection, and vulnerability

I always believed that by putting on a front, playing a role, rather than being real, I was protecting myself from humiliation or looking and feeling stupid. But I also realized that by holding back, I failed to get close to people; I could only do that by being real. Also I believed that it would be less painful to be rejected for what wasn't really me, but was a facade. But more and more I have come to realize that true joy and fulfilment come from facing and stepping through fears and no longer letting them control me.

Meltdown

A deep fear I have had is that by truly giving what is inside, I would lose myself, and go into a kind of meltdown, losing all sense of boundaries and identity. I feared I wouldn't be able to say no and would give away all the goodies in the shop. I am discovering that it is only our personality or ego that wants to keep separate, and that my heart wants to move close and connect. Little by little I continue to learn about giving and about setting boundaries.

Anger

A feeling of revenge – that other people don't deserve my best and that they won't appreciate it – goes back to feeling hurt as a child that my best self wasn't accepted and appreciated. I am discovering that I can't be hurt when I give unless I am trying to get something back in return. I am gradually getting to a place where I give for the joy of giving, and try less and less to need appreciation, agreement or feedback.

I was recently in a situation you may relate to. I had planned that at the end of the talk I was giving I would offer a prayer about purpose that I had written, but I felt very vulnerable about doing so. I had written a number of prayers, and hadn't yet shared them with anybody, so this was a first time out, truly 'from the heart'. As I reached the end of the talk I went through this inner dialogue, 'You don't need to do this, they never knew you were going to share a prayer, so there's nothing to lose and what will you gain?' I decided to do it, summoned all my courage and read it, and got tremendous feedback, and requests for copies of the prayer (copy below).

We need to be willing to be vulnerable at times, to speak from our heart, and as much as possible be willing to give and contribute regardless of the reception we get.

Prayer for Finding Purpose

Lead me to finding the purpose and passion in my soul.
Lead me to finding the gifts that you have put in my heart.
Help me find what makes my heart sing and my joy flow.
Give me the strength and direction to overcome all the obstacles I have
    created that block my awareness of my own beauty.
Give me the courage to love and shine in a world that values fear and
    hiding.
Help me find the gifts that I can uniquely give.
Thank you.

EXERCISE

◆ Why do you withhold the best of yourself in your work and your life?

◆ What benefit do you think this defence gives you?

◆ What are you willing to give now?

REVERSING OUR OWN INVERSE ARROGANCE

The highest work, in the Buddhist sense, is recreating ourselves by becoming free
and enlightened beings and helping others to do so ... The idea is not just to follow
your bliss but to create a land of bliss for all.

ROBERT THURMAN

We have already seen how we have probably been trained to think that we are *not*
that important, and if *we* are not that important, neither is our work. Yet each of
us influences hundreds of other lives every day one way or another, through our
work and our life as a whole. So what do we choose to spread through these
interactions? Indifference or love? Beauty or ugliness? Kindness or harshness? It
is our choice. We can say, 'But what can I do? I am just me, I have no real power.'
All of us have the power to spread love and kindness, to choose to live a life of
example and to inspire if we want to; we all have a sphere of influence.

Each of us has the power to *feed* other people, and I don't mean by loaves and
fishes, but through what we choose our life to be about, what we choose to
spread, and what we choose to stand for. It is our arrogance that says we have
nothing to offer. Our gifts and our self-worth are two different issues, and lack
of self-worth will blind us to what we can have and can give.

Just think for a minute how we rob the world when we withhold our
goodness through our fear, guilt or unworthiness. Consider what would have
happened if the people who had inspired us, public figures and individuals in
our private lives, had said, 'What the heck, no one cares about my talents or
gifts, no one needs me or them!' How much poorer our lives would be – how
much poorer the planet would be. What if Shakespeare, Mozart or The Beatles
had decided that they weren't very good so they wouldn't bother sharing the
gifts they had? What poverty! Let's not deprive ourselves, or other people, of the
benefit and pleasure of offering the joy of our giftedness. Let's decide to quit
withholding and turn up and shine in our own lives.

EXERCISE

◆ What contribution would and do you love to make?

◆ How do you want the earth to be a richer place for you having been here?

◆ What form(s) can that take through your work and life?

◆ Write a checklist of your skills, talents and abilities and think who you would like to contribute them to. Even something like giving blood can literally be a lifesaver.

Lessons in Giving What We Have to Give

Marva Collins is an incredible woman. She is a teacher working in a school in one of the most run-down areas of Chicago, where many of the children have parents who have drink or drug problems, are in trouble with the law or have other challenges. It is not an easy assignment and most teachers had written off these children as no-hopers, without real future or sense of purpose. This is not how Marva sees the situation. She sees children with spirits that are dimmed but not gone, children failing to get much love, support or encouragement, and children who need to be given boundaries, believed in and shown the way.

She tells her children firstly that they don't have to come to school, that they are free not to be there, but if they do decide to come they need to keep to her rules. She gives them tough love, makes them responsible for their own behaviour, and gives them boundaries, and she lets them know that there are consequences for not sticking to the boundaries.

Marva teaches them about the greatest poets, writers and leaders, and tells the kids, 'What did these people have in common? Same as you, two eyes, ears, legs, arms and feet, a mind, a body, an imagination, a will. They just put what they had to great uses, and so you can too.' She has children as young as four learning and reading aloud William Shakespeare, Walt Whitman, Martin Luther King; they learn about people such as Florence Nightingale and Rosa Parks and understand what motivated them. She knows within each child too is a great soul. I was moved to tears when I heard one of her four-year-old students reading a Shakespeare poem and discussing what it meant to them. She believes in those children so much and loves and encourages them so much that even despite their circumstances they flourish and blossom. They have a different future to the one they would have had if Marva didn't have such vision and determination. That is true contribution, creating meaning and hope where it didn't exist before.

It is important to remember that our contribution is often not so much about doing or hard work, but about our being and our presence. We can get so caught in our conditioning in work being about doing that we forget that our physical, emotional and spiritual presence have great comfort and great power.

WE ARE ALCHEMISTS

In Principle Four, on the heart, we saw how our physical body is an incredible pharmacy, literally able to turn our attitudes, thoughts and beliefs into physical counterparts. We are capable of producing the chemicals we need for our own wellness and healing within our own body. We are literally a chemical soup, constantly changing and renewing each and every moment. With each breath we inhale and exhale 10^{23} atoms, that is 100,000,000,000,000,000,000,000 atoms! Every 90 days we create a new skeleton, a new liver every six weeks, new skin every five weeks, a new stomach lining every five days and new stomach surface cells every five minutes. Within a few years every single cell of our body will be different. Our body is constantly being recreated, so the question is 'What is doing the recreating?' Our body is created and recreated by our consciousness – our mind, soul or spirit, whatever you want to call it – the inner intelligence that is our true nature.

The Unmanifest	The Manifest
The unseen	The physical
mind	matter
consciousness	molecules
thoughts/attitudes	illness
feelings	wellness
awareness	healing/disease
love/fear	physiology

We know that our experience of, and attitude towards, work affects our health. Studies show that the most likely time for a heart attack in the Western World is around 9 am on a Monday morning, as if the very thought of going back to work is making us ill and even killing us. What fascinates me, and apparently a question still not really answered by science, is how an intangible thought become its physical counterpart of illness or wellness. The connection between the realm of thought/consciousness and the realm of the physical is the least understood area of medicine and science. We have traditionally believed the mind and body to be separate, but they are one, intimately connected and constantly interacting with each other. In truth, they are a single intelligent system. When our heart is not in our work, when we hate it or are bored, we can literally turn those feelings into illness.

Similarly a profound or renewed sense of purpose can be healing. Dr Bernie Siegel has hundreds of stories from his work as an oncologist, telling how many people take their cancer as a wake-up call to do what they want with their work and life. One moving and typical story was of a young man whose passion as a teenager was playing the violin, but his wealthy parents wanted him to be a lawyer, so eventually, after fights with them, he gave up and went to study law. A bright guy, he was successful and by his late 20s was a high-flier, but he hated it. Then he became ill and was diagnosed with cancer and given six months to live. When Bernie sat down with him and asked, 'So what do you want to do now?' he thought and responded, 'Play the violin.'

He quit the law and did what he loved – play the violin, as well as other pursuits. He started to heal his life, being real, not living a role to try to please others. The result was that he recovered. His joy, love and passion became healing within him, and eventually the cancer cleared up.

A huge amount of research shows how things such as laughter, love, relaxation, meditation and prayer can produce healing chemicals in the body. This, I believe, is the medicine of the future – understanding how to stimulate the body's natural inner pharmacy through understanding how our mind affects and interacts with our physiology.

Loving our work is not just a luxury, but a necessity for wellness. Work can make us sick or keep us well. In the United States in 1996, the cost of absenteeism through sickness added the equivalent of £600 to the cost of every car manufactured by General Motors! Add to that the actual cost through the healthcare system, and the cost becomes huge. That figure is mirrored throughout the world, so just consider the increased profitability opportunities that are available by bringing our heart into our work more!

LOVE AND FEAR CREATE PHYSIOLOGY

We confuse cause and effect, as much of our physiology is created by our consciousness. We think work makes us ill or well, but it is not the only factor; of far greater impact is our attitude towards our work which in turn affects our health. This is why we need to focus on transforming our attitudes and our consciousness as well as, perhaps, the physical environment of our work.

We can take this idea to another phase. All we do and how we are affects the well-being of other people. Through our love, inspiration, motivation, encouragement, appreciation and kindness we increase the possibility of keeping ourselves and others healthy and well. Just as stress kills and immobilizes, love maintains and nourishes and supports health on all levels. We are alchemists creating changes in each other's biochemistry through our intention and communication; we can wound or heal each other. Our words, intention and behaviour become like biochemical surgical tools with which we can heal or harm.

Scientific findings are taking healthcare into a new domain, our own spirit. The new prescription includes prayer, practising forgiveness, love and surrender. We can even learn a powerful lesson from a rabbit! A research project on the effect of feeding rabbits a high cholesterol diet included one animal that seemed to defy the expected results. It had the same diet, ate the same food, but didn't fall ill like the other rabbits did. The reason, they discovered, was that the assistant who fed this rabbit didn't just throw the food into the cage like the others, but picked the rabbit up, stroked it, and talked to it. This simple act of love was enough to reverse the whole anticipated physiological response. Love, affection and tenderness overcame the poison he was fed and the same is true for us! Love, laughter, joy and finding our purpose are healing for ourselves and others.

Over 500,000 research papers are devoted to the brain each year, and I think one of the most exciting developments of the new millennium will be the growing understanding and exploration of the power of the human mind and consciousness to influence and affect our own body, and almost everything on the planet. Jon Franklin, author of *Molecules of the Mind*, recently wrote: 'A thousand years hence, when our descendants look back on this time, it will not be the name of Albert Einstein that comes to their lips. For while the forces contained within the nucleus of the atom are truly powerful, and though they may burn hot and bright, they pale when compared with the energy in the human mind.'

The power of thought alone can change the quality of our lives, but first we must radically change our thinking about ourselves and how we present ourselves to the world.

FROM 'GIVING' ROLES TO OUR REALITY

We can give from one of two places – as a role, or by being authentic. Often people I meet at workshops say to me when I talk of giving, '"Give more?" You must be kidding. I give so much already to my family, my boss and partner.' We need to remember the two types of giving:

Roles

As we saw in Principle Seven, we can be in a role in which we do what seems like all the right things, be loving, caring, supportive, efficient etc, but we are doing these things for the wrong reason. We are doing them to prove our value, which hides our deeper belief that we are of little value. We are giving in order to get. Roles are based on either inferiority or superiority. We give because no one else is going to do it, so we have to!

Real

We give for the love and joy of giving, to demonstrate our existing belief that we are valuable. We all have something valuable to give.

SO WHAT CAN WE GIVE?

Where your talents and the needs of the world cross, there lies your vocation.

ARISTOTLE (384–322 BC)
Greek philosopher and scientist

We often think that giving something has to be a doing thing or a material thing, but some of the most valuable giving can be of our time, our attention and our presence. A friend was telling me that she felt awkward at the funeral of a friend's child and didn't know how to help; I explained that her physical and emotional presence were a gift and a comfort in themselves.

Let's look at some other simple and powerful ways of contributing in the workplace:

◆ being centred, grounded and peaceful when others are flapping
◆ listening and encouraging
◆ appreciating and enjoying people
◆ being enthusiastic
◆ looking for the good
◆ not being critical or cynical
◆ simply wishing people well

EXERCISE

◆ Think of some creative ways that you can and want to make a contribution to the lives of others, such as sharing a book or a quotation, volunteering time or skills, making donations.

In truth, we will never know in its entirety the impact we have and the good that we do. I am forever reminded of the power of a small kind act. Jelka told me that when a friend was ill she sent her a book, but then she lost contact for a year. When her friend finally called, she told Jelka, 'That book saved my life.'

Esther, who works playing piano in a busy restaurant, told me how gratifying it is when a customer simply takes the time to tell her how much they enjoy her playing.

It may feel like what we do is only a drop in the ocean, but the ocean is made of millions of drops. So is love created by the millions of acts of kindness that we can all carry out. Love is exponential; our gifts multiply and spread out like ripples on a pond.

PRACTICAL WAYS TO HELP

The Talmud says that judges and lawyers are partners with God when they render just decisions … so are psychotherapists who help people take the broken pieces of their lives and transform them into something deeper, and so is anyone who takes the raw stuff of the world and turns is into something usable.

RABBI JEFFREY SALKIN

It is useful to start identifying with those we find it easy to be compassionate towards and to work up to the more challenging ones. Like a muscle, compassion may need use and practice. By asking ourselves who in the human family we feel called to help, whom we have empathy and particular compassion for, we can find our work. We also need to ask what impact we want to have and what specific difference we want to make, and at what level – individual, community, nationally or globally. Some feel called to serve one or a few, others to serve the multitudes. Numbers don't matter, only the motivation, which must be love. By learning to love, treasure and deeply accept any one person, we must be learning how to love everyone.

We discover our compassion by paying attention to the inner and the outer worlds. What outer events and activities touch us, and what intuitions and inspirations most excite us? Let ourselves be moved from within and without, by our heart and our head. Compassion is not about competing and winning, so it is a wonderful way of reaching beyond our own needs. In compassion we expand to embrace a sense of our self beyond the individual ego identity we all have; indeed we become 'bigger' people in heart and spirit.

COMMUNITY AS WORKPLACE

The goal of the community is to make sure that each member of the community is heard and is properly giving the gifts they have brought to this world. Without the community, the individual is left without a place where they can contribute. And so the community is that grounding place where people come and share their gifts and receive from others.

Sobonfu E Some
African teacher and author of *The Spirit of Intimacy*

A key element of work is the context in which it happens, which includes the physical, emotional, mental and spiritual environment in which we work or would like to work, including the intangible and very real concept of the atmosphere in which we work. I am often struck by people who tell me that they feel lonely at work, even though they are surrounded by people. We may be a square peg in a round hole and there may be more that we can do to reach out to people and connect with them.

One of the most influential experiences I have had in the area of work, community and atmosphere was when I visited the Findhorn Foundation in north-east Scotland for the first time in 1994. I had been aware of the Foundation for many years, and knew many people who had visited and lived there. I almost felt like I had been there by osmosis.

I went with high expectations. I was initially disappointed, because it didn't look any different to anywhere else I had been. Over the next week though, I came to experience the essence of the place, what is was really about, and its purpose. The Foundation was founded in the 1960s by Peter and Eileen Caddy and their family along with Dorothy MacClean, but as with most creative endeavours they didn't found a community but planted a seed. Following spiritual guidance that Eileen had received, they moved to Forres, just outside Inverness, in their caravan. Little by little, others joined them, Eileen continued to receive daily guidance, and the community began to evolve. Thirty years later it is a thriving community with around 200 people within the community and another 150 living in the area as part of the wider community. As important as the community itself is the education programme it runs. Around 10,000 people a year visit from around the world, staying from a few days to a few years.

The Foundation is based on spiritual principles, which are embodied in the way they work. Many people initially find it strange that they pay money to go stay at the community and end up working! By the end of their stay they understand though. Findhorn is based on the idea that Kahlil Gibran described beautifully in *The Prophet*: 'Work is love made visible.' I decided to work in the kitchens (rather than in the gardens or house cleaning).

The first difference was that, before any of us did a stroke of work, for a few moments a candle was lit, we joined hands and attuned. This was a way of becoming conscious, mindful and present, realizing that our work was service to other people, not just a job. We also spent a few moments checking in, saying how we were feeling and getting support if we needed it. Part of me found this all a little strange, while a deeper part of me felt I was coming home. It felt very natural to dedicate our work.

Over the following days I came to the stronger realization that I wasn't just doing a job, but working on a very connected level. Much of the food we prepared was grown within the Foundation, so I had a sense of working with nature and being grateful to the abundance of the earth and those involved in growing and preparing the food. I wasn't just making food for anonymous, ungrateful and hungry diners. I was creating lunch for the people who may have cleaned my room out that morning, or tended the garden, or for the people who would make my dinner or lunch tomorrow. I was making lunch for real people. It all had a purpose and meaning beyond filling my stomach and those of the community.

The greatest shock was that it all became huge fun; I actually looked forward to working, and by about the third day I began to experience a deep joy, cutting up carrots, cabbage and beetroot in order to make coleslaw. It was wonderful, and in some ways very confusing. Back down in London I was still rushing around trying to be Mr Successful, although in a new way. I spent much time, effort and energy trying to be happy by doing all sorts of things, and here I was simply being happy making coleslaw. The difference, I realized, was that by taking time to stop, attune and check in I was bringing my *being* into my *doing* so that my work had a purpose and a meaning. It was a priceless realization. Why did I want success? Because I thought it would bring me happiness and joy. I realized I could just go straight for joy and happiness. I have since spoken to other people who have been to Findhorn, and they reported similar experiences while working there – even cleaning the loos!

I loved many of the other activities of the Foundation. People meditate together, and have a community centre for rituals, performances and conferences. I understood very clearly that the place is built on honouring and developing the gifts and talents of all those who live and visit there. They also run several businesses – the Findhorn Press, a solar panel business, a caravan park, the education institute – turning over several million pounds and interacting with the outside world. I was struck by how all those involved with the businesses sought to run them along spiritual principles, even when dealing with conventional businesses like banks and local government.

I don't want to romanticize Findhorn. If you are not used to belonging, you can feel even lonelier there to start with. The people living there have their own angers, fears, jealousies and competitiveness – the other usual human stuff. They are not perfect, and don't claim to be, but they do consciously intend to embody spiritual and loving principles in the way they live and work, even in dealing with conflict and problems and their negative qualities. The Foundation has been a huge inspiration for me and millions of people throughout the world, and many other communities and organizations have taken Findhorn as a model and example.

THE COMMUNITY OF ALTERNATIVES AT ST JAMES'S IN LONDON

I have been director of the Alternatives programme for a number of years and have my office at St James's Church in Piccadilly, right in the heart of London. On the surface it is a 'not-for-profit' lecture series and workshop programme, but its essence lies in bringing genuine spirituality and inspiration into the capital, within a beautiful Christopher Wren church. We provide a safe and welcoming place where people can come hear some of the best-known authors and speakers on personal and spiritual development from around the world, as well as many lesser-known ones. Although we are housed in a Christian church, we are an independent trust, and have complete freedom in our choice of speakers. One week we may host a Tibetan monk, next week a Catholic priest, the next a crystal healer, a psychic, a meditation teacher, a natural health expert or a shaman. It is also a place to make friends and feel a part of the London community.

The purpose of Alternatives is to allow Londoners to hear many different ideas and to find or strengthen their own spiritual or growth path without any dogma or compulsion. On a deeper level we know we have contributed to the lives of hundreds of thousands – maybe indirectly millions – of people in a positive and life-affirming way. It is a great joy to know we have that impact.

At the beginning of all the evenings, before the speaker arrives, our staff and team of volunteers join a circle, take a minute of quiet and offer a dedication for the evening.

> We dedicate this evening to being a blessing to everyone involved
> To the speaker, to the audience, the team and all who work here
> May it contribute to all our lives, uplift us and touch us
> Thank you for the opportunity to be together as friends and have the
>   opportunity to love and serve.

And then at the end of the evening we take a moment of quiet and give thanks and gratitude for the evening. It is beautiful to do that, even though we are often so busy that it seems like a nuisance, but it helps us feel good about the work we do – it underpins it. I also run similar dedications in my mind whenever I give a talk, run a workshop or work in an organization.

THE SPIRIT OF THE WORK

> I slept and dreamt that life was joy,
> I awoke and saw that life was service
> I acted and behold, service was joy

> RABINDRANATH TAGORE
> Indian poet

The work of Alternatives is done in the spirit of service. For the first seven years of being involved with Alternatives, I didn't get paid a penny and I only started receiving a small salary in 1996. So why do I do it? 'I loved serving,' I think is the easiest answer. I have always loved the purpose of Alternatives, and enjoyed being able to hear all the speakers and go on workshops to help my own growth and development. That was such a relief and contrast to working in the commercial world.

At Alternatives we still have a team of volunteers helping out – between 10 and 15 each week – and we still do our work in a spirit of service. I often wonder why the team give so much of their time and energy for no financial reward and then I remember that I did and still do.

BECOMING A SPONTANEOUS AND INSPIRED GIVER

One of the greatest joys of life is being an inspired giver – following our hunches to give what might be needed where it is needed, when it is needed.

One day I was unloading a box of books from my car at St James's. Someone walking past glanced at one of the books on top. A voice spoke in my mind; I followed it and I asked, 'Are you interested in that book?'

'Yes,' she replied.

'Would you like to look at it?' I asked. She smiled, and then I found myself saying, 'Would you like it as a gift?' Her smile transformed into a huge grin as she left with the book in her hand. I love to give gifts spontaneously, and often do so at my talks and workshops.

A great starting point is to ask yourself how much you enjoy receiving thoughtful acts or gifts that you weren't necessarily expecting. If you love it, why not give the very thing you love receiving? A question I often ask in my workshops and talks is 'How many of you can name six people with whom you do any form of business who are inspired givers and work wholeheartedly?' Usually no hands are raised, which demonstrates that if you choose to become an inspired giver you will be remembered and most likely be successful, because the more we open our heart, the more gifts we find to give.

It only truly really works when we are unattached to the outcome, when we don't do it for a reward but because it is how we choose to live our lives, with our heart open, knowing that the source of our giving is without limits. The success comes as a by-product because we raise our energy and shine, as we discussed with regard to money. It is one the greatest joys of life, and is the best way to truly enjoy our work, because there are no limits to the ways we can make a difference. When we find a form of service that calls to us, suits our abilities, aptitudes and interests and absorbs us and draws out of the best in us, we've arrived and found ourselves.

Creating meaningful work will probably entail us changing in some way, either in attitude or the actual work we do, so let's now look at the promise, joys and challenges of change.

Simple Ways to Implement Principle Eight

* With colleagues, take an hour or two to help in the community.

* Buy a gift for a colleague or customer and give it to them for no apparent reason.

* Ask for help with something without apologizing for being a nuisance.

* Do an anonymous and random act of kindness for someone through your work.

* Next time you feel really depressed or low, ask yourself, 'Who needs my help?' Ask yourself what you could do for them, and do it.

* In your lunch break, do something totally different that you would not normally do, like clown or chat to a homeless person, to get a different perspective.

* Always keep the question 'How can I help?' in mind.

Principle Nine

WELCOMING TRANSFORMATION AND CHANGE

Within each of us there lies the power to transform both our circumstances and, most importantly, our perceptions. As we set our intention to live more fully and authentically and move in that direction, life does unfold for us, we work in partnership with the realm of spirit to dissolve our fear-based perceptions to the truth of love and creativity.

WHY CHANGE?

No one is comfortable when they begin the journey from the known to the unknown, but we can be comforted by the knowledge that the summit is not really new. We are not leaving home; we are coming home. We used to live on this higher ground a long time ago – we are simply reclaiming it. It beckons us to return.

LANCE SECRETAN
Management consultant and author of *Reclaiming Higher Ground*

Change is integral to the work we were born to do. There is, however, only one true direction of change, and that is towards our true self, little by little leaving behind fear, roles, limitations, compensations and inauthenticity and self-concepts to embrace love, creativity, spirit, integrity, wholeness and our own nature as spirit. The road from fear to love requires us to become aware of all the self-imposed and self-created blocks to love so that we can let them go. To do this we must have a beacon or a voice to follow, a truth that is our guiding light, and this truth is the voice within our heart.

Change inspires both fear and excitement, and one of our greatest talents is learning to manage both. Sometimes we have to be a little like a trapeze artist – we have to let go of one bar before we catch the new one. Think of the old trapeze bar as the stagnating job, routine, boredom, even frustration in your current work. At first we may not even see the new bar for a while. As André Gide wrote: 'One does not discover new lands without consenting to lose sight of the shore for a very long time.'

REFUSING TO CLING

Grasping is the source of all our problems. Since impermanence to us spells anguish, we grasp on to things desperately, even though all things change. We are all terrified of letting go, terrified, in fact, of living at all, since learning to live is learning to let go. And this is the tragedy and irony of our struggle to hold on: Not only is it impossible, but it brings us to the very pain we are seeking to avoid.

SOGYAL RINPOCHE
Tibetan teacher and author of *Glimpse after Glimpse*

To some extent we all cling on to whatever we think we've achieved and accumulated, thinking this is probably about as good as it gets. We think holding on will serve some purpose, else we wouldn't do it. Perhaps we think we can get some old and past need met now by refusing to let go, believing we can manipulate someone into giving us something that we didn't get before. Or we are scared to move forward into a greater level of happiness or freedom. Or holding on demonstrates how much we loved someone or something, and that we are lost without them.

We can tell we are holding on if we feel something significant is missing from our life right now, as holding on blocks present success. We aren't open to *now* when we are still holding on to *then*.

The Buddhists tell us that all suffering is caused by attachment to things of the world but interestingly not the things themselves. All change requires us to let go of attachments, otherwise when we try to change we leave precious little mental or emotional space for anything new or for the present moment. Zen teachings tell us that the practice of enlightenment is concerned with emptying out our minds, not cramming them full.

It is important to differentiate between letting go and throwing away. Letting go is concerned with treasuring and valuing what we have had and experienced, allowing ourselves to have wonderful memories and gifts from that experience. Throwing away is pretending that something or someone wasn't important when they were very significant but we can't face the pain of the loss. Letting go may initially require us to face the pain and grief of loss in order that we may become freer. In letting go we retain the value of our past experiences, relationships and people without clinging to them emotionally.

When I was bored and clinging to my old job, I was desperate to let go but scared stiff. I asked myself, 'What if I do stop clinging and let go, and then lose it all? I'll have to start the struggle up the hill all over again, and I don't think I have the stomach for it'. At that time I came across a book by Richard Bach called *Illusions*, containing a parable that seemed as if it had been written just for me:

> Once there lived a village of creatures along the bottom of a great crystal river … Each creature in its own manner clung tightly to the twigs and rocks of the river bottom, for clinging was their way of life, and resisting the current was what each had learned from birth. But one creature said at last, 'I am tired of clinging. Though I cannot see it with my eyes, I trust that the current knows where it is going. I shall let go, and let it take me where it will. Clinging, I shall die of boredom.' The other creatures laughed and said, 'Fool! Let go and that current you worship

will throw you tumbled and smashed across the rocks, and you will die quicker than boredom.' But the one heeded them not, and taking a breath, did let go, and at once was tumbled and smashed by the current across the rocks. Yet in time, as the creature refused to cling again, the current lifted him free from the bottom, and he was bruised and hurt no more. And the creatures downstream, to whom he was a stranger, cried, 'See, a miracle! A creature like ourselves, yet he flies!' ... And the one carried in the current said 'The river delights to lift us free, if only we dare let go. Our true work is this voyage, this adventure.'

This story has kept me going through many difficult times. I have refused to cling, and now I experience more and longer periods of flying, as well as a few crashes, and plenty of temptations to cling. Being open to change isn't always easy, and involves us overcoming major blocks.

THE FIVE MAIN WAYS WE BLOCK OURSELVES FROM CHANGING

1 We have no clear direction

This is a common complaint. 'I know I don't like what I am doing, but I have no idea of what I do want to do next.' Sometimes I want to add a subtext: 'Thank goodness, because if I was clear I would have to do something about it!' We may begin to realize we have an investment in being confused – clarity means decisions, change, action and commitment! Oh no, we might actually need to take responsibility for ourselves! We can find this very scary. We procrastinate and sit on the fence, and postpone decisions.

One way through this is to get inspired to change and see the possibility and benefit of it, another is to make it more painful *not* to change, so that staying caught where we are hurts and becomes the spur to change.

EXERCISE

◆ If you were really clear, which direction would you take?

◆ If you had no sense of fear or guilt, and felt free to choose, in what direction would you really want to move?

2 We fear we will not be liked or loved as much

Our ego will tell us that to have the benefit of change we must lose something – that is always its main lie to us, the need for sacrifice. We worry that if we don't live just to please others, we won't be loved anymore. At our core I expect we all have our own insecurities and fears about not being as lovable if we become more assertive/successful/happy/independent/wealthy.

EXERCISE

◆ What are some of your insecurities, the ones that make no logical sense, but can feel very real?

◆ Are you going to let them stop you?

3 We feel we have too much invested in our current situation

We are, in effect, saying to ourselves, 'This would be so painful to change.' We may feel our whole sense of self-worth and identity is tied up with our current situation, and our whole sense of who we are could be jeopardized if we changed. If we believe this, it makes sense not to change, as we don't want to experience such pain and loss. Then we tend to focus on the worst that could happen, not the joy of change and the best that could happen.

EXERCISE

◆ Have you considered the best and most wonderful things that you could experience as a result of the change(s) you are considering making?

◆ What opening to joy, happiness, creative fulfilment, freedom and abundance could be on the other side of this change?

Be clear that when we associate change with pain and loss, nobody would ever want to change! It is not the change that is painful, but it is often our resistance to change, our attachment to old ways, beliefs and concepts that causes our pain. Sometimes a letting go of an old way of being can feel like a death, but when we persevere, the rebirth always follows.

Our ego and our higher mind have very different messages for us about change. Our spirit is always clear and consistent: 'You are whole and complete and need change nothing. Just release all blocks and untrue self-concepts.' Our ego will tend to take the messages of our higher mind and spin them around. Below is a clarification of what these two voices are actually telling us.

Higher mind	Ego
we have it all now	we need, we need
release and let go	hold on
be defenceless	defend/attack
true self	self concepts
love is freedom	love is attachment
inner holiness/wholeness	inner hole
look inside	look outside
joining, unity and connectedness	independence and separation
forgiveness	judgements
being a natural loving self	doing good
innate value	having to earn and deserve value
we are love	we have to earn and deserve love
no sacrifice	must sacrifice
receive naturally	must suffer to receive
partnership	loner and independence, or neediness
surrender	fight
release	control

Letting go is like shedding a skin, sometimes a painful process but essential for growth and development, otherwise we stay constricted. When we truly let go of our emotional attachment to a thing or person, one of two wonderful things happens, either:

◆ we still have what we used to have, but with a greater level of freedom and abundance, or

◆ we don't have it any more, but we have all its memories, benefits or gifts, though something new and even better moves into our life to take its place. Nature abhors a vacuum.

Truly letting go of attachments, being willing to feel the grief that can be involved, even for a few moments, is truly heroic. In doing so we become freer and more available to life now. Remember everything that once seemed a challenge, too difficult, painful or scary is now second nature. Today's challenges can be tomorrow's ease.

EXERCISE

◆ Write down all your previous good working experiences. How much are you still holding on to the good old days? How much are you still comparing what was with what is? Close your eyes and gives thanks for those experiences, the people you've known and worked with, the closeness and team spirit you had then. Be grateful and then let go of them. Quit telling yourself that things aren't as good as they were, or should be. Be willing to be present to new and exciting work opportunities in your life now.

4 Fears of known and unknown origin

Fear is usually our biggest block to change. As we have already seen, we make fear the most powerful force in our life, letting our fearful thoughts dictate what we will and won't try, what we'll go for and what we won't attempt. Our life either shrinks or expands in proportion to our courage. The work we were born to do calls us to create a new meaning for and a new relationship with fear. If we are really honest, fear is the reason we use to stop ourselves doing practically everything in our lives, even if we often rationalize this fear into common sense and logic.

Our fears can be vague and non-specific, and keeping them secret and silent, just out of our awareness, feeds and gives them power. Our ego hates awareness, so one powerful way of diffusing the power of our fearful thoughts is simply to name them and bring them to the light of awareness.

EXERCISE

◆ Take a piece of paper and be honest and list all of your fearful thoughts concerning change, following your heart and your intuitions.

◆ If you are willing, share some of your most vulnerable thoughts with someone who you trust to be on your side, non-judgemental and supportive. See if you feel lighter and freer as a result of doing this.

◆ Fears are caused by our thoughts, so apply your best thinking to them. What steps and action can you take to deal with these fears? Take each of your worst-case scenarios and against each one say, 'If that were to happen, I would find or develop the resources to handle it, at the time.' By trying to figure out now how to deal with every future possibility, we can cripple our ability to stay centred and act in this moment, which is the only point of power. Remember, you can only solve problems if and when they happen, not now.

◆ We can choose to act, if necessary, despite our fears; as Thomas Merton wrote: 'Do it trembling, if you must, but do it.' Our fears can blind us to the paths that exist through our current situations, and by not allowing our fearful thoughts to stop us, we move through them into clearer territory.

Through habit and choices over long periods of time, we may find ourselves having fearful thoughts more easily. Within our own mind is a voice of unconditional love, trust and encouragement. We may not know this voice well, or may resist hearing it, but it is a voice that is *always, always on our side*. We need to get into the habit of listening to it.

EXERCISE

◆ In all situations where you experience a feeling of anxiety or fear, ask inside to hear the voice of love and trust, which is really the voice of the wisest and most loving part of ourselves.

5 Lack of faith

The willingness to take the first step is what is needed. Our fear can very quickly turn into a different experience when we face it head on. As I moved to the cliff edge for my first attempt at abseiling I was terrified. For 40 years I had been scared of the thought of it. We were only about 30 feet above the beach, but my heart was pounding and I was ready to walk back down to go back to sunbathing on the beach! Yet as I took that first step over the cliff, and with each step down, relief flooded in, and by the time I reached the beach I was quite excited. Within 20 minutes I was on my second attempt, and much more confident. And within the hour I had done the third, and almost had to be restrained from a fourth because I was so keen, relaxed and excited!

It really struck me how this was a great metaphor for much of life. We spend so much time and energy avoiding what we are scared of, only to discover that we actually really enjoy it and have robbed ourselves of years of joy and pleasure in the process! Remember fear is also a form of attraction, so be willing to embrace fear and see the gift that it is trying to hide.

Overcoming these five blocks to change provides a wonderful opportunity to remind ourselves that our true security comes from our very being, from the essence of who we are.

OUR SENSE OF IDENTITY AND THE PERENNIAL DESIRE FOR SECURITY

It may be that any view of life that puts security rather creativity first has misread life at its best, and thus misinterprets the cosmic process.

PROFESSOR PETER BARTOCCI

The work we were born to do is also about finding what is changeless within us and about us in a world that appears to be in such flux and change – and making a commitment to be true to that substance by overcoming whatever is in our way. Below the waves of change, like the seabed deep below the waves on the surface of an ocean, there is a place of peace, without waves or change. This is our spirit. Only who we think we are can be threatened, as our true identity is unchangeable, the solid ground on which we can always be secure, no matter what goes on around us.

The conscious desire to feel secure is, however, natural and important. Our ability to surf the waves of change hinges on our sense of identity – who we think we are. The greatest need of our ego is to maintain a consistent identity – in short, to keep itself alive – which is why change can feel such a threat to us at times. The more we identify ourselves with externals, achievements and everything impermanent, the more we tend to cling. We can put great energy into trying to maintain and defend our identity, leaving us little energy to be creative.

If we think security is a safeguard against loss, a protective barrier against going without food, clothing, shelter, heat, light, health or medical care, our best bet would be a life sentence in prison! It has been said that the only way to be safe is never to be secure! Our best advice might be to run from safety. What is rigid, secure and inflexible will die; that which adapts and evolves endures.

The bad news is that there is no security in any job, or indeed in any line of work. The good news is that real security lies deep within us, because our spirit, creativity, determination and capacity to change are truly limitless. The source, of which we are a part, is for ever flowing, but the form in which it appears is constantly changing. Think about the vinyl record industry 20 years ago. It was thriving and growing, worth about £20 billion, and if you worked in it you'd have probably felt secure. Then – boom! – the CD suddenly appeared out of nowhere, and within a couple of years record sales were declining. That must have created insecurity, yet within a couple of years the value of the CD industry had more than doubled to around £50 billion. So the industry had grown, even if its form had changed and transformed. Security lies within our own imaginations and our ability to let go of past forms and embrace new ones. It is never more than a thought away, in all places and at all times. True security means knowing that we have the creative imagination always to earn a living.

The word *secure* actually comes from two Latin words, *se* meaning 'without' and *cure* meaning 'care' – being free from anxiety and not burdened by excess cares. It invites us to remember that we are always safe, and to believe in the beauty within us. When we put our faith for security in things outside us, we can experience ups and downs, but when we put our faith in the spirit within, we are on solid ground. Faith is the bird that sings while the dawn is still dark, showing the trust in the renewing power of life.

CHANGES THAT SEEM TO FIND US

So often we wait passively for some outside force to give us permission to be who we are and to champion our cause … the permission can only come from within, from our own soul.

SONIA CHOQUETTE
Psychic and author of *Your Heart's Desire*

We may need to shed a skin in our work and life only to find that we don't have as many socially acceptable ways of doing this as other cultures. Some other cultures honour transitional life changes through rites of passage and initiation ceremonies whereas we may create forms of making major life changes indirectly: falling ill, having a breakdown, getting in trouble with the law, having a partner leave us or getting the sack. All these can ultimately give us the permission to make a big change in our life.

Illness

Illness is one of the most socially acceptable ways to change our life. When we are able-bodied and fit, we have to take immediate responsibility for what we want. When we are ill, we have a reason to put that responsibility temporarily aside and take a break from it. As we saw in Principle Eight, much – perhaps all – illness has a story behind it, and an emotional cause. As Bernie Siegel suggests, much illness is caused by pain and conflict and unresolved feelings. Our *biography* – our story – becomes our *biology*, our wellness or illness, or as Debbie Shapiro puts it, *our body speaks our mind*. The only thing worse than feeling our feelings is not feeling them, repressing or denying them, but our body has no choice but to express our unresolved emotional issues. We may have become so used to pushing ourselves hard that we stop listening to our heart, intuition or unhappiness, or cover up our feelings with busyness, food, drink or drugs. As a result we often don't notice our own dis-ease until it forces itself on us.

EXERCISE

◆ Think back on your life and the lives of family or close friends. Think of an illness and what it allowed you or the other person to do. How many people do you know or have heard of who have changed their work or made other major life changes because of an illness?

Problems

A trap is a problem for which you are afraid to get the solution because it is asking you to change in some way.

DR CHUCK SPEZZANO

We all have problems. In dealing with them we should not ask why we have problems but how we respond in the face of them. The work we were born to do is not about being problem-free and sailing off into the sunset but about choosing and gaining a new perspective on the purpose of problems in our work and life. The derivation of the word problem is from the Greek *problema*, made of the word *pro* meaning 'before' or 'in front', and *ballein* meaning 'to throw'; problems are situations, events and feelings thrown before us on our life's work journey. Problems are ways to deny our strength and natural power, and ultimately every problem is created because there is something we are withholding and not giving. Our higher mind has no problems, only our personality does; in fact our higher mind has ways out of all the dificulties we experience, even chronic problems and traps.

One of the most unhelpful and widely held misperceptions of problems is that they are a form of punishment and we somehow deserve them as retribution for previous misdeeds. But problems are our teachers. Another truthful perspective is that all problems are the result of incorrect thinking and false perceptions, signals to grow in consciousness, calling us to look at life afresh, to break through to a new understanding and to a higher ground of consciousness. Many people, for example, spend many years in psychotherapy, only to realize at the end of it that to go to another level of change requires a spiritual rather than purely psychological perspective. But we may have to undo some of the psychology before we can get to some of the spirituality.

EXERCISE

◆ Think back to some of the most challenging times in your life, perhaps times you may have felt floored, as if you wanted to give up. In retrospect how, as a result, have you now grown in consciousness into a bigger, wiser, more compassionate person?

We can have a huge investment in our problems, and we even build our lives and our identity around them. We have probably spent a lot of time trying to solve our problems. Trying can be a euphemism for not succeeding. Often, just as we are about to really change, we crash in some way, sabotaging ourselves or creating a new difficulty. On a deeper level we are scared that change will mean loss of some sort.

EXERCISE

◆ Use your intuition to pick a problem in your life now.

◆ Answer very honestly the following questions:

  (a)   What *don't* you have to do as a result of this problem?

  (b)   What *does* this problem allow you to continue doing/being?

(c)   Who are you proving wrong as a result of this problem?

(d)   What would be your biggest fear of *not* having this problem?

At the core of any problem is the belief that this problem will give us something and that if we release it we will lose out. At the heart of the problem will be the fear of loss.

EVERY PROBLEM HIDES A GIFT

It is our fear of giftedness that complicates life. All problems have at their root the fear of taking the next step in life and the fear of acknowledging our gifts and talents. These so-called problems are resolved with ease and simplicity by simply acknowledging our life-enhancing gifts and unwrapping our Presence ... Your giftedness blesses the world, for the more you receive, the more you give. It is your joy to share your giftedness, because it is a way of joining with others and creating a better world for everyone you come into contact with.

DR CHUCK SPEZZANO

We need to remember the agenda of our ego – it wants to stay in charge and keep us way from knowledge of our true nature, and one way of doing this is to create problems. 'I want to be different but I don't want to have to change' – that will keep us away from our creativity, joy and life purpose for sure! Problems can tie us up in knots for years, if not whole lives, so a new perspective to consider is that *every problem hides a gift*. Indeed, on deeper levels that are usually beyond our awareness, we actually create the problems in order to hide the gift, because we are scared of our own gifts. In essence we use problems to give us a feeling of control in our lives and over other people. If we want the gift of life at a greater level, we need to be willing to relinquish a degree of control over our life. The problem speaks of a place of confidence that we have been saying 'No' to, and the bigger the problem, fear or trauma the bigger the gift. So one of the easiest ways to dissolve a problem is to ask for the gift behind it. Here are two ways to do this:

◆ Ask yourself intuitively, 'What gift does this problem hide?' Note the answer, which may be something like freedom, love, courage or creativity.

◆ Imagine, in your mind, saying yes to receiving this gift, and open your heart and mind to receiving it. Observe this gift already received within yourself. See how your life is transformed through this gift and how the problem just begins to melt away, or is already gone. Know that the gift is within, just waiting to be born.

◆ Ask yourself, 'Who needs that gift right now? Who needs my help?' Create an opportunity to go give that gift.

◆ In your mind's eye give your problem to some spiritual master or being or even to a person that you know who you feel an affinity with, or would like to feel an affinity with, like Christ, Buddha, Mother Meera, Mary, even God. Know that it is the pleasure and delight of this being to transform the energy of the problem into a more useful energy of a gift. See the being handing the gift back to you, and start to give and share that gift in your life.

Gifts are aspects of our being, they are qualities within us. As we discussed in Principle Seven, we often hide our gifts, or were scared of them when we were younger, so dealing with a problem in our life may involves us in reclaiming a buried treasure within us.

As we progress along the path of the work we were born to do we will be given many opportunities to draw forth new and exciting gifts, and we are reminded that, above all, we ourselves are the gift, growing and expanding in our sense of who we are and what we are capable of doing. As we grow in giftedness our life develops a flow. And we will probably hit new problems and be offered bigger and bigger births.

CHANGING OUR PERCEPTIONS, SETTING NEW HORIZONS

It is the commonest of mistakes to consider that the limit of our power of perception is also the limit of all there is to perceive.

C W Leadbeater

The ability to change our perception is one of the greatest gifts we have. Our perception tells us that the earth is flat and stands still, but we know it to be round and whizzing through space at thousands of miles an hour. We can look up at the stars at night and wonder at the idea that some of the light we see is actually millions of years old. What we can begin to understand is that our perceptual apparatus creates the world we experience; there is no objective world out there that everyone experiences in the same way. We create and can recreate the world through the meaning and purpose we give it. A flower looks different to our senses than it does to those of a bee or a bird, because they have different apparatus with which to see. In effect the world out there is like a big quantum soup, out of which we create what we will. Colours, smells and tastes don't exist out there but in here. John O'Donohue, author of *Anam Cara* or Soul Friend, wrote: 'The most revolutionary thing we can do is change our perception.'

What I have come to discover is that we may undergo a process of changing our perception and strengthening our belief in our ability to change. Here are some common stages:

Wishful thinking

We'd like to change, but how on earth could we? It may work for others, but not for us. Circumstances are against us. All of this adds up to us not actually taking any risks and not taking any practical steps to change.

Belief

If we hadn't believed it, we never would have seen it. All change starts with belief in change. We can believe we can change and decide to change, and these beliefs usually come initially from outside us. This doesn't mean that we don't experience resistance within ourselves, as all beliefs have opposites and can feel like conflicts. For example, every time we say to ourselves, 'I deserve this,' another voice says, 'No you don't.' The way through these polarities is choice and putting our faith in a new possibility. As we strengthen our beliefs, our ego may throw up many doubts to try to keep us stuck.

Knowing

When we have done or experienced something, even once, we know it to be possible, but we had to believe that it was possible before we even attempted it in the first place. Through experience we know how to make love, swim, drive a car or use a computer.

I now *know* with all my heart that something that was once mere wishful thinking for me is a daily reality. When we strengthen our belief and have the courage to listen to and follow our heart and deal with the obstacles, all can turn out well and we can be supported on every possible level, including financial. This possibility exists for each and all of us, when we choose to strengthen our intention and act on what we want to do and be.

OUR CAPACITY FOR CHANGE AND TRANSFORMATION

'One can't believe impossible things.'

'I dare say you haven't had much practice,' said the Queen. 'When I was your age, I always did it for half-an-hour a day. Why, sometimes I've believed as many as six impossible things before breakfast.'

LEWIS CARROLL (1832–1898)
Author of *Alice in Wonderland*

We can easily get caught in the 'I can't do it' syndrome. Change may seem impossible, but it is a 'won't' or a 'scared to' rather than a 'can't'. Everything we now know how to do, we once had to learn. Think for a moment about the amazing journey of learning and transformation that we have already experienced: we came from nowhere in space and time, as we understand it, become an embryo in the womb, a water-living creature living inside our mother's body for nine months. Then we made the heroic journey to be born into the world as an air-breathing creature, on all fours, totally dependent on our parents for food and shelter. We grew up, we became self-aware, we learned about the world and became able to look after ourselves and even able to parent others. I think we all deserve medals to have made it through to adulthood! Then we age and become less able to look after ourselves, and eventually die and return to the nowhere that we probably came from. It is a truly heroic journey!

We are natural learners, but as we grow up we may forget how to carry on learning, and can get stuck in old patterns and beliefs. We tend to equate the known with pleasantness and safety and the unknown with fear, danger and insecurity. We need to realize that we learned this, indeed may have been taught it by parents, teachers and bosses, and that we can also unlearn it. It is not true. A far greater danger is stagnation, becoming bored, stuck and frustrated, experiencing emotional death or death of our will long before physical death.

EXERCISE

◆ Think back to the kinds of messages you received growing up. How many people told you to play safe, seek security, do as others do, be accepted by others, not take risks, seek the approval of others? How many told you to be adventurous, keep pushing out your perceived limits, find out who you truly are and what you are capable of, seek out challenges, grow, be spontaneous, live an exciting life? I would suspect that you heard more of the former than the latter.

Nevertheless, we all have the capacity for major change and even transformation in our work and lives. Parenthood, a death, marriage or divorce, redundancy, illness, addiction or even a spiritual insight may precipitate major change within us. Old values and goals seem less important, and new longings arise in our heart and mind, or old ones resurface. Nowadays we may also change as a result of a spiritual or personal development book we have read or a workshop we have attended.

Change usually results from one of two motivations: inspiration or desperation. I tend to meet more people (including myself) who have become masters at change through desperation and pain, or even worse have increased their threshold of pain tolerance and been able to put up with more and more discomfort and still *not* changed! A bit like the story of the frog which you may have heard – if you put a frog in a pan of hot water, it will jump out straight away, but if you put it into a pan of cold water and warm it up slowly, the frog will stay put and end up dying in the boiling water. The work we were born to do is not about raising our threshold to pain, but about having inspiration, vision and hope. Both motivations will ultimately lead us in the same direction, but one is much more pleasant than the other, and we do have a choice.

There can also be two types of change itself: change *within* the ego, and change or release *from* the ego. Most of what we know as change in this world occurs *within* the ego, which has been have described as like rearranging the deck chairs on the *Titanic*. Yet there is another realm of change, which is true freedom, and it is to be released from our ego.

This kind of profound inner change is a blessing, liberating us from old patterns. There is a difference between change and transformation. Change can be dull or uninspiring, or exciting and a blessing. Transformation is more about vision, freeing our self from conditioning so that we see a new possibility. Chuck Spezzano says: 'If you are not living in a visionary life, you're living a life dictated by the past, if you're not happy, it's just a life dictated by old programmes, old patterns, with old unfinished business around.' Vision and transformation can finish business and open up a new now and a new future.

Sometimes when we are about to make a major change, we will get scared on some level and create a distraction and keep us stuck, like a birth that we are refusing. When we finally break through the resistance we will have a new honeymoon period with our work and life, a new level of joy or creativity. The practice of major change is usually slow and gradual, but as long as we have our goal in mind – freedom from untrue beliefs about ourselves – then we will make it home, if not in this one lifetime, in another. Keep choosing to listen to and act on the voice for love – our heart – rather than the voices of our ego. This process of returning to the reality of who we are is not something we can do alone. The 12-step programmes that form the basis of the work of the most widespread self-help groups in the world embrace the idea of surrendering to a higher power to bring about change in our lives.

When we have grown up independently, we believe that any change has to be done by ourselves. We were hurt by being dependent when we were younger – let down, abused or betrayed – so we avoid further dependence on anything or anyone, even if it is a higher power that only has our best interests at heart.

Yet change really will occur in our life and awareness when we are willing to let love lead the way rather than needing to be in charge ourselves. All spiritual disciplines have their masters, male and female, whose purpose it is to serve humanity, acting as a bridge to lead us back from illusion to truth – Buddha, Mother Meera, Mother Mary, Quan Ying, Christ and hundreds of others – and it is a shame that we fight over whose path is the right one. We can and do develop personal relationships with any of these beings, and they will help us when we are willing to do our part too, and are ready to trust and be led. We cannot make all the changes ourselves. As it says in *A Course in Miracles*: 'You cannot undo it by not changing your mind about it. If you are willing to renounce the role of guardian of your thought system and open it to me, I will correct it very gently and lead you back to God.'

The most exquisite paradox ... as soon as you give it all up, you can have it all ...
As long as you want power, you can't have it. The minute you don't want power,
you'll have more than you ever dreamed possible.

RAM DASS

Spiritual teacher and author of *Transformation Through Our Work*

About five years into teaching the message of this book, I discovered that
without knowing it I had actually been teaching what in Indian culture is called
karma yoga, which is a practical philosophy of combining inner and outer
growth and accomplishment. Too often in modern work we feel the choice is
inner or outer work and that we must escape from the workplace if we want to
be true to our heart. Edmund Bordeaux Szekely, a modern writer on karma
yoga suggests in his book *Creative Work* that we have become too focused on the
pursuit of outer achievements at the expense of inner growth and
accomplishments. Yoga means union, so his suggestion is that we can find union
with our creator through work. My suggestion is that outer success can also
come through the expanse of our heart and soul, not at the expense of it.

DECIDING TO CHANGE

Two roads diverged in a wood, and I –
I took the one less travelled by,
And that has made all the difference.

ROBERT FROST (1874–1963)
Author of *The Road Not Taken*

But what about the parts of our personalities that don't want to change? There
is certainly a part of me that doesn't want to change, that wants to stay stuck in
old feelings and patterns. Fairly regularly I retreat into feeling hurt, angry,
depressed, worthless, useless or meaningless. What I have learned is not to stay
in those old feelings for quite as long as I used to. Here are three strategies I use,
You might want to try them:

Choice

Even when we feel so invested in feeling bad, we do have a choice, however
difficult it may feel to exercise that choice. There is always another way to see

and feel in every situation. *A Course in Miracles* reminds us that 'I could choose peace instead of this,' or as my girlfriend renamed it, 'I could choose peas instead of fish!' I remind myself that peace is available right now, and I ask for the willingness to choose it now.

Prayer

Ask whoever you believe in for the willingness to want to feel different. Here is a short prayer that might be useful:

Dear ———

I seem to want to feel this bad, but I know it is not what I truly want.

Please help me to get the willingness to want to feel differently.

I give you my willingness to be willing!

Thank you.

Sometimes we just don't want to shift, but we can be willing to be willing, and that can be enough.

Joining

On one level feeling bad can be a form of indulgence. One of the best ways of breaking through it is to ask yourself who needs your help. This is not to deny our feeling, but to make reaching out more important than licking wounds. Feeling bad blinds us to calls for help, so finding someone who needs help will enable us to shift our bad feeling, or at least a layer of it. Reaching out heals us while we also help others. It is a most powerful healing tool.

Often our conscious decisions to change are motivated by one of three forces – pain and crisis, vision and choice, or seeming chance. Let's explore these three forces.

Dreams born of pain and crisis – I had to do something ...

◆ I was sacked/made redundant.

◆ My spouse died/left me.

◆ I was so ill I had to change.

◆ I got a wake-up call.

◆ I was put down/unappreciated once too often.

◆ My spouse lost their job.

- I'd had enough – it was killing me.
- I was ignored for promotion again.
- I was sliding further into debt.
- I retired with no income.
- I had a crisis of conscience.
- My son/daughter needed me.
- The discrimination was intolerable.
- I couldn't find another job.
- I nearly died and my whole perspective changed.
- My soul was dead.

Dreams born of vision and choice – I just decided ...

- I wanted more freedom.
- I wanted to follow my heart.
- I've always wanted to be my own boss.
- I've had that idea all my life.
- We couldn't say no.
- It was too good an opportunity.
- I suddenly realized that I had nothing to lose.
- I wanted to do that since I was a teenager and the longing never went away.

Dreams born of chance – it just happened ...

- I just fell into it.
- It just dawned on me.
- It started as a hobby I loved, and people asked more and more.
- I had a chance conversation which got me thinking.
- It all started as a distraction.
- This idea suddenly came to me.
- I saw this advertisement, and thought I'd explore further.
- I just started chatting to this person on the train.
- I had this dream.

THE PROCESS OF CHANGE

Change is usually a process, not a one-off event, but there can be significant days in our lives when we choose to take our work and life in another direction. Change *can* happen in an instant, but it may take us years to arrive at that instant. My own experience and opinion is that we do have the capacity for what the Japanese call a *sartori* or an insight that literally transforms our view of life. Its implementation may take years, but without the insight or inspiration we may have no impetus to change direction. I believe that change can sometimes be amazingly quick, 'in the twinkling of an eye', as it says in John in the Bible, and some attitudes and beliefs that we carry around seem to be our life's work and almost impossible to change.

Here are examples of the days when some other people whose work is inspiring others decided to change their lives.

Dr Deepak Chopra

Born in India but living in the United States, Deepak is now one of the leading teachers of mind/body medicine and metaphysics. He became disillusioned within days of starting a fellowship in medicine in 1974, as the professor he worked for had a brilliant mind but was an unhappy and miserable human being. Although Deepak's wife, Rita, was pregnant, he quit and decided from that point onwards to dedicate his life to embracing love, laughter, harmony and peace of mind. He also vowed to live a life purpose of healing, transformation and service, living from the spirit within.

Gill Edwards

Author and founder of the *Living Magically* programme, Gill was a clinical psychologist with the National Health Service in the United Kingdom, when she had a mystical experience sitting in her garden. She suddenly became aware of an awesome feeling of being part of everything and an intense experience of joy followed, which changed her consciousness forever. Within hours she had resigned and started writing her *Living Magically* book and began to trust that spirit would guide her in her journey. Her books have now inspired and touched the lives of many thousands of people throughout the world.

Diana Cooper

Returning to England after years abroad, with a broken marriage and children at boarding school, Diana felt despairing, and threw herself into a chair and said out loud, 'If there is anything out there, help me!' She was met by an angel who took her on a journey, which among other things showed her teaching in front of hundreds of people. An hour later she returned feeling at peace. Her life changed in that instant, and seven books and 16 years later she has become that teacher, travelling the world healing and teaching.

Robert Holden

Robert's father died from alcoholism when he was 15. Out of his own pain and grief on that day he decided to dedicate his life to love and to loving, and making each and every day precious and sacred. He first founded the Stress-buster Project in 1989, then the Laughter Clinic Project in 1991, then the Happiness Project in 1997. He is the author of five books and teaches internationally.

Susan Jeffers

After a broken marriage, Susan went to Spain for a holiday and to face the pain of life on her own. She was uplifted by the beauty of Alhambra and began to experience herself as more than just her body; she experienced her being and realized that the world we see is the shadow of the substance that created it. She was filled with a deep peace and saw all the struggles and problems of her life as insignificant. This has been at the heart of her life since, and has led her to write many books and teach throughout the world.

Karen Kingston

Successful author and workshop leader on feng shui, Karen was bedridden in 1987 with a spinal disorder. Her life was degenerating – she was in debt and losing most of her friends, her boyfriend and her sense of purpose. She was lonely and depress-ed. One morning she woke and thought, 'My life can't get any worse, and if I have nothing left to lose, I can have whatever I want.' She found new hope born within her, and she began to follow her passion – feng shui, helping individuals and businesses. Her book, *Creating Sacred Space with Feng Shui* is an international bestseller.

The direction of following our heart has been travelled by millions before us and now millions throughout the planet. Those who have gone before have left trails to inspire us and give us loving support across the ages, and those around the world will be our friends and family. We can learn from them.

EXERCISE

Seek out examples of people who have made major life changes – even total transformations and miracles – in overcoming situations, illnesses or addictions, and have gone on to flourish in their lives. Let these examples give you a sense of possibility.

LEARNING AND REMEMBERING

We cannot teach people anything; we can only help them discover it for themselves.

GALILEO (1564–1642)
Italian physicist and astronomer

We talk of the need to keep changing by learning or getting the right qualification; we feel that it involves keeping the competitive edge, staying ahead of the rest else getting left behind. This is learning from fear, which is a defence, not a joy. Much learning can be fun and joyful – using a computer, mastering e-mail or the Internet, dancing or playing an instrument. As Henry Ford observed: 'Anyone who stops learning is old, whether 20 or 80. Anyone who keeps learning today is young. The greatest thing in life is to keep your mind young.' Learning is great when done for its own pleasure, but if done out of a feeling of lack or inadequacy it will not necessarily make us happy.

The learning of skills we just described is mainly of the head and body, located within time. But there is another type of learning – that of love, wisdom and truth, which are of the heart and soul, and what we learn in these lessons is perennial, beyond time and geography, and eternal. Not taught but remembered, the skills are already within us, sometimes alive sometimes dormant, so the best service we can do for each other is to is to remind ourselves and wake each other up.

But we each also have an inner cynic, and our fear is that this cynic will be proved right, which can be vicious and undermining. We can even feel a pull towards self-sabotage and failure. My experience is that it is best not to fight the inner critic's voice, as in doing so we strengthen it. Instead learn to smile at its nonsense. We should locate the voice of love and support that is also in there somewhere, and listen to that instead.

It is good to remind ourselves that while change may temporarily move us away from security, all that is now known and comfortable wasn't always. We have already changed so many times!

◆ Cast your mind back over some of the major changes you have already experienced in your life, such as careers, work, relationships or bereavements. Pick a specific one.

◆ What inner and outer resources helped you through?

◆ How were you strengthened by this change?

NINE WAYS TO LIBERATE OURSELVES TO CHANGE

Conscious decisions to change are some of the most important ways we can find the work we were born to do. We can decide to liberate ourselves to change.

1 Listen to our heart and intuition, and act on it – decide on the direction, or essence, of our change

This may be the biggest change of all – listening and honouring ourselves. The intention and direction of our change is likely to be to choose love over fear, and the starting point is as simple as that. We don't have to know how in advance – that becomes clear, step by step, as we go. Our first job is simple and powerful – to be willing and to decide. Write down a couple of intentions that seem to make sense for you; for example:

◆ I am willing to discover what I love and enjoy, and see what direction that takes me in.

◆ I don't know what to do next, but it will be something where my joy is, where I can grow, feel valued and feel like I make a difference. I will move in that direction.

We may need to take some time to explore options and consider possibilities, and then there comes a time to make decisions, which can be both scary and exciting. Our destinies are created in our moments of decision-making. Some decisions are easier because they are choice – 'Shall I have fish or meat for lunch?' or 'Shall I buy a new car or not?' We can be pretty sure what the outcome is likely to be. Many other decisions around our work and life are less obvious, like 'Shall I train as a massage therapist?' or 'Shall I take a two-month sabbatical and explore some other options?' We don't necessarily know where we will end up; these are more what I call evolving decisions, as one decision often leads to another and another, and we don't have any rule books by which to make right or wrong decisions.

The work we were born to do is concerned with getting better at making decisions. One process I would suggest you get used to using is asking your heart or intuition for guidance and trying not to work it all out logically. Find a word that feels right like *love, intuition* or *heart*, and be willing to take time to sit down and ask yourself, 'What would *love* have me decide or be or do now?' Listen for the answer. There is always a voice within us wanting to help us make the truest decisions, working for our highest good. It is a great resource that we could do well to use many times a day. Get used to deciding from love rather than fear.

Decision derives from the Latin word *decidere* meaning 'to cut off', so when we make decisions we are cutting off other options and committing to particular directions and choices. The greatest example of the decisions we have made is our life right now, the sum total of all that we have decided and are still deciding; even to do nothing and make no change is still a decision. Our ability to decide and to choose is perhaps the greatest single power we have. Decide to make some new decisions – and act on them!

2 Take baby steps

We can and do make small changes each and every day, so dispel the fantasy that we are looking for some all encompassing change that will occur at some vague time in the future and until then we'll stay stuck. We can choose small changes right now. Start where it is easiest, to build up confidence. As Thoreau said: 'Things do not change, we change.' We often worry about taking *baby* steps, thinking that nothing but major change will be significant enough, but that belief stops us making any change at all. We can learn to live by the thousands of years old wisdom of the Tao, the Chinese philosophy, which says: 'We achieve the great task by a series of small acts.' To learn and change also involves repetition, so be willing to be incredibly patient with yourself and kind as you learn new ideas or skills.

We rarely know how to do something when we start – we learn little by little. I remember in 1996 sitting down with my friend Robert Holden, who has now written five books, saying that I was getting ready to write a book. He responded with, 'Don't wait until you are ready. Start writing now, and in time you will be ready.' And he was right. I started writing paragraphs, then small essays, and a few articles, and two years later I felt at last I was ready to write my book. And when I was ready I found a publisher.

Remember that once you didn't know how to walk, eat, tie your own shoes, write joined up, multiply 12 by 16, drive a car or use a computer. You learned to do all of these things, sometimes easily and sometimes with difficulty. Make a commitment to giving yourself the joy and gift of being a lifetime learner, and give yourself permission to be really bad or inexperienced at something. As Will Rogers said: 'Everyone is ignorant, only in different subjects.' To learn it is crucial to focus on what we can do, not what we can't do. Whether we want to be more abundant, learn a new skill or make money doing what we love, it is crucial to focus on the success of small beginnings. Every success starts small. Even Marks and Spencer began as a stall in a street. A journey of any length starts with the first step.

In our effort to get *there* we sometimes forget to be *here*. People are lovable at all ages, not just when they are grown-up and competent. Babies are lovable when they don't know how to do much at all. The blossom, the bud, the ripening fruit and the fruit itself are all beautiful; we can remember to enjoy every step along the way, every moment, and remember to smell the roses.

3 Take the first steps in faith

In the film *Indiana Jones and the Last Crusade* there is a point where Harrison Ford is being chased. He reaches the edge of a chasm and there is nowhere to go; he is seemingly doomed. He is searching for the Holy Grail, and knows that he is being called to take a leap of faith, so he prays, takes the step in faith and as he does so the bridge appears. This is the metaphor for life – taking steps with faith and not necessarily knowing the outcome. We are not asked to walk off cliffs, but we may have to step off what feel like emotional cliffs. Yet this is not blind faith, it is knowing that, although we can't see it with our eyes, there is a force that responds to our intention and attention and is supporting us at all times. As the French poet Guillaume Apollinaire (1880–1918) said:

> 'Come to the edge,' he said
> 'We can't. We are afraid.'
> 'Come to the edge,' he said
> 'We can't. We will fall.'
>
> *'Come to the edge,' he said.*
>
> And they came.
> And he pushed them.
>
> And they flew.

I eventually managed to find courage in my own life by turning things around and asking how much more unhappy I would be if I stayed for another ten years. And I allowed myself to get excited and inspired about my dreams and how I could I could create my work and life. So although I was scared, I resigned.

All along the line, I have felt supported, both by people and invisible forces, which reinforces my belief that life is supporting my decision. For example, when I left my old job, I went travelling for three months. I met up with a friend in Cairns in Australia, and she checked us into the Sheraton Mirage in Port Douglas, which I then discovered was the same resort I would have visited if I had stayed with my previous employers and won the bonus incentive holiday!

I have dozens of other stories about meeting the right people, amazing synchronicities, things happening at the right place at the right time. Looking back I can see that the biggest block has been, and still is, my willingness to receive these goodies, to feel that I deserve them and give up the struggle and let life be good. When we take the plunge and commit we often have the sense of our lives being guided by some force bigger than ourselves.

4 Explore and research – you really don't know

Get more and more comfortable with the idea that you don't know. Say 'It's okay that I don't know' to yourself dozens of times until you no longer feel scared or that you have to justify yourself. We do have to be truly honest with ourselves and acknowledge that we don't know precisely where we are headed. We can get so caught up in arrival, achievement and goals that we forget that life is a journey and that travelling well is wonderful. We can do well to develop curiosity, excitement and anticipation as attitudes to live by. By pretending we know when we don't we block the possibility of being shown; in many mythological stories, the idea of getting lost in the woods is described. While scary, it also culminates in finding our way again.

Uncertainty is a great gift of life – if we were certain there would be no joy of discovery, nothing to look forward to because we would know what was coming. Yet culturally we seem to demand certainty from politicians, the medical profession, ourselves. Once we become comfortable with uncertainty, we no longer crumble under the question, 'Are you sure you know what you are doing and that this will work out?' from a concerned but fearful friend or parent. As Søren Kierkegaard wrote: 'Life must be lived forwards but can only be understood backwards.'

5 Commitment and trust – do whatever it takes

In the quest for happiness, partial solutions don't work.

MIHALY CSIKSZENTMIHALYI
Author of *Flow*

New ways of living may or may not happen overnight; they can take weeks, months, even years, and may lead us into periods of transition. But we can start right now, and the best thing about the future is that life comes only a day at a time, so we don't have to handle it all at once. As long as we commit and refuse to cling to old ways and old patterns, we will be rewarded with success.

If we are used to being independent, commitment can feel like a death sentence, or at least a lifelong prison sentence. I have found commitment very scary in much of my life, always looking for the get-out in case I needed it. I never wanted to commit to any work too far ahead. I was commitment phobic, but am getting better!

Yet there is another way of finding freedom in commitment too. When I found what I love, I wanted to commit myself to it. Commitment now is not so much about length of time but a decision to give of ourselves as fully as possible, not to hold back. I now enjoy having things in my diary a long way ahead. But commitment doesn't have to be for ever, and there are some things we want to commit to for ever from choice, not duty or compulsion. Discover that when we commit to something, it stands the best chance of turning out!

6 Relinquish some control and let life unfold

We can't demand of life that it be a particular way for us, but we can align ourselves with life though our intentions and what we pay attention to. I no longer feel I have much control in my life – I don't know what is going to happen – but I feel more in charge than ever before. This is an important distinction – we can't dictate the direction of the wind, but we can adjust our sails, determining our responses to whatever circumstances we find ourselves in.

When we are willing to let go of control, surrender a little to a greater will, amazing events can manifest. As I was completing this book, I was wondering who who may possibly give me the gift of an endorsement for my book. Paulo Coelho, author of *The Alchemist*, came to mind. Although I had met him twice, I had no way of contacting him; a friend gave me his agent's address in Barcelona, and I put contacting him on my to do list. About ten days later I was in Prague for a training course I had been invited to attend. Wandering around the city my girlfriend saw a queue and was curious, and discovered that Paulo Coelho was doing a book signing for *The Alchemist,* which had just been published in Czech. I said hello and we chatted while we walked together to his next talk in the city. I had bumped into a man I wanted to talk to who lives in Brazil while we were both in Prague, neither knowing the other was there. Coincidences, or synchronicities begin to abound as we decide to commit to our purpose and strengthen our intentions.

7 Get love and support

If you are a tough-it-out-on-your-own kind of person, be willing to start reaching out and asking for help and support. I have set up a number of support groups, including in 1999 the Heart at Work Club, which aims to support people who are or are intending to make significant work and life changes. It is partly educational, partly inspirational and partly a meeting place for like-minded people. I know from my own experiences that making significant life changes can be lonely; we can feel like the odd one out or that few people understand the change of direction that we are called to. So join a support group of some kind, or start one, or get together with friends who love and care and want to see you succeed in your life. Be willing to ask for help on inner and outer levels.

8 Be willing to have it be a good as possible – now and always

We do have a tendency to put off and to wait until – which aren't helpful. Remember that substance, the invisible essence behind all life, is here and now, wanting to love and support us now. We say to ourselves that when we get our life more together we'll deserve to be happy, but we need to remind ourselves that the essence is constantly giving to us whatever our circumstances and whatever our personal beliefs. Take time to ask for the experience of peace *now,* love *now,* happiness *now,* abundance *now* and support *now.* Spirit doesn't know of change – it is constant, and for ever giving all we need.

9 Put attention on that which is changeless

When we are going through lots of change, it can be very comforting to know and be with things that *aren't* changing, and find some stability. Here are some ideas:

◆ Nature – while it changes through its cycles, it has a predictability that can be comforting. When I felt stressed or scared I would often go back to a beach I visited as a child.

◆ Aspects of our lives – our sense of humour, home, cat, dog, family, friends, garden or chilli con carne recipe – whatever it may be that is always there for us.

◆ Some routines and time structures in the day can be comforting.

◆ Wisdom that is eternal and beyond time and different ages (cleverness can come and go). Find spiritual texts or writers that help connect to timeless wisdom, to spirit and to love; these are constants.

Remember that behind all changing appearances is a changeless spirit. Take time to focus on the source of all that changes, which itself doesn't change. Our true nature – the witness – doesn't change, only our ego believes it does. That said, one of the ways in which we can really help ourselves to change is to give our conscious minds permission to take a break from the rat race.

PERMISSION TO TAKE A BREAK

We should all give ourselves permission simply to say, 'I need a break, and am going to re-evaluate my work or life.'

Isn't it crazy to think we have to make work and career decisions at the age of 16 or so that will affect the rest of our lives, and that we are expected to carry on living and working on the basis of those decisions for the rest of our life? Isn't it mad to think that we are supposed to work eight hours a day, five days a week, 48 or so weeks a year, for around 40 years of our life? We need to give ourselves breaks, sabbaticals if possible, opportunities to take stock about who we are and where we are. We may need to give ourselves that permission, because no one else may. We all change so much, regularly, and yet we work as if we are linear beings, headed in a single direction.

You may have dismissed the idea of taking a break as an impossible luxury, but is it really?

EXERCISE

What are your fearful thoughts about taking a break?

◆ I'd never want to go back.

◆ I'd ruin my career possibilities; I wouldn't be able to get back in the rat race.

◆ I could never afford to financially.

◆ I would be so hard on myself; I'd feel so guilty for not working hard; I would judge myself.

◆ I'd miss the social contact and structure to my time; I wouldn't know what to do with myself.

◆ My partner wouldn't support me or agree with me.

Add your own fearful thoughts about why you think and believe that you couldn't take a break.

What is the best that could happen from taking a break? Why could you do it?

◆ To discover a new sense of direction and self-esteem.

◆ To be at peace with yourself.

◆ To see possibilities that you couldn't see before as you were so stressed and busy.

◆ To realize that you are happier when you take the pressure off yourself.

◆ To do all those things you've been meaning to do.

◆ To refresh, renew and revitalize yourself.

Take time to sit down and think and brainstorm how you could do it. Calculate your finances and see how much you have and would need. Simply be with the question, 'How *could* I take a career break?' Notice what thoughts come to you.

MONEY AND TRANSITION

Taking a career break or making the transition from a salary to self-employment or starting a new project may or may not mean that we have to review our finances. However, when we have natural prosperity, consciousness and self-confidence, we know that if we earned money once we can do it again and again; or even if we haven't earned much yet, we still can. But when we are governed by scarcity thinking or have attached our self-esteem to money, a financial gamble may feel challenging. We may also have a belief that we must sacrifice one thing or the other. The truth is that we can have both joy and money; it doesn't have to be one or the other.

In reality a career transition may mean we have to buy fewer new clothes, miss a holiday or eat out less, but it will be worth it as we are making a long-term investment in our happiness. What you are also likely to notice is how some of the material goodies you had grown used to were compensations for being unhappy in your work. As you become happier in your work, you need less compensation because it is more of its own reward. The Judaic tradition of the Kabbalah describes how sometimes we need to take what feels like a drop or a step backwards in order to raise the energy we need for a great leap forward. You may even realize how much money you have wasted in the past through unconscious compensation spending or by trying to keep up appearances.

Interestingly, getting by on less money for a while actually stimulates greater creativity and often leads to a greater gratitude for what we do have. And it is okay to miss some things for a while. As we build a life around new values, we often feel a new joy and gratitude for so much that we used to take for granted, and we may also begin to value quality over quantity. The joy of earning a living at doing what we love is indescribably wonderful and can feel such a blessing; it is beautiful to experience a new career unfolding, based on our creativity, talents, joy and gifts. It opens a feeling of prosperity never available through money alone, and it is the best ever pay packet. We develop a new relationship with money and a new awareness of the good it can do for each of us.

CHANGING TO A PORTFOLIO LIFESTYLE

I have learned this at least by my experiment: that if one advances confidently in the direction of his dreams, and endeavours to live the life which he has imagined, he will meet with a success unexpected in common hours.

HENRY DAVID THOREAU (1817–1862)
American writer, philosopher and naturalist

It is quite possible that the work we were born to do will be a portfolio – not a single job or place of work, but several, perhaps two, three or four strands, each allowing us to express different aspects of ourselves. Some will support us financially while others will be where our heart truly lies. When I first became self-employed I always did several things – talking, one-to-one coaching, promoting other people's talks, selling other people's books and tapes – and a nagging part of me was asking, 'When are you going to make up your mind which one you'll do?' because I still believed that a proper job was nine to five,

Letting Life Do the Hard Work

Gaby knew she was ready for major change. After eight years travelling the world as an entertainer on cruise ships, she came home to England and started to work running exercise classes at a health club. Another eight years later she had worked her way up to being general manager of the most successful branch in the chain. She was a star performer, great at her job, with a good salary, bonuses and a car. On the outside it was a job to die for, but on the inside a job that was killing her. Gaby had a recurring virus, like ME, which laid her low for days at a time. 'My problem was that I just got to hate the work,' she told me. 'I was good at it, but it just wasn't me anymore, but I didn't know what was next.' Many times Gaby and I sat down together and looked at what she could do, but she was never clear about what she wanted to do. Eventually she exercised her power of choice, found the courage together to take a sabbatical and quit her job and went off to Greece for a few months to find herself. Yet all the time her attention was focused on 'What's the next thing that I truly want to do?'

She eventually came home to Twickenham, rested and happy, but still awaiting some clarity on the next stage. 'That was the most uncomfortable bit,' Gaby explained, 'having left the past behind, being in transition and not yet having a new clear direction. My faith and trust

five days a week, 48 weeks a year. When I heard about portfolio working I breathed a sigh of relief and realized that this is a legitimate way of working, which is becoming increasingly popular.

Sue's story illustrates how a portfolio career can seem to create itself. After 15 years, Sue knew she didn't want to continue working for a building society full-time any more. Following the end of a relationship, she started to attend personal development groups and meditation classes, and to read related books. She realized that there was a whole other world out there. 'On a workshop, I told the leader about a dream I'd had, and that I thought I was in the wrong job. The leader answered, "You know you are in the wrong job!" And that was a turning point for me, I knew I wanted to change direction. I knew I wanted to take some major action, and made that intention clear, although I had no idea what form that would take. I had developed a new awareness which it was impossible to unlearn.'

were greatly put to the test, but I knew I could only move forward. I began to question my own sanity,' she says, 'but knew I had to continue to keep letting go of the past, trusting and staying open to the future. Most of all I was learning simply to enjoy the moment, which I hadn't allowed myself to do before.'

She started learning yoga, and decided to attend a course to learn to be a yoga teacher. She found she loved it more and more. Slowly Gaby began to have the creative courage to offer courses to others to learn yoga, and was amazed when people turned up! After a while she felt inspired to offer a weekend retreat in the country, and that filled up too. Gaby also worked part-time in another health club; then she was called by her old club too, asking if she'd like work as a consultant two days a week, which she knew she could do easily. She was creating a portfolio career, using her old talents more creatively, and developing new ones. 'The most challenging part was letting go of being in control, and needing to know how it would all work out. The biggest lesson I have learned out of all this is to trust, and that life is actually for me when I let it be, when I step out of the way, and don't focus on my doubts. I have let go of much of my need to be important, and found a peace and contentment in just being myself, and living day-to-day.'

Sue applied for a transfer at work and for a place on an evening counselling course, and in January 1993 she was offered them both. Later that year she also started a relationship with Roger. When her employer announced its merger with another company, she hoped she'd be made redundant, but when it became clear there weren't to be any redundancies, she set herself a target of September 1995 to have made a move by her own volition. As she made that decision everything came together: Roger found another post in the country and they decided to move there together; she sold her flat and started hypnotherapy training. 'Many people told me I was very brave to be doing this, but I knew this was their fears, not really mine. It just seemed like a big adventure for me.'

So she left with no *clear* plan other than her intentions, a feeling of rightness and self-belief. After a few months' rest she decided to approach some local computer training companies to offer her services, and one took her on to teach software skills to businesses. Initially the days were spasmodic, but then they offered her 12 days' work per month just as her money was beginning to run out. She also began to get hypnotherapy clients and was developing healing skills through a local group, and was offering them too. She had created her own portfolio career! As her confidence grew, she found more business and no longer felt she was masquerading but genuinely capable. 'One challenge I have had is lack of belief in my capabilities, but these have turned out to be unfounded, and I am thrilled at how I can do something new. It is very empowering. Also I get concerned sometimes if there doesn't seem enough work around, but there always has been. I've noticed how I always grow through the challenges.

'Looking back I can see why I did certain things, which I didn't fully understand at the time. I had to step forward in faith and trust, knowing that my intuition to leave the my old job was right, and that everything would turn out fine. I've never been good at setting goals, rather I prefer to eliminate what isn't right to leave space for the *right* to come in.'

But it is not just the freedom and fulfilment of having created her own career that Sue enjoys, but the essence of her work. She explained: 'I love helping people move forward in their life's journey, and although I teach *hard* skills I also love weaving in the *soft* skills of personal development. When I can help people overcome their limiting beliefs about learning new skills and what they are capable of, and especially help them bust their belief that they are stupid or can't learn, I am so fulfilled. I love helping people break through limits in my therapy and healing work too. I used to think that training and therapy were separate, but I have managed to combine them well now.

'My greatest joy is knowing that I can make a difference in other people's lives, and in terms of how I put together and deliver a session rather than being dictated to by an employer. I recently had a group of three lawyers who weren't expected to learn very easily. I thoroughly enjoyed helping them and I was thrilled when they thanked me for treating them as though they *weren't* stupid. They were like children with the magical "Wow!" and amazement of how much they could learn. I loved their excitement.'

Looking back, Sue is now doing what would have seemed unbelievable and even impossible to the old Sue of five years ago. 'I take one step at a time, and then look back and marvel at how far I've come.'

Michael's is another story of creative change. He initially wanted to resign from his job in drug prevention in Dublin because he wanted a break. He knew his heart wasn't in his existing work, but he didn't have clarity about what was next. He had ended up in a rut – he was told he was great at what he did but realized that it wasn't him anymore. As we talked I found that he had a really unhelpful belief: 'Do you believe you are a waster if you are not working hard?' I asked. (Waster was a word he had used himself several times.)

'Yes, I do. Although I am working 12 hours a day I am not enjoying it but feel like I'd be useless if I stopped.' He was being very hard and judgemental of himself. He'd actually been offered freelance work already, and dreamed of having a little more relaxed and freer way of working. He had the skills and opportunities to do that, but this voice in his head – his self judgement – prevented him changing. We discovered that much of this voice was the good old Protestant work ethic, also strong in parts of Catholic Ireland, and we discussed the idea that busting a gut was not God's will for him, but what many people believed to be God's will. He began to see ways forward.

Michael decided to give himself *permission to be* for a while and to take a break from work. I encouraged him to see that this was not a negative move, but a positive one to give himself time and space to be, to explore new creative possibilities and passions and decide what was true for him now. Its purpose was both a 'getting away from' the old and a 'moving towards' the new. He could afford to do this for a while financially so he resigned. He decided to muster the courage not to go back, and to seek a way forward. He is now creating a portfolio career, and is incredibly excited about his newly discovered freedom.

One of the changes most of us feel drawn to make is the call to live a more authentically creative life. To do so we need to understand more about creativity and the creative process. Let's examine that in Principle Ten – the inspiration to create.

Simple Ways to Implement Principle Nine

* Review three of the biggest changes in your life and recognize how you have grown through them.

* Take two small steps today to improve the quality of your working life.

* Write down three areas in which you feel trapped. Come up with three possible creative and original solutions to each one.

* Slow down and breathe deeply for two minutes every hour, and find the stillness at your centre as you go through change.

* Notice six things in work to be really grateful for – today, now, this moment.

* Design your ideal portfolio career.

Principle Ten

THE INSPIRATION TO CREATE

Creativity means either infusing our work with our own uniqueness or bringing ideas from the realms of our mind and imagination into physical reality. Creativity is natural to us and, as we remove the blocks we have erected to our naturalness, we will find ourselves becoming channels for creative ideas and energy, and becoming co-creators with life. Creative action is the way we turn inspiration into action.

OUR RELATIONSHIP TO CREATIVITY

The delusive idea that men merely toil and work for the sake of preserving their bodies and procuring for themselves bread, houses and clothes is degrading, and not to be encouraged. The true origin of man's activity and creativeness lies in his increasing impulse to embody outside of himself the divine and spiritual element within him.

FRIEDRICH FRÖBEL (1782–1852)
German educator and founder of Kindergarten

Creativity is at the heart of the work we were born to do and lies within each one of us right this moment. Nothing wonderful ever happened that wasn't first shaped by an idea in a creative mind. As we give ourselves fully to our work, we evolve and graduate and are given new assignments and new creative births. The next opportunities appear when we are able to let go of the old ones. Creativity is a way of saying, 'We are alive, we are here and expressing life.'

There are two forms of creativity. Firstly there is what we could call small 'c' creativity, which is about doing whatever we do with originality, in our way, putting our own gifts and talents and unique energy into our work – the report we are writing, the presentation we have to give, the way we manage our work. Creativity is the ability to act, not just react. This is work that is uniquely us, work that can be our art. The word authentic is derived from the Latin *authenticus*, meaning 'original' and 'written in the owner's hand'. This is what we all yearn for in our work – authenticity, something that is us through and through.

Then there is capital 'C' Creativity, concerned with our God-given ability to bring into existence something that doesn't currently exist, to see and create our own future. The Latin root of the word create is *creare*, meaning 'to bring into being'. It is in our nature to imagine, dream, create and shape our world, and when we do so in the spirit of love and compassion our creativity can literally bring heaven to earth. We are creators and creations.

In this way we can be said to reflect our creator's image. We can see everyday life as a miracle – we can look at a flower and see the beauty of its creation. We can become more conscious of the creative process running through nature as a whole, and bring the ideas in our own creative imaginations into reality. We can create the work we were born to do; indeed, committing to our creative energy is both *how* and *why* we evolve.

It is easy to believe that one of our creator's greatest pleasures is creation itself; there are thousands of species of plants, trees, fish, spiders, reptiles, flowers, insects, people, stars and galaxies – we live in a creative universe. There probably isn't a single one of us who hasn't at some time, even regularly, looked up at the heavens or at the latest pictures from the Hubble space telescope and felt awe at the size and beauty of creation and the mystery of everything. At one time or another we may all have wondered, 'Just where does it all come from; where and what is the source?'

The work we were born to do is concerned with making a transition from feeling like an observer of creation to recognizing that we are part of creation, not separate from but woven into it. The 12-century poet Rumi wrote: 'The intelligence that created 100 billion galaxies created me!' to which we might add: 'And still runs through me, every moment of every day.' Our brain alone is capable of processing 140,000 million bits of information every second.

Because intuitively we know that creativity is the most powerful force in the universe we can be both excited and frightened by it, knowing that in some senses it is bigger than we are. To surrender to it and let it flow through us requires something in us – some of our limits and self-concepts – to die.

EXERCISE

◆ What does creativity and being creative mean to you? Write down all the thoughts and words that come to you. It can mean many things to each of us, so it is important you get clear on what it means to you in particular. It is possible that you may develop your idea of creativity as you proceed through this principle, but it's helpful to have a starting point.

Many creative thoughts are just passing through our mind and we can't truly claim them for ourselves. They come to and through us, but not necessarily from us. After a particularly creative period of writing I described to friends that I was really in touch with my creativity, but that didn't feel like quite the right way of putting it. I then realized that creativity was more in touch with me, as I had made myself more available to it.

I often ask participants in workshops if they have ever looked at the jobs advertised in newspapers and thought that none of them appeal. Usually at least half the hands in the room are raised. This is because many of us don't want to take jobs that other people create but want to create our own work that fits with and expresses our heart's and our soul's purpose, which may or may not involve us in working for an employer. We may want to create, but most of us didn't learn much about our creative powers at school, so perhaps we feel we can't. Culturally creativity is often marginalized and seen as unimportant, irrelevant or even dangerous to our working lives, but what I am talking about is the everyday creativity that is available for each of us.

Creativity is something very natural to us; it is in our very being, but many of us lose faith in our own innate creativity along the way, unaware of the fact that once we commit to it, the life we always wanted to live can become the one we are living. We can gradually move creativity from the margins, or even from the wilderness, to the heart of our work.

OUR RESISTANCE TO CREATIVITY

Perhaps the biggest challenge is the core belief that we are not creative. Only a minority of people believe they are. A friend asked a group of 100 people how many of them could sing. A couple of hands went up, and he smiled and said, 'I don't mean can sing well, just sing at all,' and then a few more hands went up. We are not particularly educated to value and encourage creativity. We marginalize it and reward people for doing as they are told, not for being original and authentic; it may even seem as if there is an emnity between work and creativity. Yet so many us wish we were more creative, or have a sense we already are, but don't know how to get our heart and hands on it.

Let's start by exploring a few of our inner enemies around creativity – our beliefs about ourselves and creativity:

◆ I am not creative; only a special gifted few are.

◆ If I follow my creativity I will have to struggle, suffer or starve.

◆ I will lose control of my life, become bohemian and lonely.

◆ I may have a few good ideas, but not enough to sustain a career.

◆ Creativity must be fraught with insecurity, fear and anxiety.

◆ I'll look stupid because what I think is good no one else will.

◆ I'll feel things I don't want to feel.

◆ I'll discover things about myself that I will find horrible.

◆ I'll turn into a demon or an egomaniac.

◆ I'll be unemployable.

◆ My partner will leave me/I'll become promiscuous.

◆ I might get really successful and will lose control of my life.

◆ It is too late in my life; I'd have done it by now if I could.

◆ Creativity is a euphemism for doing more with less.

How many of these can you relate to? Write in your journal a few of your own personal core negative beliefs. Remember, though, that they are not facts and never have been; these are only true when we believe them. Once we discard our core negative beliefs, our creative energy will be waiting like a fresh spring for us to plunge into it again. Those beliefs only hide our awareness of and access to our creativity energy; they don't cancel out the energy itself.

We are all talented and gifted; that is not the issue. As Noel Coward said: 'Thousands of people have talent. I might as well congratulate you for having eyes in your head. The one and only thing that counts is: Do you have staying power?' The real question is whether we value and trust our creativity, and whether we will never give up on it.

CREATIVE CONFIDENCE

Love is an attempt to change a piece of a dream world into reality.

THEODOR REIK

Old ideas of confidence imply knowledge of all the answers beforehand, being in control and without doubt: there is little uncertainty. Creative confidence is not about being certain of the answers but about being certain that we will find and discover the answers ourselves. We can have a very clear idea of where we might be headed, but not of precisely how to get there. A good place to put our confidence is in the creative power that runs the whole universe, which will respond to and handle the details of our intentions and bring them to fruition.

As we grow in confidence, we may experience as many problems, but we will have the resources not to be flattened by them and to grow through them. We understand that inspiration is not a scarcity, but available to us all the time. We need simply to turn inwards and ask to be told what to say, do or be – this takes great trust, but seems to feel more and more natural as we do it more often.

COURAGE AND CREATIVITY

> Then the day came when the risk to remain tight in a bud was more painful than
> the risk to blossom.
>
> ANAÏS NIN

It can take courage and feel like a risk to follow a creative life, but it's more painful to live a diminished or uncreative life. Courage is the heart of our emotional body, giving us the emotional lifeblood that underlies all other life-affirming qualities. Courage oxygenates hope, vision, faith and trust, and allows us to act despite and in the face of fear, anxiety, doubt, conflict and even despair. Courage is willingness to act and perhaps be wrong, but most of all courage means the willingness to trust that, whatever appearances may indicate, the essence of life is really *for* us. Perhaps surprisingly, in the work we were born to do, we can grow just as much through what appear to be failures as we can through seeming successes. Our soul's purpose is to know, feel and experience itself; it doesn't care much for the circumstances.

All else in nature grows by instinct, not by choice. The acorn naturally becomes the oak, the kitten becomes the cat, the caterpillar becomes the chrysalis and then the butterfly without conscious choice. We grow physically without conscious effort, yet once we have reached physical maturity, we have the choice and ability to use the power of our will to grow emotionally, intellectually and spiritually. We can create our working lives by the dozens of decisions we make every day, and choose whether we make them with courage or from fear. Creativity requires a sensitivity to our own true nature, and a willingness to be in tune with it.

My experience of creativity is that offering our creative gifts to the world requires us to face our doubts, our inner cynics, the voices with which we say to ourselves, 'Who the heck do you think you are anyway? Who are you to think you have anything of value or use to say, write or share? It's all been done before, so why bother?' We can often use our cleverness and intellect to fuel our doubts. The most enlightened approach is simply to smile at them and know that they are tests to see if we take them seriously or not. But until then, we do tend to take them seriously, and we are learning to strengthen our will and trust in the voice for love that will support us all the way.

With my partner Helen and friend Ben Renshaw I ran the Joy Club for a couple of months. It was a place where 30 or 40 people came to be inspired, make friends and learn new ideas every week. Yet many evenings at ten past seven there would be three people there, and I would get scared thinking, 'Nobody wants what we are offering. Only five minutes to go but it won't work.' Then by 25 minutes past seven 30 people would have turned up. To stand in that empty space asking if people want what you are offering is a truly heroic act, dealing with fear of rejection or not being wanted. But when we have the courage to offer what is in our hearts, it will attract and nourish similar souls.

Another achievement that takes courage is allowing ourselves to feel satisfied! Do you ever feel that you should have done something better, or wonder why you didn't think of doing it a better way? These criticisms are ways we rob ourselves of simple but beautiful contentment. Because our ego's mantra is *more, better, best,* to learn to be satisfied with ourselves and what we do create is perhaps the greatest achievement of all. Ironically, the trappings of outer success can sometimes lead to stagnation as we might develop a sense of certainty that we know all the answers, so when this success is threatened we have no creative responses to enable us to move on.

Along the way to creating the work we were born to do, we may encounter the fear that if we give our all creatively then we'll have nothing left to give; our creative cupboard, as it were, will be empty. We need to remember that the substance from which all creativity flows is unlimited. Any experience of lack in creativity results from us having erected blocks, usually unconsciously, rather than creativity itself having dried up. To be creative, to live from our creativity and earn a living from it is the most exciting and rewarding of experiences we can have in work. Commit to giving yourself that joy and fulfilment.

CHOOSING CREATIVE SUCCESS OVER SELF-DEFEAT

At some point, we must make an active choice to relinquish the privileges of being self-defeating for the true joy of being successful. We often feel we can get more attention and support for trying (but not succeeding) than we do for being truly creatively successful. It's our choice. As we commit to being truly functional and creative, we can begin to feel very scared and threatened. We may start to sabotage or do a U-turn. Here are a few ideas about what we gain by *not* being creatively successful:

◆ We don't risk rejection, criticism or need to face the unknown.

◆ We get to stay in charge of our life, we are in control.

◆ We can stay superior and can criticize others.

◆ We don't have to learn to handle our lives more effectively.

◆ We don't have to deal with jealousy or envy.

◆ We avoid vulnerability, doubt or fear.

You may remember from Principle Six that a positive purpose involves our having the courage to face all our doubts and fears so that we may be free of them. But first we have to admit that they are there! So in a very real way the decision to live creatively can be healing because it will stimulate places in us that are tender and need attention and love. We can defend against being vulnerable or we can create, but not both.

An example of this lies in the experience of my friend Tom who works in a project at St Martin's in the Fields Church in London, which offers art courses to homeless people. The results are incredible – men and woman who are hungry and unwashed create amazing art, poetry and writing. Some of them live for their art; it gives their life meaning and purpose. Our creativity is often found as a result of going back to old places of hurt, pain, even anger and rage, and transforming that energy, turning our shit into fertilizer.

Creativity often springs from our deepest wounds, from where we ourselves stumbled. We gradually raise ourselves up and in doing so we can help others with authority. Didier Danthois is wonderful example of this: he is an inspiring performer and teacher of sacred clowning, helping people re-find their innocence and playfulness. Living in London and working throughout Europe, he helps to take clowning into hospitals and schools. As a child in France he was abused terribly by a teacher at school, and felt as if he lost his innocence. He uses the compassion of his own healing to help, touch and inspire others. Creativity is our love in action.

It is vital for us to understand that resistance is all part of the creative process; our creativity can still spring from those places and we can choose not to let them block our creativity. Don't catch yourself in the trap that you are too damaged to be creative. If you need help to deal with your resistance as you go, get it. Don't deny how you feel, simply attend to your feelings. Creating is likely to show us our broken and unhealed places as part of the creative process, and as we commit to reclaiming our creativity, we become stronger and more confident, blessed with more ideas and possibilities, new avenues and vistas.

CREATIVITY AND SEXUAL ENERGY

Work is a vocation: we are called to it. But we are also loved by it. It can excite us, comfort us, and make us feel fulfilled, just as a lover can. Soul and the erotic are always together. If our work doesn't have an erotic tone to it, then it probably lacks soul as well.

THOMAS MOORE

Author of *Care of the Soul*

The primal creative energy is, of course, sexual energy. We as beings are created through sexual energy, and many mystics say that this sexual energy pervades, infuses and directs the whole of creation. A strong indicator of where our creativity lies is in what gives us the experiences of attraction, alertness, arousal, enthusiasm, interest, curiosity, awakening, inspiration, excitement and passion. These are expressions and manifestations of creative energy.

While our culture may be less inhibited about depicting sex in the media, there is much difference between the appearance of sexuality and the essence of sexuality and sensuality. We tend to value the appearance, not the spirit, yet creativity is about nurturing the essence of sexuality, enjoying it, putting our attention on it and enlivening it. We know that when our ego gets hold of our sexuality it can hijack it into abuse and power games, but when we give our sensuality to our heart and spirit it becomes one of the most beautiful gifts available to us. It is restored to integrity and can become a blessing.

There may be parallels between any discomfort we may have around our sexuality and any judgements we have around our creativity. Both call to us to relinquish some control and open ourselves to be penetrated by an energy greater than ourselves. Yet, as with all emotions, the problem is not sexuality itself, but the way we have been taught to deny it and use it lovelessly. We may also feel inhibited by teachings that there is a split between sexuality and spirituality, which is not not true. True sexuality is spiritual, and is concerned with loving and closing the emotional distance between people, breaking down barriers and reminding each other of our true nature. We often look at what someone created and say, 'Oh, yes' because it articulates and expresses something we know to be true for us too.

◆ Note your responses, positive and negative, to the following statement: 'The creator's will for me is that I be a co-creator, and that my sensuality, aliveness and attraction are gifts to be shared.'

The writer and speaker M Scott Peck talks about the great link between a spiritual awakening and a sexual awakening. His belief is that sexual deadness and spiritual deadness go together. Similarly, he knows that spiritual awakening and sexual/creative awakening go together. He describes the experience of a priest friend who has had people explain to him that they have had some kind of spiritual awakening. His measure of how real this may be is whether the person has a sexual renaissance within the next two weeks, either within their existing relationship or by starting a new one. Awakening of any kind is the awareness of, and penetration by, spirit.

◆ Notice how you feel about strong attractions you have. How comfortable are you with strong attractions, to people, work or ideas? Are you scared away from or drawn towards what you are attracted by. Also be aware that what we are most afraid of, we are also most attracted to. Fear is also a form of attraction.

PUTTING CREATIVITY CENTRE STAGE IN OUR LIVES

> When an archer is shooting for nothing he has all his skills.
> If he shoots for a brass buckle, he is already nervous. …
> The prize divides him.
> He cares.
> He thinks more of winning than shooting – and the need to win
> Drains him of power.
>
> CHUANG TZU

I was lying on a sun lounger in Lanzarote reading Julia Cameron's book, *The Artist's Way*, when I had one of those moments of realization: 'I am an artist!' I had never thought of myself as one before, but in her wonderful book she talked about the idea of the shadow artist, someone who is in the creative area they wanted to be involved with, but hasn't yet mustered the courage to commit fully to their own creativity. We may love film and market videos, or love literature and work in a book shop, when all the while what we truly want to do is make or produce films or write books.

It hit me – for many years I had organized and marketed talks and workshops for other people, but had done my own workshops almost as a tertiary activity. The realization was that I wanted to commit to talking, presenting, broadcasting, writing and developing my own services full-time. I wanted to put myself in the limelight, not other people. I wanted to commit to developing, enjoying and sharing my own creativity. It was as if my mind became unified and I took a huge leap forward in my career. I was both scared and excited.

We may have the experience of wanting to put creativity centre stage in our life, but fear that this will somehow change our enjoyment of what we have loved or, as Chuang Tzu says, our aim will be less straight because money is involved. We may believe that we will have to prostitute creativity, what we love and enjoy, for money. We need to remember, money has no power other than the power we give it. Pieces of paper, metal and plastic only have the power we endow them with. When we are aiming to earn a living from our creativity, we obviously have more invested and develop a stronger attachment to the financial outcome. The more we are attached, the more our aim may be affected.

We need to remember that when we put our trust in creativity, we are also putting it in the power that created and runs everything that is, was and will be. Do you wake up in the morning and say, 'Oh my God, has life forgotten to bring the sun up?' Do you suddenly think after a good meal, 'Oh no, I have forgotten how to digest my food?' Of course not – we trust the intelligence of life to run those things for us without us even having to consider it. Yet when it is our career we believe we have to do it all by ourselves, or it won't get done at all. As we commit to a creative life and developing our own creative skills for our joy and the benefit of all, we are aligning ourselves with the creative intelligence behind all things. We only struggle when we try to separate ourselves from it. Holding ourselves back from the creative spirit within all of us is likewise a kind of self-deprivation.

EXERCISE

◆ Why do you think life wouldn't support you in following your creative purpose?

Your answer to this question will reveal some of your unhelpful beliefs about work, creativity and your purpose.

We are all artists of one fashion or another; each of us contains a naturally creative being, and each of us may have a different medium for our creativity and a different way of expressing it. It may be singing, writing, dancing, laughing, storytelling, reading, drawing, painting, solving problems, listening, being a parent, being a lover, gardening, homemaking or flower arranging. There is an unlimited number of ways to be creative.

EXERCISE

◆ Take some time to be still, and ask yourself the question, 'If I were to put creativity, my creative ideas and my creative power centre stage in my life, what might that look like?' Note the ideas and thoughts that come to you.

INNER VISION AND IMAGINATION

> The key to life is imagination. If you don't have that, no matter what you have, it's meaningless. If you do have imagination … you can make a feast of straw.
>
> JANE STANTON HITCHCOCK

No one can stop us being creative, but we may still have to tread the path of reclaiming our natural creative power and abilities. The real blocks are our own doubts, negative beliefs, fears and our inner critic. When I eventually found the courage to quit my old job, I told myself, 'Now I am free to be creative; no one can stop me.' What I discovered was that I wasn't free to be creative, because I had sold out on and not developed my own creative skills. I had left what I didn't want, but hadn't yet created what I did want; indeed I wasn't even all that clear about what I did want.

Our imagination, the mind's eye, is the starting point of all our creative impulses and ideas, although it may have some hard graft and sweat before their fulfilment. Yet we need to regain our imagination so that we can choose our direction and so that the hard work has meaning. Reclaiming our creativity is about re-establishing the connection with the child within us, where the source of much of our creative energy is.

◆ What creative endeavours did you most enjoy as a child at the ages of 7, 12 or 15? Did you enjoy singing, art, pottery, crafts, music, drawing, acting, dancing, writing, flower arranging? List all the things you have creatively enjoyed during your life. How many are you actively involved in now?

As a child our imagination knew few boundaries. We could transport ourselves to different times and places, we could find 101 uses for a cardboard box, we created imaginary friends and worlds. Our imagination was our magic carpet. Without our moving a muscle it would to take us wherever we wanted to go and back again.

Without consequences, we could do and be whoever and whatever we wanted. We had the power to create our own imaginary world and no one would stop us or even question us. Ask children at the age of eight whether they think they could do anything with their lives, and 96 per cent respond positively, but by the age of eighteen this has reduced to 4 per cent. We tend to lose rather than broaden our sense of possibility as we grow up. The chances are that because of work and family pressures you may be doing less creatively now than you have done in the past. But it is vital to be involved in creative activities somewhere in our lives, for the sheer pleasure and joy of being creative if nothing else.

Even as adults our imaginations never stop sending us powerful messages about our dreams and purpose and changes that we'd love to make in our life. By adulthood we may have learned to value facts and information over fantasies, data over dreams. We may have become so immersed in work that we have forgotten how to imagine it being any different. But, as Einstein said: 'Imagination is more important than knowledge.' In order for us to make an outer change in our working life we will need to forge our ideas in the fire of our imagination. No amount of skilful invention can replace this essential element because the world of reality has its limits, but the world of imagination is boundless.

Vision is the capacity to see into the boundless, beyond the limits of our conditioning, to what could be. A visionary is one who goes into the darkness and turns on a light, who shines bright and shows the way home. True vision is not of the eyes of the body, but of the eyes of the mind. That power is still within us at every age of our lives; we all have the capacity to be visionaries, and imagine a different future for our working lives. In vision we can see life with the scarcity removed, and true creativity is concerned with what *could* be, and not just what has been. Vision is our willingness and ability to see the present and the future, not as the same as the past or the future, but as being able to be qualitatively different. As far we know, we are the only creatures able to think about, imagine, influence and create our future. What an awesome power we have – to see in our minds and then create that vision in physical reality! Visionaries show the way home, and one person living the vision in their hearts warms the fire in all our hearts.

A story from the medieval Christian tradition illustrates vision and intention: A traveller came to a work site and saw two men carrying large blocks of stone, one looking bored and frustrated, the other looking happy and fulfilled. He asked the first one, 'What are you doing?', and his response was, 'Moving stones.' When he asked the other one the same question, he responded, 'Building a cathedral.'

EXERCISE

◆ What is the boldest vision you have ever had for your life? Write it down even if it feels like a mad or arrogant fantasy.

◆ Write down your positive and negative responses to the following *true* statement:

I, [insert your name], am a gifted, talented and creative individual, and have access to the creative energy that has been available to every person that ever walked this planet. It's nothing special; we all are, by right of the way we've been created. I can find, follow and discover ways of being creative and support myself financially from my creative impulses and creative ideas.

ASPIRATION AND VISION

Without this playing with fantasy no creative work has ever yet come to birth. The debt we owe to the play of the imagination is incalculable.

CARL JUNG

Several years ago I was listening to DJ Steve Wright's afternoon show on Radio 1. He was interviewing Sir John Harvey Jones, ex-Chairman of ICI. Half jokingly, Steve asked what Sir John thought was the biggest problem with British management today. I loved the answer: 'Poverty of aspiration ... We don't aim high enough.' There is a Bible quote that says: 'Without vision, people perish.' Develop a vision for yourself and, if appropriate, your colleagues. The key is to make it something that touches the heart and soul, something that truly motivates you, so that you are willing to face the obstacles that may appear.

Sometimes the bigger the vision, the more beautiful it is, the more important it is, the greater the resistance to it. The resistance may be fear, uncertainty or doubt, and we learn to use resistance as a sign, and can tell ourselves, 'If I am resisting something this much, there must be something good here, a new birth, that my ego wants to keep me away from.' Struggle is not itself valuable, although there is a widely held belief that creativity must involve struggle, and we have to suffer for our art and creativity. This is a myth. Creativity demands no sacrifice; we don't have to give up anything, other than control, to be creative. The struggling artist is not a compulsory role.

One of the most beautiful stories of following a dream is that of the character in Paulo Coelho's book *The Alchemist*, who sets off in pursuit of his dream. The story follows his triumphs and apparent failures, joys and sorrows, until he finally makes his dream come true. Paulo's own life was a mirror of his character. He always dreamed of being an author, wrote *The Alchemist*, and eventually managed to have it published in his home country of Brazil. After a year or so it had sold only a few hundred copies, so the publishers, in polite 'publisher-speak', told him, 'We are obviously not the right publisher for your book,' which can be a euphemism for, 'It is not a very good book.'

His dream was in tatters, it seemed. Yet he didn't give up, and eventually a new publisher bought it. It has now sold over 4 million copies throughout the world, and Paulo has had success with many other novels. Paulo is a humble man, simply grateful for his success and the possibility of making a living doing what he loves. The character in his book summed up his message: 'When you want something, all the universe conspires to help you achieve it.' But the path may not *seem* smooth, and a few of our rough edges may need to be knocked off first.

When we have a vision we are working towards we experience joys and challenges, but somehow the challenges have more meaning and purpose to them and become ways to learn and grow. Ultimately the joy of vision is that there are no losers: true vision has no cost, it can only bless. We may have forgotten how to cherish our visions and our dreams, but they are the children of our soul; the blueprints of our ultimate achievements.

EXERCISE

◆ What can/do you imagine yourself doing or being in work?

◆ What do you do to realize this dream? What regular action do you take?

◆ What dreams have you had over the years, since childhood, that you have abandoned or forgotten?

◆ What do you aspire to?

TRUSTING AGAIN IN THE BEAUTY OF OUR DREAMS AND IDEAS

I am certain of nothing but the holiness of the heart's affection and the truth of Imagination.

JOHN KEATS (1795–1821)
English poet

Electricity, art, music, language, software, electronic mail, none of it existed once, until the possibility – the idea – existed in someone's imagination and was brought into physical existence. Nothing exists that wasn't once an idea, which William Blake echoed when he wrote: 'Everything starts in the imagination.' Everything in the natural and human world starts as a seed, and ideas and visions are seeds of potentially great things. I have often used the image of the acorn, a seed, and how when it sprouts into a sapling, it needs protecting from damage. As it grows stronger, it needs less protection, gradually becoming more self-sufficient. In time it becomes a mighty oak, beautiful, strong and offering life and protection to other animals, plants and humans. So too with our ideas and dreams. The chick is hatched naturally from the egg, not smashed from it. In time we can bring into being amazing and beautiful dreams when we commit to creating them and are determined to deal with all obstacles, inner and outer, that come our way. Not everything will bear fruit, but we may only need one good idea that we commit to putting our heart into.

We can do well to regain our sense of awe at creative potential. Hold an acorn in your hand, and wonder at where the oak tree is, look at a tomato seed and try to find the vine of tomatoes. Where is this potential? The answer is *nowhere* – it doesn't exist in time and space as such. Science can tell us how cells replicate and how information is stored in DNA, but it can't tell us who created the DNA and who put the information in the DNA. Even scientists have a sense of awe and mystery, as the source is beyond this world of time and space.

In our age of wanting everything either fast or instantly we may forget that our dreams take time to come to fruition. In the spiritual realm, everything exists now and it has been said that time is God's way of preventing everything happening at once. We have become so trained to expect things instantly that if we can't have them straight away we don't bother, which is a confusion that the ego creates around now. External pressures often keep our attention on too many short-term goals and we spend our whole life firefighting, throwing buckets of water on our problems but never feeling able to take a longer term view and figuring out how to make sure the fires don't start. More organizations have to report to shareholders monthly or quarterly, let alone yearly; governments are always looking to the next election. All these pressures discourage and damage true creativity.

Over and over again people drop creative ideas that don't come to immediate fruition, not realizing that if they stay focused on their goal it will eventually become real. In Greek there is a word *chronos*, meaning linear time, and a word *kyros*, meaning at the right time. It does require determination yet when we set our sights on our creative vision based on beauty, love, service and contribution, all the forces of life can get behind it. When we hold the vision constantly in our mind's eye and follow our purpose, we become less distracted, like a missile that won't stop until it hits home. Our creative inspiration blesses others and reminds them of the beauty that is in their hearts and inspires them too. I love the story concerning invitations for tender to manage a beautiful natural park; they received many proposals, mostly with five- and ten-year plans. Another proposal included a 200-year plan! That is true vision, planning not just for our own needs, but those of our children and future generations that aren't even born yet. That is real love too.

We may need to lengthen our timescales, but delays are not denials. Committing to the work we were born to do is a project that takes as long as it takes. It can be quick, or may take six or 12 months, or several years to come to fruition. Nelson Mandela spent 26 years in prison before he saw his dream come true, but we probably won't have to wait that long, because our only prison is our own thinking.

Setting Your Heart, Valuing Yourself

Jackie was bored with the company where she was working as a graphic designer. After attending a talk of mine, she decided to examine who would she like to work for and what she would like to be contributing to a new employer. She sat down and identified her ideal job and its attributes on paper, and then in her imagination. She shortlisted six organizations she would love to work for, and made the shift to believing that she had a lot to offer. She wrote to all six with her profile; within two weeks she had three interviews, and within a month she had two job offers. She took the one that felt best, not paid best, and that allowed her to make the most valuable contribution.

We can learn to value our dreams at all stages of their evolution and growth – we don't throw babies away because they don't come out fully formed and fully educated. We can learn to love the formation, growth and evolution of our creative endeavours too. Ideas and beginnings are beautiful too.

CREATIVITY PRINCIPLES AND IDEAS

Here are some key principles and ideas to help you redefine the concept of creativity in your life.

Creativity Principles

◆ Substance or essence is the natural order, the building block of life and infusing all life; creativity is consciously working with this substance.

◆ This creative energy is ever present and ever available to all of us.

◆ The purpose of our ego is to deny or pervert this; all blocks to creativity are acts of self-will, however unconscious we are of this.

◆ We are both creations and creators; all our dreams and visions have a divine source and as we lovingly extend our creativity we know our own divinity.

◆ Creativity is a gift from our creator to us and what we create is our gift back.

◆ As we open ourselves up to creative energy we open ourselves to our creator.

◆ As we open we may well experience resistance as gentle but powerful changes take place within us; we begin to be transformed, and it is safe to do so; only resistance causes pain.

◆ We don't even need to believe in a creator; we simply need to commit to the process and watch it unfold.

Creative Idea 1: Discover and Follow Creative Passion

You can wait, delay, paralyse yourself, or reduce your creativity almost to nothing.
But you cannot abolish it.

A Course in Miracles

Simply get excited, inspired, passionate, enthusiastic, moved and creative in some area of your life. We don't get creative just by reading about it or watching it: we need to throw ourselves into it somehow. The first step is to connect with that creative energy. Do something new – with a friend or partner if that works. Take up a salsa class, a creative writing class, flower arranging, a martial art, film-making, musical appreciation, or whatever. Simply decide and resolve to find what makes you feel creatively alive.

A producer I met when giving a radio interview explained that she had joined the local amateur dramatics group and found that the creative self-confidence she discovered through that really helped her in her work too. Another person, Chantelle, had to give up her job when she was pregnant, and partly out of boredom started drawing and discovered that she was actually very good. Four years later she has had three children's books published simply because she tried something new. We have no idea of what talents and gifts each of us has just sitting underneath the surface, so get in the habit of trying out new skills and creative endeavours. Be willing to discover what you could do. You are already sitting on your talent and gifts – go explore for them, and determine not to give up looking for them!

◆ Try something new regularly.

Creative Idea 2: Be Authentic and Creative Now

Ask yourself, in whatever work situation you are now, 'How can I be, and would I like to be, more creative and self-expressive?' Also ask. 'If I were being fully creative right now, what would that look like?'

Unique Gifts

Becky works on a flower stall within St James's where I have my office and picks and wraps flowers. She does it so beautifully, in a way that no one has ever been able to put a finger on. The recipient of each bunch of flowers I have bought there has said how beautiful the appearance of the flowers was. Somehow Becky has a way of picking, arranging and wrapping flowers that is unique, creative and wonderful.

Often we stop ourselves being more creative by saying that *when* we get the new job, are self-employed, have more money, a new boss or a new team, *then* we'll be more creative. These are just excuses, covering some fear or another or a lack of motivation. Creativity is not limited by circumstances, even harsh circumstances. Imagine living in the Arctic and thinking to yourself, 'All we have is this snow, ice, a few fish we have to saw through the ice to catch, and maybe a few plants a few weeks a year. Can't do anything with that.' Creativity is often evoked and inspired by harsh circumstances. The Eskimos have a culture rich in art, spirituality and crafts, finding the creativity within their own souls and imagination, then using what is available from the environment for that creative expression. We've all seen incredibly wealthy and uncreative people and organizations driven by the belief that throwing money and resources at any problem will solve it. We know that doesn't work: creative solutions – new ways of thinking – are what are needed.

EXERCISE

◆ Take a creative risk every day. Put more of *you*, your originality, your love, fun, humour, whackiness, heart or care into whatever you do. Do, or suggest doing, a few of the things that you've always dreamed of at work. Build up your creative muscle.

Creative Idea 3: Commit to Creativity

Decide what you will make a creative commitment to, not just in the early stages of your honeymoon and excitement about your own creativity but also when the initial glow has worn off. Decide what you will stick with during the power struggles, the dead times when you feel like you've lost it, no one cares and you wonder if even you care. Make a commitment to hang in no matter how exciting, challenging, scared or successful you get, and even when you want to give up and sabotage yourself.

FINDING A DIRECTION FOR OUR CREATIVITY

An invasion of armies can be resisted, but not an idea whose time has come.

VICTOR MARIE HUGO (1802–1885)
French poet, novelist and playwright

We may want to know what we are supposed to be doing with our lives or how to defend ourselves against the future, but there is no future as such and nothing that we are supposed to be doing. The future is not there waiting for us. There are no external guarantees. Our determination, our love, our spirit, our heart are the guarantee. If we don't live by, and are true to, our own imagination, our life is determined by other people's choices.

GET FASCINATED!

The imagination is where all invention is born, and it needs to be unleashed with sensuality and abandon. By doing this you will create the necessary passion to set your dream in motion.

SONIA CHOQUETTE
Author of *Your Heart's Desire*

We often underestimate the power of our own minds. When we picture something in our mind it has great power. Perhaps only 5 per cent of our mind is consciously available to us and up to 95 per cent of our mind is unconscious. Many of the keys to our motivation lie in the unconscious, which doesn't know the difference between something that we vividly imagine and something we actually experience. When we see a film, we can feel scared, excited, happy, inspired, angry, joyful by what is in truth simply a piece of plastic running over a light bulb! We know that and yet we react as if it were real. That is the power of the unconscious. These days the power of visualization is being used to reduce and heal cancers and other illnesses, to relax and build the immune system and to create success in athletics and business. Through visualization we can begin to project our dreams on to the universe.

The universe is one big creative dream-manifesting machine. The source, the unmanifest, is infinite, a field of all and unlimited possibilities. We come along and our mind is plugged into the big mind. We decide the story of our life through the pictures and the ideas we keep making in our thoughts and our mind. Like magicians we create the mental, emotional and subsequently physical reality of our life. It is said that we create our own reality, which is partly true. We didn't create love, peace, wholeness, happiness and truth, the essence of creative power; that was done for us by the creator. We *do* create our horror stories and dramas. As Jesus said: 'As we think, so we become.'

The major tool we use – consciously or unconsciously – to create the story and daily experience of our life is that which we are fascinated by and give most attention to, spending our time thinking and fantasizing about and worshipping. As we saw in Principle One, through our attention on these objects or ideas we create more of them. What we are fascinated by is given more power.

It is as if our attention has a cable attached to the universal power supply; wherever ever our attention goes, that power is directed according to certain laws or principles. This power supply is non-judgemental and has only one purpose – to go where *we* direct it, through the application of these principles and by strengthening *our* thoughts. Stuart Wilde likens it to a cosmic conveyor belt; we put in our order – our fascination – and in time we get a kind of cosmic DHL delivery service. It matters not whether we are fascinated by dreams of horror, fear, lack, pain, drama and death or by beauty, joy, peace, abundance, unfolding love and limitless joy. The life force is non-judgemental and delivers our hearts' desire or horror.

Fascination and attention are magnets with only one purpose – to attract. A magnet will attract rust, filings and old cans, or coins, objects of beauty and useful tools. The wise people throughout history have always known this, and taught us only to place our thoughts and attention on what we want. This is how we manifest and create, and we all have this power. Most of us have been unaware of how it has worked and unwittingly lived out our bad dreams.

Once we understand the process, we realize that we are the writer, director, star, projectionist and audience in this production called *Our Life*. If your life was played on a cinema screen, what kind of production would it be? A love story, comedy, tragedy or thriller? How long would you stay to watch? Would you recommend it to friends?

One question we can all answer is 'What shall we be fascinated by?' Do we want to change the object of our fascination, or are we happy with how we are now? Literally, the direction and quality of our life is determined by the quality and direction of our attention. By deciding to be fascinated by what we have, love and enjoy now, by what we are grateful for, by what we are touched, inspired and moved by, we will create happiness in our work and love.

I decided to become fascinated by the question, 'What creates happiness and true fulfilment in work?' I began to ask people I met what they most enjoyed about their work, what they would love to do if they were truly free of other financial or family pressures. I would seek out books on the subject, which in Britain was not easy, I have to say. On a trip to Hawaii I went into a Borders book store on Kauai and within 30 minutes was weighed down with new and exciting titles. I felt like a kid in a toy shop, suddenly hitting a vein of gold. I made several more visits there during the trip, and had to buy another suitcase just to bring back my new book collection!

I discovered networks of business people dedicated to bringing spirit into work, conferences around the world, workshops, tapes and newsletters. By reading and researching I discovered hundreds of beautiful quotations on work from different traditions throughout the world and throughout history. By focusing on what I wanted and was fascinated by, I made huge discoveries, and in the process my own creativity, confidence and inspiration were fuelled. The quality of my own work – my talks, workshops, broadcasts and writing – increased greatly.

We don't reap a harvest of positivity by sowing seeds of negativity, just as apple seeds don't produce oranges. What we pay attention to, we start to become.

EXERCISE

◆ Decide what you want to become fascinated by. Decide what you would like to become a student of or an expert on. Start immersing yourself in that area and start an inner and outer discovery process. Become a student of what you want.

Becoming a Sand Artist – and the Lessons of Attachment

I love the example of Buddhist artists who make mandalas, beautiful pictures, out of sand on the ground. They take many days of effort, talent, concentration, skill and hard work to complete them, perhaps for an exhibition, and when it is over they simply brush them away and let the sand be taken on the wind or in the rubbish. They let go of attachment to their creation. The important point is that while they are making the mandala they give themselves to it totally. They are fully present, despite knowing it will not last. We have probably all asked ourselves at some point, 'Well, what is the point? If it won't last, why bother?' The answer is simply, 'To express beauty'. We are, at heart, beauty ourselves.

At the end of a retreat I ran, a lovely man gave us the mandala example as his philosophy of life – unattachment. Something didn't sit right with me, and it wasn't until several days afterwards I realized why not. He was not unattached, but distant and withdrawn. Of all the people on the weekend he had probably contributed and given least, risked least and had been quite cynical. He may have guarded himself, but he didn't seem happy. He tried to stay safe but by not risking his heart, by withholding, he only succeeded in staying lonely.

CREATING OUR OWN WORK

Never give up on what you really want to do. The person with big dreams is more powerful than one with all the facts.

H JACKSON BROWN

The most exciting creative act is to bring the work we were born to do into being – to take an idea from the realm of thought and imagination into the realm of making it truly happen in the physical world. One of my greatest joys in my work is having ideas for a talk or workshop, offering them, and then having a roomful of people turn up, because I had the idea to offer and run it. My next greatest joy is actually giving the talk or workshop, which I love, and then having people tell me that they found it useful and were inspired. And then to get paid for it – well, that's another joy! I had the dim vision that I wanted to do inspiring work for most of my life, but it took me until I was 30 to actually decide to listen and follow and realize the creative power that resides in each and every one of us, rather than override my heart.

Below is a brief action strategy for creating your own work:

◆ Have a vision in your mind's eye – something that excites, inspires you, touches your heart and something that you know will help other people.

◆ Be clear about the essence, not the form, of the vision – what qualities do you want to give and share? Keep your inner and outer attention on this essence.

◆ Be willing to face and step through all your doubts, fears, and questions about self-worth, and to embrace your true divine nature. Be willing to face any old hurts, and keep going, however hard it may seem to get. Know that grace and love are on your side.

◆ Live the paradox of wanting to create your vision, and at the same time let go as much as possible of your emotional attachment to the outcome. Tell yourself, 'This or something better.'

◆ Grow in your awareness that life is for you and that when you commit to intentions based on love life orchestrates opportunities for their fulfilment.

◆ Develop the awareness that you are in co-partnership with the creative power in head office.

There is no path – we create it once we set out to walk it. It cannot be mapped out in advance, but will naturally unfold as we commit to living by our values and our principles. Then we move from a job to an adventure.

We can make a mistake in linking creativity and the commercialization of our creativity too soon. If we ask ourselves as soon as we get excited about something, 'But how on earth can I make a living out of this?' or we tell ourselves, 'But I can't see a way that I could make a living out of this' we put too much pressure on our fledgling creativity. It takes discipline and skill to reap material rewards from the form of the work we were born to do. Before we can start we may need to have completed the first stages of our inner awakening, adapting our own consciousness and the consciousness of those around us – which has its own subtle yet profound benefits.

THE CREATION OF OUR UNIVERSAL CONSCIOUSNESS

The most exciting area of study over the next decades will be the exploration and understanding of human consciousness – the exploration of 'inner' space. We seem to have been through three separate eras of belief about the nature of consciousness:

Era 1

The 'truth' taught in all universities in the Middle Ages was that everything – people, animals, buildings – had souls and nothing was inanimate. The soul was believed to hold the potential for, and ultimately determined the physical forms of, everything. Indeed the word *animal* comes from the Greek word *animus*, meaning 'soul'. Spirituality continues to contain elements of these beliefs, having always taught that consciousness is a function of the soul, not just of the brain.

Era 2

Within the last 200 years we have developed the view that we don't have consciousness. According to conventional science, thought is merely the random effect of chemicals reacting in the brain. The mind and the brain are one and the same thing. The idea that the mind could exist beyond the brain doesn't even exist. Science, since Descartes, views all of the universe as a big machine, and our brain as a very clever computer. He drained the soul from everything but the brain, so science hasn't really believed that there is anything to study in the field of consciousness.

Era 3

Consciousness definitely exists and is not merely confined to our own brain or body. On the face of it there has been a split between science and spirituality for 200 years, but quantum physics is changing this by showing us that we actually live in a universe that is alive, conscious and evolving, not just full of inanimate objects. Modern science is showing us that intelligence and consciousness exist throughout our body, that our organs think, each cell thinks, that our whole body is an intelligent system, constantly communicating between cells and organs to regenerate itself, heal and maintain optimum wellness. Our whole body is beautifully conscious.

Vast numbers of experiments have demonstrated that consciousness even exists outside the limits of our body and beyond the limits of time itself. Thousands of experiments on prayer, healing, Reiki, ESP, remote viewing, meditation and positive thinking demonstrate that we are able to influence our physical environment with our thoughts. Isn't that an amazing idea? Just as a single drop of water has all the characteristics of the ocean, so our divine essence has all the characteristics of the whole ocean of divinity.

An even more mind-boggling idea is that creative consciousness exists everywhere; our consciousness is not even in our body, because ultimately consciousness is beyond time and space. The way we tune in to this consciousness is through our brain, the transformer of universal thought into individual thought. Just as a radio picks up signals that are throughout the ether and transforms them into music and words in our home, office or car, our brain captures our thinking and our ideas and allows us to execute them through our body. We are used to this idea in radio – we don't listen to Simply Red and expect to find the singer Mick Hucknell inside the radio. The radio waves can extend for hundreds of miles, and we can tune into them anywhere the waves extend to. What if the 'I', the choice-maker who we truly are, is elsewhere, not in space and time, not actually in our body at all, like the radio wave, and we just shrink ourselves and reside in this body for a lifetime, even if it is not our true home. We are a field of intelligence, both local and non-local, and we can eavesdrop on the Universal Mind through silence, prayer and meditation.

CREATIVITY, EVOLUTION AND THE MIND
BEYOND THE BRAIN

The 100th monkey syndrome describes one monkey on a tropical island who learned to wash his sweet potato before eating it. After a while other monkeys copied him or her, and then it was discovered that other totally unconnected monkeys had started washing their potatoes, even on other islands. There wasn't a monkey potato-washing school, so how did they learn?

The theory put forward by Rupert Sheldrake, a biologist and mystic scientist, is the idea that each species in nature has a collective memory that he calls *morphic resonance*. This idea would account for personal and collective evolution, such as the monkey evolution. For example, in the last 50 years general IQ has increased by 3 per cent every decade. The IQ tests are just as difficult as they ever were, but people are finding them easier to do, perhaps as a result of the memory of the millions of people who have already done them. This idea is compatible with Carl Jung's idea of a collective unconscious, whereby ideas pop into many people's minds at similar times. The most exciting realization is that we are not alone in our own parcel of skin and bone. Through our own mind we are connected to the universal mind, the collective consciousness of life.

Each of us moves in the direction of joy in our work, and thanks to the millions who have already followed their joy we make it easier for each other and everyone who comes after. At a deep level, all our minds are joined, and as we are healed we are not healed alone, so as we all move towards personal wholeness we make it easier for each other. Our individual healing and evolution are not selfish acts, but ones of genuine help to everyone. We are blazing a trail for others to follow.

The more we get in touch and in tune with our creative ideas and impulses, the more we come to realize that they are truly limitless. Out of the human mind comes such unlimited creativity. We can bring characters, events and ideas to life through stories, films and songs that then go on to enter deeply into the minds of millions of people. There is literally no end to these possibilities – they are in abundance, so let's now turn our attention to how we can begin to live more in and from this abundance.

Simple Ways to Implement Principle Ten

✳ Take a creative risk today in work. Be original, or whacky, or set a creative idea in motion.

✳ Take or give a "wellness day" – take a day away from work being well and happy, so as to avoid a future illness. Refresh and recreate yourself.

✳ Listen to an inspiring tape on the way to work and notice how your day is different.

✳ Be creatively authentic today – do something your way.

✳ Find a form of creative expression that is new and exciting to you, and pursue it.

✳ Do something really beautifully.

✳ Ask for creative inspiration in your sanctuary time.

Principle Eleven

ABUNDANCE AND INNER RICHES

Abundance is our natural state, a consciousness where we are open to receiving and sharing the gifts of spirit, but which most of us have blocked through guilt and feelings of unworthiness. As we reclaim our own sense of self-worth and choose to put ourselves back in the flow of giving and receiving, we will release thoughts of lack and reclaim our abundance.

THE EXPERIENCE OF ABUNDANCE

No miracles are required. It is the way you have been created. You are a rich and creative spiritual being. You can never be less than this. You may frustrate your potential. You may identify with that which is less than you can be. But within you now and always is the unborn possibility of a limitless experience of inner stability and outer treasure, and yours is the privilege of giving birth to it. And you will, if you can believe.

ERIC BUTTERWORTH
Author of *Spiritual Economics*

The first time I spoke on the telephone to Robert Holden, founder of the Laughter Clinic, Stressbusters and the Happiness Project, we had a strong connection, like we were soul brothers. At the end of our conversation he had agreed to come speak at Alternatives, and said to me, 'You're a trainer, aren't you? I have been very successful over the last three years. I will send you a copy of all the clients on my database, and you are welcome to contact them and see if they would like to hire you.' Within a week, he'd sent me a list of 200 clients, and I subsequently sent them my brochure and I was hired by several of them.

Those of us with any commercial background know that client databases are precious, like gold, to be protected not shared. Yet Robert's example shows a different attitude, a desire to share, not hold on to, what is precious. His attitude has continued to bring him incredible success in his personal and professional life.

Richard Wilkins, author of the *10/10* series, his self-published books, sent me as a gift a list of all the shops that had ever bought his books. It turned out to include over 300 shops, which I was then able to contact to offer them my first tape. It had taken he and his wife Gillian over two years to compile the list, a huge effort of research, and yet he willingly shared it freely, asking nothing in return.

Liz was asked by the publisher of the new magazine that she was editing, 'How much budget do you want for setting up and market research?' She gave a figure, and a few days later he came back to her and said, 'I don't think that is enough,' and offered her nearly a third more than she had asked for.

These are examples of people who know and live by a simple truth – the more you give and share, the more you receive. They all know the amazing truth – that the cupboard can never run bare. They know the greatest simple truth of a happy life – the supply side of abundance is never the issue as it is guaranteed and unlimited; we need to see where we are standing in the way, and then get out of the way. They know that abundance is natural, created from love and blocked by fear, guilt or resentment.

The root of the word 'abundance' is in the Latin term *abundare*, meaning 'to overflow', or 'flow away from'. We are our own source of incredible abundance, which can flow from us and through us, while our conditioned self would have us believe we are lacking. There are no limits to ideas for fashion, food, stories, pop songs, news, shops. The form of creation is utterly limitless, although the source is a single universal intelligence – the invisible substance from which all flows. We see with our eyes what is perishable and what won't last, but the source is invisible to the eye; it will never perish or run out, and is for ever fresh and new. We begin to be in awe of the incredible abundance that is creation, yet this is our natural inheritance. When we say 'Yes!' to this abundant creative energy, I have an image of the creator doing the cosmic equivalent of cartwheels of joy, as we start to channel, not resist, life energy.

A simple way to trigger abundance in our lives lies in the simple choice to notice, be aware of and be grateful for what *is* in our lives, the good things and blessings that we have right now. Abundance is the willingness to receive and to keep receiving and sharing the endless gifts of life. The secret of abundance is to quit paying attention to what we don't have and to decide to focus on an appreciation of all that we are and all that we have.

WHAT IS TRUE ABUNDANCE?

Imagine having an unlimited bank account where we never even have to make deposits and can draw out as much as we want, whenever we want, all the time. That is our inheritance, our source and true nature. That is abundance – a state of awareness and consciousness in which we are aware of the all-infusing substance as being the source of everything. Mostly we don't know even know how to make a withdrawal and forget we even have the account; we don't believe we deserve it or we don't touch it just in case it does run out. Abundance is not a matter of deserving but of willingness to receive. We are all the inheritors of the kingdom of plenty, but may live like paupers for lack of awareness and our past conditioning in lack and scarcity.

EXERCISE

Imagine a world where all our material and financial needs are freely met. If we want a car, we ask the garage and it gives us the one we want; if we want money, the bank gives us whatever we need; all the food we need is available free, if we just go and help ourselves.

◆ What thoughts and feelings does this bring up for you?

◆ What would be the purpose of life and work for you if that were true? What would be the purpose of your life if not struggle?

What we really need to know about abundance is that it is an ever present reality. We each can draw in unlimited amounts. Its power is literally mind blowing, yet each of us has been conditioned in our own way to cut ourselves off from this supply of abundance.

EXERCISE

◆ What was there an abundance of in your family of origin? For example, love, money, fun, appreciation, support, criticism, worry, neurosis, debt.

◆ What are your images of abundance? For some they may be the horn of plenty, an ever opening flower, the loaves and fishes miracle, nature. What are yours?

◆ What is your relationship with abundance? You may believe in it, but think it is not for you; it doesn't exist; it is a cruel joke, an unattainable idea; you don't know how to access it; or you rely on the abundance of others, but deny being your own source. Capture your thoughts.

OUR BLOCKS TO ABUNDANCE

Through beliefs in our own unworthiness, guilt or fear, that abundance is outside us, or doesn't even exist, we end up in struggle, the sure sign that we have cut ourselves off from our heart and the natural flow of abundance. It demonstrates that we have decided to do it all ourselves, from our own power, rather than let abundance and grace flow through us, cutting ourselves off from the natural generosity of life and trying to do everything by the power of our own ego. We simply can't do all this and truly succeed.

CATCHING SCARCITY THOUGHTS

Go within and you'll never go without. Poverty is made by us in our minds, and based on no natural laws. The universe is built on abundance, and we simply erect barriers to our awareness of it with our own thinking and conditioning. Our egos will actively fight abundance, because they are invested in lack, so we may therefore be used to thinking thoughts of scarcity, and may not even recognize them for what they are, taking them for reality. Here are some clues to help you identify them. Begin to change your thoughts if you find yourself thinking along the lines of:

◆ I might miss out on something.

◆ There is never enough of ...

◆ I am in a hurry; there's not enough time.

◆ I need desperately ...

◆ I feel empty, lacking or incomplete.

◆ It will all run out/go wrong.

◆ I can never get enough.

◆ This is a one and only chance.

◆ Yes, they could, but not for me.

◆ Opportunity only knocks once.

◆ It is good now, but will never last.

◆ I've only a little money.

◆ I have to hold on to this ...

◆ There may only be a few ideas in me.

◆ My luck won't last.

We've been trained in scarcity and lack most of our lives. We can't all pass the right exams, get to the good schools, there is only so much love and money. We are trained to compete right from the beginning, and are educated that we live in a win/lose world, so you have to make sure you are a winner or accept your lot as a loser. We focus on what is missing from the world and our lives.

EXERCISE

◆ When you were young, at home or at school, what did you feel that there wasn't enough of? For example, time, money, opportunity, love?

◆ What did you decide about yourself and the world as a result of those thoughts?

◆ Identify six areas of your life where you experience a sense of lack now. This includes a sense of emptiness or neediness. What do you think will fill these areas of lack? How successful have you been so far in removing this sense of lack?

We take lack and scarcity as a fact, and on a surface level we'd be mad not to. Just look at all the evidence. Too few people do what they love for a living; there is mass unemployment; too many graduates are chasing too few vacancies; hundreds if not thousands of applicants chase some jobs; perhaps two-thirds of the world lives in poverty; there is competition, battles and strife; firms are going bankrupt all the time; there are limited supplies of oil, gas and coal. This seems to be our reality.

Yet we get cause and effect the wrong way around. These are not the causes of lack but the consequences of our belief in lack and scarcity. They are caused by our thoughts of lack. And because we believe in it we create lack and most importantly experience lack. Of course we live in a limited world. We tend to treasure what is in short supply; indeed scarcity seems to create value. What is abundant isn't valuable. We don't value air or water because we are surrounded by them but, as Ben Elton described in his novel *Stark*, the way to make anything financially valuable is to create a shortage of it.

CHOOSING BETWEEN SCARE CITY OR ABUNDANCE UNLIMITED

Although billions of us work in millions of different physical workplaces, emotionally and spiritually there are only two inner places to work: in Scare

City Limited, a frightening, competitive, threatening place, or Abundance Unlimited, a more happy, co-operative and inspiring workplace. (This idea is inspired by Alan Cohen.)

Scare City Limited

Here the key concern is survival – of the individual and of the company. People are very independent, taking care of themselves, always looking over their shoulder, armoured against the harsh competitive realities of commercial and business life. It's a tough and harsh world in Scare City Limited, and the best chance of survival is damned hard work and lots of it. This proves what a worthy person you are and is the best chance to defend against the unfairness of life. You never know when a disaster will strike, so you'd better be prepared. Competition and when necessary manipulation are techniques taught at the business schools that feed staff into Scare City Limited. Everyone knows that it's a win/lose place, and few people want to lose.

Accumulating more than you need is another way of keeping the tough world at bay. There never seems to be enough of anything in Scare City Limited – time, support, sales, money, opportunities, resources – and even if there is enough now, it could all run out and go pear-shaped very quickly. In the wider world there are always stories of lay-offs, foreign competition, natural disasters, criminals, terrorists, environmental poisoning and other bad news. It always looks tough, and people wonder what happened to the good old days. They are pretty stressed out most of the time, and dare not relax too much or take their eye off the ball, as someone may see their vulnerability and take what they have away, or they may lose their edge.

People at Scare City Limited are treated as components, just like money, desks, computers, raw material or information. While it is important to treat them well and take care of them as the law dictates, they are still resources that cost the company money and therefore need to be used as efficiently and effectively as possible. Good relationships too are important for productivity, but people in Scare City Limited never get too close because they have to compete and be tough with each other, so emotional involvements are kept very separate from business activities. People's hearts are rarely, if ever, shown at work. That would be seen as weakness, and weakness isn't tolerated.

Scare City is based on a hierarchy, and the goal is to get as high up it as you can, accumulating financial and status power as you go, the belief being that the more you have the happier you'll be. This never quite seems to be true, as the most powerful people don't seem to be happiest, but that is usually explained away as some character defect. Most people still secretly believe that the power would make them happy.

Fear is the greatest motivator in Scare City – fear of losing your job, being passed by or simply not being important – so management use fear when necessary to get hard work. As the people who work in Scare City Limited have been well trained in fear since birth, the management's job is already done in their minds.

Most people never quite make the grade anyway. Work is a constant series of tests and hoops to jump through. Self-improvement is a great tool in Scare City, as no one feels good enough. Everyone feels they should make themselves better to hold on to their job, and they are always trying to make themselves more efficient, useful and attractive to employers. Nobody really feels safe and secure, and many people simply fail to make it and fall by the wayside – but that is the way they believe it must be.

Success in Scare City depends on proving that you are not a waster or useless, and the main two ways of doing that are:

◆ making money and financial survival

◆ the outer appearances of success – the trappings, cars, house, status, achievements and external power

Money in Scare City Limited is the major force on which human energy is focused – making, accumulating and keeping it. Because money is so important, most people in Scare City are doing work they don't enjoy, holding the erroneous belief that that these things will make them happy, or at least less unhappy.

Religion or spiritual practice of any kind has no place in work in Scare City. God, if He exists, is outside, distant and of no use to them in their day-to-day activities. It would be an inefficient use of their time, if not a downright waste.

Perhaps you have worked at one of the brother and sister organizations of Scare City Limited? Or in Scare City itself? It has branches throughout the world, in the public and private sectors, in all business areas, in the caring professions, in local and central government. Even many self-employed people have signed up to the culture. That is the one abundance related to Scare City Limited – its abundant manifestation!

Abundance Unlimited
Only a thought away from Scare City Limited is another organization called Abundance Unlimited. It operates under very different principles, but is very

much more successful, even though both places have the same resources.

People in Abundance Unlimited usually love their work because they know that they are most motivated and successful when they do what they enjoy, what they feel called to do, and what serves themselves and their customers. They know that when they bring the best of themselves to their work, any work can be enjoyable. If they hated their work they'd know they were in the wrong place and simply let go and find another job; they wouldn't cling. At school, children are encouraged to discover what they want to do, and supported in whatever they show interest in and enjoy most.

In Abundance Unlimited people don't need to be commanded and controlled. There is no hierarchy, as they are encouraged and appreciated, educated and guided, and shown how to rectify their mistakes. Through this and through listening to the intuition in their hearts, they have a natural sense of what is appropriate in most situations. They are largely self-correcting. Some people have more power and responsibility than others, but this comes through choice and agreement; they are not regarded, nor do they regard themselves, as superior, but simply more suited and gifted to take on these responsibilities.

In Abundance Unlimited everyone knows that everyone can win, because happiness and fulfilment come from within. They experience this as a result of finding and contributing their gifts and strengths, being creative, serving and being authentic. It is not arrogant to be good and to shine, but the goal of everyone. People collaborate, co-operate and share to create win/win situations. There is plenty of room at the top in Abundance Unlimited, because the top is a state of mind available to everyone, and they celebrate each other's successes, how they have grown and developed and have more to contribute to life in the organization.

Through sharing, people in Abundance Unlimited always have a sufficiency, and are always discovering more. There is no point in hoarding or accumulating, and no one competes, because there is also no point in competing for what you can freely have, but they do celebrate excellence. They know that each of them has access to spiritual power, which is the source of all they ever want, so their joy is drawing from this spiritual reservoir and sharing the bounty, so no sacrifice is necessary.

There is just as much money available in the economy in which Abundance Unlimited operates as there is in Scare City, but people see it differently. They know that money will always come as a by-product of loving, serving and doing what they enjoy most. For them, money is not an objective to pursue with all their energy, but an object that helps them facilitate their exchanges. It is a joyous expression of abundance, of the good done for each other. Money is never hoarded, because the more it flows, the more exchange is occurring.

Viewed from above, both places look the same and have the same resources available to them. Both places are actually states of mind – we can and do create either of them through our beliefs and attitudes. Likewise we can consciously choose to get over the blocks obstructing the way out of Scare City.

UNDOING BLOCKS TO ABUNDANCE IN WORK

When I was working on my Business Studies degree, part of the course was economics. On the first day we were taught 'economics is the study of the distribution of scarce resources'. This belief in limited resources is accepted as true by much of the world, but it is simply not true. Indeed in economics, things only have value because they are scarce, and that which is freely available is usually not particularly valued. All politics could be seen as the way we decide who gets what, how these scarce resources are to be distributed. For many of us we see no other reality than scarcity, so we cling, fight, battle and compete in the rat race; but, as Lily Tomlin rightly observed: 'Even when you win in the rat race, you're still a rat!'

We struggle when we believe in lack and scarcity, that there isn't enough to go around and that the supply is unlimited. But abundance is not about our circumstances but about developing the awareness of inner prosperity. Abundance is not a miracle, but a natural principle, experienced by identifying and removing the blocks that we have learned and created.

1 The Belief in Scarcity

We've all been to school in Scare City, and our culture seems to prove lack, with haves and have-nots. The world of the market is the arena of winners and losers. Scarcity says that we think the creative force of the universe failed to create enough to sustain the needs, wants and desires of all its creations. That is an odd idea of a creator, a kind of cruel cosmic joke. When we genuinely believe in scarcity, it makes great sense and is logical to hoard, battle and accumulate more than we need, leading us into competition and guilt about what we do have. This is one of the deepest aspects of our cultural conditioning. It is discovered and undone layer by layer.

As you affirm abundance, deeper levels of resistance may rise into your awareness. Our ego mind is invested in scarcity, and will do all it can to prevent us realizing and experiencing the truth of abundance. Keep focusing on what is present, not absent. When I first set up as self-employed in 1990, my deep fear and belief was that I would have to fight and compete to be successful in my business as trainer: 'There are thousands of people doing what I do now, how am I ever going to beat them?' Over the years I have come to know that as my scarcity belief. Now living more from abundance, I experience success by simply being me and giving my best, which detracts from no one.

2 Competition

Most, but not all, competition has its roots in lack, and our belief can be that the only way to get what we want in life is to compete, even fight, for it. If we truly believed there was enough for everyone, why compete when there is no shortage of supply? A certain amount of competition is fun and does bring out the best in us, but we can't compete for and win abundance. We can start to receive instead. *A Course in Miracles* tells us that we actually ask for too little: 'Would you be content with little, which is all that you alone can offer yourself, when He who gives you everything will simply offer it to you? He will never ask what you have done to make you worthy of the gift of God. Ask it not therefore of yourself. Instead, accept His answer, for He knows that you are worthy of everything God wills for you.'

The whole business world has its roots in lack. Interestingly competition blocks receiving, and we truly succeed by giving up competition. The concept of winning and losing is demonstration of belief in limitation, as is any form of inferiority or superiority. Competition says the creator plays favourites, and we must do many things to earn love and rewards. Undoing this starts by considering the idea that getting has nothing to do with competing, but much to do with being willing to receive.

The way out of competition is to find our own unique way of expressing life, our purpose, the things that no one does like we do. When we win through competition, we may get what we want as a trophy, but don't always receive fully and enjoy what we got. It isn't true that competition is an absolute necessity to stimulating the best in ourselves. We can bring the best out of ourselves because of love and inspiration, by wanting to love and help others, by wanting to create more beauty in the world, by wanting to add to the richness of life. These are responses to the call of our spirit, not to the desire to win over others. Spirit gives without ceasing, without limits or conditions.

3 The Jolly Green Giants of Jealousy and Envy

Envy and jealousy are two of the feelings that I personally find most difficult to deal with in creating the work I was born to do. I am coming to realize that I am not alone in this. When we genuinely admire someone, we can celebrate their talent, be grateful for it and even aspire to be like them. When we are jealous, deep down we feel that they don't deserve what they have, or that we are capable of having it either. Jealousy has its roots in the Latin word for *zealus*, meaning 'to seethe, boil or ferment', so it eats away at us. Envy is derived from the Latin word *inuida*, meaning 'to see' or 'to look upon', but in a bad sense. Our heart and spirit genuinely celebrate the success of others because they know abundance, but our ego can be so invested in scarcity that it tells us that anyone else who is a success has taken something away from us, and is a form of enemy. We can see someone else's success as our loss, even as an attack on us.

We are often ashamed or guilty about our jealousy, so we hide it even more, but this simply compounds the problem. I have had many friends whose achievements have felt it like daggers in my heart, when they were nothing even to do with me! Somehow I have felt that their success diminished me – but it didn't, even if it felt like it. Jealousy blocks receiving and creates scarcity.

4 Lack of Self-Worth and Asking for Too Little

Centuries of conditioning in being not good enough and the notion of us being sinners in the eyes of God leave many of us feeling unworthy to some degree or other. We all have limits to what we are willing to have before we feel guilty or even push away the very things we say we want. 'The meek shall inherit the earth,' we have been taught – by one of the wealthiest institutions in the world. Receiving is not an issue of deserving but of willingness. Undoing low self-esteem can be an incredibly challenging and rewarding path. When we lack self-worth, we tie up our self-esteem in what we have or don't have – we judge ourselves by our material accumulations, or lack of them. We may also believe that by not receiving now, we will be rewarded in a world to come instead.

5 Lack of Willingness to Receive

Being unwilling to receive is a huge block. Either through a feeling of moral superiority or that others are more deserving, we erect a barrier to natural abundance. To receive can pull us into being out of control, even threaten our self-image. An addiction or a sense of being a victim can become a major part of our identity and how we define ourselves in the world. We don't predict life any more, and however wonderful the new opportunities, we may be threatened and choose to stay with our old ways.

Scarcity in any area – money, work, fulfilment, satisfaction, play, sex or fun – usually has either guilt or fear at its root, manifestating a way of punishing ourselves for some past mistake, or a means of getting revenge on someone else. True abundance is a demonstration of innocence, that we are naturally deserving and willing to receive. Here is a powerful exercise to help you discover your hidden agenda for refusing abundance.

EXERCISE

◆ What major scarcity story are you running in your life right now?

◆ When and why did you decide it wasn't safe to receive in your life?

◆ Who are you proving wrong by indulging in your current scarcity story? And why would you want to do that; what are the benefits and purpose of this behaviour?

◆ What are you even more scared of?

Identify an area in your life where you are experiencing lack. Be very honest with yourself and answer the following questions about that lack:

Given your present situation around, money, career or life purpose, what are you communicating to:

◆ your mother?

◆ your father?

◆ your partner?

◆ any previous partner?

◆ any brothers/sisters?

◆ your boss?

◆ your colleagues?

◆ the creator?

6 Doing What You Hate or Are Bored By

The belief that we can only earn money by doing things we don't enjoy can run deep in us. When we stick with dull work, or refuse to change our attitude, we are effectively saying that life is largely joyless. By not exploring other opportunities and ways of working, we are affirming scarcity. I worked with Kate, who was incredibly successful in material and financial terms but didn't actually enjoy what she did. To compensate she pushed as hard as she could to manipulate the corporate system to get as many perks as possible; she was an expert at it, getting one of the best reward packages in the organization. But it was evident that although she was wealthy and successful, she was not prosperous because she didn't enjoy what she did. She was still very unhappy, because she wasn't using her creativity in a joyful way and using it to contribute to others. She never got to fill her inner feeling of lack.

7 Unwillingness to Take Risks

When we do what we've always done, we get what we've always got. When we don't stretch ourselves, try new things and put ourselves in new territory, we have no way of knowing what else we might enjoy; we fail to create any new space for more to enter. We can't know all the answers beforehand, so we have to explore.

8 Fear

As we've already seen, fear lies behind all the other blocks to abundance. Where there is fear, there can't be abundance. Fear creates limits, strings and conditions, and is manifest as scarcity. Consider why you might be scared to have abundance in your life.

9 Blame

To blame any outer situation for our lack of abundance is to fail to recognize that abundance is a mental state, a way of thinking and acting that is under our charge. When the economy picks up, when interest rates come down, when there is less unemployment or any other excuse (however logical they may sound) – these say that the natural flow is affected by external circumstances. In fact the natural state of abundance is always available, fully, at every moment, when we align our thoughts with it. We don't get depressed because we have recessions – we have recessions because we lack confidence, are scared or get depressed. Again, we mistake cause and effect.

We may have felt that we had to fight for what we needed and wanted in our family, that there was not enough love to go around. Desirée, whom I met in Switzerland, had 12 brothers and sisters! She had certainly grown up believing that that there wasn't enough love to go around in her family and had quite given up on believing that she could get the love she needed. Yet during the course of our 14-day workshop we shared our experiences in our family group, and she began to see that none of us has to compete for love and attention, but instead we could be the source of love. She began to see that each of us was not the enemy or the competition for a limited amount of love but a source of love, inspiration and support. By sharing and not competing we created more good experience! She took this new belief into her life and work and has moved to new levels of success.

10 Perfectionism

Needing our work, a situation or a client to be perfect automatically blocks abundance, because perfectionism focuses on what is is wrong rather than what is present and correct.

11 Pay-offs for Scarcity

We may have grown used to getting lots of sympathy, support and understanding for the lack in our life. We may even use our own lack and problems to control and manipulate the emotions of others. We may also wonder if we will lose many of the rewards we currently receive.

12 Attachments and Hoarding

Abundance is a flow, yet we have been taught that the only way to have anything is to hold on to it or own it. When we are emotionally attached to expectations, people, situations and events, we block that flow, making life fit our needs rather than simply letting it work naturally for us. Holding on is a way of trying to beat lack, and the emotional attachment is actually a form of fear. When we release emotional attachments (not the things themselves), we find that we have greater freedom or have something new and better.

To choose to stop clinging to old ways of working and being may initially feel like a descent into hell. Many workshop participants describe their experience this way initially, as they let old jobs and careers go. Then, in time, as they begin to let go and refuse to cling more, they find that there is another force at work in their lives – this is the organizing force of abundance. Abundance is intelligent; it knows how to match us up with the right situations, people and events, when we take the time to listen to it, have the wisdom to act on its guidance and free ourselves from many of our attachments. One person described it to me is as like 'clinging by your hands to a window ledge for all you are worth, for fear of falling, with nails breaking and muscles aching. Then eventually you let go and decide to face the worst, only to discover you were only ever six inches off the ground.' Abundance is always there to catch us when we quit clinging.

13 Only Certain and Special People Can be Abundant

This is another myth stopping us knowing our true nature. There are no special people; what one person can do, anyone can do, with time, patience and awareness. The power of abundance is available to all of us, irrespective of age, gender, religion or our past.

14 Pretending to be Abundant Out of Fear

True abundance has no fear. I meet many people who have thought that by denying their fear and acting abundantly they would experience abundance. They spend more than they have, make commitments they can't honour, and say that life is abundant so they must be supported. This is bordering on recklessness, and has nothing do with true abundance, because its motivation is fear. Abundance has integrity.

15 Limiting the Sources of Abundance

Often people in workshops describe that the culture of their existing employment is based on lack and fear, and say they feel unvalued or held back in their work. Yet they are scared to leave. I get them to contemplate the idea that there is either an employer that wants them just as they are, with their skills and experience, or that they can create the work they want themselves, or that they can develop the skills or confidence they feel they lack now. Employers are not the source of abundance; the source is within us. As someone once said, 'There is no future in any work or job; the future is within us.' Just because we are not experiencing abundance now doesn't mean that we won't experience it up the road. Remember that our problem is not in the supply side of abundance; the source of abundance is truly without limits; the problem is in the blocks we have created, our knowledge about how to draw forth abundance, and in our willingness to receive it. We need to affirm life, not exist numbly in denial of its gifts.

AFFIRMING LIFE

The most powerful visualization would have been one that saw all the beauty of nature and the abundance of the universe already residing *within* their hearts. We seek external riches only when we have forgotten the riches *inside* of us. Truly the only quest is for spiritual awakening, which reveals to us that what we sought is what we are.

ALAN COHEN
Author and workshop leader

Abundance is life-affirming, how we celebrate the wonder of life, and there are unlimited ways to do this. What are your favourite ways of loving life? Of being kind, loving, generous, inspiring, creative and humorous?

Abundance is a quality – even *the* quality – of the Source. Everything in the world is a symbol of the abundance of the source, not the cause of it. All creativity, all art, all wealth, all imagination, all love, peace and joy have their source in the Source. Abundance is the decision to call forth these qualities from our own connection to the Source.

I have always been fascinated by the sunflower as a symbol of abundance. One sunflower seed can produce 500 new seeds, as well as a beautiful flower, each year. In five years alone, a single sunflower seed can cause another 62,500 million more seeds to exist ... Break open a sunflower seed and you don't see millions of other seeds, you simply see the potential for all these flowers and seeds. We can count the number of seeds in an apple but ultimately how many apples are there in one seed? The answer is infinite – there is no limit, just as our own potential is without limits.

We are all seeds, within each of us are unlimited ideas, unlimited emotions, unlimited thoughts. Just as lack is in our minds, so is the potential. Everything in this world is a symbol of either the belief in lack or the reality of abundance. We have, it has been estimated, between 60,000 and 90,000 thoughts a day, but most of them are the same as the ones we had yesterday, preoccupied with lack, shortage, what's missing or fearful thoughts. Just imagine the potential of creating just a few hundred more abundant thoughts. Our body seems to be a symbol of limits. Yet the biggest parts of who we are – our mind, our thoughts and our imagination – are unlimited. There is nothing we cannot think about. Who we truly are is therefore endless.

The Flow of Abundance

Abundance is natural, and it is only through our own mind that we block this connection. A wonderful story illustrates this. A little girl is helping her father water the garden, and is holding the hose. Suddenly, she cries to her father, 'It's stopped, Daddy.'

Her father looks across and sees that she has trodden on the hose with her foot. He calls across, 'Take your foot off the hose!' She does, and the water flows again.

A little while she cries out again, 'Daddy, the water has stopped again,' and he looks again and notices she has her other foot on the hose.

'Take your other foot off the hose,' he cries, and she does, and learns the lesson. We are like that little girl – without realizing it, we block the source, cut ourselves off from the ever present flow of life, and then turn to God and say, 'Look what you've done, how could you do this to me?' We feel victims when we did it to ourselves!

We truly live in a universe of natural plenty: there are now estimated to be eight galaxies for every person on this planet, and each galaxy contains billions of stars; our sun alone – there are thousands of other suns – has generously given us light, heat and life for millions of years and will do so for many more; the universe is endless and infinite, it never stops; on this planet there are 5 billion people and they could all stand on a land mass the size of the Isle of Wight, so there is no shortage of space; there is enough food to feed everyone; as much energy comes into this planet in one minute from solar energy and electromagnetic sources as the whole of humanity uses in a year, so there is no shortage of energy; the estimated financial wealth of the planet is over £10 million billion – enough for everyone to be a millionaire; there is an incredible abundance of natural flora and fauna, animal, fish and insect life, which is forever replenishing itself. Where is the lack? In our thinking and attitudes – *in our minds* and in cutting ourselves off from the flow!

In truth there are unlimited opportunities every moment. Thousands of new business ideas are created every hour, thousands of new jobs are created each day, new books are written; new software, new songs and new technologies are produced, new dreams and visions are realized. We live in a world of unlimited potential and unlimited creative opportunity. New opportunity is an every moment reality, when we stop letting fear and lack cloud our vision. Fear squeezes out the truth that the universe has an infinite supply of opportunity. When we replace fear with excitement and willingness, our perception of any situation can transform into abundance.

I was invited to run a day with the alumni of women MBA students at Cranfield University. These women were all mature students, successful in their own right, but many were dissatisfied and wanting to make changes, but feeling resistance to making these changes, having worked hard to get where they were. During the afternoon, one of the women stood up and said to some of the others who were expressing some of their fears, 'Come on, women! We are all very talented and successful; do we really think that having created what we have in our lives we can't make a change and create it all again? There are thousands of opportunities just waiting for us, we just need to believe in ourselves.' When we have self-belief and self-confidence, an abundance of opportunities await wherever we go.

We are only just beginning to understand the power of our mind. We learned earlier in this book that the thoughts we hold become real – what we focus on in our mind, we create in our lives when we consistently hold those ideas and act in accordance with them.

The Store of Plenty

I love the story of a man who died and went to heaven. God showed him around all the wonders but, going past one room, God said, 'You don't want to look in there, it is such a sad room.'

The man asked, 'Why, what is in there?'

'Don't ask,' was the reply. After the man pushed and persuaded, God eventually capitulated and let him see inside. The man was astonished, because the room was packed with treasures of every conceivable kind, love, tranquillity and beauty.

'Why is this such a sad room?' the man asked.

'Because these are all the treasures that I have offered people but they have refused to accept.'

WHAT DO WE WANT MORE OF?

Remember that we don't prove prosperity and abundance by having lots of money and things. The world is full of rich people who don't feel prosperous. The legendary Getty died a paranoid billionaire, recluse and not trusting a soul; even Barry Manilow said that despite his fortune he was still scared of losing all his money. True prosperity is a mental and emotional state, a way of thinking and a level of consciousness. We can be incredibly wealthy, yet feel poor, scared and fearful of losing what we have; we can be materially poor and feel like a king or queen. Money does not take away fearful thoughts. It is all in the way we choose to perceive and think.

We have come to believe that things will make us feel particular ways, so we want money to feel secure or free, the work we were born to do to feel fulfilled or a relationship to feel happy. These things can certainly encourage us to have those experiences – a sunny day can help us feel cheerful, and a rainy day miserable, but they don't directly make us cheerful or miserable. When we realize that we have an abundance of what we are looking for already within us, we can start to change our focus of attention. We can shift from needing money to feel secure to drawing forth the resources and experiences we seek from within ourselves; then we will be freer to have anything of the world we want.

EXERCISE

◆ What do you expect to experience as a result of finding and creating the work you were born to do? They may be things like joy, fulfilment, a sense of purpose … List them in your journal.

◆ Focus on where in your life you already have some of these experiences, maybe just in small quantities at the moment. By noticing them and putting attention on them now we will experience more. Otherwise we can be like the person on his deathbed saying, 'I had a great life, but I didn't notice at the time.'

◆ Spend time in meditation or your sanctuary time contemplating those qualities, building an awareness of them. Start to build a stronger relationship with them. Realize that they are already there within you in abundance, and through nurturing your awareness of them you can experience them more.

Our inner consciousness is like a smorgasbord – we have an abundant number of choices of experiences and we can begin to choose which ones we bring forth.

STRATEGIES TO BRING ABOUT THE EXPERIENCE OF ABUNDANCE IN WORK

1 Have intention

Emerson wrote, "The ancestor to every action is a thought.' Hold the thought in your mind that you have decided to live abundantly, so that your intention will start to manifest. This breaks the waiting game, that we tell ourselves we'll be abundant when things get better. When we decide to live abundantly and act accordingly, we will witness the unfolding harvest of an abundant life. The inner shift precedes the outer manifestation.

2 Affirm 'I am willing to be abundant'

The words 'I am' and 'I have' are probably the most powerful words in the world. Whatever words and ideas we repeat and act in accordance with, we become. Begin to affirm 'I am abundant' mentally to yourself, and then become an expert at noticing the existing truth of that statement. While your logical and critical mind may speak loudly about what is missing from your work, determine to notice what is present in your life. As you continue to affirm 'I am' two things will happen. Firstly it will be as if a veil begins to lift, and you see how blessed you already are and always have been. Secondly you become a magnet to more abundance, and in time will consciously manifest people, situations and events. The expression 'To those who have, more will be given' refers to the state of mind of abundance, not just to material things. John 1:1 says, 'In the beginning was the Word …' This is the power of 'I am'.

3 Be for, not against

We give power to whatever we don't want or are against, helping it survive. In many organizations where I have worked, they have wanted to eliminate or reduce stress. I have often asked the question, 'So what would you like to experience instead?' After a few strange looks and some 'Don't knows', we compose a list of qualities such as fulfilment, appreciation, balance, support, encouragement, co-operation, trust, openness, even joy. We don't get what we want by getting rid of what we don't want. We get what we want by focusing on it and creating it. Instead of looking at how to get rid of stress, we move to looking at creating the work experiences we want.

4 Notice what you notice

Be aware of what you notice for two days. Do you notice what is missing and what is not good enough? Remember that whatever we focus on expands, and what we withdraw energy from gradually, in time, diminishes and even disappears. Focusing on problems keeps problems going; focusing on solutions, or asking for solutions, creates solutions. Powerful and empowering questions create solutions.

5 Be thankful – focus on what is present, not on what is missing

Most of us have an almost unlimited capacity to see what is missing from our work and our life. Write a list down now of everything you think is missing. Now notice what you do have. However little money or food you may have, give thanks for it, as well as for your work and opportunities. Focus on the miracle of your own life, that you can walk, talk, breathe and see. There are people in the world who can't do these things. What we focus on enlarges, so continue a diet of daily gratitude.

6 Do what you love, and love what you do

> No matter what your work, let it be your own. No matter what your occupation, let what you are doing be organic. Let it be in your bones. In this way you will open the door by which the affluence of heaven and earth shall stream through you.
>
> RALPH WALDO EMERSON (1803–1882)

We must work in our right mind, with our right consciousness, and let our work follow from our being. When we choose and commit to our work, regardless of the compensation or the thoughts of others but because we do it for the health of our own soul and to benefit others, we open the door for true affluence to flow in in unlimited supply. We will not experience abundance when we are resentful, angry and bored. Practice beginning to enjoy whatever you have to do. The choice to hate or enjoy is yours, so make new choices. Instead of *having to* do the report, *choose* to do the report; do it with love, do it as beautifully as possible and with the intention of it being a gift to the other person. We can all reclaim our power. Yes, we have to work, but we can choose the attitude we do it with, resentment or gratitude. When we do work that we hate just to pay the bills or get out of debt, we are focused solely on what we dislike, which will then be enlarged because of our belief in scarcity. We believe we don't have enough time, skill, talent, qualifications or connections to do what we enjoy. When we believe in abundance, we know we can find what suits our gifts and talents, and we do whatever we need to create or find that work. We know that work involving pain is not truth, but that working with joy is truth.

Start choosing to do things in life and work that you enjoy. Joy is the key to abundance, inside us in unlimited quantities, and it is our duty to discover what external activities connect us to our inner joy, and do more of them. Joy and pleasure are the fuels that gives us energy to work and create. By focusing on what you love, enjoy and cherish, it will expand and the loathsome activities of your life will begin to diminish.

7 Stretch – give more when it pinches, not less, and receive more when offered

The source of abundance is unconditionally available at all times. Our only job is to align ourselves with it naturally and remove the blocks that we have created in our awareness. So, when we feel inclined to hold back, we should stretch *into* abundance. When we do that regularly, from a genuine desire to be abundant rather than from a fear of lack, we experience the abundance underneath the fear.

8 Affirm abundance daily

The source of abundance is ever present, and it should be affirmed even when you experience the total opposite. Affirm that behind whatever appearances you see, fullness is available. Look at what you have in your life, the doors that are open to you, the opportunities you have, the abundance of the natural world around you.

9 Ask for abundance

Thomas Merton wrote: 'The biggest human temptation is to settle for too little.' Ask for what you want. Mostly we've been conditioned that those who ask don't get, which just serves to block abundance. Our greatest security in life is our own connection to the unlimited source of abundance, but we can forget to ask for that abundance. We draw forth what we ask for and what we consistently focus our attention on. When faced with a situation that seems difficult to resolve because of some issue of lack, ask yourself an empowering question like, 'What would an abundant solution to this situation be?' A wonderful example is of two chefs fighting over the single orange they both needed for their recipe. A third chef looked at their recipes, and recognized that one needed the flesh and the other needed the juice. The orange provided what they both needed.

10 Remember we are stewards, not owners

I remember reading about a businessman who threw a party for his employees just after he sold his business for about £3 million. What he didn't tell them was that during the party he was to give away most of that fortune to them. He had come to realize that although on paper he had owned the business, it was also everyone else's love, energy, support and effort that had created its success, so he shared the abundance with them.

It is worth remembering that in 50 or 100 years everything that we are now so scared to lose or have taken away will belong to someone else or won't exist anymore. That should help us to lighten up our grip a little, and be a little less attached.

11 Be affluent

To be affluent means to be in the flow. Life is sustained by the flow of blood through our heart and around our body, not just by having blood. We have come to equate affluence with an abundance of material goods and comforts, but it also means being in the flow of giving and receiving, opening up as a channel for the flow of goodness. Ultimately, we own nothing; we come into this world with no things, and leave with no things, yet we spend much of our lives worrying about getting and holding on to things. Look around your office or home and identify some things that you don't love or use, and let them go. Give them away to a friend or a charity shop but don't wait for the 'right' recipient – give to those around you now! We can still value and treasure what we let go of. You will feel clearer, freer and probably amazed at how quickly something new will enter your life. To get flow going, give something. It may be your time, energy or money. Whatever your skills are, offer them for free to someone who could really use them.

12 Practise luxury

Notice where you make do. Choose not to, but go for the best of whatever you can – even in minor matters.

13 Practise the joy of holy receiving

Write this in big letters and keep it above your desk or dressing table: 'It is just as holy to receive as it is to give.' Go on a receiving spree! If there is a Judgement Day, we are going to get our wrists slapped for refusing to enjoy and care for the precious treasures that life gave us, rather than for having too much. God's greatest joy is giving, and we rob God of that joy when we don't receive through each other. It is holier to give *and* to receive.

EXERCISE

◆ Notice when you don't accept and receive things you are offered in any form, be it money, love or help.

◆ Ask yourself why, and notice which of your beliefs you are playing out.

14 Give for the sheer joy of giving

Work is not usually associated with being a place of natural generosity, but seen as a place of competition and getting what you can, often at the expense of others. Naturalness, openness and generosity are often seen as weaknesses, as you are fair game for being taken advantage of. We often give in order to get something in return, like approval, love, recognition or gratitude. A good practice is to give with absolutely no expectation or desire of any reward but for the sheer joy of it.

One great way is to practise random acts of kindness – do something to enhance someone's life without being asked, without reward and even anonymously. It needn't be much, and you can start small. Start treating colleagues to cups of tea or cappuccinos. Notice if you can do it without any expectations of a thank you. It is not what you give, but the spirit in which you give it that is vital. What you give can be intangible, like silent good wishes, a compliment or an appreciation. Then move to bigger acts that stretch you more.

15 Cultivate freedom in our work

Freedom in work may sound like a contradiction in terms, but it is not. It comes as a result of choice rather than compulsion. Joy also is a by-product of genuinely committing ourselves to our work, giving ourselves fully to it in each moment. When we are not motivated by fear, we are free.

16 Everything we are looking for is inside

We are the presence of everything we are looking for as all experiences are in our own mind. We blame external circumstances, but in fact we create them through our own perception and our desires for anything outside ourselves. Buddha, Jesus and all the other mystics across the ages and the oceans have said that the kingdom is within. They all describe those wonderful experiences of joy, bliss, peace and happiness that just bubble up from within. We can learn this too through meditation, prayer, or just sitting quietly. Abundance comes from within, we need do nothing other than peel off the layers of conditioning.

17 Celebrate the successes of others

My conditioning in lack caused to me find it hard to celebrate the successes of other people. I almost felt as if their achievement was an attack on me, as if it held up a mirror to my inadequacy and deep feelings of failure. Learn to celebrate that other people's accomplishments and creations show what is possible, and let them be an inspiration and encouragement to us. The Buddhists have a lovely concept of sympathetic joy, which invites us to feel the joy of others not as an attack on us but as a gift to us. We can share in their joy without taking it away from them.

18 Unlimited opportunities

Abundance means that there literally no limits to life and its opportunities. We can find or create the niche that is right for us and not just take what isn't true for us.

Opening up to abundance – mentally, emotionally and spiritually – is one of the greatest adventures we can embark upon. I would liken it to experiencing an ever opening flower at the heart of the work we were born to do. It can keep on becoming more beautiful, and may also take us to a few scary emotional places as we face the voices of fear, doubt and lack and become willing to move beyond them. As we learn to align our thoughts with the existing reality of abundance and draw from the source, our work can take on a more magical and joyful quality.

We come into this world with nothing material, and leave with nothing. Perhaps the true measure of a successful life is how much we allow ourselves to receive and to share throughout our lives. Know that our creator celebrates our abundance.

OVERCOMING ANY LINGERING DOUBTS ABOUT ABUNDANCE

The well of Providence is deep. It is the buckets we bring that are small.

MARY WEBB

Most of us have major doubts about abundance, because our experience of life is often governed by scarcity and lack, but just because something is very deeply ingrained that doesn't mean it is true. We affirm and experience abundance not by waiting for it to come true, but by knowing it to be true already, choosing to activate it and draw it forth from ourselves in our life. There is no scarcity of opportunity to make a living doing what we love, only the scarcity of will to make it happen. True wealth is measured by what we have found in ourselves, shared and given in our lives, not just by how much we've accumulated, so let's now complete our journey by discovering the true meaning of success.

Simple Ways to Implement Principle Eleven

* Take a big tin of biscuits into work and share them with everyone.

* Make someone laugh at work.

* Share some of your most inspiring quotes with people today.

* Choose to give willingly more than is expected of you.

* Ask for something that you really want but have never asked for before in work.

* Offer to help someone else today.

* Give some positive feedback that is overdue to someone.

* Notice when you feel nervous or anxious about contributing. Do it anyway.

Principle Twelve

EXPERIENCING THE TRUE MEANING OF SUCCESS

Success might be measured by what we achieve materially, but more importantly it is the sum of who we become aware of being in the process of discovering and loving the work we were born to do. True success means finding our heart and soul and bringing them into whatever we do while having the material and financial support we need. Ultimately true success is not of this world, but is in the realm of spirit. It means knowing ourselves as children of our creator, as spirit.

CONGRATULATIONS!

What lies behind us and lies before us are small matters compared to what lies within us. And when we bring what is within out into the world, miracles happen.

HENRY DAVID THOREAU (1817–1862)
Writer and social critic

You have already achieved great success simply by being willing to open your mind to so many new ideas. How do you feel, having come so far? And how can you take the next steps towards truly beginning to enjoy your success?

True success depends not on what we know but what we do with what we know. It's about how we discover our true power and innocence by gradually releasing guilt and fear. How big a leap are you willing to take? What have you come to give the world that would make you so happy, so thrilled, and probably so scared? Whatever it is, be sure that it is a great thing!

We've now learned how much lies within us – the incredible power and inheritance that is ours. So what shall we do with our newfound inner power? Having come this far, you are probably in a place of excitement and doubt, motivation and fear, which must mean you're still human! In this last principle we'll look at how we can take all the ideas we've been introduced to in the previous principles forward into our lives to create the work we were born to do. While I can offer you all these suggestions, their true power lies in your application of them in your own life, knowing that they work as you actually experience them. There is an old joke about somebody who is lost asking the way to their destination and being told, 'Oh, I wouldn't start from here!' That is often how we feel – we should be starting from somewhere else. We think, 'If only I was a few years younger/older' or 'If only I had more experience or hadn't done that work for so long' … The truth is that right now is the ideal starting point. Whatever your current financial or emotional position, you can and will start from accepting how and where you are, not by resisting it.

EXERCISE

◆ Think about and list all your options, at this moment, as you currently perceive them.

◆ Which one(s) most appeal to you and inspire you?

◆ If you don't have one that really appeals, make discovering what really appeals an ongoing project.

◆ Decide on six positive steps that you can take over the next 28 days to explore or create these options.

◆ Create an 'everything is possible' type of work/ job description for yourself. What would be ideal for you?

Creating the Work You Were Born to Do

You simply don't know what you are capable of until you start going for it. I met a woman who had a desire to bring three seemingly separate loves of her life together into work – she was a trained youth worker who loved working with young adults; she loved clubbing; and she loved art. She created a job working for an art gallery, taking art to young adults in the clubs where they met.

Success in experiencing the work we were born to do is achieved through a process of daily decisions to practise the ideas we have talked about in this book. Many times every day we are offered opportunities to step either into new ways of working, living and being, or to stay with or slip back into old familiar habits. Remember that there is no 'right' or 'wrong' way – there are simply choices and consequences. There is no one with a cosmic clipboard keeping your score and awarding you a winner's or loser's medal. The greatest reward of all for the work we were born to do is how we get to experience ourselves, our work, our life and the people around us.

The work we were born to do is greatly concerned with realizing success, but perhaps in a different way. Do you actually have a definition of success for yourself? Interestingly the vast majority of people don't have a clear definition of success, but without this what compass do we have to live our life by? Most of what we have come to know as success is what we believe we *should* want, and is largely concerned with our outer world and what we have achieved, bought and accumulated.

EXERCISE

....

◆ Firstly, look at what you believe you must do/achieve/have in order to be successful. As usual, be honest with yourself, and complete the following statement: 'To be successful I must have ...' Would it be, for example, no debts, no anger, my own business, a large house, fame, three holidays a year, £100,000 in the bank? ... Let the list roll. You may be amazed at just how many things you think you need or must have, and how many can be incompatible.

◆ We've looked a little at outer success, so let's now turn our attention to inner success. If you left out all mention of money, achievements, fame and material possessions, how would you define success for yourself? Would any of the following statements ring true? For example, success is 'feeling on purpose in my life', 'feeling confident in my ability to handle the situations of my life as they arise', 'feeling free to express love', 'to be in touch with my creativity and know that I am loved', 'stepping through my fears to be more and more authentic'.

◆ What does success mean to you in your life now?

....

Here is a summary of how we may be changing our perception of what success means to us.

Old paradigm for success	New paradigm for success
Success is 'outer'.	Success is an inner experience.
We are incomplete and lacking. We want success to complete us.	We are complete.
Success as compensation.	Success as contribution.
We want success to 'get' something.	Success is about giving our heart and receiving in abundance.
We have to 'act on' the world to make things happen.	Our thoughts are creative. We are creative beings.
We are separate from the world around us.	We are all interconnected, part of the web of life. The basis of everything apparently physical and separate is consciousness.
Physical reality is all there is.	All physical reality has a non-physical essence.

It's basically an unfriendly world.	The universe is friendly.
Not everyone can win, so we have to fight, compete and struggle.	Every being can experience success, success is co-operation, joining.
Our success is usually achieved at somebody else's expense.	We can all 'win'.
Success involves suffering.	Success can be graceful, growthful and joyous.
It's all about achievement.	Success is creation.
Domination and control. Power *over*.	Co-operation and alliances. Inner power *with* people.
Use people and resources.	Everything is sacred.
Can't relax – must keep trying.	There can be ease.
Accumulation.	Flow, let things come and go.
Fear-based.	Love and creativity.
Heirarchy.	Interdependence.
Deny and control emotions.	Appropriately express emotions.
External power references.	Inner references, personal responsibility.
Need to be special.	We're all 'special' and holy.
Playing roles, doing out of duty and sacrifice.	Being our true best selves, being naturally.
Split between commerce and spirit.	Work can be holy.
Control and have goals.	Inner goals, let life unfold and emerge.
Cling and be attached.	Release, let go and flow.
Success is by comparison with others, is relative.	Success is unique to each of us, is absolute.
We're limited.	We're unlimited.
Life is random.	Life has meaning and purpose.
Success is rigid.	Success is growth and expansion.
Success is needed to 'prove' worth and esteem.	Worth and esteem are integral to our being.
Always wanting more, more is better.	Enough, satisfaction, contentment. Sometimes less is more.

IT'S ALL ABOUT COMING HOME TO OURSELVES

We shall not cease from exploration

And the end of all our exploring

Will be to arrive where we started

And know the place for the first time.

T S ELIOT (1888–1965)

Author of *Four Quartets*, dramatist, poet and Nobel Prize winner

The work we were born to do brings us home to our own being, a place we may have forgotten but never left. When our work springs from our naturalness, it is authentic and beautiful and, like a guitar string that we play, creates a resonance in the strings close to it. Our naturalness and light resonates with other people, and helps them remember their magnificence, the secret we keep from ourselves.

My friend Ansy is a classical singer, trained in all the techniques over the years. She told me, 'I struggled with many teachers, and with all the techniques, all the right and wrong ways of singing and breathing. Then I met a teacher who just said, "Be natural, and sing naturally." It was so refreshing and liberating to be given permission to be myself. I stopped struggling and it all started to flow. My singing got better, doors opened and opportunities manifested for me like never before.' Ansy still has to put effort into her singing, but it's now much less about struggling to get it right. Our work is great when it is easy and natural.

Being natural, being ourselves, is the one permission that we can give to ourselves. As we do so our work will spring forth from that inner, special place. We will finally experience what it really means to be in our element.

12 FINAL STEPS TO HELP YOU CREATE THE WORK YOU WERE BORN TO DO

1 Continue developing and trusting your inner knowledge over your doubts

Shakespeare said: 'Our doubts are our traitors.' Doubt is one of the biggest guns of our ego, the slayer of so many dreams, visions and good ideas. The word 'doubt' has its roots in the Latin term *dubitare*, meaning 'to be of two minds', and I would very much expect that you are in at least two minds (if not several!) about the work you were born to do. This is perfectly natural and to be expected. With respect to doubts the only real question is how we can learn to deal with them. Imagine growing up in an atmosphere of certainty with no doubt, simply being told with absolute certainty from birth that you are precious, powerful and able to manifest your heart's desires. How different your life would be! This energy of knowing through banishing doubt is described beautifully by poet Robert Frost: 'We all sit around in a ring and suppose, while the secret sits in the centre and knows.'

So start to develop that sense of certainty today! Instead of 'being of two minds', begin the practice of being of one mind. Put all your love, energy and resources in a single direction, and make a commitment; as Mark Twain said, 'Put all your eggs in one basket, and then watch the basket!' Nothing great has ever been achieved through ambivalence. We can become single-minded, which doesn't mean becoming hard or fanatical, but simply remaining focused on our desired goal, not swayed by inner or outer doubting voices.

We have learned much about the power of our intention and attention which can be summarized: 'As we think, so we shall we become'. So the goal is not to fight or deny doubts, but simply not to give them our attention. How different our lives could be as our doubts ceased to become self-fulfilling!

The antidote to all doubt is faith, which in a way is the acceptance of what our five senses and our reason deny. Acting in faith, our doubts begin to dissolve. We do not progress in our life through knowledge alone, but by our willingness to step forward in faith and courage. I coach and counsel so many incredibly well-qualified people who know so much – except what inspires them, what they love and what they want to do with their lives! I have discovered that what is most rewarded in life is not knowledge or cleverness, but vision, courage and moving boldly in the direction of our heart's desire. I love the idea that faith is the bird who sings while the dawn is still dark.

2 Develop self-belief

While it is all very well knowing that the ideas in this book have worked for me and other people, you will want to know that they work for you too. You need to believe in them, and to do this you may need to develop your self-belief. This can be achieved as a gradual expansion through:

◆ having a success in moving beyond a limiting belief, idea or obstacle and enjoying and celebrating that, and

◆ having a creative success, having an idea and vision and bringing that to fruition, in small ways to start with, and

◆ being kind to and loving yourself, regardless of the outer aspects of your life.

My heartfelt advice is to start small and to celebrate all the small steps in the intended direction. Move into an upward success spiral; overcelebrate your small achievements and emotional shifts, and undercriticize yourself for any mistakes. Because the work we were born to do is an unfolding process, there is no *there* to get to; the journey is the destination, so enjoy every *here* along the way. In time you will be somewhere else, but you will have enjoyed the journey to such an extent that you want to keep moving. We can't grasp and hold happiness, but we can carry it in our hearts and souls. Begin now! And now! and now! It is never too late – unless we never start. As we start moving in the direction of our intentions, we move from wishful thinking to belief and finally *knowing*.

We also need to know which self to believe in – our ego or our true self, our spirit. Pierre Teilhard de Chardin said: 'We are not human beings having spiritual experiences, but spiritual beings having human experiences.' Let's place our trust and faith where it belongs – in our divine nature. If we do trust in our self-created concept of who we are, we have every reason to feel nervous, afraid and concerned that we may run out of steam, but when we put our faith in divine nature we are putting our trust in the power and intelligence that created all that is. That is a much safer bet, even a dead certainty.

Self-belief is not about ignoring or overriding our human vulnerabilities, but about embracing them as parts of ourselves. We can be both great and fragile, joyful and depressed, angry and tender. We can achieve great things despite our human foibles; perfection is definitely not required for greatness. I, for one, have found my life's work, but I still can feel depressed, insecure and very scared. We are all forever recycling and healing old emotional issues at deeper and deeper levels, and healing is simply our release from fear.

3   Stretch yourself a little every day, act on your inner knowledge

We all live in what some people call a 'comfort zone', but which I prefer to call a familiarity zone – an area that we know well. Its edges are where we feel fear, doubt, anxiety or even terror, the places about which our ego cries, 'Don't go there!' We often mistake these edges for the limit of what is possible, or at least of what is possible for us, and manufacture them through our conditioning. Remember the barracuda in Principle Two, on conditioning, which would rather starve to death than go beyond its learned limits?

The work we were born to do is about sometimes choosing to stretch out beyond our beliefs and perceived limits, which is why it can be so exciting. It is about throwing off old concepts to realize we are all important, can all have happiness, experience abundance. Stretching ourselves may be about actively *doing* something, or it equally could be about *not* doing something.

A concept called *active laziness* means that we keep busy to avoid issues and inner work. One big lesson will probably be to *do* less and *be* more, not to give in to the voices in our head that nag us to keep on achieving. We must realize that a sense of self-worth exists within us that has nothing to do with any accomplishments; we have a core value as a living being.

EXERCISE

◆ On a daily basis, do something that will positively enhance your life but that you feel scared about. Try to do it with as little attachment as possible to the outcome. This stretch may even be *not* doing something, just *being*, especially if you are a workaholic or addicted to activity or achievement. For example, start writing, ask for help, enrol in a new class, ask for a pay rise or for the means to enhance your job; also take time simply to *be* and not *do* all the time. When our real sense of being is underpinning our life, we can begin to infuse all we do with it rather than slog our guts out in vain in order to attain a contrived state of being through being busy.

◆ Tell yourself daily, 'My value is not something to prove but something to accept. I am loved, valuable and precious right this moment, now and *need* do nothing to prove it, nor *can* I do anything to be of more value. My value has been decided by the one who created me.'

Creating heartfelt success *is* cumulative, not a one-off event. It is best experienced as a result of consistent movement in an intended direction in our work. As the saying goes, 'It can take a few years to be an overnight success,' but know that every effort is worth it. By consistently stretching – or trusting – ourselves in new ways, we can alter the direction of our lives dramatically in small and simple ways. The fulfilment of our true vocation can be a whole life's work. As we find our true work, words like 'winning' and 'losing', 'success' and 'failure' begin to lose their significance; we are constructing our life, and we simply see the results, learn from them and adapt our course as necessary. We also become more and more guided.

Perseverance is important, as it requires commitment to authenticity; however, authentic focus is the living font from which perseverance flows; attention is power and inner power grows as we grow more intimate with our loves.

The work we were born to do is also a spiral path: we may appear to keep going back over old ground, and indeed we will. We will be offered lessons until we eventually learn them, although each time we will be taught them at a higher level, although one of our ego's goals is to have us believe that we've made no progress at all even though we are always progressing, even when we feel stuck. The key is to keep applying all the principles we have learned, including when we least want to and when we feel they are least working. This form of discipline is extremely useful. There are frustrations and obstacles, joys and breakthroughs at every level along the way, and we learn that all our pain is actually caused by resistance to love and abundance. Every obstacle and problem is actually a call to a new creative birth, a shedding of an old skin and an old self-concept and a step further into a greater sense of ourselves.

We must also ensure we have long-range goals so that we stop ourselves from feeling too frustrated with any short-term disappointments.

4 Aim to demonstrate, not prove

Whenever we try to create anything in our life in order to prove something, this implies doubt, which means there is a basis of fear. Our ego will always give us ideas of things we have to prove, and fears that we are not good enough until we have done so. We are great now – this minute perhaps in embryo – but still *now*. Proving and disproving are unnecessary and unhelpful, as Sarah found. She wanted to create a successful career to show her parents that they were wrong when they suggested that she couldn't do it. Her motivation and intention were not to demonstrate that she was talented, wise and clever. As we talked further, she confided that her deepest doubt was that maybe she *was* useless, and that her parents may have been right. Like a castle built on sand, any work or career based on proving or disproving can tumble down in turbulent times. We may fight and defend, but we always have a vulnerability there.

Deep within our heart, we should all remember that we are complete, precious and whole. Our work can flow from that space of value, and simply be a blessing for others. Within our spirit there is no lack, but our ego will continue to implore that we lack things or experiences. Within this physical experience of life, we can have as much abundance as we want and as many things as we want, but the key is to remember that having as many material things as we want doesn't *mean* anything at all. It doesn't make us any better or worse but simply demonstrates that we are a powerful and creative being.

I often wonder if the greatest human achievement is actually very simple: to be satisfied and content and to say 'enough'. This can take many forms – 'I am lovable enough and happy enough', 'I have enough money', 'I have given enough', 'I have enough time', 'I have helped enough', 'I have enough friends', 'My creativity is good enough', 'I have done enough work and worked hard enough'. Our ego's call – *more, better, best, keep striving* – is a smokescreen to keep us away from the experience of being at peace with ourselves.

Our whole culture seems to be built on wanting more money, more power, more material possessions, more love, more, more, more … and we are almost regarded as suspect if we *don't* want more, if we aren't ambitious, lean, mean and hungry. So much of our culture is built on creating and then satisfying needs, discovering new ways that we didn't even know of. Our spirit wants nothing more: it is already whole and complete, calling to us, 'You are enough.' We need to listen.

EXERCISE

◆ Think about where in your work and life you feel *enough*. What does 'enough' in these contexts mean to you?

◆ Develop some strategies for experiencing *enough*:

   (a) Continue to notice what you have in your life and not what is missing.

   (b) Ask your spirit to guide you to what you seem to need. Ask yourself if this is your ego or your spirit talking.

   (c) Keep telling yourself each and every 'You are enough' and continue through any resistance you may experience.

   (d) Notice who in your life enjoys and accepts you just as you are.

   (e) Continue to develop a consciousness of prosperity and abundance.

All things flow from a peaceful heart, so continue to cultivate inner sanctuary and time to be with your heart and soul. Blaise Pascal wrote: 'Most of the evils in life arise from man's being unable to sit still in a room,' and Picasso said: 'Nothing can be achieved without solitude.' Learning simply to *be* can be challenging at first and takes perseverance. Continue to contemplate and meditate on the invisible energy behind the whole of creation. As we move our ego out of the way more and more, it will help us to manifest our hearts' desires. As we continue with this practice, we will begin to realize that this source is the essence of our own true nature: we too are a well of infinite possibilities, ideas, emotions and energy.

5   Integrate inner and outer success

We have learned that the outer world is a result of our inner attitude and state of mind, and that success in the work we were born to do is about cultivating our awareness of our inner nature and watching our outer lives unfold as a result. We need to let go of the idea that inner and outer success are in conflict or incompatible, and realize instead that the two are totally interwoven. They need not be in conflict but should be in balance. While we are on the path to discovering the work we were born to do, we still need to feed, clothe and house ourselves; we are not being asked to sacrifice but to change our perceptions.

Experiencing success is about making new decisions about where we place value; it is about deciding to value essence and spirit over form. True success is ultimately not about money or outer achievements. Although these things can be fun – we don't need to discard them – they are not at the heart of it. The rewards that we really take with us lie in who we've become aware of being in the process of living – the love we've given and received, the amount of light we've shone into the dark places of ourselves and the world, how much we have forgiven, how we have grown in consciousness through our life. The only thing we really take with us, and that is really ours, is what lies in our heart – what we have given with love. We don't have to spurn, but we should attempt to integrate.

Finding and following the work we were born to do may well bring us financial and material success, neither of which we need deny, but by far the greatest reward is that we get to know and experience the greatest treasure of all – our own being, our own heart and soul. We revive our powers as we find and regain our lost loves, our truest aims, our true values and potentials and our authentic desires and most precious feelings. No particular amount of money is required, no hoops have to be jumped through, no amount of shows of success are needed, no material possessions are required or have to be relinquished. All that is needed is continued willingness to change our mind about who we are.

6 Decide what you will make more important than fear

Continue to trust in the beauty of your dreams. Know that life is on your side, but that you will probably face fearful thoughts all the way – each one an opportunity to recognize that you have a choice – to let fear rule, or to make something else more important. Don't deny fearful thoughts, as they will remain, but acknowledge them and choose again. Keep remembering they are only fearful thoughts; they only exist when we misperceive ourselves as ego and not spirit. Sometimes it can feel like we don't have a choice, but we can always choose love in its many forms over fear.

A great antidote to fear is simply to find and keep committing to our purpose. As we do so we get so absorbed in living fully and in each moment that we forget to be scared! And we have such support all the time; we are never alone. *A Course in Miracles* reassures us that 'if you knew who walked beside you on the way that you have chosen, fear would be impossible'. We only experience fear because we forget how loved and supported we all are; we have never been and never will be left alone or abandoned. As we remember and become aware of this constant presence, our fear will dissolve.

Also remember that there is only one life force that is the cause of all life and infuses every aspect of creation, so whatever we may feel fear about is simply an aspect of ourselves.

7 Keep stepping through the biggest fear of all – the fear of happiness, joy and true success

It has been said that there is only one thing worse than not getting what we want, and that is getting what we want! Our biggest fears can actually be the very things we claim we want so much – happiness, joy, love, abundance and freedom! The question is not 'How good can it get?' but 'How good will we let it be?' All these wonderful experiences exist right now, but we resist them. How willing are we to put down our defences and let bounty in?

Many of us seem to have been conditioned to confine and squash ourselves yet our soul yearns to sing free of constrictions. Much of our religious programming dictates that we are bad, so if we stay invisible and hide our light, this angry God might overlook us and leave us alone. Our deep fear is that if we turn up, be joyful and shine our light in our own lives, we'll be exposed; God will come to get us and we'll be punished. Hiding can seem like a survival issue, as if our very existence depends on us hiding out.

Yet in continuing to heal our own life, embracing happiness and abundance is the greatest gift we can give and the best hope we can give to others. As we shine and show our greatness, even for a moment, we become a mirror in which others see themselves; our joy and freedom is a gift and a service to a world that can be very dark. As we see the genius of our own soul reflected in others, truth shines and recognizes itself.

All fear only stems from one single thought – the doubt we have about our divine nature and our ego's attempt to keep us in doubt and away from true self-knowledge. Fear only exists in our mind, and it only exists because we have lost the awareness of love. The only antidote for fear is love, and the greater the fear the greater the amount of love called for.

We can choose to release ourselves from guilt, for it is we who condemned ourselves in the first place. By forgiving ourselves we restore the memory of our own wholeness and innocence. One of the best ways of releasing ourselves from the chains of guilt is to release others from them first. Practise seeing colleagues, friends, bosses and customers as innocent, however justified you can feel in proving them to be guilty or wrong! As we free them, we free ourselves, and our own life comes back to life again and flows more easily and gracefully. Guilt can be a form of indulgence and is a defence against having to move forward in our lives.

8 Resist the urge to sabotage

Sometimes, just as we are about to make a breakthrough, we grow scared and return to old habits; we refuse a new birth. Without being conscious of it, we've all set our limits, like a thermostat, basically our rules and beliefs about how good we can have things. So when things get *too good* the thermostat kicks in to cool us down again and to bring us back to our comfort zone; we resist anything more. We can only have so much happiness, so much appreciation, so much money, or success, or gifts. We set our own limits on the supply of abundance, but it never stops wanting to give.

Sabotage shows up in many ways, such as:

◆ having a brilliant idea but not following it through

◆ fighting with someone who wants to help you

◆ not contacting people who are interested in you or your worth

◆ not returning telephone calls

◆ not turning up for meetings or appointments

◆ withdrawing

◆ 'rationalizing' all the 'logical' reasons why something wouldn't work

◆ keeping yourself too busy with other things and not giving yourself time for what is precious to you

◆ refusing work or money

◆ constantly believing you *can't* do something

All sabotage has its roots in either guilt or fear of loss. The guilt is based on the belief that we don't deserve something, and the fear is that if we do have it we will lose something in the process. Both have their roots in feelings of low self-worth, so the way through is to increase our self-esteem. No matter how attractive, intelligent or skilful we are, we need a high sense of self-worth to let in the true goodness and treasures of life.

Although giving up these old habits is rarely seen as fun, the success of breaking them will increase our self-confidence, reclaim our power and enhance our self-worth. We are constantly offered the choice to be in control or to be happy.

I often wonder if we stop ourselves going for what we truly want in our working life because we fear on a deep level that even if we achieved these successes we still wouldn't be happy, This can give rise to despair and the feeling of 'So what is the point?' The truth needs repeating – nothing of the world will make us happy, but it can encourage us to be happy. Ultimately happiness is from within, from loving ourselves. If we can usefully face some of our disillusionment we will be free of it. Be willing to face disappointments; give up trying to *get* and choose to *be*; give and extend the abundance within.

We need to keep releasing the erroneous belief that it is good to love others but not to love our self. Self-love is not vanity but fulfilment of love's natural desire. Our genuinely loving ourselves – our preciousness and celebrating our existence – is everybody's win. Nothing is stronger than the loving spirit that is holding us together.

9 Practise unattachment

To be unattached means to be genuinely without need. One of the greatest lessons I ever learned about being unattached was at the Samye Ling Buddhist monastery in Scotland, which I mentioned in Principle Four. The monastery seems to be a miracle in itself; you turn a corner in the Grampians and suddenly you see what looks like a piece of Tibet! I was amazed by the place, and also began to get a little confused. I understood that Buddhists believed that all suffering comes from emotional attachments to things of the world, and wondered how they could reconcile that with this amazing place, with its intricate decorations, incredible beauty and the £750,000 it had taken to build.

So I asked Lama Yeshe how he reconciled this, and he told me that firstly, 'You must have vision,' and explained that you must do all within your power to make that vision come true – meditate on it, visualize, take action, raise money and build it. And then, paradoxically, 'You must let it go, let go of the emotional attachment.' That was the lesson. In the West we believe that the only way to get something is to be like a dog with a bone – fight, compete, struggle and strive, invest our whole identity in something so that we feel awful if we don't get it – which means that we feel increasingly driven and will sacrifice almost everything else for our success. And we are not supposed to give up until we get it. The stress and strain of this process is awful, and we pay a huge price for it in terms of our health, peace and well-being.

The alternative way is to create from a place of wanting rather than needing. As Lama Yeshe explained, this still requires effort, but when we can little by little let go of need and emotional attachment we become freer and life flows more easily. A crucial point here is not to confuse emotional unattachment with disinterest. We feign detachment when we act disinterested, as we are actually holding back in order to protect ourselves from hurt, rejection or disappointment. True detachment means giving our all, not out of naïveté, but out of truth, yet not knowing what the outcome will be. It means not holding back for fear of getting hurt, but is not a guarantee of not getting hurt, though it demonstrates our willingness to deal with situations if and when they happen. With the detachment that lead to true success, we live more *now,* and we know that 95 per cent of our fears never come true so we'll probably have fewer fantasized problems, as well as a few real ones that we learn how to deal with.

EXERCISE

◆ Close your eyes and imagine yourself giving of your heart and your best, holding nothing back and having no attachment to the outcome. Imagine truly not needing to be agreed with, not needing recognition and not needing anything. How free would you feel?

Being genuinely unattached is what psychologist Abraham Maslow called 'being independent of the good opinion of others'. It is a prerequisite for real success in the work we were born to do. A great teacher of mine has been Dr Wayne Dyer. I once accompanied him to a radio interview at Greater London Radio, and sat in the studio listening to him on air. He spoke of the importance of love, of God, forgiveness, how each of us is a precious divine being. But what touched me was his openness and how free he was of defensiveness or embarrassment. Later I asked him, 'How can you be so relaxed and open, and seemingly so fearless?'

He told me, 'I am genuinely unattached; I am not trying convince them of anything, change their minds or even get them to like me. Because I am only choosing to be being real, I am free to speak my truth.'

I learned a lot from his example, including how trying to manipulate and distort ourselves to be liked just doesn't work. Being real and authentic is the ultimate experience and, precisely because we don't need the approval of others, many people will warm to us. When we are attached we create need and fearful thoughts. What if it doesn't turn out? What if they don't hire me? What if they don't like me? We won't allow ourselves to get excited in case we are disappointed or we won't allow ourselves to dream in case we discover it was all a dumb fantasy. And if we reach a point of desperation we never seem to get what we want. I have this image of trying to catch a bird. Try to chase it (be needy), and it will always fly away from you; place some bird seed in your hand and stand still and it will come to you. This is the key – desire, be determined, let go of attachment as much as possible and we will become attractive; opportunity finds us. Attachment is born out of scarcity thoughts. When we know there is an abundance we can loosen our grip on life and live a little more lightly.

Unattached Vibes!

My friend Bets told me that she was desperate to get a date, and dressed up to the nines on a Friday night to go to the disco in Corby where she lived, determined to meet a guy. Guess what? She came home on her own, because she had the equivalent of a flashing blue light on top of her head saying, 'I am desperate!' It pushed away the very thing she wanted. The following morning she went down to the newsagent to get a pint of milk in her jeans and without make-up, and she was asked out on a date! She was detached, and that made all the difference.

When we are attached, we tend to put our life on hold until we get what we think we need; when we are more detached, we keep our intention in mind and take the necessary action but then just get on with living our life. We can be detached and connected, as expectations are premeditated grievances.

We also need to have love and compassion for the many parts of ourselves that are very attached. Opening our hearts enough to experience joy, love and happiness again does also expose us to the risk of the pain and sorrow of loss. We need to embrace all our lost and broken parts, and love them all. Pain is inevitable in life, but prolonged suffering is more of a choice.

10 Know that the ultimate success is not what you achieve, but who you become aware of being in the process

This may seem like a fairly radical idea. We are so trained and conditioned to believe that the purpose of life has something to do with our success in the world out there, and how much we get of it. What if the true purpose of life was actually simply to know ourselves, who we really are behind all the ideas of who we think we are? We would do this through letting love be the most important thing in our lives.

Through the work we were born to do we can become aware of our own inner nature, that we are essence, we are substance, and always have been, and as such have been created with all power within us. The intelligence that created the whole creation is in us, and it is us. We are like the musk deer who spend their life seeking the source of their own fragrance, it *we* that we are looking for – self-realization – we are the prize!

The purpose of this life is to realize that we are already whole and complete and to withdraw the value we have placed on anything outside of our own being. This doesn't make the world wrong or bad, just without any real meaning. We can be fully in this world, but not of it. *A Course in Miracles* describes it this way:

> No one who comes here but must still have hope, some lingering illusion, or some dream that there is something outside of himself that will bring happiness and peace to him. If everything is in him this cannot be so. And therefore by his coming, he denies the truth about himself, and seeks for something more than everything, as if a part of it were separated off and found where all the rest of it is not … And thus he wanders aimlessly about, in search of something that he cannot find, believing that he is what he is not.

We are simply here to wake up from the dream that we are little and limited. We are the witnesses of all human experiences and can learn to embrace all experiences, but also we can be less and less attached to any of them. Our greatness *is* a gift, but it is also a decision we need to make daily.

As we continue to open our heart, we eventually begin to lose our desire to compete and win, but not our desire to achieve, which starts to take on a new hue. We become more motivated not just by our own personal gain and meeting our own needs but by a desire to go beyond our separated selves and ask questions like, 'How can I love others and make them happy?' not out of sacrifice, but out of our will to extend the love that we are.

A familiar feeling for many people is *littleness;* there are *big* people in the world but we are not one of them! In truth we are all the big people, although some of us are frightened, hiding and playing small. Identify who in your life you identify as big or grown-up, and be willing to take that projection back little by little and own the bigness and greatness in yourself too.

11 Move forward in faith

Doubt and fear are partners – what we doubt will cause us to experience fear, and what we fear creates doubt in our mind about our ability to deal with it. We can believe in a universal intelligence but one of the greatest injunctions we have is against knowing this intelligence. When we move forward in faith we are required to be out of control and to surrender to an invisible but tangible force.

Surrender is not a passive giving up and acceptance of our lot but involves very actively cultivating and developing our attitudes and mind to take action to achieve what doesn't currently seem to exist. This is true vision, and calls on us to summon up and employ our courage. It is about working in partnership with the energy and force of creation.

We can move from belief to knowing. With knowing there is no doubt, because we have direct inner experience. We can sense and know the energy that flows through everything. Whatever changes we experience in our life, our inner self will remain; there is no future in any one type of work, the future is always within us.

We have faith that this intelligence runs the stars and the heavens, that sunrise will come in the east tomorrow, that spring will follow winter, that this intelligence will turn our food into the nutrients that our body needs. If we can have faith in that, why not simply extend that faith to our daily life, career, work, relationships and finances? We don't have to see this energy and intelligence to believe it, just know it, be grateful and be aware of it. Simply begin to develop the awareness of this energy, and know that it runs through each of us, night and day, without ceasing.

Probably the hardest part of this knowing for us will be relinquishing our struggle, disbelief and doubt. This does not mean that we will not experience obstacles and challenges, but with a vision of faith we can begin to see that all difficulties are somehow for our highest good, not punishments but opportunities to know that we are being called to exchange our limited view of life for a greater and grander awareness.

Here are some suggestions for cultivating your inner knowing.

◆ Make sanctuary time. Be alone and meet this invisible intelligence within you, which is found in the silence of your own being. As you sit with this silence you will start to become aware of its richness and power. Give up any need to talk about or share this experience with anyone else.

◆ Notice, but let go of, doubt, judgement or inner criticism. Know that they are like the disturbance on the surface of a pond, while the stillness is unaffected underneath.

◆ Give up the doubt that we can know the energy and intelligence that is behind all of creation. To know it is actually natural and the easiest thing in the world, because it is who we are. We have simply been severely misled about our nature and the nature of divine intelligence.

◆ Know that this intelligence does not come and go, even if our awareness of it does. It is constant, eternal.

◆ Remind yourself that doubt is not true, however real it may feel. Clouds are real, but they don't destroy the sky. Night-time is real, but it doesn't destroy the sun. Our true nature still *is*, however much we may doubt.

I have always enjoyed the following poem by e e cummings, which speaks of the endless giving of this power and energy:

O sweet spontaneous
earth how often have
the
doting

      fingers of
prurient philosophers pinched
and
poked

thee
,has the naughty thumb
of science prodded
thy

     beauty   .how
often have religions taken
thee upon their scraggy knees
squeezing and

buffeting thee that thou mightest conceive
gods
     (but
true

to the incomparable
couch of death thy
rhythmic
lover

     thou answerest

them only with

        spring)

In the Bible the power is described this way: 'It is something very near to you, already in your mouths and hearts; you have only to carry it out.' (Deuteronomy 30:14.)

The Native American leader Sitting Bull described the power in the following words:

> Behold, my brothers the spring has come;
> The earth has received the embraces of the sun
> And we shall soon see the results of that love!
>
> Every seed is awakened and so has all animal life.
> It is through this mysterious power
> that we too have our being.

The work we were born to do is about getting to know this power, energy and intelligence that flows through everything and through each of us in our very being. It is about stepping through each doubt, fear and limit that we may experience, so that we eventually remember who we really are.

12 Experience the joy and fulfilment of letting love be your guide

So much of our energy can go into getting people to like us, accept us, approve of us and not reject us. We try to buy the love of those around. As we grow in awareness, we realize that love is within us and we can give love and encouragement, appreciation and support to the very people we used to demand it from.

We may have been used to the drug of fear in much of our life. When we choose more creative and loving thoughts, we may go into cold turkey and experience some withdrawal. We may initially just want to go back to familiar but uncomfortable old ways and thoughts.

A Course in Miracles tells us: 'Teach only love, for that is what you are.' Being a teacher of love is not something to *do,* but something to *be,* born in the realization that love is not something to get out 'there' but experienced by extending, sharing and giving the love that is 'within' us. We are like a ray of sunshine, extended from the sun, but still with the sun as its source, connected to the sun and every other ray. We only truly have what we share and extend, so we let love express itself and flow through us. We don't have to understand love and how it works, just as we don't need to understand electricity to keep warm by the fire. We are all here to teach love – the only question is when we will accept the assignment.

Be aware that we may teach and demonstrate what we most need to learn, and that the sole purpose for teaching anything is to reinforce our own belief and experience of what we teach. I teach everything in this book because I am learning it too! I experience fear, doubt and guilt most days of my life! So basically we don't have to be perfect before we start teaching love, but in teaching love we will learn about it and experience it. Love is a power that we don't really understand at all; we can't touch it, weigh it or measure it, but we can experience it and see its results.

To teach love, firstly we need to believe that there is a voice for love, a voice that is constantly available at all times at all places, either in words or as a feeling. Love knows that what is always called for is correction not judgement, and that we are always free to ask how to teach and demonstrate love in any situation. In this way the voice for love will become our true teacher, whereas our ego will always tell us that guilt, fear, greed, hatred, judgement or revenge will buy us something.

True success is all about degrees; there will always be new levels to open to, new opportunities and challenges. As we keep committing the way will be shown, as long as we don't give up and are willing to receive more.

EXERCISE

◆ On your epitaph, what would you like to have been known for giving?

◆ What message would you most like to have delivered to the world?

Whatever your life story so far you have greatness and genius within you; we all have the mind of the universe buried deep within us. We are God's great ideas.

Success is not something to get but to be. You will have success by giving your heart, by receiving love, peace, joy and abundance, and by sharing it. Success is not about being in control but about being open and guided. It is not about winning, but about being your best self, opening up to being your best self, giving and receiving all, opening a voice for spirit. Your natural success is a blessing to yourself and those around you. Be bold – take your place centre stage in your own life.

The great joys for all of us lie in finding and developing our gifts, listening to our inner guidance and trusting it, gradually banishing our doubts and seeing the work we were born to do unfolding from our inner vision into physical reality. Whether this be a radical change of attitude in your existing work or new work, you can transform your work as you can transform your consciousness. The fulfilment will come from your attitude, not what you do; as the Zen proverb says, 'Before enlightenment, we chop wood and carry water. After enlightenment, we chop wood and carry water.' Our work may never change, but the sense and the experience of ourselves that we bring to our work *can* be transformed.

The sheer joy of having faced and stepped through our fears and doubts is enormous and wonderful, and the gratitude of feeling so blessed is beautiful. This sense of joy is a peak experience, not always available, and it comes as a great gift to us. We can all feel the beauty available in every moment though, whatever we are doing, as it springs from our very being. We are all destined to choose love over fear; the only question is when. As we choose to surrender our plan for happiness for love's plan for our happiness, the work we were born to do will continue to unfold in our heart and in our life.

I wish you all the love and inspiration on your journey home to your heart.

Simple Ways to Implement Principle Twelve

* Celebrate yourself. Write down, for yourself, ten things that you are good at and that you contribute through your work.

* Ask for, and be willing to receive, a miracle in your working life.

* Ask for a miracle in the working life of someone you know who is facing challenges.

* Choose to be at peace rather than right but critical.

* Celebrate something that is not special but that has gone well.

* Notice one of your biggest doubts and step right through it.

* Affirm to yourself today 'I have incredible creative power and gifts within me.'

In Conclusion

As soon as your subconscious accepts any idea, it proceeds to put it into effect immediately ... Sometimes it seems to bring about an immediate solution to your difficulties, but at other times it may take days, weeks or longer ... *Its ways are past finding out.*

DR JOSEPH MURPHY
Author of *The Power of Your Subconscious Mind*

You can begin now, this moment, to create your own future, living the work you were born to do.

EXERCISE

Imagine a future day in your working life, living the work you were born to do. Write about this day in the past tense, as if you had already lived it. Describe your experiences, what you enjoyed, your successful relationships, your accomplishments and achievements, your sense of fulfilment. Write with a sense of excitement, passion and possibility. Imagine only what would interest and inspire you. By writing in the past tense, your unconscious mind will feel that these events have already happened, that they are possible, and it will therefore support your actual creation of them. Begin *now* to take action to make this working day a reality. What beliefs do you need *now* to start to create that way of living and being?

The journey to creating the work we were born to do is full of rewards on every level, and is not always easy; it may involve some of the toughest and, at the time, scariest decisions we ever make. But don't be afraid to go out on a limb – that is where the fruit is. The first step up the ladder is to remember that *life is on our side*, and that spirit is our invisible friend and ally, silently working to make our heart-felt dreams become reality, never giving up on us. We just need get out of our own way. All our achievements are brought to fruition by a constant series of small steps, so keep taking small constant steps in the direction your heart calls you.

You are not alone in your quest to discover the work you were born to do. We are all learning to work in true and equal partnership with everyone else around us. Be willing to open to new and greater levels of love, friendship, support and co-operation, even when you feel doubting or lost. Be willing to give and receive more than ever before, and to become more abundant. Ask for whatever help you need, be willing to let more flow through you, for your benefit and the benefit of those you love. There is always help available; we just forget to ask. Be willing to do whatever it takes, face whatever needs facing and risk your heart again and realize that there is nothing to get, but everything to be; everything truly valuable is already in your own heart and spirit.

Finding the love that is within us is what it is all about. From my heart to yours, I wish you every success in every area of your life. You are worth it; we all are.

Useful Contacts and Partner Organizations

UK

Nick can be contacted through Heart at Work:
Nick Williams
Heart at Work
PO Box 2236
London W1A 5UA
tel: 07000 781922
website: www.heartatwork.net
email: success@heartatwork.net

Heart at Work support products and services

Heart at Work, founded by Nick Williams, aims to serve the needs of three key groups:

1. Individuals seeking career inspiration and guidance. Nick gives talks, workshops and coaching.
2. Individuals considering or already running their own small businesses, based on their passions. See www.dreambuilderscommunity.com.
3. Organizations in the public, private and voluntary sector who want to inspire the best from their staff and appreciate them. Nick has worked with many household-name companies including BT, IKEA, PricewaterhouseCooper, WH Smith and many NHS trusts, as well as providing individual executive coaching for members of these companies.
   - Heart at Work runs regular events around the UK and internationally. We'll happily send you a programme or you can visit our website.
   - We offer a free monthly e-newsletter with inspiration and ideas.
   - We offer year-long email coaching programmes. Every week for 52 weeks you will receive email coaching direct from Nick Williams to help you create unconditional success and the work you were born to do. These cost only £35 for a whole year. See www.dreambuilderscommunity.com.
   - Contact us for full information on how we can work with your company or conference, from a 60-minute presentation, to a year-long programme. See www.nick.williams.uk.com.

For further information, contact us at:

Nick Williams
Heart at Work
PO Box 2236
London W1A 5UA
tel: 07000 781922
website: www.heartatwork.net
email: success@heartatwork.net

SOUTH AFRICA

Richard J Nefdt
tel: 00 27 82 804 2000
website: www.heartatwork.co.za
email: richard@heartatwork.co.za

USA

Barbara Winter
tel: 001 952 835 5647
website: www.barbarawinter.com
email: babswinter@yahoo.com

IRELAND

Michael Daly
The Barnabas Project
9 Linnetfields
Dublin 15
tel: 00 353 1 827 0806
email: barnabas@gofree.indigo.ie

Organizations mentioned in the book:

Alternatives
St James's
197 Piccadilly
London W1J 9FF
tel: 020 7287 6711
website: www.alternatives.org.uk
email: post@alternatives.org.uk

Psychology of Vision
France Farm
Pewsey
Wiltshire
SN9 6DR
tel: 01980 635199
website: www.psychology-of-vision.com
Supports the work of Chuck and Lency Spezzano, Jeff Allen and Julie Wookey

The Miracle Network
12a Barness Court
6-8 Westbourne Terrace
London W2 3UW
tel: 020 7 262 0209
website: www.miracles.org.uk
email: info@miracles.org.uk
*Supports students of **A Course in Miracles**.*

Index

belief in 322–3
and ego 42–3, 317, 322
as 'giving' block 230
and guilt 325
and money 131–2
pay-offs for 327
as spirit squashing belief 42–3
in workplace 319–20
Schweitzer, Albert 228
science
and consciousness 308–9
and spirituality 59, 61–2
Secretan, Lance 246
security, desire for 253–4
self-attack, as 'purpose' block 171–2
self-belief, development of 347–8
self-defeat, and success 289–90
self-denial 38–9
self-discovery, process of 3–5
self-esteem 14, 48
self-expression 74
self-improvement 15
self-involvement 224–5
self-love 103–4
self-worth 13–16, 35, 324, 355
service
genuine 225–7
myths about 220–5
and spirituality 227–8
true nature of 219–20
sexual energy, and creativity 291–2
shadow work, reasons for 207–8
shadows, facing 187–93
shadows of light 193–5
Shakespeare, William 346
Shapiro, Debbie 255
sharing, and abundance 321
Shaw, George Bernard 128
Sheldrake, Rupert 310
shen (feeling heart) 93
Sher, Barbara 97

Shintoism 60
Siegel, Dr Bernie 235, 255
silence 66, 96
Sitting Bull 362
skill development 148–9
Sneed, Catherine 227
social roles 186
Solzhenitsyn, Alexander 191
Some, Sobonfu E 239
soul 159–60, 308
sources of money 138–40
special, striving to be 16
Spezzano, Dr Chuck 102, 153, 178, 255, 257, 261
Spinoza, Baruch xviii
spirit
and appreciation 87–90
and courage 83–5
and the ego 68–70
enhancing beliefs 48–50
essence and form 62–4
of fear and love 86–7
and happiness 78–81
injunctions against 67–8
inner 65
nurturing the 66–7
and science 61–2
squashing beliefs 36–44
of work 58–61, 70–8, 81–3, 242
spiritual inheritance 86
spirituality
and compassion 227–8
and money 125–6, 134–5
and self-belief 348
spontaneous giving 243
Springsteen, Bruce 111
stability 274–5
stagnation, danger of 260
Stanford University report (on intention) 7
Stark (Elton) 318

living a 166–7
visualization 52, 79, 204, 304
vulnerability, as 'giving' block 230
Wagner, Abe 199
Watts, Alan 54
wealth 135–6
Webb, Mary 339
Whitman, Walt 218
wholeness 182–213
Wilde, Oscar 137
Wilde, Stuart 200, 305
Wilkins, Richard 102, 314
Williamson, Marianne 13, 178–9
willingness
    lack of 324–5
    prayer for 263–4
    and service 220–1
Wilson, Paul 148
Winfrey, Oprah 110
wisdom 275
wishful thinking 54, 259
witness position, and beliefs 52
women, and appreciation 87
Wood, Victoria 144
Wordsworth, William 182

work, spirit of *see* spirit, of work
work ethic
    and money 137–8
    new 47
    and original sin 41
    and punishment 38–9
    and self-worth 15–16
    and service 222
work place
    abundance in 75, 320–2, 333–9
    community as 239–42
    giving in 237–8
    repression in 197–200
    scarcity in 319–20
World Bank 84
World Watch Institute 131–2
Wright, Joel 22
Wright, Steve 297

Yogananda, Paramahansa 73, 106
Young, Margaret 5

Zen philosophy 193
Ziglar, Zig 100